Heidegger, Authenticity, and Modernity

Heidegger, Authenticity, and Modernity

Essays in Honor of Hubert L. Dreyfus, Volume 1

edited by Mark A. Wrathall and Jeff Malpas

The MIT Press
Cambridge, Massachusetts
London, England

This book was set in New Baskerville by Best-set Typesetter Ltd., Hong Kong, and printed and bound in the United States of America

Library of Congress Cataloging-in-Publication Data

Heidegger, authenticity, and modernity : essays in honor of Hubert L. Dreyfus / edited by Mark A. Wrathall and Jeff Malpas.
    p. cm.
    Includes bibliographical references and index.
    ISBN 0-262-23207-3 (v. 1 : alk. paper)—ISBN 0-262-73127-4 (v. 1 : pbk. : alk. paper)
—ISBN 0-262-23208-1 (v. 2 : alk. paper)—ISBN 0-262-73128-2 (v. 2 : pbk. : alk. paper)
    1. Dreyfus, Hubert L. 2. Heidegger, Martin, 1889–1976—Influence.
3. Philosophy, European. 4. Philosophy, American—20th century. 5. Computers.
6. Cognitive science. 7. Dreyfus, Hubert L.—Influence. I. Dreyfus, Hubert L.
II. Wrathall, Mark A. III. Malpas, J. E.

B945.D764 H45   2000
193—dc21   99-056942

Contents

Contents

Contents

Foreword

Richard Rorty

No one in our day has done more than Hubert L. Dreyfus to make American philosophy less parochial. For some forty years, he has helped the rest of us understand what our European colleagues are up to, introduced us to them, and encouraged the study of their works. By commenting on them, by organizing conferences about them, and most of all by weaving their works together with work being done by anglophone analytic philosophers, Dreyfus has rendered invaluable service to the international philosophical community. It is no exaggeration to say that without Dreyfus the gap between European and anglophone philosophy would be, at the end of the twentieth century, far greater than it in fact is. By behaving as if the analytic-Continental split were of no great importance, he has done a great deal to narrow it.

My own acquaintance with European philosophy owes almost everything to Dreyfus. Back in the late 1950s, when I was at Wellesley and Dreyfus was at Harvard, he encouraged me to read Merleau-Ponty and tried to convince me that Husserl was not nearly as pointless as I thought. Had I not been intrigued by his account of Husserl's break with Descartes, I should never have taught *Cartesian Meditations.*[1] By helping John Wild and others translate the early portions of *Sein und Zeit*[2] and letting me reproduce copies of the result, Dreyfus made it possible for me to assign bits of that book to my Wellesley classes. (This underground, unauthorized, mimeographed translation was the basis for most teaching of Heidegger in the

United States prior to the publication, in 1962, of the Macquarrie and Robinson translation. People whose German was weak but who knew Dreyfus had a big head start.)

Toward the end of the 1960s, when I started reading Derrida, Dreyfus was one of the few friends with whom I could hash over *La Voix et le Phénomène*[3] and who could explain to me what was going on in Paris. Later on, in the 1970s, Dreyfus helped me to get acquainted with Jürgen Habermas and with Michel Foucault. Many other American philosophers owe their personal acquaintance with these two men to Dreyfus's mediation. He made it his business to ensure that not only Berkeley, but the U.S. academic community as a whole, realized that exciting and original philosophical work was being done in non-anglophone countries. He encouraged students to work on these figures, and he became one of the very few senior figures in American philosophy on whom young philosophers who were interested in Heidegger or Foucault could rely for support. Students whom Dreyfus trained at Berkeley have become influential and important commentators on European philosophy and, in their turn, have encouraged and supported the efforts of a third generation of scholars. When intellectual historians track the gradual flow of postwar French and German philosophical thought into the United States, Dreyfus's archive will be one of their principal sources.

Dreyfus would not have been able to do all this without amazing reserves of energy and great personal charm. But his achievements are due above all to his inexhaustible intellectual curiosity—his willingness to read anything that comes along with the hope of finding something new and important in it. The sheer joyous optimism of his approach to philosophy, his assumption that there is probably something useful and interesting in any new philosophical publication, is primarily responsible for his contribution to our country's intellectual life. In a period in which it has sometimes seemed that American philosophers read less and less in every generation, and in which specialization in philosophy has reached hitherto unheard-of extremes, Dreyfus has remained a colleague with whom one can profitably converse all along an amazingly wide spectrum of philosophical topics and authors.

Starting in 1980, Dreyfus (with help from his wife Geneviève and his friends Jocelyn and David Hoy) staged a series of summer institutes, sponsored by the National Endowment for the Humanities. These brought Husserlians together with Searleans, Heideggerians together with Davidsonians, Foucauldians together with bourgeois liberals. Some of the most fruitful teaching I have ever done, and some of the most instructive intellectual encounters I have ever had, were at these institutes. Hundreds of American philosophers who spent their summers in Berkeley or Santa Cruz, talking with the others whom Dreyfus had assembled beneath the redwoods, had similar experiences. Nothing else that the Endowment has done so far for American philosophy compares with its sponsorship of those institutes.

So far I have concentrated on Dreyfus's role as mediator, commentator, and impresario. But of course he has another persona: he is an original, heretical, systematic philosopher. I have often resisted his views, and still resist many of them, but over the years I have often had to concede that he was right all along. In an era when flow charts captivated the imagination of most analytic philosophers, Dreyfus's 1972 book *What Computers Can't Do*[4] was shrugged off by many people, including myself. Twenty years later, when I read *What Computers Still Can't Do*,[5] I realized that I had come around to agreeing with Dreyfus at almost every point. I first heard about connectionism and parallel distributed processing from Dreyfus, and, like many others, I owe to him my understanding of the significance of this new way of thinking about what computers will, and will not, eventually be able to do.

When they write the history of the sub-area of philosophy called "philosophy of mind" (an area that was born in 1949 with Ryle's *The Concept of Mind*,[6] and that I predict will die when the neurologists finish doing to the cognitive psychologists what the atomists did to the alchemists), Dreyfus's work will loom large. For the computer-mind analogy has dominated this field for decades. Throughout those decades Dreyfus has been the philosopher who has insisted, strenuously and lucidly, on the disanalogies. He has helped make the rest of us realize the need to develop a nonreductionist account of the relation between minds and brains, and he has given us reason to wonder whether neurology ever will play the role that I and others still fondly envisage for it.

As the 1990s approached, Dreyfus began to reach both beyond exegesis of European philosophers and philosophy of mind, and to offer original and provocative contributions to other areas of discussion, notably those concerning modernity and postmodernity. I find myself reacting to these more recent writings with the same mingling of admiration and doubt with which I have long read his interpretations of Foucault and Heidegger.

For whereas Dreyfus reads these authors as talking about real issues, struggling to get things right, I read them as offering interesting, and possibly useful, alternative descriptions of what is going on—descriptions between which one need not choose. Instead, one can pick them up, use them for various occasions and purposes, and lay them down again. Dreyfus and I have always held divergent metaphilosophical views: we have differed about whether to read our favorite philosophers as telling you how things really are or as recontextualizers—people who do not reveal the essential nature of anything, but simply tell you how things look when rearranged.

Dreyfus tends to read for adequacy, but I usually read for edification. For example, it would not occur to me to ask whether the phenomenology of Dasein in Part I of *Being and Time*[7] gets human existence right. Despite all Dreyfus's efforts, I remain deeply suspicious of the claim that some phenomenologists get something right that others have gotten wrong. I still see Husserl's attempt at strict science as being as bad an idea as Russell's attempt to make logic the essence of philosophy. Dreyfus has never been able to persuade me that Husserl said anything about intentionality that Wilfrid Sellars did not render obsolete. I long ago became convinced that philosophers should leave off talking about experience and should talk about language instead, and that is an issue on which Dreyfus and I will probably never agree.

Foreword

The range of Dreyfus's publications is astonishing. They begin with interpretations of Dante and Cervantes and end, for the moment, with work on socioeconomic globalization. I can think of no other contemporary American philosopher who has done so many different things so well. The gratitude I feel for forty years of Bert's friendship is matched only by my gratitude for his having turned me on to so many fascinating authors, so many novel lines of argument, and so many fruitful topics of speculation. The authors who have contributed to this volume are only a few of the many philosophers whose intellectual lives are richer thanks to his work.

Acknowledgments

The editors would like to give special thanks to Geneviève Dreyfus, without whom this volume never would have appeared, as well as to Larry Cohen at The MIT Press. Preparation of the volumes was completed while Jeff Malpas was a Humboldt Research Fellow at the University of Heidelberg. A number of students at Brigham Young University and the University of Tasmania have assisted in the preparation of this manuscript, including Amy Jensen, Heidi Poulson, Stacy Day, Hillary Warner, Angela Rosier, and especially Julie Murdock.

Introduction

Mark A. Wrathall and Jeff Malpas

A first glance at Hubert L. Dreyfus's bibliography can leave a rather confused impression. He has written on *Don Quixote* as well as artificial intelligence. He has written on Heidegger, Merleau-Ponty, Foucault, Husserl, Kierkegaard, and Sartre, but also on psychology, cognitive science, ethics, entrepreneurship, and expert systems. Indeed, it is Dreyfus's remarkable breadth that inspired us to create two separate volumes in his honor. There was no other way, we reasoned, to begin to pay an adequate tribute to Dreyfus's remarkable contributions to philosophy and related fields while maintaining some thematic coherence.

The diversity of Dreyfus's interests was already evident in his undergraduate career. Arriving at Harvard College in 1947, his initial interests were in physics rather than philosophy. He discovered, however, that he had an aptitude for work in the humanities, and the lectures of C. I. Lewis, then at the end of his career, awakened in him a real interest in philosphical inquiry. In 1951 Dreyfus did his *senior honors thesis* on "Causality and Quantum Theory" (W. V. O. Quine was the main examiner awarding the thesis *highest honors*), but by the early 1950s he had, partly through the influence of John Wild, started to read Heidegger and Merleau-Ponty.

A Harvard Sheldon Travelling Fellowship enabled Dreyfus to visit Freiburg, Germany, in 1953–54 (a visit that included an interview with Heidegger himself), and when he returned to Harvard, he began teaching at MIT while also looking around for a dissertation topic and supervisor. In 1955 Aron Gurwitsch influenced Dreyfus to start reading Husserl, and he spent 1955–56 at the Husserl Archive at the University of Louvain. In 1959 a French government grant took Dreyfus to the Ecole Normale Supérieure in Paris, where he made the acquaintance of Michel Haar among others. It was not until 1962, with Dagfinn Føllesdal as his supervisor, that Dreyfus finally settled on a topic for his dissertation: the opposition between Gurvitz and Føllesdal on the concept of the noema in Husserl. He completed the dissertation in 1964, and in that same year, while still at MIT, he was engaged as a consultant to the RAND Corporation to review the work of Allen Newell and Herbert Simon on artificial intelligence. It was this job that eventually led him to write *What Computers Can't Do*, which appeared in 1972.

In 1968, Dreyfus moved to the University of California at Berkeley. Here he and his students began to explore a vast range of topics, from cognitive science and philosophy of mind to existentialism in literature and the progress in our culture from gods to God and back. From the beginning Dreyfus has enjoyed a mutually productive relationship with his Berkeley philosophy colleague John Searle—notwithstanding the philosophical differences between them.[1] In the late 1970s, Dreyfus came into contact with Paul Rabinow, who was in the anthropology department, and the two collaborated on a number of projects reflecting contemporary French theory, particularly the work of Pierre Bourdieu (who met with Dreyfus and Rabinow in Paris in the late 1980s) and Michel Foucault (with whom Dreyfus and Rabinow became friends after he visited California in 1979 and 1980).

As this sketch suggests, while it was his critique of artificial intelligence that originally established Dreyfus's public reputation (*What Computers Can't Do* has been translated into ten languages), it was the study and interpretation of "continental" philosophers that came first in the order of his philosophical interests and influences. As he explained in the introduction to the MIT Press edition of his book entitled *What Computers Still Can't Do*, his early work "can be seen in retrospect as a repeatedly revised attempt to justify [his] intuition, based on [his] study of Martin Heidegger, Maurice Merleau-Ponty, and the later Wittgenstein, that the GOFAI [Good Old-Fashioned

Artificial Intelligence] research program would eventually fail."[2] And much of Dreyfus's writing on other issues can be seen similarly to derive from his study of Heidegger and others. It is appropriate, then, that the first volume of this set of essays should focus on the dialogue with the continental philosophical tradition, and particularly the work of Heidegger, that has played such a foundational and ongoing role in Dreyfus's thinking.

From the perspective of many Heideggerians, of course, analytic philosophy, with its emphasis on logical analysis as a basis for answering traditional metaphysical questions regarding the nature of language, mind, and world, is a part of the problem of modernity, which needs to be overcome. From an analytic perspective, on the other hand, continental philosophy in general, and Heidegger in particular, have often been viewed with extreme disdain—as Searle writes in his contribution to volume 2 of this festschrift, "Most philosophers in the Anglo-American tradition seem to think that Heidegger was an obscurantist muddlehead at best or an unregenerate Nazi at worst."[3] Dreyfus, as much as anyone, has contributed to breaking down such antipathies. His clear, jargon-free reappropriation of Heidegger and other Continental thinkers has made their work accessible, as well as respectable, to the analytic world. At the same time, rather than dismissing it as hopelessly mired in metaphysics (in Heidegger's sense), he has taken the analytic tradition seriously as offering insights and approaches to the same sort of problems that have troubled continental philosophers. His commentary and other papers draw frequently on the work of Searle, Davidson, Wittgenstein, and Quine to illuminate issues in Heidegger's work.

Dreyfus's engagement with thinkers such as Heidegger has played a crucial part in opening up academic philosophy, particularly in North America, to continental influences. The publication of Richard Rorty's *Philosophy and the Mirror of Nature* is often viewed as a watershed event in this process.[4] Rorty and Dreyfus have been friends since the 1950s, and there was undoubtedly a certain amount of reciprocal influence. But even before Rorty's book appeared, Dreyfus's own influence was having its effect, not only through his appropriation of continental thought in relation to the AI debate, but also through his role as an energetic and committed teacher and through his involvement, often in company with Rorty or another old friend, Charles Taylor (whom Dreyfus first met on a visit to Oxford in 1954), in various lectures, colloquia, and seminars.[5] As an award-winning teacher of undergraduates[6] Dreyfus has been responsible for motivating many students to include philosophy in their life pursuits, and as a supervisor of graduate students he has helped produce a generation of ecumenically minded scholars. To cite just two examples from among the contributors to this volume,[7] John Haugeland and Charles Guignon were both students of Dreyfus at Berkeley in the early 1970s, and even if their views often diverge from his, still Dreyfus's influence is clearly evident in their work.

Around the same time as Rorty's book appeared, Dreyfus was organizing the first of a series of Summer Institutes that were to focus on topics crossing the analytic/continental divide. The inaugural Institute, "Phenomenology and Existentialism—Continental and Analytic Perspectives on Intentionality," was held in 1980 in Berkeley and brought together a quite amazing range of presenters including Robert Brandom, Rüdiger Bubner, Dagfinn Føllesdal, J. N. Mohanty, Paul Rabinow, Richard Rorty, John Searle, and Wilfrid Sellars. Between the first of the Summer Institutes in Berkeley in 1980 and the second held at Santa Cruz in 1988 (by which time David Hoy's involvement was an important part of the event), Dreyfus organized a number of Summer Seminars at Berkeley. The second Summer Institute included among its participants Thomas Kuhn, Clifford Geertz, Richard Rorty, Charles Taylor, Stanley Cavell, and Alexander Nehamas. Subsequent Institutes (in 1990, 1992, 1994, and 1997) have been no less broad either in the range of participants or in the issues discussed.[8]

In the preface to the second edition of his *Kantbuch*, Heidegger writes that "In contrast to the methods of historical philology . . . a thoughtful dialogue is bound by other laws."[9] It is never, of course, the case that one can forego attending to the historical context and meaning of a text, but the significance of a real philosophical dialogue between thinkers can never be measured in terms of historical correctness alone. Dreyfus's engagement with Heidegger—like his engagement with Kierkegaard and Merleau-Ponty, with Foucault and Bourdieu, with Homer, Aeschylus, Dante, Dostoevsky, and

Melville—has never been geared just to a set of exegetical or historical concerns. Neither, of course, are such concerns forgotten: Dreyfus aims to let the texts speak for themselves. He is always concerned to learn from the philosophers he reads and teaches (as he is also concerned to learn from his students and teaching assistants), not to make them mere mouthpieces for views he holds already; and to learn from them is both to attempt to understand and to appropriate what they have to say.

One of the important features of the dialogue with continental thought that has characterized Dreyfus's work is its orientation to contemporary philosophical concerns. As Dreyfus has said of his approach to teaching, "according to my students, I am always trying to relate what I am reading to what difference it makes to the world or in their lives, so that they see a connection. They see that philosophy is not just an abstract scholastic debate between me and some commentator or between me and some basic text. And I also hear from my students that I am concerned about treating a text, like Heidegger's text, with great respect for what's in it, trying to get the truth about it, but not a kind of worshipful respect. I am ready to criticize it or make jokes about it too."[10] Dreyfus's engagement with other thinkers has always been driven by his desire to understand certain basic questions about ourselves and our world, and so the philosophers on whom his teaching and research have focused are just those whose work seems to him to reveal phenomena that advance that understanding—philosophers whose work seems "to make a difference" to the world and to our lives.

Both of the volumes that make up this festschrift can be seen as honoring Dreyfus's own efforts to "make a difference," not only in the lives of his students but also in the broader world—and not just the world of academic philosophy. This is especially evident in the essays that make up volume 2. But even in this volume, whose focus is much more traditionally philosophical, the emphasis of a great deal of the discussion is on issues that engage with our contemporary situation, with our sense of who we are and what we can be.

One of Dreyfus's most important contributions to our understanding of Heidegger is his influential commentary on Division I of Heidegger's *Being and Time*. In the preface to the commentary, entitled *Being-in-the-World*,[11] Dreyfus explains his belief that Division I is "the most original and important section of the work, for it is in Division I that Heidegger works out his account of being-in-the-world and uses it to ground a profound critique of traditional ontology and epistemology."[12] Many reviewers have disputed Dreyfus's claim that Division I can be understood apart from Division II, although to our knowledge no one has pointed out which elements of Dreyfus's interpretation of Division I would need to be changed in the light of Division II. Dreyfus is now convinced, however, on the basis of what he has learned from his students, his teaching assistants, and the participants in this volume, that by treating Division I independently of Division II he has failed to comprehend the importance to the Heideggerian project of a higher form of intelligibility than everyday intelligibility. This is something Dreyfus takes up in his reply at the end of the volume and that he will develop further in the second edition of *Being-in-the-World*.

Dreyfus's general approach to Heidegger (including his readiness to correct Heidegger where mistaken, and his distaste for jargon-ridden obfuscation, whether by Heidegger or others) has struck many Heideggerians as sacrilegious, and they have seized on Dreyfus's prefatory comments as an excuse for disregarding his reading of Heidegger as a whole. But a less dismissive study of Dreyfus's work—one that reads beyond the preface of his commentary—finds that his thorough and clear account of being-in-the-world underwrites an extremely powerful and suggestive analysis of the existentialist portions of Heidegger's work, which are perhaps the most obscure sections in *Being and Time*. For instance, Dreyfus's powerful accounts of the structural fallenness of Dasein and of Dasein's indebtedness to public intelligibility make it possible to make sense of Heidegger's discussion of the source of Dasein's tendency to lapse into inauthenticity.

The problem of authenticity that is raised here is the focus, in differing ways, for the papers in the first section of this volume. All four papers, in the spirit of challenge that Dreyfus encourages in the classroom, argue for deficiencies in Dreyfus's account of authenticity. Taylor Carman, for instance, suggests a resolution to apparent tensions Dreyfus has noted in Heidegger's accounts of structural falling, fleeing, and authenticity. Randall Havas criticizes another feature of Dreyfus's account of authenticity—his glossing of authenticity in terms of the openness to the ungroundedness of human existence. Havas argues that Dreyfus is drawn into this mistaken view by his attempt to read Heidegger as grounding intelligibility in communal norms.

John Haugeland's paper raises the question of the relationship between Division I of *Being and Time* and Heidegger's "existentialist side." Haugeland argues that Heidegger's account of authentic being-toward-death, as the condition of disclosedness, far from being severable from Division I, is "the fulcrum of his entire ontology".[13] Haugeland thus argues for the inadequacy of Dreyfus's and Rubin's reading of authenticity, falling, death, etc., as secularizations of Kierkegaard. Where Haugeland focuses on authenticity and resolute being-towards-death as substantive bases for his account of discovery and everyday being-in-the-world, Guignon concentrates on the phenomenon of involvement in the concrete situation and the narrative structure of human life as the foundation on which all philosophical inquiry must rest.

Heidegger's epochal account of being—and in particular the loss of meaning in the understanding of being that prevails in the modern and technological ages—is a central theme, not just in Dreyfus's reading of Heidegger's post-*Being and Time* works,[14] but in Dreyfus's own teaching and writing on other figures in philosophy. Dreyfus teaches what is perennially one of the most popular undergraduate courses at Berkeley—a course he calls "Existentialism in Literature and Film"—in which he offers a Heideggerian account of the religious response to the Enlightenment, at first reinterpreting, and then grieving, the loss of the Judeo-Christian God. Dreyfus brings home modernity's distress at the prospect of a loss of meaning by combining a reading of philosophical works such as Pascal's *Pensées*, Kierkegaard's *Fear and Trembling*, and Nietzsche's *Gay Science* with an interpretation of literary works such as Dostoyevsky's *Brothers Karamazov* and films such as Alain Resnais's *Hiroshima mon Amour* and Carol Reed's *The Third Man*. Not surprisingly, the course has many offspring taught by Dreyfus's former students and teaching assistants at other universities.

Mark A. Wrathall and Jeff Malpas

In the second section of this volume, "Modernity, Self, and World," we present six essays responding, in various ways, to questions of modernity. Alastair Hannay argues against Dreyfus's reading of Kierkegaard, in which Kierkegaard is seen as responding to the loss of meaning resulting from the leveling of distinctions in modern society. Michael Zimmerman takes up Dreyfus's and Charles Spinosa's argument, presented in "Highway Bridges and Feasts: Heidegger and Borgmann on How to Affirm Technology,"[15] regarding the possibility of Dasein preserving its world-disclosive essence in the technological age. Taking Dreyfus's work on technology as a starting point, Michel Haar's subtle and suggestive reading of Nietzsche and Heidegger deepens our understanding of the threat posed to our essence by the technological epoch. Béatrice Han, in a related fashion, explores the possibility of preserving the meaning and value of truth in the face of modernist rationality through a revival of archaic forms of the idea of the "Master of Truth." Both Jeff Malpas and Julian Young respond to the challenge presented by Heidegger's thinking in relation to questions of place and dwelling. Malpas focuses on the way such questions might be illuminated by consideration of Heidegger's problematic treatment of spatiality in *Being and Time*, while Young focuses more directly on Heidegger's later thought.

The four essays in the third section of this volume pay tribute to Dreyfus's ability to bring Heidegger into a productive dialogue with other philosophers. William Blattner responds to Rorty's reading of Heidegger, contrasting Dewey's view of coping with Heidegger's practice-based account of unconcealment to show how fundamentally different Heidegger is from pragmatism. Dagfinn Føllesdal, on the other hand, argues that Dreyfus's reading of Heidegger overstates the originality of Heideggerian coping. In particular, Føllesdal suggests that Husserl anticipated Heidegger's work and that Heidegger, far from breaking with Husserl, was merely continuing in the path he had opened up. David Cerbone, in differentiating between Heidegger's and Searle's attempts to undermine the philosophical urge for a proof of the existence of an external world, shows how Heidegger's insistence on the priority of ontology undermines the epistemological tradition in philosophy (of which Searle remains a part). Mark Okrent uses Davidson to illuminate another important feature that distinguishes Heidegger from the analytic tradition. This distinction between Heidegger and Davidson and, for that matter, between Heidegger and the whole analytic tradition, Okrent argues, is the way in which for Heidegger all intentionality intends the intender.

There is no doubt that Hubert Dreyfus's work has made a difference in a great many ways. And the work of his friends and students —work such as that gathered together in this volume—has also made a difference to Dreyfus's own thinking. Philosophy, for Dreyfus, is always a matter of engagement and exchange. Indeed, Dreyfus's commitment to such a conception of philosophy, and the passion and enthusiasm with which he pursues that commitment, as well as the generous and open-minded spirit that is so characteristic of his work, is a model of what philosophy can and ought to be. For Dreyfus, philosophy can never be an abstract academic activity. It is as personal and as consuming as any other part of our lives—an activity that is as rewarding as it is demanding. As Dreyfus writes, "Philosophy . . . only has itself as its subject matter. There are no facts, there are no rules, there is not even a corpus of accepted interpretations. It has to be reinvented every day. Some days you fail, some days you succeed, and when you do, then you and your students know something of what is exciting and important about philosophy."[16]

I

Philosophy and Authenticity

1

Must We Be Inauthentic?

Taylor Carman

Individuum est ineffabile.
—*Goethe*

I Introduction

Hubert Dreyfus and Jane Rubin describe Heidegger's account of
authenticity in *Being and Time* as a "successfully secularized version
of Religiousness A,"[1] Kierkegaard's notion of a kind of spiritual self-
annihilation before God. "To comprehend this annihilation is the
highest thing of which a human being is capable," Kierkegaard
writes; "a human being is great and at his highest when he corresponds to God by being nothing at all himself."[2] Religiousness B,
by contrast, represents genuine Christian faith in the recovery of
individual selfhood and eternal happiness "based on the relation to
something historical," paradigmatically Jesus Christ.[3] Dreyfus and
Rubin argue convincingly that Heidegger's account of authenticity
takes over a version of the self-abnegating ideal of Religiousness A,
but forgoes the faith, unconditional commitment, and consequently
the more robust conception of selfhood that define Religiousness B.
"Care itself, in its very essence," Heidegger writes, "is permeated with
nullity (*Nichtigkeit*) through and through" (*SZ*, 285), so that authenticity (*Eigentlichkeit*) just amounts to "owning up" to that essential
nullity in an attitude of openness and resolve.[4]

Dreyfus and Rubin point out that this partial appropriation of Kierkegaard comes at a great cost, however, for "the very success of Heidegger's description of an authentic life makes his account of inauthenticity incoherent."[5] This is so, they say, because Heidegger advances two separate, indeed incompatible, accounts of "fallenness" (*Verfallenheit*), that is, Dasein's absorption in and fascination with the world and its own average everydayness (*SZ*, 175). According to the view that dominates Division I of *Being and Time*, falling (*Verfallen*) and fallenness constitute a permanent *structural* feature of being-in-the-world that constantly inclines us toward an inauthentic mode of existence. According to the version that emerges in Division II, by contrast, fallenness is the *motivated* result of Dasein's temptation to "flee" from its own nullity in the face of anxiety. Given his equivocation between the structural and the psychological accounts of fallenness, Heidegger's position "runs into a double contradiction; inauthenticity becomes both inevitable and incomprehensible."[6] On the one hand, if fallenness is motivated by a flight from anxiety, "then, since absorption is essential to Dasein as being-in-the-world, Dasein becomes essentially inauthentic."[7] On the other hand, if authentic resoluteness itself affords Dasein a kind of "equanimity" and "unshakable joy," as Heidegger himself insists (*SZ*, 345, 310), then "resoluteness is so rewarding that, once one is authentic, falling back into inauthenticity becomes incomprehensible."[8]

Dreyfus and Rubin are right that the structural and the motivational stories are incompatible as competing wholesale explanations of fallenness. I want to propose, however, that a properly reconstructed version of the structural story taken by itself renders inauthenticity neither inevitable nor incomprehensible. For while falling and fleeing are indeed formally distinct, they are from a practical and phenomenological point of view wholly continuous, differing only in degree. Anxious flight is not just some random psychological aberration, but an "intensified" or "aggravated" modification of falling (*SZ*, 178). There is a straightforward conceptual distinction between falling and fleeing, then, but what the distinction marks is a merely gradual difference.[9]

II Falling, Fallenness, and Fleeing

The challenge facing any interpretation of Heidegger's concept of falling is to spell out its relation to what Heidegger describes as Dasein's "turning away" (*Abkehr*) or even "flight" (*Flucht*) in the face of itself (*SZ*, 184–186). For falling is an "ontological-existential" structure of being-in-the-world as such,[10] whereas inauthenticity is just one of Dasein's "ontic-existentiell" modes, along with authenticity and finally "indifference" (*Indifferenz*), which is neither authentic nor inauthentic (*SZ*, 43, 53, 232).

Dreyfus and Rubin are therefore right to insist on a formal or conceptual distinction between falling and fleeing, since in principle no existential structure of being-in-the-world can be identical with one of Dasein's merely existentiell modes. One way to appreciate the distinction is to see that the effort to flee oneself is teleologically incoherent and doomed to failure, since nothing could count as having managed to do it. There is no such thing as a Dasein that has escaped itself. Fleeing in the face of yourself, then, is like trying to pull yourself up by your bootstraps: no amount of effort advances the cause. But neither does the impossibility of success render the effort impossible, and it is the effort itself that concerns us phenomenologically, notwithstanding the incoherence of its intended effect. Falling and fleeing are at least formally distinct, then, for while there is no such thing as *not* falling, neither is there any such thing as having managed to flee.

At this point Heidegger cautions that "with such phenomena, the investigation must guard against conflating ontic-existentiell characteristics with ontological-existential interpretation" (*SZ*, 184). Yet he himself seems to collapse the distinction between falling and fleeing throughout *Being and Time*. More precisely, as Dreyfus observes, he offers two very different accounts of the relation between fallenness and fleeing: one structural, the other psychological or motivational. According to the structural story, falling generates an abiding tendency, even "temptation," to flee (*SZ*, 177).[11] On the psychological account, by contrast, Dasein's flight from itself in the face of anxiety is what generates fallenness: "The turning away of falling is grounded . . . in anxiety" (*SZ*, 186).

I think Dreyfus and Rubin are also right that if fallenness were merely a function of Dasein's spontaneous flight in the face of anxiety, as the motivational story suggests, then Dasein would be doomed to inauthenticity. For then our fallenness could only mean that we are forever and constantly responding to anxiety by fleeing, rather than owning up to our existence resolutely. But Heidegger clearly does not regard inauthenticity as an inescapable fact of existence, so fallenness cannot just be the result of a motivated flight. Rather, as I shall argue, fleeing figures prominently in Heidegger's account as a kind of limit case, an aggravated mode of falling, not an inevitable ongoing syndrome. This is not to say that the very notion of a flight from onself makes no sense, only that it cannot explain Dasein's fallenness as such, as Heidegger at times seems to have intended. If fleeing in anxiety is one of Dasein's ontic-existentiell possibilities, it must be understood as a structurally conditioned yet ontically contingent inclination or tendency. In short, falling must explain fleeing; fleeing cannot by itself account for fallenness.

It is the burden of the structural story, then, to make sense of Dasein's tendency to flee itself and become "captivated" or "fascinated" (*benommen*) by entities in the world around it (*SZ*, 113, 176). Unfortunately, Dreyfus tells us, "On the stuctural account, the tendency toward fascination remains unaccounted for,"[12] and in a note he adds, "One could try to fill out such a structural account, but Heidegger in *Being and Time* has recourse to a motivational account and so never faces the problem."[13] It seems to me, on the contrary, that Heidegger does face the problem, although his response to it is admittedly somewhat underdeveloped. The structural account does require some filling out, but there are also considerable clues in *Being and Time* concerning how the elaboration might proceed.

Actually, Dreyfus suggests a partial solution to the problem himself. In chapter 13 of his commentary on *Being and Time* he points out that Heidegger need not revert to the motivational story to account for fallenness itself, since fallenness is just a function of the public nature of intelligibility: "Simply by being socialized," Dreyfus writes, "Dasein takes over the fallenness of the one" (*das Man*).[14] And as he quotes Heidegger saying, "First and for the most part the self is lost in *das Man*. It understands itself in terms of the possibilities of existence that 'circulate' in the contemporary 'average' public way of interpreting Dasein" (*SZ*, 383). Dreyfus's partial reconstruction of the structural account of falling, then, consists in pointing out that no motivational story is required to account for Dasein's already having fallen into average everydayness, since such fallenness is a condition of intelligibility as such and so always a kind of *fait accompli*.

But this partial solution can only be partial, as Dreyfus admits, since it only explains why Dasein initially—or as Heidegger says, "first and for the most part"—finds itself in its everyday fallen condition. It says nothing about why, once having gotten a taste of the "unshakable joy" and "equanimity" of authentic resoluteness, Dasein perpetually finds itself relapsing or *falling back* into inauthenticity. Granted, we are constantly thrown into social contexts whose norms transcend us. Yet something more seems to be at stake in Heidegger's description of falling as a force that somehow constantly steers us away from ourselves: "Falling is an ontological concept of movement" (*SZ*, 180); "This 'agitation' (*Bewegtheit*) of Dasein in its own being is what we call the *plunge* (*Absturz*)" (*SZ*, 178). Falling is not just a prior condition of intelligibility, but an ongoing dynamic tendency, a perpetual pull away from authentic existence:

The movement of plunging into and within the groundlessness of inauthentic being in *das Man* constantly tears the understanding away from projecting authentic possibilities and drags it into the sedated presumption of possessing or attaining everything. This constantly being torn away from authenticity, yet always feigning it, along with being dragged into *das Man*, characterizes the agitation of falling as *spiraling* (*Wirbel*). (*SZ*, 178)

Like being closed off and concealed, then, "It is part of Dasein's facticity that, *as long as* it is what it is, it remains in the throw (*im Wurf*) and is whirled (*hineingewirbelt*) into the inauthenticity of *das Man*" (*SZ*, 179). Indeed, "Being closed off (*Verschlossenheit*) and being concealed are part of Dasein's *facticity*" (*SZ*, 222). "To be closed off" is essential to Dasein's "disclosedness" (*Erschlossenheit*), which Heidegger here famously identifies as the existential-ontological meaning of truth (*SZ*, §44).

It is therefore not that Dasein just happens to find itself "first and for the most part" fallen, rather disclosedness always remains to some extent essentially closed off, and all facticity involves a kind of constant pressure drawing Dasein away from authentic resoluteness. This pressure is what Heidegger wants to describe in his structural account of falling. "Which structure," he asks, "exhibits the 'agitation' of falling?" (*SZ*, 177). What is this peculiar force that seems to drag Dasein away from authentic existence? As Dreyfus says, "we need a structural account of why Dasein *yields* to the pull of the world it is absorbed in . . . so as to let itself be *turned away from* what is primordial in the world and in itself."[15] How are we to understand falling in a structural way that makes sense of Dasein's *letting* itself be pulled into inauthenticity? Given that Dasein "constantly delivers itself over to the 'world' and lets the 'world' matter to it," then, why does it do so, as Heidegger says, "in such a way that Dasein somehow evades its very self" (*SZ*, 139)? Why should falling tend toward self-evasion? The reason, I want to suggest, has to do with Dasein's concrete particularity, and its relation to the discursive—that is, the expressive and communicative—conditions of interpretation.

III "Mineness" and the Generic Drift of Discourse

Dasein's concrete particularity is, of course, fundamentally different from that of any entity that is not essentially self-interpreting. Being-in-the-world essentially consists in having an understanding of being. But it is also crucial that in its facticity Dasein "is delivered over to *its own* being" (*SZ*, 41–42, emphasis added), and not just to being at large. "The being of this entity is *in each case mine*" (*SZ*, 41), Heidegger insists. Indeed, Dasein in general "has the character of *mineness*" (*Jemeinigkeit*) (*SZ*, 42). What this means is that human existence exhibits an essential concrete reflexivity, for I must make sense not just of the being of entities at large, but of *my own* being. This irreducible dimension of particularity inherent in the structure of existence grounds all self-interpretation, authentic and inauthentic alike.

At the same time, Dasein's interpretation of its own particularity is essentially conditioned by "discourse" (*Rede*). Discourse, in Heidegger's sense of the word, is not restricted to language, nor indeed to any system of signs or symbols. It is rather the entire domain of Dasein's expressive and communicative possibilities in virtue of which things become interpretable for it, and by it, as such. Discourse is expression and communication in the broadest sense, including all our spontaneous and unsystematic means of conveying something about something to someone. Heidegger thus analyzes discourse according to its three "constitutive moments": "the about which of the discourse (what is talked about) (*das Beredete*), what is said (*das Geredete*) as such, communication (*Mitteilung*) and intimation (*Bekundung*)" (*SZ,* 162).[16] Since discourse is not necessarily linguistic, its content or "what is said" need not be propositional, "what is talked about" need not be the referent of a singular term, nor must communication or intimation be overt. "*Hearing* and *remaining silent* are possibilities belonging to discursive speech," Heidegger says (*SZ,* 161). "Hearing is constitutive for discoursing" (*SZ,* 163). Indeed, another "mode of discourse," according to Heidegger, is the "call of conscience," which one might otherwise be tempted to identify with some essentially private domain of ethical subjectivity (*SZ,* 269, 271).

But just as the call of conscience turns out not to be as private as one might think, neither is discourse itself limited to overt verbal and nonverbal speech acts. Rather, both conscience and overt linguistic behavior inhabit the shared social and semantic space in which entities are collectively intelligible to Dasein as the things they are. More specifically, then, "discourse" in Heidegger's sense refers to the abiding repertoire or practical vocabulary of spontaneous expressive and communicative comportments into which we are habituated and in virtue of which our everyday practical world is always more or less readily interpretable for us. "*Discourse is existentially equiprimordial with affectivity [Befindlichkeit] and understanding*" (*SZ,* 161), Heidegger says. Indeed, he defines "meaning" (*Sinn*) as "that which is articulable in interpretation, *thus even more primordially* in discourse" (*SZ,* 161, emphasis added). If discourse is equiprimordial with attunement and understanding, and even *more basic* to meaning than interpretation itself, then all interpretation must be conditioned by discourse, that is, by expressive and communicative practice.

It is widely acknowledged among readers of *Being and Time* that Dasein finds itself and its world always already interpreted, and moreover finds its own interpretations conditioned by and permanently indebted to the anonymous social normativity governing intelligibility at large, a normativity that Heidegger calls *das Man*. It is less widely understood why this must be so. The answer, it seems to me, lies in conceiving of discourse in concrete pragmatic terms. For if interpretation is itself a kind of practical comportment, and if it is conditioned by the discursive dispositions and habits into which we are socialized, then it is no wonder that we find ourselves in our very comportment spontaneously and constantly reliant on the interpretations always already at work in the social world that gave rise to those dispositions and habits in the first place. Discourse thus constitutes the bridge between the anonymous social normativity of *das Man* and the concrete interpretive practices of individual human agents.

Yet the anonymity and banality generated by what I shall call the *generic drift* of discourse, which at its most mundane devolves into "idle talk" (*Gerede*), naturally tends to obscure the particularity of Dasein's own unique situation: "Idle talk is the possibility of understanding everything without any prior appropriation (*Zueignung*) of the matter" (*SZ*, 169). This kind of generic obfuscation leads to what Heidegger, borrowing from Kierkegaard, calls "leveling" (*Einebnung*), that is, the socially sanctioned, habitually enforced averageness of daily life (*SZ*, 127), and "ambiguity" (*Zweideutigkeit*), the fact that "it soon becomes undecidable what is disclosed in genuine understanding and what is not" (*SZ*, 173).[17]

Recognizing the discursive conditions of interpretation, then, promises to shed light on Heidegger's characterization of falling as a kind of constant movement or agitation in which Dasein is perpetually torn away from authentically owning up to its own existence. For it is not a matter of indifference, structurally speaking, whether Dasein's interpretations proceed farther and farther in the direction of some repertoire of prefabricated public meanings or return instead to a more concrete grasp of its own factical particularity, or "mineness." Mineness is a formal condition of interpretation but is otherwise empty of concrete expressible or communicable content. It is discourse that provides the only vocabulary in which interpretation can in fact proceed. There is no alternative to expressing and communicating one's understanding in the given idiom of one's social and cultural milieu. To make sense of oneself at all is to make sense of oneself on the basis of the banal, indeed flattened out and levelled off, language of *das Man*. And yet to settle on some generically intelligible, and so more or less normatively sanctioned, interpretation of oneself in one's being is precisely to forego, or even to evade one's own factical particularity, which nonetheless remains an abiding condition of interpretation itself. Settling on some definite self-interpretation means, at least temporarily, setting aside the necessarily unsettled particularity of thrown projection itself and the perpetual need to make sense of one's own being futurally as what one "has" to be, as an ongoing issue. It is the conventional settledness and determinacy of the very resources of discourse itself, then, that belies the unsettledness and indeterminacy of existence as such.

There is in this sense an inherent tension between Dasein's factical particularity and the generality of the discursive terms in which it must express and communicate its understanding. Precisely because it is rooted in discourse, interpretation is constantly subject to a kind of generic drift, since articulations and elaborations of meaning essentially move in the direction of common intelligibility. What is intelligible is precisely what "one" understands. It is constitutive of making sense that one do so according to the standards of *das Man*. Interpretation has no choice but to accommodate and exploit the prevailing criteria of intelligibility, which means at least to some extent trading the irreducible particularity of one's own factical situation for generally adequate, but always more or less loosely fitting means of expressing and communicating it. The effort to make oneself intelligible in discourse therefore tends to drift into ever shallower waters, eventually bottoming out in sheer banality and cliché. It might be tempting to suppose that the generic drift of discourse is just some contingent, perhaps deplorable tendency. But the point is precisely that averageness and generality are positive phenomena, constitutive of interpretation. The only intelligible interpretations are those that to some degree accommodate the averageness of common understanding.

Yet Dasein's factical particularity remains recalcitrant to such accommodations. As we have seen, Dasein finds itself first and for the most part lost in *das Man*, whose sheer averageness obscures and renders indeterminate Dasein's very freedom of choice:

> With its lostness in *das Man*, Dasein's nearest factical ability-to-be . . . has already been decided upon. Grasping these possibilities of being is something *das Man* has always already taken away from Dasein. *Das Man* hides even its own silent discharge of the explicit *choice* of these possibilities. It leaves indeterminate who "actually" (*eigentlich*) chooses. (*SZ*, 268)

Heidegger is emphatically *not* arguing that Dasein has chosen its own lostness in *das Man*, and has then subsequently deceived itself about having made such a choice. Again, in ambiguity, Heidegger says, echoing Kierkegaard, "it soon becomes undecideable what is disclosed in genuine understanding and what is not" (*SZ*, 173). Yet this tendency is not a psychological syndrome; it is instead social and discursive in nature: "ambiguity in no way first arises from an explicit intention toward disguise and distortion . . . it is not summoned up by the individual Dasein. It lies already in being-with-one-another as *thrown* being-with-one-another in a world" (*SZ*, 175).

Dasein is essentially free, then, but freedom is the existential condition both of choice and of the force of habit and blind compulsion. Choice as such emerges only when Dasein "reclaims" it by coming to interpret itself as capable of choosing. Getting lost in *das Man* in the first place, by contrast, is something that happens by itself, involuntarily, by default.

> This unchoosing being-carried-along by the nobody, in which Dasein gets ensnared in inauthenticity, can only be undone by Dasein's own fetching itself back to itself from its lostness in *das Man*. This fetching back must however have that mode of being *by the default of which* Dasein has lost itself in inauthenticity. Fetching onself back from *das Man* means that the existentiell modification of the *Man*-self toward *authentic* being oneself must occur in the form of *reclaiming a choice*. Reclaiming a choice, however, means *choosing this choice*, deciding on an ability to be, out of one's own self. In

choosing the choice Dasein first *makes possible* its own authentic ability to be. (*SZ*, 268)

Heidegger does not conceive of Dasein as having freely chosen its inauthenticity from the outset, but as having fallen into it, and only then "becoming free" in surrendering itself to an attunement or responsiveness to its own factical particularity: "Letting oneself be called forth to this possibility understandingly involves Dasein's *becoming free* for the call: readiness for the ability to be called. In understanding the call, Dasein is *in thrall to its ownmost possibility of existence*. It has chosen itself" (*SZ*, 287). Dasein's "ownmost possibility of existence" is precisely the understanding of one's own factical particularity as a condition of all self-interpretation. To be authentic, then, is not to retract or reverse some initial voluntary act, but rather to become responsive to one's factical particularity as calling for a decision of some kind: "Resoluteness means letting oneself be called out of the lostness of *das Man*" (*SZ*, 299).

IV   How Is Authenticity Possible? Why Is Anyone Ever Inauthentic?

One might object that this account of the generic drift of discourse once again renders authenticity impossible, since it implies that as a matter of principle no general terms can ever do justice to the particularity of Dasein's factical condition. Conversely, one might maintain that the tension I locate between generality and particularity is bogus, since all intelligibility involves the subsumption of particulars under general terms or concepts. The mere generality of a predicate like "red," for example, hardly prevents me from seeing the unique brightness and saturation of this particular apple. These objections reiterate the criticisms that Dreyfus and Rubin level against Heidegger himself, namely, that an overly robust conception of fleeing threatens to make Dasein essentially inauthentic, while a merely structural account of falling seems to relegate full-fledged inauthenticity to an inexplicable aberration. I will consider these two points in turn.

How then is authenticity possible at all, if discourse inclines all interpretation in the direction of banality and cliché? Dreyfus and

Rubin argue persuasively that Heidegger is wrong when he occasionally seems to reduce fallenness to a mere artifact of some anxiety-driven flight, and that such a view would render Dasein essentially inauthentic. Fallenness therefore cannot be an artifact of fleeing, rather fleeing must be understood as an essentially contingent effect of falling. But why only contingent? On my account, is it not unavoidable?

No, for banality and leveling do not by themselves necessarily amount to the evasion and obfuscation characteristic of inauthentic existence. As we have seen, Heidegger insists that the existential analytic in Division I of *Being and Time* is an interpretation of Dasein in its "average everydayness," which is as such neither authentic nor inauthentic, but modally undifferentiated (*SZ* 43, 53, 232). Authenticity and inauthenticity are both modifications of the "indifference" (*Indifferenz*) of mundane life. All interpretation is cast in more or less general terms, falling or slipping away somewhat from the ecstatic temporal structure of existence into an absorption with the things we encounter in the temporal present under the horizonal schema of the "in-order-to." Falling is constitutive of encountering anything at all, just as discursive generality is constitutive of interpretation. Yet falling constantly directs us to an understanding of the being of things in the present, just as discourse perpetually casts our interpretations in more or less generic, commonly intelligible terms. There is therefore an inherent tension between Dasein's ecstatic temporality and concrete particularity on the one hand, and the generic character of discourse on the other.

But to say that there is an inner tension between existentiality and discourse is not to say that all interpretation is therefore false, distorted, or inauthentic. Understanding authenticity as a genuine possibility requires that we conceive it in negative rather than positive terms. Resoluteness is not a stable, self-sufficient mode of existence, but a perpetual struggle against the reifying and banalizing forces inherent in discursive practice. Authentic existence is thus constituted by the very forces against which it has to push in its effort to grasp itself in its facticity. Being resolute is like swimming against the current: there would be no such thing absent the forces resisting it. At the same time, there is only so far you can swim upstream before you run out of river. Similarly, authenticity consists in nothing over and beyond our ongoing resistance to the banalizing, leveling pressures that pull us away from any explicit recognition of the "mineness" at the center of our existence. At the same time, there is no such thing as a pure apprehension of existence as one's own outside of the mediating conditions of discursive practice. Falling, then, does not by itself compromise the potential authenticity of Dasein's interpretive response to it.

One could say likewise that there is a kind of tension between gravity and jumping, yet far from rendering us utterly prostrate and inert, gravity is precisely what makes jumping possible, by hindering it. The most graceful leap is at once conditioned and inhibited by gravity. So too, Dasein's most authentic self-interpretations are at once facilitated and constrained by discursive idioms that impose a kind of leveled significance on its factical particularity, which always remains to some extent recalcitrant to such generic appropriations. Just as a good jump at once resists and is shaped by the force of gravity, so too authentic resoluteness consists in resisting the "movement" or "agitation" of falling from within the leveling process that is at work in all discursive idioms. Authentic resoluteness is no less compatible with the generic drift of discourse than upward jumping is with the downward force of gravity.[18]

And just as resisting gravity never amounts to escaping or transcending it, so too it would be incoherent to imagine Dasein bypassing the discursive field altogether and confronting its existence immediately in some private sphere of meanings. The world Dasein inhabits thus lies between two reefs on which its self-interpretations forever threaten to run aground: the empty generality induced by mundane "idle talk" (*Gerede*) on the one hand, and the structural zero point of Dasein's "mineness", which is hermeneutically vacuous, on the other. The generic drift of discourse and the essential averageness of everyday understanding do not by themselves render authentic existence impossible. Inauthenticity is a contingent, if prevalent, modification of falling.

On what, then, is inauthenticity contingent, and why is it so common? If falling does not lead inexorably to fleeing, why does Dasein flee itself at all? As Dreyfus and Rubin argue, in the absence of a compelling structural account of falling, and in light of the putative "equanimity" and "joy" of authentic resoluteness, Dasein's lapse into inauthenticity seems inexplicable. Especially pressing for my own account is the question why there should be any tension at all between the generality of discourse and Dasein's mineness. General terms in natural languages do not inevitably obscure the particularity of the objects denoted by singular terms, so why should the generic drift of discourse tend to conceal Dasein's factical particularity?

The answer, I believe, lies in what Heidegger describes as the "rebound" or "counterthrust" (*Rückschlag*) of possibilities back upon Dasein (*SZ*, 148). What this means is that Dasein's projection onto the possibilities that constitute its future cannot be understood as a pure spontaneity or unconditioned freedom. Heidegger's view therefore stands in direct opposition to the radical voluntarism in Sartre's conception of consciousness as pure negation. For Sartre, consciousness is literally nothing beyond the emptiness of its own freedom, so that, as he puts it, "There is no inertia in consciousness."[19] The "rebound" of projected possibilities back upon Dasein amounts to precisely the kind of existential friction or inertia that Sartre's voluntarism excludes as a matter of principle. More precisely, it is the condition of the possibility of the kind of explicit and elaborated understanding that Heidegger calls "interpretation" (*Auslegung*).[20] Interpretation, in Heidegger's sense of the word, is possible only because projecting into possibilities has immediate internal effects on the very situation into which one is thrown, and over against which one must continue to project.

Interpretation thus has consequences for Dasein's self-understanding that are altogether different from any of the effects it has on entities not engaged in discursive practices. Interpretation characterizes things in the world, but then also feeds back into Dasein's ongoing expressive and communicative comportment. Dasein is thus constantly absorbing and acting on the discursive implications of the possibilities it finds itself committed to, whether tacitly or explicitly. Interpretation, that is, has an irreducible normative dimension from which Dasein both inherits and forms interests concerning itself and the things it deals with. To interpret yourself in terms of your social identity, for example, is not simply to settle on some factual or observational determination of who you are. It is also to direct and orient your actions in light of the point, or what Heidegger calls the "for-the-sake-of" (*Worum-willen*), that constitutes that identity. Interpreting yourself in some definite way entails a commitment to actions that continally reflect, confirm, alter, and perhaps challenge that self-interpretation.

This is why so much self-interpretation has the character of a self-fulfilling prophecy, acquiring genuine inertia from its own practical consequences. The normativity and inertia of interpretation are rooted in Dasein's projection and thrownness, respectively. Nor is the momentum with which we are thrown into our own self-interpretations a mere illusion perpetrated by bad faith. On the contrary, it is precisely what gives the lie to Sartre's claim that we choose ourselves and our projects *ex nihilo*, just as Descartes's God sustains reality through a continuous act of will.[21] Instead, interpretation produces genuine friction for further interpretive practice, which stands in constant need of some background discursive repertoire from which to construe things under definite aspects. If authentic resoluteness consists in maintaining an effort to resist the drift of discourse into sheer superficiality, then inauthenticity and irresoluteness simply amount to flagging in that effort and going along with the degeneration of authentic talk into idle talk.

Moreover, the momentum is cumulative, for the more we are immersed in the present, drifting into increasingly generic interpretations, the harder it becomes to extricate ourselves, to survey the full scope of our ecstatic temporality, which embraces the givenness of our situation as well as our being-unto-death, and finally to reclaim a sense of ourselves as factical particulars never exhausted by the discursive vocabularies that render us intelligible to ourselves. The "temptation" to lapse irresolutely into inauthentic existence thus requires no independent explanation, since it is just an artifact of falling itself, in pronounced or aggravated form: "The tempting sedation *intensifies* the falling. . . . The tempting-sedating alienation of falling leads *by its own movement* to Dasein's getting *entangled* in itself" (*SZ*, 178, emphasis added). It is falling itself that generates the momentum of Dasein's anxious, self-evading flight.

V Conclusion

If this reconstruction of Heidegger's account of inauthenticity is right, then the best response to the challenge posed by Dreyfus and Rubin goes something like this. First, authentic resoluteness is not a self-sufficient mode of existence standing outside Dasein's essentially self-evading inclinations. It is instead a kind of internal resistance to the obfuscating tendencies inherent in the generic drift of discourse, which constantly turns Dasein away from an explicit, problematic attention to its own ecstatic temporality and finite particularity. Second, inauthentic irresoluteness is a common phenomenon not because Dasein elects to take it up as a matter of spontaneous free choice, but because being irresolute just consists in relaxing the effort to put up active resistance to the force of falling. Authenticity is conceivable, then, since it is possible for Dasein to resist the force of falling *while* falling, just as one can resist the force of gravity while remaining continuously in its grip. Conversely, inauthenticity is intelligible as an abiding inclination, since it does not essentially consist in some freely chosen form of motivated irrationality, but in a failure to muster adequate resistance to the generic drift inherent in discursive practice as such.

Of course, one can press the question one step further by asking why Dasein should ever fail to put up the necessary resistance and lapse into any irresoluteness at all. Even granting that inauthenticity is an extension of falling, and so is continuous with it, why should the hermeneutical effort to hold fast to one's mineness ever flag or fail in any way? Why are our efforts imperfect? I think the only adequate answer to that question will lie in the contingent "ontic" limitations on the bodily and psychological resources we actually have at our disposal in any of our endeavors. Why is anything imperfect? What I hope to have shown is that inauthenticity is at once intelligible and yet contingent, since it flows not from any motivated act, but from a merely imperfect effort to resist the force of falling.

2

The Significance of Authenticity

Randall Havas

In the second essay of *On the Genealogy of Morals,* Nietzsche suggests that two conditions must be satisfied for there to be meaning and understanding in the sense that concerns him—for there to be what he calls "the right to make promises". First, our behavior must be "calculable, regular, and necessary"; it must have what is sometimes called a "normative" dimension, such that it makes sense to speak of someone's getting it right or wrong.[1] Second, the individual must take responsibility for what he or she says and does; he must, in other words, be responsive to the norms in terms of which his activity has the significance it does. In Nietzsche's view, such responsiveness is always the business only of each individual, guaranteed by nothing more or less than his individual willingness to go on. By its very nature, however, such individuality aims at a form of community. As Nietzsche sees it, it is our tendency to confuse our responsibility for meaning with guilt—to *moralize* it[2]—that prevents us from establishing the form of human community he identifies with the capacity to make sense.

In this chapter I want to recommend an interpretation of Heidegger's *Being and Time* very similar to the one I have just sketched of the *Genealogy*. I begin with a brief statement of what seem to me to be the chief philosophical and interpretative benefits of this sort of reading. After laying out in a little more detail Nietzsche's conception of what I call the first condition of intelligibility, I go on to explore the idea of community as it functions in the first half of

Being and Time. In this part of the chapter, I take issue with one part of Hubert Dreyfus's influential interpretation of Heidegger's appeal to that idea. The importance of Dreyfus's reading of *Being and Time* cannot be denied. He has done the most by far to make clear the significance for traditional philosophy of Heidegger's investigations of being-in-the-world: the sort of philosophical detachment on display especially in Cartesian epistemology makes sense *only* as a deformation of average, everyday intelligibility. Dreyfus correctly insists that such intelligibility cannot be accounted for in terms of the private contents of individual consciousnesses; it is something we "always already" share and is, in that sense at least, something public. I suspect, however, that Dreyfus's eagerness to defeat his Cartesian opponent may at times obscure for us the real significance of what he rightly takes to be *Being and Time*'s central insight. In particular, on Dreyfus's reading, Heidegger held that a background of shared practices and institutions *explains* how meaning is possible. I will argue, on the contrary, that an appeal to community cannot do this sort of work. No such explanation is forthcoming, because, on Heidegger's view, no such explanation is needed. I suggest that this fact encourages us to reconsider the role Heidegger assigns to the notion of community. In the second half of the chapter, I will consider the conception of individuality indicated by an appropriate understanding of the idea of community—what Heidegger calls "authenticity". My aim is to show that, for Heidegger, only once we give up the idea that facts about how we take things are the source of intelligibility will we be in a position to understand the content of individuality.

Reading Heidegger in the light of the *Genealogy* helps us to see that, contrary to one tempting reading, his insistence on what he calls "world"—on the shared context in terms of which our activity makes the sense it does—does not imply that he believes public practices and institutions play a constitutive role in intelligibility.[3] For Heidegger, as for Nietzsche, responsibility for meaning lies solely with the individual; for both, the idea of a source or a ground of meaning has significant application only in this context. For neither thinker, however, is such responsibility properly conceived in the sorts of "constitutive" terms favored by the philosophical outlook they reject.

The principal interpretative benefit of reading *Being and Time* in the way I am suggesting we should is that it suggests a natural understanding of the relationship between the first and second halves of that book, one obscured by the "constitutive" interpretation of human community I believe both Nietzsche and Heidegger reject. On the reading with which I will shortly take issue, because the meaning of a person's life is constituted entirely by the understanding of human being he inherits from the culture at large, Heidegger supposedly concludes that a well-lived life is one that renounces all attempts at self-determination. That, contrary to what we might like to believe, we are not in this sense self-determining animals is Heidegger's cue to interpret human being in terms of what he calls "originary temporality".[4] On this reading, we are what we do. But because the meaning of what we do is not up to us in particular, nothing makes what we do what *we*—as individuals—do. Consequently, an authentically lived human life can only be one in which the *way* we do what we do manifests our acknowledgment that nothing we do can possibly serve to provide us with a determinate identity. Human activity has a (temporal) structure, but no content.

This sort of reading tends to reinforce the impression that Heidegger's discussion of authenticity is more or less an existentialist after-thought—as though once Division I had demonstrated that community is the source of intelligibility, Heidegger went on in Division II to ask about the status of the individual. In other words, on this reading, it is difficult to understand why Heidegger insisted that Division II carries the investigations of Division I a step deeper, why it makes them, in his word, more "*primordial*".[5] But the interpretation we are considering begs the question of whether in fact Heidegger thought that the problem about intelligibility with which he was wrestling was a problem that *could* be solved by an appeal to community in the way the interpretation imagines. I will suggest that Heidegger's interest in authenticity is *continuous* with his attack on Cartesian individualism in Division I. Individuality and community are, for him, two sides of a single coin. Neither is meant to explain the other.

I

Let me begin by saying something about the *Genealogy*'s first condition on intelligibility: what Nietzsche calls "calculability, regularity, and necessity". Nietzsche says, "The task of breeding an animal with the right to make promises evidently embraces and presupposes as a preparatory task that one first *makes* men to a certain degree necessary, uniform, like among like, regular, and consequently calculable."[6] To understand something (an action, utterance, or gesture) is to be able to say—even if only by responding appropriately to it— what it *counts* as—for example, that it is a gesture of greeting. To be able to mean it is to be able to *make* it count as such. But the ability to say what something counts as depends in part on there already being a pattern of regular usage in place.[7] Such uniformity is not something Nietzsche deplores; there is no point of view from which to do so, and, contrary to popular opinion, he shows no inclination to believe that there is. Meaning is impossible where there is, in this sense, nothing to mean, but we should not rush to assume that the notion of possibility here packs any philosophical punch.

To say that necessity as well as regularity is involved in our ability to make sense is to say that what counts as what is not *up* to anyone. In particular, *I* do not decide that such-and-such a gesture in such-and-such circumstances counts as taking one's leave. Nor do *we* decide that this is so. We can, naturally, make various things up, and we can agree to abide by them and to sanction those who do not. But no fact about me or you alone—nor indeed about the two (or more) of us together—determines that such-and-such is the custom around here.

What counts is what is necessary only "to a certain degree", however, because what is an appropriate response to what is of course subject to change over time. Nothing rules out invention or conceptual originality in this picture. Moreover, our sense of what is appropriate has a complex natural history.[8] Nietzsche is perhaps best known for his insistence on precisely both these points. He is equally adamant, however, that one cannot mean something just once.

Nietzsche therefore speaks of "calculability" to underscore the fact that where nothing counts as an *appropriate* response to something, nothing can count as a response to it at all.[9] The point of talking about calculability is thus that the human capacity to make sense depends upon a shared grasp of what counts as an appropriate response to what. But Nietzsche is not endeavoring to raise calculability up to the status of a mysterious something that distinguishes our responses from those of animals or inanimate objects. It is of precisely the sense of mystery here that he seeks a diagnosis.

In saying that one must *become* calculable, regular, and necessary—that one must be *made* so[10]—Nietzsche means in part to remind us of the fact that while no sense has been given to the philosophical demand to know what makes the norms that govern the significance of our activity *binding* on us, calculability is nevertheless a purely human phenomenon, one that, as such, has a history. There is, for him, no friction between the view that intelligibility requires both regularity and necessity and the view that it is a wholly *natural* phenomenon. Indeed, as he sees it, the very idea of calculability makes sense only in "naturalistic" terms; it can *only* be a human phenomenon. It is our "human, all too human" wish that things were otherwise that he wants most to understand.

It seems to me that considerations remarkably similar to these are at work in the first half of *Being and Time*. We do not go far wrong if we take Heidegger's target there to be modern (Cartesian) epistemology, with its first-personal account of our relationship to the world around us.[11] Specifically, he is trying to undermine our confidence that we can make good sense of the epistemologist's individualism, of the idea that facts about the individual can serve to ground his relationship both to the world at large and to other individuals within it. His attack on this picture has two parts. In the first, he contests the primacy of knowledge; in the second, he questions the intelligibility of the epistemologist's construal of the first-person standpoint. Heidegger insists that the epistemologist's emphasis on knowledge as our most basic means of "access" to the world ignores the fact that we are "in the world" first and foremost by way of our practical concerns. Concerns with knowledge grow out of these as further practical concerns with specialized conditions of satisfaction of their own, but our fundamental involvement with the world cannot be understood in the terms appropriate to our more detached dealings with it. Not only is our relationship to material objects not to be understood in broadly perceptual terms, but neither is our relationship to ourselves. We ourselves are not primarily—either for ourselves or for others—objects of knowledge. Rather, we are fundamentally part of a *common* world.[12]

It is this insistence on the idea of a common world that we need to understand. In his commentary on Division I of *Being and Time*, Hubert Dreyfus argues that the success of the second part of Heidegger's attack on traditional epistemology depends upon his ability to show that the significance of an individual's activity depends upon a shared background of institutions, customs, and practices.[13] Dreyfus contends that if Heidegger fails to demonstrate convincingly that this is so, his attempt to overturn the Cartesian setup will come to grief, because he will have shown only that the source of intelligibility is practical rather than theoretical, but not that it is non-individual.

Dreyfus takes seriously a challenge leveled by Frederick Olafson in his *Heidegger and the Philosophy of Mind*.[14] As Olafson reads him, Heidegger recognized the importance of a shared background in terms of which the individual's dealings with the world make sense. He failed, however, to explain adequately how our familiarity with the appropriate forms of response to the world is actually shared by us. Thus, in *Being and Time*, Olafson complains, "There is no real account of the way in which my uncovering an entity as an entity depends on someone else's doing so as well".[15] On this reading, unless Heidegger has an account of how *my* sense of what is and what is not an appropriate way to go depends on yours, I will have no way to rule out the possibility that any apparent convergence between us is anything but accidental. For all Heidegger tells us, there is no *common* world, only a set of incidentally overlapping ones.

According to Olafson, only a "strong conception of *Mitsein*"[16]—of what I am calling "community"—would remedy this defect. It is this "strong" conception of community that Dreyfus thinks can be found between the lines of Heidegger's condemnation in Chapter 4 of *Being and Time* of the everyday "inauthentic" understanding of human being embodied in public practices and institutions. As Dreyfus admits, Chapter 4 seems at first blush to be little more than a rather disjointed discussion of the problem of other minds and of the evils of conformism.[17] He thinks, however, that he can tease out an answer to Olafson's challenge by distinguishing what he calls the "positive" from the "negative" functions of what Heidegger calls "*das Man*"—the average understanding of human being embodied in our public practices and institutions. In Dreyfus's view, it is the positive function of "*das Man*" to provide the theory of community Olafson demands.

As Dreyfus understands him, Heidegger's insistence on the notion of a common world into which each individual is socialized is meant to show that "[s]ociety is the ontological source of the familiarity and readiness that makes the ontical discovering of entities, of others, and even of myself possible".[18] On this reading, Heidegger tries to show, first, that the individual human being is by and large not an isolated, detached subject of mental states, but rather a "mode of comportment" and, second, that sense can be made of such comportment only in terms of essentially public practices.[19]

According to Dreyfus, then, the agreement in our practices that insures there is one public world rather than a plurality of individual worlds can be thought of as conformity to norms. Such conformity is said to be "constitutive"[20] of intelligibility, because—apparently—without it, there would *be* no "common world". Thus, "For . . . Heidegger . . . the *source* of the intelligibility of the world is the average public practices through which alone there can be any understanding at all."[21] Dasein is what it does, and what it does is to be understood primarily as what "one" does or is disposed to do in similar circumstances. But how shall we understand Dreyfus's talk of a "source" of intelligibility? What is it for something to "constitute" intelligibility?

Let us consider Olafson's challenge once again. He believes Heidegger needs an account of the dependence of the intelligibility of the individual's activity on the intelligibility of that of others if he is to avoid the unwelcome conclusion that the sense we make is inevitably plural. But what would an account of this "dependence" actually look like?[22] What *kind* of explanation does he think is needed here? To whom, more specifically, does he imagine it is to be given?

Let us consider what kind of question might be asked about a practice—for example, that of shaking hands to seal an agreement. Suppose someone asks, "why does shaking hands in these circumstances seal an agreement?" In certain contexts, we might well appeal to what we do around here, to our "shared sense" of what's appropriate, to "agreement" in our comportment. The point of such an appeal would most naturally be either to remind someone of or to instruct him in the appropriate ways of dealing with certain sorts of people in certain sorts of situations. So far, the questions and answers here are perfectly ordinary and practical. Someone has forgotten how to do something, or someone needs to be taught. However, an appeal to "what is done" would hardly satisfy a more philosophically minded interlocutor like Olafson. The latter would surely greet the news that this is what we do with indifference; for him, it would be of anthropological interest at best to learn that "people like us" seal agreements by pumping their joined hands up and down.

The basic difficulty here is simply that an appeal to what we do has force as a philosophical justification of why doing *this* is the right way of doing something only to the degree that we have some way to specify the content of the "we" independently of the practices we are trying to explain.[23] In an ordinary context, the circularity of appeals to community agreement is not a problem, for we are not ordinarily trying to provide *philosophical* justification for what we do. I suggest, then, that Heidegger's talk of a "common world" either blatantly begs Olafson's question or is intended precisely to question our sense that the philosophical demand for justification makes sense here. The latter reading seems clearly preferable: Heidegger does not mean to answer that demand either directly or indirectly. And while he cannot simply *claim* that the philosopher's demand makes no sense, he is certainly in a position to insist that its sense be made plain—something it seems clear to me Olafson has not done.[24]

Olafson wants a "theory" of human community, an account of why *his* way of using a hammer in such-and-such circumstances is the *right* way. He is, however, not confused about how or when to use a hammer. He knows, for example, that one does not pound screws with hammers, eat with them, and so on. Confusion—say, a child's —about that sort of thing is intelligible enough, and, in these contexts, appeals to *"Mitsein"*, if we want to talk that way, are perfectly in order. It is clear, however, that no such answer will satisfy Olafson. But then what is the difficulty supposed to be?

Dreyfus contends that the public practices in terms of which we make sense of the activity of individual human beings are "the source of significance and intelligibility,"[25] but he insists that Heidegger has not *directly* answered Olafson's challenge. He claims that, for Heidegger, community is not a source of significance in the traditional philosophical sense. It is not an "absolute" source or ground, but rather an *"Un-grund"*. Heidegger can call it what he likes, but why should we suppose that there *must* be some extra-ordinary, non-traditional sense in which we can speak of community as the source of significance? Whence, in other words, Dreyfus's insistence that community, in Heidegger's view, must be a source of significance in *any* sense other than in whatever sense is at stake when we instruct or remind someone about the appropriate ways of using, say, a hammer?

Dreyfus maintains that conformity to norms cannot provide the kind of intelligibility whose ground or "source" has traditionally been sought.[26] It is, I take it, the idea that the intelligibility we do have is not the intelligibility we may have wished for that Dreyfus believes we will find unsettling. The suggestion is that we hoped for intelligibility rooted in something more than facts about our human, all-too-human lives. From the traditional philosophical point of view, intelligibility without that kind of support is intelligibility in name alone.[27]

But why suppose that the philosopher's account of our wishes for grounding makes sense? The thrust of *Being and Time* as a whole is that the traditional philosophical description of our situation is *empty* and not simply mistaken, because it is offered from a point of view whose very intelligibility has not been accounted for. It is difficult to see where Heidegger might have believed there was room to articulate the idea of a "relative"—as opposed to an "absolute"—source of intelligibility.

And yet, Dreyfus insists, "The one is surely *something*"[28]: community is not intersubjectivity, not Hegelian *Geist*; and certainly not mere behavior; but it's not *nothing* either. Why suppose, however, that

Heidegger was trying to carve out a special sense of community at all? Why suppose, that is, that the One plays any role in his account other than that of the 'agent' of conformism? Certainly, the fact that Dreyfus must struggle as hard as he does to disentangle a positive from a negative function of community from a discussion that by his own account appears uniquely focused on the latter suggests that Heidegger himself was not trying to do so. In any case, neither Dreyfus nor Olafson has given reason to believe that community must be either something *or* nothing. My suggestion in the second half of this chapter is that Heidegger means his discussion of authenticity in effect to show why it is neither.

Dreyfus contends that the account of community he finds in chapter 4 of Division I is the last nail in the coffin of the Cartesian tradition. But his interpretation seems, on the contrary, to breathe new life into the corpse, for it supposes, wrongly, that Olafson's question about intelligibility is one that *demands* an answer, even if only a "nontraditional" one.

I think, therefore, that we should reject the attempt to demarcate a constitutive function for the public practices in terms of which an individual's activity makes sense. Such a reading is certainly less of an interpretative strain on the text. If Heidegger is read in the way I suggest, there is no friction between a view according to which conformity to norms is the source of intelligibility and a view according to which conformism to the leveled down understanding of ourselves expressed in the average understanding of those norms is the source of *un*intelligibility. There is conformity. And there is—sadly— conformism. But these facts are not in any way at odds with one another. More important, such a reading avoids saddling Heidegger with an answer to a question there is no reason to suppose has been endowed with a definite sense.

This interpretation has the virtue of making clearer why Heidegger is interested in authenticity in the first place: perhaps surprisingly, his interest in that notion is precisely Nietzsche's. To see that this is so, let us begin with an alternative interpretation of Heidegger's account of authenticity in *Being and Time*.

II

An authentic individual, it is frequently suggested, is someone whose way of living expresses an acknowledgment of the "groundlessness" of the sense she makes; an inauthentic individual, on the other hand, is someone who "flees" in the face of this groundlessness. There are, I think, at least two things wrong-headed about this approach to the nature of authentic individuality in Heidegger. First, it takes for granted the intelligibility of the claim that the sense we make is "grounded" or "ungrounded", "necessary" or "contingent", with or without "foundation". Second, it forces us to treat authenticity in terms of a misleading distinction between form and content. Let us start with the first point.

The idea that Heideggerian anxiety reveals the groundlessness or contingency of the sense we make is common in the literature,[29] but Dreyfus's is the most powerful version of this reading. According to him, Heideggerian anxiety reveals "the essential truth, accessible to all human beings, that, since reality is relative to human practices, and nothing can define the self, human beings can never find a foundation for their lives, and can never feel at home in the world."[30] But from what point of view are we supposed to recognize the groundlessness or contingency of our lives? Heidegger's aim in *Being and Time* is, in large measure, to undermine our temptation to speak in these ways. Let us briefly consider one example of his strategy.

In Division II, Heidegger describes human being as a nullity in the sense that there is no way for us to escape the fact that the sense we make depends upon the cultural practices into which we are, as he says, "thrown". Such dependence, however, "has by no means the character of a privation, where something is lacking in comparison with an ideal which has been set up but does not get attained in Dasein."[31] A radically self-determining human being is not a human being at all: there is no self and no determination of it without a sense of what's worth doing. It is the tendency to think that there is something to bemoan in this fact that Heidegger, like Nietzsche, finds at the root of the inauthentic ways of life he deplores.

It is true enough that Heidegger finds there to be *something* unsettling about being human. But the text does not suggest that he believes a description of human life as groundless or contingent is anything other than symptomatic of a misunderstanding of the phenomena. What I will want to urge in conclusion is that the truth of the matter is more or less the opposite of what this sort of interpretation would have us believe. Before we turn to this point, however, let us examine what I said was the second principal shortcoming of this interpretation of authenticity: that it treats authenticity as a matter of form, not content.

What seems to many commentators to motivate the talk of groundlessness or contingency is the insistence that, for Heidegger, an individual human being makes sense of his life only by taking over some role from the set of roles his society offers him. Worries about groundlessness seem to creep in when we reflect on the facts that, first, neither he nor anyone else is responsible for the possibilities with which he's presented, and, second, that therefore there is no philosophically respectable justification for claiming that any of these possibilities is definitive of *him* in particular. On this sort of reading, an authentic individual must manifest his recognition of this sort of groundlessness in the way he lives his life, but nothing about the content of his actions—nothing about being a janitor, say, rather than a jet pilot—serves to express the relevant sense of groundlessness. Rather, it is the form or "style" of the individual's activity that does so.

It is the temptation to assign a constitutive role to community that leads commentators to think that, for Heidegger, authentic individuality is at best only an *attitude* one adopts toward what one does. It is this view that drives Dreyfus, for example, to the conclusion that "[t]he *form* of acting on *any* possibility is all that is absolutely essential for constancy, and constancy is all that is essential for authenticity."[32] And it is the latter interpretation that impels Dreyfus to look for clues in chapter 5 of Division II as well as in Heidegger's later thought for a way of life that "is not merely formal but acquires specific content."[33] If, on the other hand, we reject the constitutive view of community, then it is not obvious that Heidegger has *any* account of "the relation of the individual to the universal". For it is not clear that, in this sense, there is any such relation to be accounted for.[34] This reading suggests in turn that, for Heidegger as for Nietzsche, it is the category of the individual that should have pride of place in our reflections on the nature of intelligibility, and not just any individual but rather the very one that is each of us.

If we jettison the categories of form and content, how then shall we think of authenticity? As the second essay of the *Genealogy* makes clear, the relevant notions for an understanding of intelligibility are not groundlessness and contingency, but responsibility and conscience. Nietzsche's insistence on this point can seem like the better part of common sense. For the heart of our most run-of-the-mill intuitions about what gets called authenticity and inauthenticity is surely not that an authentic person faces up to groundlessness while his inauthentic counterpart flees it, but rather that the former takes responsibility for himself while the latter seeks to avoid it. That there are an indefinite number of ways in which we fail to take responsibility for what we say and do suggests that there is no one thing that constitutes responsibility in the first place. But that there is in this sense no "essence" of responsibility clearly ought not to be taken to imply that the difference between responsible and irresponsible action is "merely formal". On the contrary.

The *Genealogy* tells us that the "sovereign individual" is "like only to himself."[35] This does not mean that he speaks a language different from that spoken by the herd. It does not mean that he says or does outlandish and original things. Nietzsche's point is rather that only the individual truly *speaks* at all. But speech, as the *Genealogy* conceives it, manifests not primarily the inner life of the individual speaker, but rather his sense of standing for all men—what Nietzsche calls "a sensation of mankind come to completion."[36] The rest of us are mired in our privacy and merely mouth our words. Once again, because there is no one way in which this aping of humanity occurs, there is no one thing that counts as individuality. The distinction between authenticity and inauthenticity is not meant—by Nietzsche or by Heidegger—to supply that sort of information.

What grants the individual the right to make promises—to speak for all men in the sense of representing for them the best they can become—is what Nietzsche calls "the extraordinary privilege of *responsibility*."[37] It is this last point I wish to stress. The *Genealogy* claims that, in taking responsibility for what he says and does, the individual expresses his responsibility or indebtedness to community.[38] It is important to notice, however, that, for Nietzsche, there are not two different things going on here: an acceptance of the individual's indebtedness to something like community at large, on the one hand, and, on the other, an acknowledgment of his relationship to those to whom he is speaking on a particular occasion. In Nietzsche's view, prior to the latter, there *is* no community to speak of. In other words, community is not presupposed by intelligibility, but is instead the very fact of it. It lasts no longer than our responsibility for it—a responsibility that is "in each case mine". And this is why, for Heidegger, what community we can achieve is neither a something nor a nothing.

3

Truth and Finitude: Heidegger's Transcendental Existentialism

John Haugeland

In their lengthy and powerful appendix to Dreyfus's *Being-in-the-World*, Dreyfus and Rubin argue that the "existentialist" portions of *Being and Time*—those having to do with authenticity, falling, anxiety, death, conscience, guilt, and resoluteness—are an attempt to secularize Kierkegaard's notion of Religiousness A, while also incorporating certain features of his Religiousness B (though *without* the latter's essential risk or vulnerability). They conclude, however, that, for all its ingenuity, this attempt results in an inconsistent position and is therefore a failure.

It is undeniable that Heidegger drew most of these terms and much of what he says in their regard from Kierkegaard. I believe, nevertheless, that his uses of them, and the larger endeavor within which they fit, are farther removed from Kierkegaard's than Dreyfus and Rubin allow. In particular, they are deeply integrated with the explicit and overarching aim of *Being and Time*, which is to reawaken the question of being. For instance, Heidegger says about *Being and Time* in 1930:

It was never my idea to preach an "existentialist philosophy." Rather, I have been concerned with renewing the question of ontology—the most central question of western philosophy—the question of being.[1]

Accordingly, I take it as a sign of the incompleteness (at best) of Dreyfus and Rubin's reading that they do not so much as mention the understanding of being until their last few pages, and then only in the context of discussing how Heidegger's position evolved in subsequent decades.

In the present setting, I will undertake neither to summarize the Dreyfus/Rubin interpretation nor to criticize it in any detail. Rather, in the space available, I will sketch an alternative approach that may better unify the various themes in *Being and Time* and perhaps thereby illuminate them severally. In so doing, I will give pride of place to Heidegger's extensive and central treatment of death, surely one of the most striking and puzzling "existentialist" notes in the book. (Indeed, it is so puzzling that the foremost exegetical question is what it's doing there at all—that is, in a technical treatise on the question of being.) Yet I will maintain that death, as Heidegger means it, is not merely relevant but in fact the fulcrum of his entire ontology.

Toward this end, it will be necessary to expound in outline that larger metaphysical project; and here it seems to me that Kant is at least as important and illuminating a predecessor as Kierkegaard. Specifically, Heidegger's inquiry into the disclosing of being as the condition of the possibility of comportment toward entities as entities is a direct descendant of Kant's inquiry into the forms of sensibility and understanding as conditions of the possibility of knowledge of objects as objects. In Kantian terms, this could be called the *transcendental* question of the possibility of *objectivity*. In Heideggerian terms, that would become the *existential* question of the possibility of *truth*.

I   Traditional and Heideggerian Concepts

Heidegger is inevitably and self-consciously a follower in the western philosophical tradition. But he is also attempting to advance and hence transform that tradition. This effort entails generalizing and/or transforming various traditional concepts, as well as introducing new ones. The most basic of Heidegger's innovations—in the sense that it's what all the others turn on—is his "reawakening" of the question of being. So that will be my main topic in this introductory section. Before undertaking to explain what "being" means, however, I need to review briefly four of Heidegger's other characteristic words—"entity", "comportment", "Dasein", and "disclosedness"—and how they relate to their traditional predecessors.

Entities are all and only what there is: *everything* that there *is*—no more, no less. Thus, if Quine were right that to be is to be the value of a bound variable, then entities would be all and only the values of bound variables. Now, the term "object" can be used in broader and narrower ways. Heidegger usually reserves for it a recognizably Kantian sense: objects (*Gegenstände*) are the entities that can be known in explicit, theoretical judgments—paradigmatically, the knowledge attained in natural science. He also often calls such objects *occurrent* (*vorhandene*) entities. But, according to Heidegger, not all entities are occurrent objects. Two other sorts of entity are discussed at length in *Being and Time*: (i) *available* (*zuhandene*) entities, which include tools and other equipment and paraphernalia; and (ii) *existing* entities (in Heidegger's proprietary sense of "existence"), which include Dasein and such "Dasein-like" entities as sciences and languages. Thus, all objects are entities, but not all entities are objects. So Heidegger's term is a generalization of Kant's.

Corresponding to that generalization is another. Heidegger is concerned with the possibility of *comportment toward* entities (as entities). Husserl (following Brentano) had already generalized theoretical knowledge to intentionality, which includes other cognitive attitudes besides knowing, such as those characteristic of action and perception. But Heidegger maintains that everyday uses of equipment and interactions with other people aren't usually *cognitive* at all, even in Husserl's broad sense. Yet they are still ways of having to do with entities *as entities*—that is, not just interacting with things physically (as do sticks and stones), or even just actively and sentiently (as do animals), but in some way that involves understanding them as what they are. Thus, he speaks instead of comportment-toward, which is even more general than Husserlian intentionality (though still not so general as to include whatever it is that animals do.)[2]

The generalization from intentionality to comportment-toward is important not merely because the latter encompasses a wider range of relevant phenomena, but also and mainly because, according to Heidegger, the further phenomena that it embraces are more basic.

Comportment-toward is not exclusively or even primarily a mental phenomenon, but rather, in the first place and usually, an active and competent "taking care of business." *Cognitive* comportments (that is, intentional "attitudes"—including but not limited to knowing) are a special case that is not only different from but also *founded upon* noncognitive comportments—such as skillful engagements. Thus, the generalization is not made simply in the interest of thoroughness, but rather in the interest of addressing what is most fundamental.

Dasein is Heidegger's word for what essentially distinguishes the human from the nonhuman (whether animate or inanimate). This is not definitive of Dasein, but only an indication of its evident scope; in other words, it is not ruled out that there may be nonhuman Dasein (perhaps on other planets), but we don't know of any. It is *definitive* of Dasein that it is the entity that understands being, hence can comport itself toward entities *as entities*. (This is not the most basic definition of Dasein, but it follows from it.) Thus, Dasein is a distant successor of the logos and the immortal soul, and a not-so-distant successor of the transcendental subject or spirit. (As it happens, I disagree with most readers of Heidegger about the individuation of Dasein; in particular, I don't think there is a separate and unique Dasein for each person. But that won't matter for most of what follows; so I won't discuss it except in passing.)

Dasein's essential characteristic, as the entity that understands being, is what Heidegger calls *disclosedness*. I am going to argue that disclosedness is a successor, albeit fundamentally transformed, of Kant's transcendental apperception. Apperception, for Kant, is consciousness of an object that is, or at least could be, conscious of itself as conscious of that object. Apperceptive consciousness is the consciousness that is distinctive, and prerequisite to the possibility, of synthetic judgment—hence of empirical knowledge. In particular, the fact that it could be conscious of itself in being conscious of an object is prerequisite to the possibility of its being conscious of the object *as an object* at all. This is why apperception is *transcendental.*

There are many conspicuous and important differences between disclosedness and apperception. (I will mention several in a footnote to a later passage.) The reason that I nevertheless want to emphasize their kinship is that disclosedness has the same sort of interdependent duality in what it is "of" that apperception has. Any disclosing is *at once* a disclosing of Dasein itself *and* a disclosing of the being of entities. It could not be either without being also the other. But, as we shall see, disclosing the being of entities is the condition of the possibility of any comportment toward them *as entities*; and, moreover, this depends on the fact that it is always also a self-disclosing. Therefore, disclosedness too is *transcendental*, and for a structurally similar reason.

One disanalogy, however, is quite fundamental. Whereas apperception, as self-conscious, is conscious also of objects, disclosedness, as self-disclosing, does *not* disclose also entities, but rather the *being* of entities. This is not a minor difference. If there is any single thesis that can be picked out as Heidegger's most emphatic, basic, and original, it is this: "The being of entities "is" not itself an entity" (*SZ*, 6). This expresses what he calls "the ontological difference"—the difference between being and entities. It is the central thought of Heideggerian philosophy.

Kant could not have seen this profound difference between apperception and disclosedness because he did not thematize the difference between being and entities. For the same reason, he could not have raised the question of being. Heidegger claims that, apart from a few dark glimpses, all of his predecessors since the earliest Greeks have *forgotten* the question of being (and he has an account of how and why that happened). But he also claims that the disclosedness of being (as self-disclosing too) is the condition of the possibility of any comportment toward entities as entities. That is why the question of being now needs to be *reawakened*—the principal aim of *Being and Time*. Thus, disclosedness lies at the heart of the whole project.

It is all too easy to get baffled or intimidated—not to say exasperated—by the way Heidegger talks about being. But that's not necessary; the basic idea is in fact fairly straightforward. The *being* of entities is that in terms of which they are *intelligible as entities*. The qualifier "as entities" (as I am using it) is short for this: with regard to the fact *that* they are (at all) and with regard to *what* they are. Understanding an entity *as an entity*—and there is no other way of *understanding* it—means understanding it in its *that*-it-is and its *what*-it-is. Disclosing the being of entities amounts to letting them become accessible in this two-fold intelligibility—that is, as phenomena that are *understood*. When taken with sufficient generality, a pretty good colloquial paraphrase for "disclosing the being of" is *making sense of.*

I can illustrate and clarify this by reciting a familiar special case. Consider the entities that are investigated by fundamental mathematical physics—electrons, quarks, photons, the properties or states they can have, the basic forces by which they interact, and so on. These are all *physical* entities (in a specific sense of "physical"); that is, they are things that there *are*, according to fundamental physics. Now, in terms of what are these entities *intelligible* as entities *that* are and as *what* they are? Obviously, they are intelligible via physical theory, especially the basic laws that specify how they can and must relate to one another. For instance, *what* the electromagnetic force is—its *essence*—makes sense in terms of, and only in terms of, the laws of electromagnetism; and so do electric charge, magnetic moment, and what have you. More subtly, perhaps, but just as clearly: *that* there is such an entity—its *actuality*—is intelligible as its current, particular standing in just such relationships, at determinate locations in space and time.[3] In sum, the *being* of the physical—the essence and actuality of physical entities—is spelled out by the laws of physics.

This being, in terms of which those entities are intelligible as entities, is *disclosed* by Dasein—more particularly, by what might be called *physicist*-Dasein. (On my controversial reading, physicist-Dasein is not individual physicists, or something that they all "have," but rather the scientific theory and practice of physics that they develop and carry out; but never mind that.) We, physicists and their disciples, comport ourselves toward physical entities (as physical entities) in terms of what is thus disclosed—that is, in terms of their being. No one could observe or measure an electron or an electric field (or even talk about them) *as such*, except in terms of that being, as spelled out by the relevant laws. It is only in such terms that they so much as make sense to us as entities at all. In other words, disclosure of the being of the physical is the condition of the possibility of comportment toward physical entities as physical entities.

This example of physics and physical being is mentioned by Heidegger (*SZ*, 9f., 362f.), but not elaborated. On the other hand, he discusses the being of *equipment* in considerable detail. Everyday equipment is primarily understood in the skillful mastery of its proper use—what we might call a "hands on" intelligibility. *What* an item of equipment is (its "essence") is what it is properly to be used *for*—what Heidegger calls its *employment* (*Bewandtnis*), which is tantamount to its equipmental *role*. Its "actuality" is what he calls its *availability* (*Zuhandenheit*)—that is, its current, particular capacity to be so used. These two, role and availability, make up the *being* of equipment, in terms of which it is intelligible as equipment at all. Our primary mode of comportment toward equipment as equipment is, of course, using it as the equipment that it is; but there are other modes, such as making it, repairing it, looking for it, talking about it, and so on. The condition of the possibility of any of these modes of comportment is that the equipment make sense to us *as equipment*—which just is the disclosedness of its being (by lay or professional Dasein).

Now, physical *being*—physical*ness*, we might call it—is clearly not itself a physical entity. It's not a physical particle, a physical property, a physical force, a physical interaction, or anything of the sort. Likewise, equipmental *being*—equipmental*ity*, we might call it—is not an item of equipment. Are physicalness and equipmentality *entities* of *any* sort? Heidegger insists that they are not—they're not *anything* that there *is* whatsoever. This is precisely the point of the ontological difference.

The idea that being "is" not anything *at all* can be hard to get used to. It's even hard to express: given the point, one strictly shouldn't even use the copula "is" to talk about being—yet, the copula is built into the very structure of ordinary language (much as the quantifier is built into the structure of predicate logic). Accordingly, philosophers have tried to say that, although physicalness isn't a *physical* entity (or equipmentality an *equipmental* entity), they—and with them various other sorts of being—must be entities of some further and somehow "special" sort. Perhaps the being of ordinary entities is an "abstract," "ideal," or even "divine" entity. But, then, what of the being of *these* entities (in terms of which alone they could be intelligible and accessible)? Nor is a possible regress the only problem with such traditional suggestions. Another that Heidegger is concerned to avoid is the implication that they make being somehow *eternal.* (It's no accident that the title of his book is *Being and Time.*) But the real payoff for recognizing the ontological difference and reawakening the question of being will lie in the insights it affords us into ourselves and our comportments toward entities as entities.

So far, I have mainly been introducing some Heideggerian terminology, including some of the relationships within it and between it and traditional terms. Now it is time to get down to business and see how these things really work.

II Disclosing Being and the Grounding of Ontical Truth

We comport ourselves toward entities *as entities.* From one point of view, the whole question is what that means and how it is possible. Heidegger calls such comportments *ontical* comportments, because they have to do with *entities.* This is to distinguish them from *ontological* comportments, which have to do rather with *being.* Disclosing being is an ontological comportment. *Discovering* entities is the corresponding term for ontical comportments. What we want to see is how disclosure makes discovery possible.

Discovery presupposes a species of truth—what we can call *ontical* truth (truth regarding entities—which is the only sort of truth most of us ever consider). This is implied in the pivotal qualifier "as entities": it means that ontical comportments must undertake to get the entities in some sense "right." The *feasibility* and *requirement* of ontical truth is what distinguishes human (ontical) comportments from the behavior of animals and inanimate things. Thus, in wanting to see how disclosure makes discovery possible, we want to see how it makes ontical truth possible. I will call this issue the *grounding* of ontical truth; and I will structure my exposition of Heidegger's transcendental philosophy as a three-stage response to it—that is, a three-stage grounding of ontical truth.

The first stage (the remainder of this section) spells out in more detail *why* discovery of entities presupposes disclosure of their being.

In so doing, it shows also, though only in a preliminary way, how discoveries are *beholden* to the entities they discover (the "feasibility" of ontical truth.) Stage two (section 3) shows how disclosure of being is inseparable from self-disclosure, and thereby shows also, though again only in a preliminary way, how ontical truth is *binding* on Dasein (the "requirement" of it). Finally, the third and deepest stage in the grounding (sections 4 and 5) will reveal why and how all of this depends on the so-called existentialist elements in *Being and Time*—especially the doctrine of death. In particular, it will fill in what is missing from the first two stages, in virtue of which they are each only "preliminary". (It must be conceded that Heidegger himself does not lay out the stages in quite this way, or develop any of them quite fully. But he does say more as the stages get deeper and more difficult, and is particularly fulsome at stage three).

In Heidegger's analysis, discovery and disclosure each have three moments—understanding, telling, and sofindingness. The fact that they each have this same structure evinces the fact that they are closely related phenomena; indeed, we could as well say (though Heidegger does not) that discovery just is *ontical* disclosure.

Heidegger's basic conception of *understanding* is *competence* or *know-how*. Thus, everyday ontical understanding is knowing how to use, manage, or otherwise cope with everyday entities and situations. For instance, understanding hammers is knowing how to hammer with them, understanding a language is knowing how to converse in it, understanding people is knowing how to interact and get along with them, and so on. Even everyday self-understanding is characterized as one's "ability-to-be" who one is—that is, to carry out one's various personal, social, and professional roles. This is not to deny that there can also be theoretical or intellectual understanding; but these are seen as dependent upon "practical" understanding in at least two ways. First, as many have pointed out, theoretical understanding is almost always derivative (perhaps via several intermediaries) from prior pretheoretical understandings, themselves rooted in practical mastery and difficulties. And second, even grasping a theory itself involves technical mastery of various formalisms, methods, vocabulary, models, and such.

"*Telling*" is my translation of "*Rede*", a word which usually just means "talk". But Heidegger introduces *Rede* as the *foundation* of language, and then explicitly defines it as the *articulation of intelligibility* (where "articulate" carries its original connotations of joints and separations between things). Now, "tell" comes from the same root as "talk" and often means much the same—as in telling others about something, telling them what to do, telling a story, and the like. But it also has other uses that have to do more with distinguishing, identifying, and even counting—such as telling apart, telling whether, telling what's what, telling one when you see one, telling how many, and so on. These latter senses clearly echo the image of articulation, and are plausibly prerequisite to the possibility of putting things into words. So, for example, in skillfully hammering, I can *tell* whether I am swinging hard enough, whether the nail is going in straight, or whether the board is splitting; and these distinctions *articulate* what, in knowing how to hammer, I understand. And they also underlie my ability to talk sensibly about hammering—at least insofar as I "know what I'm talking about."

"*Sofindingness*" is my contrived rendition of Heidegger's contrived word "*Befindlichkeit*". This bizarre term names the feature of human life that it is always responsive to what *matters* in its current, concrete situation—it *finds* the situation as thus mattering to it. For instance, if I am absorbed in hammering, I will be responsive to the heft and recoil of the hammer, the fit and integrity of the boards, the position and angle of the nail; these all matter to the hammering. But I'm likely to be oblivious of the sawdust on the floor or the flicker of the lamp (unless, of course, they interfere with the work). Moods are Heidegger's favorite example of a response to what matters in a situation, at least in part because they are so pervasive, intrusive, and uninvited. A mood makes manifest not only (i) how things are going (here and now), but also (ii) the way in which this matters, and (iii) the extent to which it just has to be accepted (put up with). But I think that sofindingness must also include more than Heidegger explicitly mentions, such as the fluid involved rapport of a craftsperson or athlete with the current work or play situation, and even the attentive responsiveness that is prerequisite to "disinterested" observation.

These general characterizations of understanding, telling, and sofindingness have been neutral between discovery (ontical) and disclosure (ontological); but the examples have all been ontical. What would be examples of *ontological* understanding, telling and sofindingness—that is, of disclosure properly so called? Heidegger is perfectly clear about the essential point: understanding, he says, always projects entities onto their *possibilities*. Ontical know-how masters entities as they are or are not *in fact*. Ontological know-how masters entities as they *could* or *could-not* be. In other words, disclosing the being of entities involves grasping them in terms of a distinction between what is possible and impossible for them.

This should not come as a complete surprise. After all, specifying what is possible and impossible for physical entities is precisely what the laws of physics do. (Indeed, they specify the possible relationships among the values of physical variables so precisely—that is, strictly—that it is often easier to think of them as specifying what is necessary; but that's just another way of saying the same thing). So, understanding physical entities in terms of these laws is projecting them onto their possibilities. Projecting entities onto their possibilities is the same as projecting them onto their being. (Heidegger uses both expressions). So, the ability to project entities onto their possibilities is the ontological know-how that is the understanding moment of disclosedness.

Notice that, for sciences like physics, the essential connection between understanding and possibility is a commonplace in the philosophy of science, even though it is expressed in a different vocabulary. The usual focus is explanation; but *explaining* something (perhaps something already known) is nothing other than a way of rendering it *intelligible*. And standard models of explanation always involve subsumption under lawlike generalizations—where "lawlikeness" amounts to some sort of modal force (necessity or possibility).

The possibilities and impossibilities for equipmental entities are not so strictly definable as for physical entities; but they are just as fundamental to understanding. What is possible for an item of equipment is how it *can* properly be used and how it *ought* properly to function in such use. Thus, stirring paint with a hammer is ruled out, and so is a hammer that shatters when it hits a nail. Of course, neither of these is "physically" impossible; but they are ruled out for this equipment as the equipment that it is. Clearly, equipmental possibilities and impossibilities are in some way normative. Yet, just as with the physical, the equipmental is intelligible as such in terms of—as projected onto—what is possible and impossible for it in the relevant sense. We can see, therefore, that standard accounts of scientific explanation are effectively special cases of Heidegger's more general formulation.[4]

Ontological understanding, like any understanding, is essentially integrated with a telling (articulation of intelligibility) and a sofindingness (responsiveness to what matters in the current situation). Manifestly, the articulation of ontological intelligibility is at least making the many determinate distinctions between the possible and the impossible for the entities of the relevant sort.[5] Without these distinctions, the ability to project would be vacuous. In effect, the ability to project is nothing other than the ability to "apply" these distinctions in particular and specified kinds of cases. Just as clearly, those distinctions would come to nothing—would not in fact be drawn—if there were in general no ability to "apply" them. So, the understanding and telling that belong to disclosedness belong essentially together.

Sofindingness is responsiveness to what matters in the current situation. What is it that matters for *ontological* sofindingness—the sofindingness that belongs properly to disclosedness? What *matters* is that the entities, as ontically discovered, be in fact *possible*—that is, *not im*possible—according to the understanding of their being. I will explain this point in a way that is not explicit in Heidegger's texts, but lies, I believe, just behind the scenes. It is quite fundamental to the first stage in the grounding of ontical truth.[6]

If ontical truth, "getting the entities right," is to be a distinctive possibility and aim of ontical comportments, then there must be a difference between those comportments that are true in this sense and those that are not, a difference that depends on the entities themselves, and that the comportments undertake to be on one side of. The effect is that comportments must be, in a distinctive way, *beholden to* the entities toward which they are comportments. Thus, apart from all other questions of success or failure in a comportment, there is this *distinctive* question of success or failure: has the comportment "got the entity right"?

This will all seem less cryptic if we revert for a moment to more familiar territory. Suppose the comportment in question is a description of the state of some physical particle. Such a comportment (description) might succeed or fail in any number of ways: in impressing the graduate students, in securing a grant, in adhering to the grammar of English, or whatever. But there is a distinctive kind of success that descriptions *as such* must aim at—one that depends on the described entity itself. In our example, it depends on whether there *is* such a particle and whether it *is* in that state. This amounts to saying, of course, that a description as such undertakes to be *correct* or *true* (truth in the sense of correctness). Thus, truth, in the sense of descriptive correctness, is a special case of "getting the entities *themselves* right."

Heidegger uses the word "truth" for a more general phenomenon of which descriptive correctness is a special case. For example, using a hammer properly as a hammer is also true in this more general sense—it *discovers* the hammer as an entity and "gets it right." He also says of such true comportments (including but not limited to correct descriptions) that they "let entities be," "let them show themselves," or "set them free." The idea is that entities first lie *hidden,* either because they have not yet been noticed, or because they have since been somehow disguised or even forgotten. *True* comportments bring them out of this hiddenness—out into the *open.* It is no coincidence that the terms "discover" and "disclose" both have connotations of unhiding and bringing into the open.

Now, if there is to be a significant distinction between "getting an entity right" and failing to do so, there must be some way—some feasible and nonarbitrary way—of telling it in particular cases. For instance, for a descriptive comportment (judgment or assertion), there must be some way of telling whether that description is true (correct) of the entity described—not in every instance, of course, but as a rule. Comportments in themselves, however, do not wear their ontical truth on their sleeves. Therefore, something else, some further comportment or comportments, must be involved in telling whether they are true or not. So the question at this point resolves into these: how can some comportments impugn the ontical truth of others? And, supposing they can, how can the choice among them be nonarbitrary?

Comportments can impugn the ontical truth of others if their respective discoverings of entities as entities are mutually *incompatible*. Hence, such incompatibility must itself make sense and be tellable (identifiable) in practice. In general, discoverings of entities are incompatible just in case the entities themselves, as (ostensibly) discovered, would be *impossible*. And this, at long last, is why the difference between the possible and the impossible *matters*—matters, in particular, to the aim of ontical truth. Ontological sofindingness is *responsiveness* to ostensible impossibilities in the current situation as something that *matters*.

More specifically, the response must be a *refusal to accept* any current apparent impossibility. Impossibilities matter by way of being *unacceptable*. This is familiar enough: if you discover both that your son is now at school and now at home, then something must be *wrong*, for he *cannot* be two places at once. Likewise, if you discover that something is a hammer but shatters against a nail, or that something is an electric current but generates no magnetic field. Since that would be impossible, *something* is wrong. So, you have to ask: *what* is wrong? You double-check, reexamine your means of discovery, find alternative ways to discover the same entities, seek confirmation from other people, and so on. Soon enough, other things being equal, it becomes clear *which* of your earlier *apparent* discoveries was wrong—was *merely* an appearance—and perhaps also why. By such perfectly ordinary procedures, the choice among the incompatible comportments becomes *nonarbitrary*. To put the emphasis another way, these procedures make feasible a nonarbitrary distinction between (mere) *appearance* and *reality*—that is, the ability to get the entities *themselves* right.

But that means we have shown how comportments can be beholden *to entities*—that is, can be comportments toward entities *as entities*. This, however is just to show how they can undertake to be ontically true. Thus, ontological sofindingness, as the refusal to accept ostensible impossibilities, belongs together with ontological

understanding (projecting entities onto their possibilities) and ontological telling (articulating the distinction between the possible and
the impossible) in making true ontical comportments possible. And
that is exactly what we wanted to show: disclosing the being of entities is a condition of the possibility of discovering them *as entities*.

In this first stage of the grounding of ontical truth it has been
shown why any discovering of entities presupposes a disclosing of
their being. In particular, it has been shown (though only in a preliminary way) how ontical comportments can be—feasibly and
nonarbitrarily—*beholden* to the entities toward which they are comportments. This beholdenness belongs to the essential aim of any
comportment toward an entity as an entity—namely, that it get the
entity itself "right." In other words, beholdenness to entities belongs
to ontical truth as such; and it is *this* that has been grounded in the
disclosing of being.

III Disclosing Dasein and Ontological Responsibility

Whenever any entities are discovered, they are discovered *by Dasein*.
It is Dasein that, in comporting itself toward entities, undertakes to
get them right. Thus, really, it is Dasein that is "beholden" in any
beholdenness to entities. This beholdenness *of Dasein* must also
belong to any adequate account of ontical truth. To avoid confusion,
I will refer to this second essential side of beholdenness as the *bindingness* of ontical truth—namely, its bindingness *on Dasein*. Explaining the essential bindingness of ontical truth is the second stage in
its grounding.

As I mentioned at the outset, disclosedness is analogous to apperception in two ways: first, it is the condition of the possibility of comportment toward entities as entities; and second, it is *at once* a
disclosing of the being of those entities *and* a self-disclosing. It is to
the latter of these two parallels that we now turn. We have just seen
what disclosing being means, and how it is prerequisite to ontical
comportments toward entities as entities. But what does that have to
do with *self*-disclosing? In this section I will give an initial account of
self-disclosing and then explain why it is and must be integral with
disclosing the being of entities. And that will enable us to see (though

again in only a preliminary way) how ontical truth is binding on Dasein.

In the first place and usually, Dasein does not "discover" itself by, say, using, observing, or measuring itself. Rather, in each case, it simply lives its life—mostly by taking care of its daily business. ("Dasein *in each case*" means each individual person, whether or not one accepts my controversial suggestion that Dasein *as such* is not individual or personal.) As Heidegger says, we *are* what we *do* (*SZ*, 126, 239). That is, in each case, we comport ourselves toward ourselves as ourselves (that is, as the entities that we are) by living our lives as *our* lives. As with any comportment toward entities as entities, we do so in terms of a disclosing of being—our being. This disclosing too has the form of an articulated sofinding understanding in terms of possibilities—our possibilities. In seeing what this means, we will see why Dasein's self-disclosing is inseparable from a disclosing of the being of *other* entities.[7]

Dasein's possibilities are ways in which it *can* live—what Heidegger calls its *ability-to-be*. In the first place and usually, these are individual capacities that are governed and defined by social norms and practices, as further specified in each case by individual social roles. Thus, "we" (end-of-millennium westerners, say) *can* use money to buy food and clothing of our choosing, *cannot* run around in public without clothing, *must* pay taxes, and *need* licenses if we are to operate automobiles. If we are academics, we can (and are "expected to") teach classes, assign work to students, and evaluate that work; on the other hand, we cannot issue traffic citations (unless we are also police officers). And I, in particular, can and am expected to teach particular classes (with a certain leeway in how I teach them), at particular times, and with particular students. It is in such terms that we understand *ourselves* as entities and as the entities that we are—that is, as *who* we are.

These are all worldly possibilities. They are possibilities for an entity whose basic make-up is being-in-the-world, which means (among other things) being in the midst of entities, and comporting ourselves toward them. I could not be a teacher, for instance, without comporting myself toward students, lessons, assignments, and the like. Thus, in knowing how to be me, I must know how to deal with the entities amidst which I work and live—indeed, these are often just two ways of looking at the same know-how. But that's not all: since what I can and am expected to do (in the roles onto which I project myself) depends on which entities there are and what they are, my comportments toward those entities must be ontically *true* (at least mostly). My *self*-understanding, therefore, *presupposes* that I understand the being of the entities amid which I live.

In fact, the connection is closer yet. My self-understanding is my ability-to-be who I am—the skillful know-how that enables me to project myself onto my own possibilities (as a teacher, for instance) and, in those terms, to live my life. But, if my self-understanding depends on my understanding of the being of other entities, then I must also *be able to* project those entities onto their possibilities. *This* ability, therefore, belongs essentially to my ability-to-be *me*. My ability to project those entities onto their possibilities is not merely another possibility onto which I project myself, but is rather *part of* my ability to project myself onto my own possibilities at all. In other words, my *self*-understanding literally *incorporates* an understanding of the being of other entities. And since, conversely, there could also be no projection of any entities onto their possibilities if that were not something that someone is able to do, neither self-understanding nor understanding of being is possible except insofar as they are integrated with one another.

Obviously the same goes for articulative telling. Projection onto possibilities, whether possibilities for one's own living or possibilities for the entities around one, is for nought if the respective possibilities are not distinguished from impossibilities—that is, from something that is ruled out. Making such distinctions is the relevant telling; and there would be nothing to tell if there were no projections. Therefore, since the corresponding understandings are possible only as integrated, so are the tellings.

Sofindingness is more interesting. In understanding myself as a teacher, I project myself onto the possibilities that go with that role— possibilities that I distinguish from impossibilities. Moreover, I am responsive to that distinction as something that matters in each current situation, specifically in that impossibilities are not acceptable to me. That's the sofindingness that belongs to self-disclosing.

But, since *I* am the entity that I'm comporting myself toward, what matters is whether *I* am "possible" or not—which is to say, whether what I am *doing* is ruled out or not. For instance, in comporting myself toward myself as a teacher, it matters to me that, so far as I can manage, I do everything that's prescribed to me as a teacher and nothing that's proscribed. Stretching the terms a bit, we could even call such propriety the "ontical truth" of being a teacher.

Now, we saw earlier that comportments toward entities as entities *undertake* to be ontically true, because impossibilities are *unacceptable*. In the context of *self*-disclosing, however, what I *undertake* is to *do* what I am supposed to—that is, never to *act* in a way that is ruled out; that's what matters in this sofindingness. But a responsiveness that finds what is ruled out in the responding entity's *own* actions to be unacceptable *to that entity itself* is *responsibility*. So, for instance, one can say of a hammer or other worldly entity that is found to be impossible (ruled out) that it is unacceptable; but one cannot say that it is irresponsible. By contrast, one can and does say exactly that of a teacher—or any other person—who is out of line in terms of his or her role. Therefore, the sofindingness that belongs to *self*-disclosing amounts to responsibility.

But, as we have also seen, performing as one is supposed to in a worldly role always involves comportments toward entities as entities, comportments that need, that is, mostly to be ontically true. I cannot carry out my responsibilities as a teacher, for instance, if I cannot reliably tell whether I have my notes with me, whether I am in the right classroom, and a host of other such things. Telling *reliably* means mostly *truly*. It follows that the responsibilities implied by self-disclosing *include* the responsibility to, in a broad sense, *tell the truth*.

This responsibility does not extend merely to everyday comportments toward, say, equipment or other people, but rather to all ontical comportments. Suppose, for example, a physicist discovered an entity that, according to certain experimental results, appeared to violate some law of physics (that is, was impossible according to that law). How should this physicist, *qua physicist*, respond to such a discovery? Well, in real life, there may be many reasonable alternatives; but nonchalant indifference is not among them. No one who simply didn't give a damn whether experimental results accord with theory could be a proper scientist—it would be scientifically *irresponsible*. But this is just to say that every scientist as such must acknowledge the scientific responsibility (perhaps in concert with the larger scientific community) to see that such matters are cleared up, that is, to figure out what's true.

Since getting the entities right depends on the disclosure of their being, the ontological sofindingness that belongs to the disclosure of being is likewise not merely responsiveness but responsibility. That is, finding impossible entities unacceptable is not just a response but a responsibility—a further part of the responsibility that Dasein in each case has as self-disclosing. And, moreover, there clearly could be no such responsibility except as part of Dasein's self-responsibility. In other words, the sofindingness of self-disclosure and that of the disclosure of being are inseparable. Inasmuch as this responsibility is responsibility for ontical *truth*, it can also be called *ontological* responsibility. (Ontical responsibilities are just one's ordinary duties and the like).

With this conclusion, we have shown for each of understanding, telling, and sofindingness that, as belonging respectively to self-disclosing and disclosing the being of other entities, they are inseparable. But, since these three moments are jointly constitutive of disclosing, to have shown that for each of them is to have shown it for disclosing itself. In other words, we have *shown* that disclosing as such is *at once* a self-disclosing *and* a disclosing of the being of entities. This was the first goal of the present section. (Among other things, it completes the justification of the analogy with transcendental apperception.)

And the second goal now follows easily. Responsibility is intrinsically a kind of bindingness: one is "bound" by one's responsibilities. Therefore, in showing that Dasein is *responsible* for ontical truth—for "telling the truth"—we have shown (at least in a preliminary way) how ontical truth is *binding* on Dasein. And that completes the second stage in its grounding. What remains is to see why these first two stages have only been "preliminary"; and second to supply what is still needed for a full grounding of ontical truth. That will take us into the thick of Heidegger's "existentialism."

IV Owned Disclosedness: Resolute Being toward Death

The most pervasive and basic of Heidegger's "existentialist" concepts is that of *ownedness* (*Eigentlichkeit*). The usual translation of "*eigentlich*" is "real" or "authentic" (as opposed, for instance, to fake or counterfeit). But Heidegger explicitly warns that he has chosen his expressions "*Eigentlichkeit*" and its opposite "*Uneigentlichkeit*" in "the strict senses of the words" (*SZ*, 43)—which I take to mean their etymological senses. The root word "*eigen*" is broadly equivalent to (and cognate with) the English word "own" (as in "a room of one's own"). This suggests that Heidegger's terms (neither of which is an ordinary German word) might better be translated "ownedness" and "unownedness"—and that's how I will translate them (and correspondingly for the adjectives and adverbs). But the ultimate justification for this must be philosophical.

The first clue to a proper understanding is Heidegger's further remark (in the same passage) that ownedness and unownedness are *both* grounded in the fact that Dasein at all is defined by *in-each-case-mineness* (*Jemeinigkeit*). The point here is that each person's life *belongs to* the person whose life it is: each person can say "this is *my* life," "*my* decision," "*my* responsibility," and so on. It is not Dasein *as such* that is "mine" (or can say "my . . ."); rather, Dasein *in each case* is (respectively) "mine." Dasein *as such* is defined by this fact that in each respective case it is "mine." Ownedness and unownedness are *modes* of Dasein's being; and they are both grounded in that fact about Dasein as such, that it is in each case mine.

Thus, ownedness and unownedness are alternative *ways* in which Dasein, in any given case, can be respectively "its own" ("mine"). Dasein is invariably *its own* (mine) in each case. But it may or may not be *owned*—ownedness is something over and above mineness that varies from case to case. (I think Heidegger should also have said that ownedness varies in degree from case to case, and that, in any given case, its degree can differ in different respects; but he did not.) Unownedness is, so to speak, the default: in the first place and usually, Dasein is unowned. Ownedness, by contrast, is distinctive and special. But the *possibility* of ownedness is universal (implicit in mineness), and is moreover, as we shall see, essential to Dasein as the entity that comports itself toward entities as entities.

The difference between ownedness and unownedness is a difference in modes of disclosedness. Unowned disclosedness (the default) is called *publicness*; owned disclosedness (Dasein's distinctive possibility) is called *resoluteness*. But, given the way Heidegger uses the word "existential", it can also be called *existential* disclosedness. Thus, we will understand what this is all about—what it has to do with the transcendental question concerning the possibility of ontical truth—when we understand resoluteness. It is in Heidegger's lengthy explication of resoluteness that all of the notorious existentialist notions—falling, anxiety, individuality, death, conscience, and being-responsible ("guilt")—come to the fore.

Falling is the basic characteristic of Dasein that, in each case, it inevitably tends toward unownedness—specifically, unowned disclosedness (publicness). This is why publicness is the default. In the special case of scientific Dasein, *fallenness* (unownedness) is exactly what Kuhn calls *normality* (as in: *normal* science). So falling is a generalization of the tendency toward normality in science. Kuhn has a lovely explanation for *why* a dogged, even sometimes dogmatic, tendency toward normality is *essential* to science.[8] Heidegger, too, says that falling is not a derogatory concept, and that it is essential to Dasein; but he lacks Kuhn's developed explanation of why. Given this essential tendency toward unownedness or normality (what Heidegger also calls everydayness), there must also be some push in the opposite direction, if there is ever to be anything else. Kuhn's and Heidegger's accounts of this opposing push likewise have much in common, the former's being richer in historical example, the latter's more general and more worked out philosophically.

Resoluteness, as a mode of disclosedness, has the same basic structure that we've already seen: a sofinding and telling understanding. Each of these three moments has an owned (existential) mode that belongs to resoluteness as owned disclosedness.

The owned sofindingness that belongs to resoluteness is *readiness-for-anxiety*. Anxiety is a mood that manifests a profound breakdown in an individual's way of life. Nothing makes any sense or means anything anymore—nothing matters except the overwhelming fact that nothing (else) matters. (Thus, anxiety is analogous to Kuhn's sense of crisis). Heidegger says that anxiety *individualizes* Dasein. This does not mean that Dasein is not, in each case, already an individual, but rather that, in anxiety, a person's individuality is "brought home" to him or her in an utterly unmistakable and undeniable way. Falling back into public life (normality) is a way of escaping anxiety, and the public culture encourages this. Indeed, the culture offers "common-sense" interpretations that tend to minimize anxiety itself—turn it into (confuse it with) some weak-kneed or adolescent self-indulgence. Thus, the very possibility of genuine anxiety is publicly confused and covered up—disguised and forgotten.

Readiness-for-anxiety is not the same as anxiety, but it does run directly counter to this public (falling) tendency to disguise and forget anxiety. Readiness-for-anxiety is an individualized mode of sofindingness in which anxiety is held open as a constant possibility—a possibility that currently matters to that very individual. This does not mean that the person is hoping or striving for anxiety—far from it—but only that he or she is determined not to hide or run away from it. (If we were to invent a Kuhnian analog for this, it would be openness to the possibility of scientific crisis).

The owned telling that belongs to resoluteness is *conscience*—or, rather, that *reticence* (muting the public babble) in which conscience can be "listened for" and "heard." According to the common public interpretation, conscience is an "inner voice" that mainly warns and reproves—tells you when you would be or have been naughty. (A so-called "good" conscience merely reassures you that you haven't been naughty). But, as with anxiety, Heidegger claims that this fallen interpretation disguises and forgets what conscience really articulates, which must be (Heidegger is not explicit here) the difference between one's whole life "working" and its breaking down or failing to "work"—the very difference that matters in readiness-for-anxiety.

What Heidegger *is* explicit about is that (in articulating this distinction) conscience *calls upon* Dasein in each case to *take over responsibility* for its whole life—a call that the public interpretation likewise disguises and forgets. This is not the same as what I earlier termed *ontological* responsibility, which is perfectly intelligible in terms of public norms and expectations, and which concerns only particular events. Rather, the responsibility that existential conscience gives Dasein in each case to understand—namely, *existential* responsibility—is responsibility for its *own self as a whole*, for *who* it is. Thus conscience, like anxiety, individualizes.

Heidegger's formulation of this point takes advantage of some relationships among German word-senses that can't be reproduced exactly in English. The term that I am translating as "responsible" is "*schuldig*". The two most common senses of this word are guilty/at-fault/culpable and obliged/indebted/liable. "Responsible", in English, is not as specific as either of these senses, but is broad enough to cover them both. Clearly, the common theme is how one ought and ought not to behave. (It is helpful to remember that "*schuld-*" is cognate with "should"). Thus, Heidegger can say that, according to common sense, conscience mainly tells us that we are *schuldig*—guilty or obliged. But he can then go on to say that guilt and obligation are merely fallen public interpretations of being *schuldig*—interpretations that track only public norms and statuses, keeping score on everyone's credits and debits, points and infractions. As fallen, however, these "normal" interpretations are but forgetful disguises of a more originary *self*-responsibility—one that cannot be public but can only be taken over by an individual. Conscience, understood existentially, calls upon Dasein in each case to take over and own *this* responsibility.

The owned, existential understanding that belongs to resoluteness is *projecting oneself onto being-responsible*. Thus, *being*-responsible, like anything onto which Dasein projects *itself*, is a possibility for how it can live—an ability-to-be. Heidegger calls it Dasein's *ownmost* (*eigenste*) possibility or ability-to-be. Now, Dasein, as that entity that comports itself toward entities as entities, is *always* in each case responsible. (Irresponsibility is just a deficient mode of responsibility). This was shown already in the second stage of the grounding. So the *being*-responsible (onto which owned Dasein projects itself, and which conscience gives it to understand) must be something over and above that invariable responsibility that always characterizes Dasein—something that is a *possibility* for it, but not necessary.

An individual's *being*-responsible is its *taking over* responsibility for its *whole self*. But, what does that mean? Here we have "existentialism" in its full flower. Yet, according to the passage I quoted in my pro-logue, Heidegger does not want to preach an existentialist philoso-phy, but rather to renew the question of being. Does that mean that being-responsible has something to do with the question of being? Yes, of course! Ultimately *everything* in *Being and Time* has to do with the question of being—and, with it, truth. The existential concepts are introduced for this reason and this reason only. Our task as readers is to understand how.

That task will take us through the most remarkable of detours—or, rather, what at first *seems* to be a detour—Heidegger's doctrine of death. As with anxiety, conscience and guilt/responsibility, Heideg-ger claims that the understandings of death handed down to us by our culture are mostly fallen and forgetful disguises. He singles out two versions of these popular conceptions for particular attention, so as to contrast them with his own, and thus to set them aside. The first of these he calls *perishing*. This is the ubiquitous and all-too-familiar biological phenomenon that is the cessation of systematic biological function in an organism (and, typically, the onset of organic decay). All organisms eventually perish: plants, animals, fungi, and what have you, including all specimens of Homo sapiens. But *Dasein never* perishes—not because it is immortal or everlasting, but because it is not a living organism in the biological sense at all.

The second popular conception of death Heidegger calls *demise*. Unlike perishing, demise is not a biological phenomenon, but per-tains exclusively to Dasein. It is instead a social-cultural phenome-non. Roughly speaking, demise is that social event upon which you cease to be countable in the census, your spouse becomes a widow or widower, your property ceases to be yours and passes to your heirs, criminal charges against you automatically become moot, and so on. Although demise typically coincides with the perishing of an organ-ism, these are not at all the same. The relationship between demise and perishing is loosely analogous to that between marriage and mating (which likewise are not at all the same).

What is important about these is only that neither is to be identi-fied with death, *existentially* conceived. Without attempting a full account, I will relate a few of the most salient and significant things that Heidegger says about death (as opposed to perishing and/or demise).

- Death is *not an event*: it is not something that happens—*ever* (*SZ*, 240, 250, 257).
- Death "is" only in *being toward* death; that is, death is intelligible only as a certain sort of being-toward (*SZ*, 234, 245, 259).
- Death is *a way to be* (Dasein is *constantly* dying); in other words, death is a way of life (*SZ*, 245, 251, 259).
- Death is Dasein's *ownmost possibility*—a possibility that it is called upon to *take over* in each case, and so one that *individualizes* Dasein (*SZ*, 250, 263f.).
- More specifically, death is the *possibility of the impossibility* of Dasein's existence at all—that is, of any comportment toward entities as entities—and is thus the possibility of giving itself up (*SZ*, 250, 262, 264).
- In its being toward death, Dasein *decides* or *chooses to choose* itself (*SZ*, 259, 264, 384; and see also 188, 268, 287f.).
- Death is Dasein's *finitude* and *ability-to-be-whole*; that is, in being toward death, Dasein exists *finitely* and *as a whole* (*SZ*, 264, 309, 329f., 384–386).

It is clear from the wording of several of these (especially the fourth) that death is related to resoluteness. But Heidegger makes the connection explicit and even stronger. On the one hand, at the conclusion of his existential interpretation of death (*SZ*, 266), he acknowledges that, as so far described, being toward death remains a "fantastic exaction," and that it has not been shown how Dasein is *capable* of it. On the other hand, following his initial account of resoluteness, he suggests (*SZ*, 302f.) that it has not yet been "thought through to its end." The solution is that each discussion fills the lacuna in the other: thought through to its end, resoluteness must be resoluteness *toward death*, and it is *as* thus resolute that Dasein is *able to be* toward death.

Accordingly, he offers (*SZ*, §62) a further elaboration of resoluteness. As resolute, Dasein projects itself onto its ownmost being-responsible—that is, understands itself as responsible for its whole life by *owning* that responsibility and "taking it over." *Owning* responsibility, however, means taking it over not as something occasional or incidental, but rather as constant and essential; that is, it projects *itself* onto being-responsible *as a whole.* To put it another way, it understands itself as responsible *no matter what.* But, *as finite,* Dasein simply *cannot* project itself "no matter what." The "whole" as which it projects itself must be a *finite* whole—which is to say, the projection must be in some way limited, and must project itself *as* thus limited. (Resolute Dasein does not hide or run away from its finitude). As Heidegger puts it, resolute Dasein projects itself as self-responsible "right to its end" (*SZ,* 305).

Such whole-but-finite resolution means resolution toward death. Death—which is intelligible only as being toward death—is Dasein's ability-to-be-whole and its finitude. Conscience and anxiety exact this resolute responsibility of Dasein (*SZ,* 307f.); so, while indeed an "exaction," being toward death is not "fantastic."

The word "resolute" means firmly and unwaveringly determined or decisive. Heidegger expresses as much by saying that resoluteness resolves to "repeat itself"—that is, to keep at it or stick to it by, as it were, constantly "re-resolving." But he makes this point in the context of making another: resoluteness cannot become rigidly set in its ways about its situation, but rather must be held open and free for whatever its current possibility is. In particular, it must hold itself free for a possible—and, in each case, necessary—*taking it back.* Taking a resolution back means retracting or withdrawing it—that is, giving up on it. These two points are made together and as belonging together (*SZ,* 307f., 391). Resoluteness *as such* resolves to repeat itself (stick to it) *while also* holding itself constantly free for the possibility of taking it back (giving it up). Clearly (and as Heidegger immediately makes explicit), the possibility of "taking it back" refers to death. This is what is meant by saying that resoluteness is resolute being toward death.

But building this into the structure of resoluteness as such—as something it "holds itself free for"—sounds incoherent. Sticking to it is, of course, a possibility onto which Dasein projects itself—which just means that it rules out the contrary, not sticking to it, as unacceptable to itself. But this seems flatly incompatible with holding itself free for the possibility of taking it back. Including them both in the definition makes being "resolute" sound like making a promise with your fingers crossed—which is not to make a *promise* at all.

So we have to ask: how can resoluteness be *resolute* if, as such, it must be resolute *toward death?* What kind of *responsibility* could that be? And, in the meantime, what can it have to do with the question of being and the grounding of ontical truth?

V Truth and Finitude

We are not, after all, unprepared for a connection between resoluteness and the questions of being and truth. Resoluteness is a mode—the owned, existential mode—of disclosedness. Disclosing is at once a disclosing of the being of entities and a disclosing of Dasein itself. We have seen how these can be described separately, but also how they are essentially united. As thus unitary, disclosedness is the condition of the possibility of comportment toward entities as entities—hence of ontical truth. That was the substance of the first two stages of the grounding. Resoluteness, as a mode of disclosedness, is likewise at once a disclosing of being and of Dasein. What we have focused on so far is resoluteness as the owned disclosing of Dasein. Therefore, in order to complete the story, we must see how, as the owned disclosing of Dasein, resoluteness is essentially also an owned disclosing of being.

In *Being and Time* as we have it, Heidegger does not fully work out this crucial chapter of the account. But it is implied in everything that we do have. So the omission cannot be mere negligence, nor can it be that he thought it unimportant. I conjecture, therefore, that it is one of the topics to have been addressed in the never published third division of part one. (The *main* topic to have been addressed in that division is temporality as the "sense of being," which might have amounted to a fourth stage in the grounding of ontical truth.) Accordingly, I propose to sketch out in the remainder of my chapter how resoluteness is an *owned* disclosing of being. That will complete the third—and for now final—stage in the grounding of ontical truth.

A moment's reflection shows that the possibilities onto which entities are projected—hence, their being—is cultural and historical. Physicists learn the theory and practice of physics at school and from their peers, as part of their cultural heritage; and what they learn today is not what they learned a hundred or a thousand years ago. After all, except in times of crisis, the standards for scientific investigation and getting the entities right are established by normal science; and what is *normal* is cultural and historical. Though less dramatically obvious, the same is true for the possibilities and being of ordinary, everyday entities.

Heidegger emphasizes that Dasein is essentially historical (*geschichtlich*), not merely in the sense that it always "has" a history, but rather, and more basically, in the sense that its being (existence) is constituted by historicalness (*SZ*, 382). Accordingly, insofar as Dasein is owned, it is owned as historical. This means, among other things, that resolute Dasein discloses its current possibilities from out of a heritage that it *takes over*—that is, takes responsibility for (*SZ*, 383). In responsibly handing possibilities down to itself from out of its heritage, it *explicitly* chooses them for itself (*chooses to* choose them) and this explicit handing down is *repetition*—the repetition that belongs by definition to resoluteness (*SZ*, 384f.). (Heidegger adds that this repetition of an inherited possibility is not mere reiteration but also makes a "reciprocative rejoinder.")

As we saw in the second stage of the grounding, since Dasein's basic makeup is being-in-the-world, its self-disclosing is inseparable from its disclosing of the being of the entities toward which it comports itself. Therefore, resolute Dasein, in handing down possibilities to itself from out of its heritage, is handing down *at once* the possibilities onto which it projects itself *and* the possibilities onto which it projects those entities. Though the wording is peculiar, the point is easy to see: physicists, in becoming physicists, inherit *both* the possibilities for working as physicists *and* the possibilities for the physical entities with which they work. Neither makes sense without the other. In other words, the being of the physical is just as historical as the practice of physics. And a resolute physicist takes responsibility for both.

How can a physicist take responsibility for the *being* of the physical? Heidegger, unfortunately, declines to say. After briefly discussing the scientific projection of entities (especially in mathematical physics), and concluding with a quick invocation of resoluteness, he remarks: "The origin of science from out of owned existence will not be pursued further here" (*SZ*, 363). Whether he intended to pursue it further later is not made clear. Be that as it may, I think we can pursue it further now, and moreover we must if we are to complete the grounding of ontical truth that is so strikingly and thoroughly prepared in the text we have.

Resoluteness not only repeats itself, but also holds itself free for the possibility of taking it back. But this freedom is not irresponsible license—precisely not. It is the freedom of *responsible* decision. To *what* is this free decision responsible? Cryptically, yet not incorrectly, we can say that it is responsible to *itself*. Less compressed, this says: it is responsible to that very disclosing of self and being that, as a resolute decisiveness, resoluteness as such is. How that can be will come into focus if we think again about disclosedness and responsibility.

In the first stage of the grounding, disclosing the being of entities makes intelligible a nonarbitrary distinction between appearance and reality via the entailed refusal to accept apparent impossibilities in entities as discovered. That refusal stands behind all the double checking, and so on, that ferrets out which apparent discoveries are wrong and so vindicates those that are right. In the second stage, in which that same disclosing is seen instead from the side of self-disclosing, that same responsive refusal manifests itself as ontological responsibility—that is, responsibility for ontical truth. For unowned Dasein, that's as far as responsibility for the truth goes.

There is, however, and can be no antecedent *guarantee* that all that double checking and whatnot, no matter how assiduous, will ever actually succeed. That is, no matter how hard the relevant individuals and community try, they may not find a way to reconcile their apparent discoveries with what they know to be possible. What then? Well, of course, there can be appeals to magic, miracles, and mysticism. There can be denial, disinterest, and decline. And, in the meantime, everybody's busy: if the impossibility is remote or arcane, maybe the best thing is to ignore it and see if it goes away.

But, what is the *responsible* response? Notice that this question cannot be about *ontological* responsibility. What that responsibility requires—the double checking and ensuing corrections—has already been exhausted. So we're looking for another and *further* responsibility—"further" because it only comes up after whole-hearted ontological responsibility has exhausted itself. This further responsibility too must take the form of a *refusal to accept* any discovered impossibilities. ("Accepting" them is simply irresponsible.) A discovered impossibility rests on two factors: what is in fact discovered and what is ruled out by the projection onto possibilities. The careful and persistent double checking has eliminated the discoveries as the culprit. That leaves the possibilities—in other words, the *being* of the entities discovered. So, our further responsibility must be responsibility for the projection onto those possibilities, which is to say, for the disclosing of that being.

Taking responsibility for something is not only taking it as something that matters, but also *not* taking it for granted. Taking the disclosure of being for granted—whether explicitly or tacitly—is characteristic of fallen Dasein and normal science. *Owned* Dasein, as taking over responsibility for its ontological heritage, no longer takes it for granted. It *reawakens* the question of being—as its *ownmost* and sometimes *most urgent* question. In other words, it holds itself free for taking it back. That doesn't mean it *does* take it back, still less that it does so easily or casually. The freedom to take it back is not a liberty or a privilege but rather a burden—the most onerous of burdens. That's why everyday Dasein runs away and hides from it, and even denies that there is any such freedom. Hence, conscience and anxiety must *exact* it of Dasein, and resolute Dasein must *hold* itself free.

Giving up on a disclosing of being is not a matter to be taken lightly; and the reason is not hard to see. Heidegger, like the early Kuhn, concentrates on extreme cases—maybe even more so (it's hard to be sure, since, unlike Kuhn, he does not offer examples). An extreme case is one in which a disclosing is given up more or less wholesale, or, as is sometimes said, radically. The trouble with giving up the roots is that you forfeit also the branches. Put less figuratively, the point is that the means of discovering entities—what Heidegger calls "modes of access" and Kuhn calls "experimental procedures" and "puzzle-solving techniques"—themselves *depend on* the disclosure of the being of those entities.

The design of scientific instruments and experiments and the interpretation of their results depend *essentially* on the very laws and theories they sometimes test. Without a great deal of accepted physics, for instance, no cloud-chamber image or statistical pattern from a cyclotron could so much as make sense, let alone reveal anything. But this means that, if intransigent discovered impossibilities undermine a disclosure of being, they pull the rug out from under themselves as well—and along with them, any other discoveries and abilities to discover in that region. The disclosure, the discoveries, and the abilities to discover all stand or fall together—as a *whole*. So, giving up on a disclosing of being is, in effect, giving up on *everything*—including the self-disclosing that makes possible that way of life.

This is why Heidegger speaks of death—or, rather, of resolute being toward death. Taking responsibility resolutely means living in a way that explicitly has everything at stake. Heidegger's way of saying this is: Dasein is the entity for which, in its being, that very being is an issue (*SZ*, 12, 191, 240, 263). This is the most basic definition of Dasein; all the others follow from it. It follows, for instance, that Dasein's basic makeup is being-in-the-world, because its being couldn't be an issue for it if its life were not essentially at risk, and this risk presupposes the potential intransigence of intraworldly entities. And it follows that Dasein is the entity that discloses entities in their being, since entities could never be intransigent if they were not projected onto possibilities, nor if impossibilities weren't unacceptable. *Existence*, in Heidegger's proprietary sense, is the *being* of Dasein; hence, it means all of these.

Fallen, everyday Dasein runs away and hides from the issue of its being (though it can never escape it); resolute Dasein faces up to it by taking over responsibility for itself—that is, by resolving to repeat itself, while holding itself free for taking it back. "Refusing to accept" intransigent impossibilities has a double meaning. One way of refusing to accept is bullheadedly refusing even to *see*—blinding oneself. *Existentially*, that kind of refusal—running away and hiding—is *irresponsible*. Thus, holding itself free for taking it back belongs just as essentially to existential responsibility as does sticking to it as long as one reasonably (responsibly) can. The existential *understanding* that belongs to resoluteness—self-projection onto being-responsible—just *is* perseverant being toward death.[9]

It is crucial, therefore, not to lose sight in this context of the other clause in the formula for resoluteness as a responsible way of life: it resolves to *repeat* itself—that is, to *stick to it*. Since most apparently discovered impossibilities are *merely* apparent, it would be wavering and irresponsible ("irresolute") to give up too soon—that is, so long as there is any way that it might *responsibly* be avoided. Thus, double checking and ontological responsibility are entailed by resoluteness. Resolute Dasein too is responsible for getting the entities right—indeed, as we shall soon see, all the more so.

What differentiates owned from unowned disclosedness is its holding itself free for the possibility, *in extremis*, of taking it back. In so doing, it takes over responsibility not only for ontical truth itself but also for that disclosedness that is the condition of its possibility. Since this disclosedness is the projection of those entities onto the possibilities that determine their *being*, we can, in parallel with the phrase "ontical truth", call it *ontological* truth. Heidegger himself calls disclosedness *originary* truth; and he calls the owned mode of disclosedness (that is, resoluteness) *owned* truth and the *truth of existence* (*SZ*, 220f., 297–299, 307, 397). Thus, in these terms, resolute Dasein takes responsibility not only for *ontical* but also for *ontological* truth. But, in what sense can disclosedness be called a sort of *truth* at all? What could be counterposed to it as a sort of "falsehood," and what are the feasible and nonarbitrary responses that tell them apart?

Falsehood is a *failure* of truth, a *fault* of it, not merely in the sense of an error (waywardness) but more in the sense of a breach or lack. So the "opposite" of ontological truth would be a failure, breach, or lack of disclosedness. That is exactly the sort of breakdown that manifests itself in anxiety, is told by conscience, and onto the responsibility for facing up to which owned understanding projects itself. Therefore, resoluteness, as both resolving to repeat itself and holding itself free for the possibility of taking it back, takes responsibility—*existential* responsibility—for the difference between *ontological* truth and falsehood, while undertaking to stay on the side of the former.

Ontical truth and the responsibility for it presuppose a disclosing of the being of entities, because the need for responsible double checking arises only in the face of apparent impossibilities, and *only so* are ontical comportments feasibly and nonarbitrarily beholden to entities. But there can be no comparable account for *ontological* truth and the responsibility for it, because there is no "meta-disclosedness" for them to presuppose. The possibilities for entities are not themselves projected onto "meta-possibilities" in terms of which there could be apparent "meta-impossibilities." How, then, and to what is ontological truth *beholden?*

Ontological truth is beholden to *entities*—the very same entities that ontical truth is beholden to, and via the very same means of discovery. The difference lies in the character of the potential failure and the required response. A failure of ontical truth is a misdiscovery of an entity, such as a factual mistake. With more or less work, it can be identified and corrected; and life goes on. A failure of ontological truth is a systematic breakdown that undermines everything—which just means a breakdown that *cannot* be "fixed up with a bit of work." So the only responsible response (eventually) is to take it all back; which means that life, *that* life, does *not* "go on." But this response too is a response to discovered entities, and only to them—a refusal to accept what we might paradoxically call "*real*" impossibilities among them. Intransigent impossibilities can *only* show up among entities as ostensibly discovered. To be sure, they may turn out in the end not to have been discovered entities after all; but that eventuality *presupposes* ostensible discoveries of entities.

This is an important result, for it means that ontological truth, though historical, is not arbitrary. Therefore, Heidegger's (and Kuhn's) "historicism" about being does not imply relativism. Discovery of entities does indeed presuppose—hence is "relative" to— Dasein's disclosure of their being (or a "paradigm"), which is historical. But whether a way of life with its ontical comportments *works* or not is not ultimately up to Dasein, either individually or historically. So that disclosure itself, in turn, is *beholden* for its "success" to those very entities as discovered—entities that are independent of it in the concrete and inescapable sense that they are *out of control*. And that beholden disclosure is *binding* on Dasein in that its very life depends on it. Resolute Dasein *takes over* that beholden bindingness—binds *itself*—in existential responsibility. Therefore, resolute being toward death is the condition of the possibility of *ontological truth*.

The first and second stages of the grounding showed in a preliminary way how ontical truth is feasible and nonarbitrary, and how, as such, it is beholden to entities and binding on Dasein. Those demonstrations were only preliminary, however, because the status of the presupposed possibilities for those entities was left out of account. If those possibilities themselves (the disclosed being of the entities) were to remain arbitrary, and therefore neither beholden nor binding, then the achievement of the first two stages would be hollow at best—even ontical truth would not be a sort of *truth* after all. The demonstration that ontological truth (disclosedness) is itself feasibly nonarbitrary and, as resolute, also bound and beholden, closes that gap. It constitutes, therefore, the third and most fundamental stage in the grounding of ontical truth. The existential conception of finitude—death—that is its crux is accordingly *transcendental*.

Kant understands human knowledge as *essentially finite*. Only in terms of this finitude does a transcendental grounding of its objectivity so much as make sense. But the finitude of knowledge is itself grasped only in contrast to and as falling short of infinite knowing. The relationship between any knowing and what is known in it can never be merely arbitrary. Infinite (divine) knowledge is perfect-in-itself in that it is not in any way *limited* by what it knows. Infinite just means unlimited: unbounded and unbound. Such knowledge is therefore originary or creative; that's how the relationship to what it knows is nonarbitrary (in effect, what is known is bounded and bound by the knowing of it).

Finite human knowledge, *by contrast*, is *not* perfect-in-itself. Since it is not originary, it can only be knowledge insofar as it is bounded and bound by what it knows. But that means that whatever it knows must stand over against it as an *object* (*Gegenstand*). So, finite knowledge can *only* (at best) be *objective*—it falls short of being creative. In order to be objective (bounded and bound), it must be responsive to objects, which means it needs a passive faculty of receptivity. But since mere passivity does not suffice for objectivity (it suffices for boundedness, but not for bindingness), finite knowledge *also* needs an active faculty of spontaneity—a faculty that can somehow *bind itself* to what is accessible in receptivity. The entire problem of the transcendental analytic is to delineate the conditions under which this *self*-binding is possible—an issue that arises only because human knowledge is only finite.

Heidegger calls his analysis of Dasein and disclosedness an *existential* analytic, not because the grounding of ontical truth is not transcendental, but because it can *be* transcendental only *as* existential. Death, as Dasein's finitude, plays, as we have seen, a starring role in this drama—not, however, as the antagonist who makes the dramatic resolution necessary, but rather as the protagonist who makes it possible.

4

Philosophy and Authenticity: Heidegger's Search for a Ground for Philosophizing

Charles Guignon

In the late 1960s Bert Dreyfus taught a year-long course called "Phenomenology and Existentialism" that focused especially on Husserl, Kierkegaard, and Heidegger and was taught in the energetically polemical style that has characterized Bert's life's work. The first third of the course was devoted to a reading of Husserl so illuminating and compelling that the class was convinced Husserl had the answers to all interesting questions posed by philosophers. For the rest of the course, Bert went on to show how Kierkegaard and Heidegger had undercut Husserl's ideas and moved toward a radically new conception of our predicament. As I look back on the past thirty years, I can see how these lectures determined the questions and outlook that motivate my interests to this day.

Three important questions were driven home in my mind in Bert's lectures. The first starts from the contention that Husserl's ideal of doing philosophy from the standpoint of a "theoretical attitude" is untenable because, as Kierkegaard and Heidegger argue, only a being who *cares* about something has the ability to pick things out from the field of experience in order to get an understanding of the world. But if we agree that care is crucial to understanding, and grant that people care about things in different ways at different times, the question arises whether we can ever get a "correct," or even intersubjectively agreed-upon, view of things. The second question arises from the supposition, which seems inescapable on a close reading of Division II of *Being and Time*, that one must be authentic in order to do fundamental ontology. Bert was quite genuinely puzzled by this question: what could it possibly mean to say that only authentic people can do philosophy? The third question, posed at the end of the course, was why Heidegger seems to end his magnum opus, after 436 pages of systematic analysis, by undermining everything he has said so far. On the last two pages of this massive work, Heidegger suddenly tells us that the account up to this point has been only *preparatory*, and that the existential analysis which has been central to the story so far "remains only *a path*," one "way" (*Weg*) of going. The assumption, central to the book from start to finish, that the question of Being has to be answered through an examination of Dasein is suddenly dropped as Heidegger questions whether this is the only way to approach the topic: "Whether this is the *only* way or even the right one at all, can be decided only *after one has gone along it*."[1] And in the marginal notes written in his own copy of the book, next to the words, "We must look for a way," Heidegger adds cryptically: "Not the 'sole' way."[2]

These thoughts and questions preoccupied me long after Bert's own thought moved on to the interesting views for which he is best known. As I looked at Heidegger's early lecture courses and read accounts of his lecture style,[3] I found that this tendency to put everything said so far into question at the end of a long course of thought is actually quite common. Concerning Bert's third question, I began to suspect that the inconclusiveness and self-undermining quality of *Being and Time* might be less a proof that the inquiry into the Being of entities undertaken there has failed than it is an indication that Heidegger's path of questioning is unavoidably open-ended and inconclusive. What if we were to regard *Being and Time* as one among many way stations on a long and winding path, a path with no final destination? What if we took seriously Heidegger's succinct conclusion at the end of his life that "*Alles ist Weg*" ("All is way")[4] with its implication that there is no such thing as arriving at a final or correct account of Being?

Looking at the end of *Being and Time* in this way helped me to address the first two questions raised by Bert's lectures. In what follows, I want to explore the suggestion that, for Heidegger, the inconclusiveness of philosophy is an unavoidable consequence of the fact that philosophical questioning has to reflect on its own stand-point in asking philosophical questions, and that this reflection invariably leads to a transformation of the questioning itself. Hei-degger himself made this point in 1929 when he said, "every meta-physical question can be asked only in such a way that the questioner as such is present together with the question, that is, is placed in question."[5] This is why genuine philosophical inquiry is different from the sorts of "proving" one does in mathematics and science. Whereas traditional proofs assume that "the one who understands remains the same," Heidegger says, "In philosophical knowledge, the first step begins a transformation of the human being who under-stands. . . ."[6] What I want to show is that, with each transformation of the questioner and the understanding of the vantage point for ques-tioning, the inquiry needs to be repeated at a new level, and this fact explains why Heidegger, especially in his early works, is constantly concerned with getting clear about where he stands when he engages in philosophical reflection.

My aim here is to give a rough overview of the evolution in Hei-degger's reflections on the authentic standpoint for philosophy between 1919 and 1935 by looking at a few of the key developments, leaving to a longer study a full treatment of Heidegger's writings on method. As my story turns to the notion of authenticity in *Being and Time*, some of what I say will necessarily be at odds with Bert's thoughts about this subject as presented in the Appendix of *Being-in-the-World*.[7] Yet I see no point to calling attention to specific points of disagreement between my account of authenticity and Bert's latest views; these issues will be evident to anyone familiar with Bert's book. I would like to believe that the opposition that arises here is not so much between me and Bert as between the early Dreyfus and the later Dreyfus. Whether or not Bert will accept this description, I hope he will consider the following inquiry as my way of paying homage to his always stimulating ideas.

I   The Critique of Objectivity: Heidegger's 1919 Lectures

Thanks to the publication of Heidegger's Freiburg lectures of 1919,[8] we can now see how Heidegger's thinking from an early date was already preoccupied with the "question of Being." The War Emergency seminar in 1919 explores the idea of a "primal science" (*Urwissenschaft*) that will bring to light "the experiencable in any sense," what is called the "primal something" (*Ur-etwas*). Shortly after this seminar, this primal science is called "ontology," and philosophy itself is defined as "phenomenological (existentiell, historical-cultural) 'ontology' or *ontological phenomenology*."[9]

In undertaking this ontological inquiry, Heidegger is especially sensitive to the question of the standpoint from which such questioning should be undertaken. Philosophy must always ask: where do I stand when I say these things? As in *Being and Time*, Heidegger suspects that both the "common sense" standpoint made manifest in everyday life and the "objective" theoretical standpoint are inadequate for such an inquiry. The standpoint of ordinary "common sense" cannot be trusted to give us a clear insight into things, because the sense of reality that arises in day-to-day existence is warped by public interpretations and by the disjointedness of preoccupied absorption in mundane affairs. If we are to avoid the distorted outlook of "common sense," then, we must begin from a deeper and more original experience of life than is found in everyday existence.

At the same time, however, ontology cannot start out from the cool, disengaged standpoint of traditional philosophy. Heidegger holds that, ever since the Greeks, philosophy has operated with a set of rigid, unquestioned concepts that force our experience and thought into calcified grids, and thereby present things to us in one-sided and distorted ways. The result is a deformed interpretation of things, which arises not just because of the influence of scientific modes of objectification, as Husserl had claimed, but because of the effects of *theorizing* as such. As Heidegger says, "It is not just naturalism, as [Husserl] thought, it is the general domination of the *theoretical* that deforms the genuine problematic" (*ZBP*, 87). Heidegger's point is that, as soon as we adopt a detached theoretical standpoint, the world, as it were, goes dead for us. In place of the dynamic flow of life-in-the-world characteristic of lived-experience, we encounter reality as a collection of brute objects that are simply *present*, on hand for a perceiving subject. The result is a "de-vitalizing" (*Entlebung*) of experience that bleaches out the richness and complexity of what we actually experience in the "stream of life" as it is prior to reflection and theorizing.

This means that the sense of Being we arrive at through the objective standpoint of disengaged theorizing is not at all the kind of "primal" truth about beings a "primordial science" seeks, but is instead a misleading perspective on things generated by the tradition. In Heidegger's view, the ideal of theoretical objectivity is wrong on two counts. First, its way of disclosing beings is one-sided and deceptive, since it presents things to us only in the objectified form they have after they have been worked over to fit the template of the theoretical outlook. And, second, to the extent that objectivity presents itself as a purely neutral stance toward things, it conceals the fact that its vision of reality is made possible by a set of interests and motivations that preshape what we encounter. The theoretical standpoint therefore produces a double concealment: theorizing conceals the most fundamental aspects of beings by forcing all experience into the grid of objectification, and it then conceals its own concealment by creating the impression that, as dispassionate and impartial, it alone has privileged access to the truth.

For Heidegger, as for Kierkegaard before him, our ability to experience *anything* at all—that is, our ability to discern things within the field of what we experience, to distinguish one thing from another— is made possible by the fact that we have motivations and concerns in terms of which things can stand out for us as *counting* or *mattering* in some way. In other words, discernment and differentiation are possible only for a being that *cares* about what it encounters. It is our *care* that generates the anticipations and general orientation that lets the world sort itself out into what is relevant and trivial, noteworthy and petty, central and peripheral. In the vocabulary of *Being and Time*, we can say that our care lets things show up as *significant* in determinate ways. If there were no care about things, then the world would recede into gray indifference, and experience of any sort would become impossible. A being that was not motivated by concrete concerns in addressing the world would be no more capable of having experience, properly understood, than is a photoelectric cell.

Heidegger's critique of "objective truth" bears striking similarities to Kierkegaard's defense of "subjective truth" in *Concluding Unscientific Postscript*. There Kierkegaard observes that "the way of objective reflection" makes both the subject and his subjectivity a matter of indifference. By making the subject indifferent, however, "the truth also becomes indifferent, . . . for all interest, like all decisiveness, is rooted in subjectivity."[10] Although Kierkegaard is willing to grant the validity of objective inquiry in a number of areas (for example, mathematics), he holds that the stance of objectivity is inappropriate in dealing with questions that are of pressing importance to a person's life. For these questions, the only truth-revealing stance is that of *passion*—a stance of intense commitment to something that gives one's life a content and meaning. Kierkegaard says that it is only in "the moment of passion" that the individual can "realize existentially a unity of the infinite and the finite," and, by becoming what he or she is, is able to see what life is all about.[11]

Although Heidegger parts company with Kierkegaard's vocabulary of "subject" and "object," he is in fundamental agreement with the idea that primal science must start out from a stance of committed engagement in life. In an appendix to the 1919 lectures, titled "On the Essence of the University and Academic Studies," there is a discussion of the different stands one can take within the context of university life. Heidegger tries to think through the specialized modes of inquiry that arise in the different sciences as variants on what he calls a *situation*. A situation is defined as "a specific unity in natural life-experience" (*ZBP*, 205), a cohesive, self-contained unity within the ongoing flow of life. According to this account, what gives *unity* to the situation is not the fact that it occupies a series of contiguous moments in objective time, for a situation might unfold through a number of contexts and times. Rather, what defines a situation is the cohesive meaning a set of events have within a life— for example, "a day at school," or "a tour of duty," or "learning to drive." When Heidegger says, "Every situation is an 'event' (*Ereignis*) and not a 'process' (*Vorgang*)" (*ZBP*, 206), he means that a situation cannot be thought of as a mere sequence of physical movements in a causal nexus. To say that a situation is an event is to say that it is a meaningful totality in which the three temporal aspects of

the event—the point of origin, the way it unfolds, and its culmination or realization—are interwoven into a lived, coherent unity.
Using Paul Ricoeur's reading of Heidegger, we might say that the
situation has a *narrative* structure.[12]

As an example of a situation Heidegger considers the event of
climbing a mountain to see a sunrise. Reaching the opening at the
summit, one is totally absorbed in the situation. The sun, clouds, and
rock ledge fill the moment and have a distinctive quality that is sharp-
ened and brought into focus by the long climb. This situation is a
situation *for* someone, but the self who experiences the situation is
not experienced as some "thing" distinct from the situation. On the
contrary, in such a situation the self is out of sight: "it swims together
[with everything else] in the situation" (*ZBP*, 206). The structure of
the situation is defined by a background of *motivation* (what later
comes to be called "thrownness"), a *tendency* that impels the course
of events in a particular direction (later called "projection"), and a
fulfillment that binds the whole together and defines it as a unity. Like
a well-crafted story, there is a beginning, a development, and an
ending that gives the whole its *point.*

To be in a situation, then, is to be part of an unfolding story
with a distinctive temporal structure: as Heidegger says, "the I is
'historical'" (*ZBP*, 206). Watching the sunrise at the top of the mountain, I experience myself not as a subject having experiences, and
certainly not as an organism functioning in a geographical location.
Instead, I experience myself as the climber who prepared for days,
who rose before sunrise, who braved the cold, who reached the
summit after a difficult climb, and who is now in touch with the
beauty of nature. Far from being one item among others *in* this
scene, my identity as a human is *constituted* by the entire lived context
that makes up my dwelling in the world.

After presenting his description of the situation, Heidegger considers how a situation can be extinguished or "exploded" as a result
of shifting to a theoretical attitude. In adopting a theoretical standpoint, he says, "The situation-character disappears. The unity of the
situation explodes. The experiences, no longer possessing a unity of
meaning (*Sinn*) or a unity of content, lose the unity the situation
gave them" (*ZBP*, 206). Now things around us can obtrude as brute,

meaningless objects with no defining connection to any context, and events can present themselves as causal "processes" occurring in objective time. When the situation explodes, the self comes to appear as a detached spectator making observations—one item among others in the space-time coordinate system. Through this "breakdown" and "change-over" (to use the vocabulary of *Being and Time*), the world is "dis-worlded" and the stream of life is robbed of its character as living. To the extent that this objectified picture presents itself as the way things have been all the time, it gives us a misleading picture of reality and our own selves.

The 1919 lectures make it clear that genuine philosophy must be carried out from the standpoint of the most basic way of being-in-a-situation, where this is understood as a full and intense life-experience. In a discussion of how phenomenology can disclose the "sphere of life-experience," Heidegger refers to Husserl's "principle of all principles," a principle which demands that all philosophical pronouncements be grounded ultimately in something immediately and fully presented to us (*ZBP*, 109). Heidegger interprets this as meaning that only a stance of intense, committed involvement in a situation can give us access to a "primordial" insight into life and the world. As examples of "genuine ways of experiencing life (*Lebenserfahrungen*) that grow out of a genuine life-world," Heidegger points to the lives of certain artists and religious people. For such individuals, life is driven by "genuine motivation-possibilities" which are fully realized in the course of living out the life (*ZBP*, 208). In their intense experiences, such people fulfill the possibilities they undertake, and so can genuinely *be* what they are.[13]

That is why Heidegger's radicalized phenomenology refuses to see itself merely as a "standpoint" (*Standpunkt*) with a pregiven method established in advance. Since "phenomenology can only authenticate itself by itself and through itself" (*ZBP*, 110), there can be no procedure or technique that determines the course of inquiry totally independent of the concrete findings uncovered along the way. Instead, Heidegger suggests, phenomenology should start out from a way of life that fully actualizes and manifests life in its concrete reality. Only by living a life of this sort can we vividly display the "contents" we are seeking in this investigation—we can fully *be* what we are looking for. This is perhaps one of the reasons why Heidegger turns again and again to Pindar's injunction: "Become what you are."[14]

Since achieving clarity about life is likely to lead one to transform one's understanding of what is needed to gain such clarity, however, the nature of the inquiry itself is constantly subject to revision as it is carried out. The open-endedness and lack of external foundations in this form of inquiry indicate that the phenomenologist must constantly reflect on his or her own position in undertaking the phenomenological investigation. The "basic attitude" (*Urhaltung*) of the investigation is something that comes to be realized and defined "only when we live it in itself." Phenomenology, thought of in this way, is not a "method"; it is a way of life, a "total immersion into life." Such an immersion in life is necessary, because "genuine insights . . . can be obtained only by an honest and unreserved immersion in life itself in its genuineness, and this is ultimately possible only through the genuineness of a personal life."[15] This explains why Heidegger says in *Being and Time*: "The ontological 'truth' of the existential analysis is developed on the ground of the primordial existentiell truth" (*SZ*, 316). As the questioner achieves ever greater clarity and genuineness in living the phenomenological way of life, he or she will see the need to renew the inquiry again and again.

It should be obvious that a number of questions arise from the claims made in these 1919 lectures. For example, we might ask; what precisely *is* this "primal attitude" that philosophy is supposed to achieve, assuming that the philosophical life is not identical to that of the artistic or religious person? We might also wonder whether there is not something suspiciously circular and self-fulfilling about the idea that you can disclose the primordial truth about life only by living it, and that you will know the truth when you see it. And what exactly does "primordial" mean here? Moreover, how can we *sustain* a "primal attitude" in our lives if, as Heidegger claims, we are constantly "falling" into the busy-ness and self-loss of everyday activities? Finally, what assurance do we have that *any* stance is going to disclose to us *the* meaning of Being as opposed to particular "perspectives" on things relative to particular sets of feelings, interests, and goals?

Heidegger's constant efforts over the years to think through the point of departure from which he conducts his questioning reflects his sensitivity to questions of this sort.

II From the "Truth of Existence" to Truth in the Artwork

In his religion courses of 1920–21, Heidegger examined primal Christian experience as a privileged way of experiencing factical life.[16] Since "Christian religiosity lives temporality as such," it is especially well suited to displaying the historicity of the "historical I." According to these lectures, primal Christian religiosity is grounded in eschatology and the question of the proper stance to take in relation to the prospect of salvation. For St. Paul, Heidegger claims, salvation is not a matter of waiting for a future event, but rather of decisively assuming one's context of becoming a Christian in order to be prepared for the Event which is already happening. Such a moment of decision[17] contains in itself a moment of vision, a *kairos*, in which one lucidly grasps all that has come before and all that is yet to be in one "twinkling of the eye" (*Augenblick*). The studies of religion therefore portray the "moment of vision" as the ideal standpoint from which one can grasp the temporality of life in its tripartite, "ecstatic" structure.

Though Heidegger sees the religious life as providing a clue to an authentic understanding of existence, he holds that philosophy cannot simply take over this Christian experience as a model of philosophical life, because philosophy should not presuppose anything from what might be called "regional" modes of experience. As a result, he must find a correlate of the Christian disclosure of temporality which is accessible to anyone. This correlate, spelled out in the 1924 lecture, *The Concept of Time*, and developed in detail in the second division of *Being and Time*, is the experience of being-toward-death.[18] Like the Christian confronting the eschatological promise, the human being (now called "Dasein" rather than "life") stands before an event which is "not yet," but is nevertheless constantly *there* as a life-defining possibility: the possibility of running out of possibilities, of being "at the end." Though in average everydayness we tend to "flee" from this fact, Heidegger suggests that a person can face up to this "uttermost possibility" in life with lucidity and integrity. Confronting the possibility of death, he suggests, will bring one face to face with the finitude of life, the fact that at its core Dasein is *zum Ende*.

Not surprisingly, the experience of temporality that results from this confrontation with death is structurally identical to that of primal Christianity. Dasein does not "await" death as some future "occurrence," but instead "runs forward" toward it by living in a distinctive way. Instead of tumbling into the frenzy and preoccupations of day-to-day existence, the individual who faces up to death lives each moment as part of the totality of life, and carries forward the past as part of a coherent, cumulative narrative. In contrast to the dispersal and endless "making-present" of everydayness, such a life is authentically *futural* to the extent that it clear-sightedly faces up to the inevitable truth of its own finitude and lives each moment as an integral component of the overall story it is shaping in its actions. In this authentic "living-forward" toward the end, one is *resolute* in the way one takes up the task of living to which one is "delivered over" by acting in a focused, coherent way. Dasein's Being "becomes accessible as *simplified* in a certain manner" as it is pulled back from "the endless multiplicity of possibilities which offer themselves" and is brought "into the simplicity of its *fate*" (*SZ*, 182, 384).

In becoming authentic, the barriers created by self-deception and dispersal in everyday "falling" are torn down, and Dasein is brought into a "moment of vision" in which the whole of life—stretched out from beginning to end—is transparent in its temporal structure. Resoluteness, Heidegger says, constitutes "the primordial *truth* of existence."[19] In resoluteness, there is not simply an empty intending of some ultimate possibility of Dasein's being. On the contrary, in *living out* such a possibility, the intention is fulfilled: Dasein *realizes* its temporal being by clear-sightedly taking over its factical "situation" and taking a stand on its being-toward-death in a concrete way. The disclosedness here is "primordial truth" because it is a way of life in which what is revealed comes into being *through* the very act of revealing. This is what Heidegger means when he says that, in resoluteness, "Dasein is revealed to itself in its current factical ability-to-be, and in such a way that Dasein *is* this revealing and being-revealed" (*SZ*, 307).

In other words, one has *become* the very thing one hoped to find in this search for the truth about what it is to be human.

In the same passage of *Being and Time,* Heidegger goes on to make a series of moves that come very quickly and are not easy to follow. He first draws a distinction between the *truth* that is revealed in resoluteness and the *mode of comportment* one has to that truth, a mode of what he calls "holding-for-true." The "holding-for-true" correlated with this primordial truth about Dasein's being, according to Heidegger, is "being-certain": what is disclosed in resoluteness (the temporal unity of a "simplified," finite life span) presents itself as absolutely *certain* so long as one *is* resolute.

Heidegger then goes on to ask whether there is a form of being-certain "in which one *maintains* oneself in what resoluteness discloses" (*SZ,* 307, my emphasis). In other words, since there is the constant danger that what is revealed in this moment of insight might soon be lost, the question arises whether there is a mode of existence that will sustain the "primordial truth" revealed in resoluteness in its full clarity and certainty. Heidegger's answer is that the stance of being-certain can be sustained and carried forward only if Dasein lives in such a way that it "*gives* itself the current factical situation, and *brings* itself into that situation" (*SZ,* 307). The point here is that one must constantly renew one's commitment to the current situation, appropriating the situation in a coherent, focused way, in order to keep alive that mode of being which realizes the "primordial truth." This distinctive form of existence is called "repetition." In Heidegger's words, "holding-for-true . . . is *authentic resoluteness which resolves to keep repeating itself*" (*SZ,* 308). Only by reaffirming one's resolute stance in the face of death throughout one's life can one sustain the clarity and insight achieved in the moment of vision through resoluteness.

How exactly is resolute involvement in the current situation to be understood? To be resolute is to be totally committed to something, to focus your whole being in a clear-sighted way on something in your current situation that thereby comes to have world-defining importance for you. But how are you to know *what* you should commit yourself to? This is Heidegger's question when he asks, "On what is [Dasein] to resolve?" His answer is quite simple: "*Only* the resolution itself can give the answer" (*SZ*, 298). In other words, since things can stand out as really *mattering* or *counting* only for someone who already genuinely *cares*—that is, for someone who has made a resolute commitment to something—it follows that only someone who has already made such a commitment will be able to encounter a world in which anything can stand out as being *worthy* of commitment. Thus, it is only through something like a Kierkegaardian leap of faith that you can see the possibilities within your current situation as counting in some way and so as worthy of choice. In Heidegger's words, "*The resolution is precisely the disclosive projection and determination of what is factically possible at the time*" (*SZ*, 298). Once you make a resolute commitment, then, you are granted a moment of vision which "makes the situation authentically present," and which discloses "the authentic historical *constancy* of the self" (*SZ*, 410).

Needless to say, Heidegger does not believe that any commitment is as good as any other for this purpose. At the end of *Being and Time*, he turns to an examination of how a clear-sighted grasp of the current situation is bound up with an understanding of our belongingness to a shared "heritage" and our participation in a communal "destiny." A detailed analysis of these passages is not possible here.[20] What becomes clear from this discussion of historicity is that Dasein's being as a temporal unfolding is found to be enmeshed in the wider unfolding of a communal history in such a way that what counts as a meaningful choice will always be determined by the historical context in which one finds oneself. In other words, though there is no algorithm that dictates one's choice in acting in concrete situations, there are guidelines and directives within one's heritage that help one understand what choices make sense.

Nevertheless, there is something deeply dissatisfying about the final picture that emerges in *Being and Time*. For one thing, it might seem that the description of primordial truth as produced by Dasein's own way of existing threatens to embroil Heidegger's question of Being in a form of self-fulfilling idealism: the attempt to ground all ontology in something like the total transparency of self to self. It goes without saying that such a foundationalist standpoint would run counter to the awareness of worldliness and thrownness that is central to *Being and Time*. The problem is hinted at toward the end of that work, when Heidegger discusses the need to take into account the "hermeneutic situation" of the interpreter (*SZ*, 397) who engages in historical inquiry. This reference to the hermeneutic situation raises questions about the prospects of ever disclosing a "primordial truth of existence" with any finality and certainty. For if every inquiry starts out from the hermeneutic situation of a historically situated interpreter, then the idea that there can be a moment of total clarity becomes questionable. This might be why, as I shall argue in the next section, Heidegger's writings immediately after the publication of *Being and Time* turn to the issue of working out a deeper understanding of our own status as questioners in asking the question of Being.

A second source of dissatisfaction with *Being and Time* results from its account of resoluteness. From the discussion of resoluteness in that work, it is tempting to conclude that Heidegger is advocating a form of "decisionism," the view that one should make a commitment to some cause or thing with no other basis than the need to make a commitment itself.[21] Such an instrumentalist approach to commitment runs the risk of slipping into an extreme subjectivism, for it seems to keep the individual trapped within the closed circuits of his or her own will and concerns. Why this is so will become clearer if we reflect for a moment on what is involved in making a commitment. To make a commitment is not just to leap one way or the other for the sake of leaping; rather, becoming committed to something is most often experienced as *answering a call* or *responding* to something outside ourselves, something that makes a demand on us.[22] It would seem, then, that any picture of resoluteness that ignores this dimension of being called will fail to capture what is most fundamental about our actual experience of being committed. For this purpose, some account needs to be given of *what calls us*, and this requires a move beyond the descriptions of Dasein's own projections and disclosedness to an account of something that can exert a pull on us from outside ourselves.

One way to understand the shift that occurs in Heidegger's writings in the mid-thirties is to see these works as addressing this problem. In the 1935 essay, "The Origin of the Work of Art,"[23] for example, truth is described not just as a matter of what Dasein does, but as something that happens to Dasein through Dasein's being in a relation to a particular entity—a work of art—which "sets truth to work" and thereby discloses a world. In Heidegger's central example, the Greek temple, we see how a world-defining artwork provides a focus and a sense of orientation for a people, and so gives them an understanding of who they *are* and of what courses of action make sense for them. The temple, Heidegger says, "first fits together and at the same time gathers around itself the unity of those paths and relations in which birth and death, disaster and blessing, victory and disgrace, endurance and decline acquire the shape of destiny for human being" (OWA, 42). By giving concrete content to human life, the temple defines what it is to be a human in this world. It is only *through* the clearing opened by such an entity that we humans gain "access to the being that we ourselves are" (OWA, 53) and so emerge-into-presence in a determinate form. The Athenians, for example, only became the Athenians they were by encountering themselves in the light of the temple of Athena and the tragedies of Aeschylus and Sophocles. Since the temple-work and the works of tragedy first allowed them to *be* the people they were, there is no way to think of truth as something produced by humans. On the contrary, "truth occurs only by installing itself within a particular being" such as an artwork (OWA, 69). Even the artist, as the artist he or she is, first comes into being through the artwork (OWA, 57).

The art essay therefore points toward a conception of authentic existence as a matter of coming to be defined and oriented by virtue of one's relation to a world-defining entity.[24] It is a view of authenticity that bears certain similarities to Kierkegaard's picture of the knight of faith as someone who gains a positive content for his life and an insight into the "truth" of existence through a defining relation to something outside himself. Here, clarity about the human situation is achieved not through some sort of intense self-concentration, but by way of a detour through a form of life that looks like complete self-loss: the act of giving oneself over to something outside oneself. Thus, the kind of insight Heidegger had sought in Dasein's resolute "individualized" being-toward-death now comes to be seen as arising from a total involvement in something outside the self—a world-defining work of art.

III Concealment and Dasein's Finitude

With its account of the relation to a world-defining entity, "The Origin of the Work of Art" captures the experience of being oriented and given a sense of direction by something outside the self. But this essay also brings to light the fact that, as dependent on something that lies outside ourselves, we are always thrown into the midst of things in such a way that we can never achieve total transparency about beings in general or even about who we are. Because we are enmeshed in a context we can never totalize and comprehend, Heidegger says that every revealing and opening of a world is accompanied by a *concealing* in which beings "refuse themselves to us down to that one and seemingly least feature which we touch upon most readily when we can say no more of beings than that they are" (OWA, 53). What is important about the work of art, according to this essay, is that it accomplishes something that neither equipment nor present-at-hand objects can accomplish. In setting up a world, the work sets forth that "which is by nature undisclosable, that which shrinks from every disclosure and constantly keeps itself closed up," something Heidegger now calls the *earth* (OWA, 47). Because it sets forth the earth in this way, the artwork displays the inevitable concealment bound up with every lighting and opening—the fact that every lighting is achieved only in conjunction with a darkening.

It should be obvious that there was no place in *Being and Time* for the idea of something that remains totally opaque and defies comprehension. The primary example of nonhuman entities that Heidegger discusses in that work, ready-to-hand equipment, is said to be "transparent" to the extent that it remains unnoticed and unobtrusive when everything is running smoothly. And even though Dasein is described as "thrown" and consequently "in the untruth," this dimension of opacity and uncertainty seems to be pushed into the background as Heidegger concentrates on Dasein's capacity for authentic self-transparency (*Durchsichtigkeit*).

Nevertheless, in Heidegger's lectures and writings after the publication of *Being and Time*, we find him thinking through the status of the questioner in all philosophical questioning and so rethinking what seems like an ideal of total transparency in *Being and Time*. In fact, a profound sensitivity to the situatedness of all inquiry was already evident in the early lectures. His 1921–22 lecture course, for example, emphasizes the fact that philosophy always starts from "factical life," that is, from a concrete "cultural-historical situation." The concrete context of the interpreter makes up the "hermeneutic situation" of the inquiry, a frame of reference that contains "factical tendencies of expectation and preconceptualization" which structure and direct the inquiry (*PIA*, 161). These tendencies and motivations pervade all thinking as the tacit and only partially articulable assumptions underlying inquiry.

Heidegger also examines the situatedness of inquiry in the 1922 text, "Phenomenological Interpretations with Respect to Aristotle."[25] According to this study, "factical life moves always within a determinate *interpretedness* which has been handed down [to it]" (PIRA, 363). Because of this background, "the philosophical hermeneutic of facticity necessarily makes its own beginning within its factical situation, and it does so within an already given particular interpretedness of factical life which first sustains the philosophical hermeneutic itself *and which can never be completely eradicated*" (PIRA, 369–370, my emphasis). Since there is no vantage point outside this concrete cultural-historical situation of interpretation, there is no way to get totally clear about the motivations and understandings underlying and guiding one's inquiry.

Concerning his own attempt to understand Aristotle, Heidegger says that every historical inquiry is preshaped by a background of assumptions and motivations determined by the present situation, a background that can never be fully mastered or disclosed. What is needed in undertaking such an inquiry, then, is a "decisive choice" about how the interests and motivations of the present are to be understood. This stance toward the present will in turn provide the framework for interpreting the past. As Heidegger says, "The past opens itself only according to the resoluteness [*Entschlossenheit*] of the ability-to-lay-open [*Aufschliessenkönnen*] which a present has available to it" (PIRA, 358). The aim of understanding the past, then, is "not simply to accept established knowledge, but rather to *repeat* primordially that which is understood *in terms of [one's] own situation and for that situation*" (PIRA, 360, my emphasis). In this context, then, repetition is thought of as a matter of taking up what has come down to us from the past and reinterpreting it for the purposes of the current situation. In other words, it is what *Being and Time* calls "retrieval."

The strong sense of the situatedness and limitation of all inquiry in this Aristotle study is obviously at odds with the image of full illumination that seems to be implied by *Being and Time*'s notion of the "primordial truth of existence." If we are always thrown into the midst of beings, caught up in a historically mediated interpretedness in such a way that we can never break clear of this situatedness in order to totally comprehend it, then the belief that there can be a moment of total insight—what seems to be a correlate of the Cartesian clarity of self to self—must be an illusion. The best we can hope for is an ongoing working out of the understanding embodied in factical life, an inquiry that is inseparable from historical reflection on our background assumptions.

In the writings and lectures that came immediately after the completion of *Being and Time*, we find Heidegger intensely concerned with addressing this embeddedness and "finitude" of philosophizing.[26] In *The Metaphysical Foundations of Logic* (1928), he says that "philosophizing is essentially an affair of finitude," which means that "every concretion of factical philosophy must in its turn fall victim to . . . facticity."[27] Recognizing the finitude of philosophy leads us to see "the intrinsic necessity for ontology to turn back to its point of origin" (*MFL*, 156), where this point of origin is described in a way quite alien to *Being and Time* as "the factical being-present-at-hand of *nature*" (*MFL*, 156, translation modified). Whatever this means precisely, it shows that Heidegger is not regarding humans simply as centers of illumination, but as part of the "totality of beings," where this is described as the wider context of "nature" as a whole. It is because of this expanded conception of Dasein's finitude, which goes well beyond the constraints of what has been called the hermeneutic situation, that these lectures talk about Dasein's body and embodiment, about sexuality and being part of nature.[28]

The concept of earth in *The Origin of the Work of Art*, together with the correlated account of concealment, is the culmination of this new sensitivity toward the facticity and finitude of inquiry. The artwork differs from equipment to the extent that it sets forth and sustains that which cannot be totally mastered and made intelligible, that which always resists the attempt to swallow everything up into the opening or clearing of world, namely, the earth. The concept of earth refers to something that confronts us as ineradicably "Other" to all our attempts to comprehend and appropriate. Through the artwork, we catch a glimpse of the all-encompassing realm of nature that human works can light up in particular ways (*Gestalten*) but can never exhaust or fully comprehend. With this powerfully articulated notion of the earth, Heidegger subverts any attempt to arrive at *the* answer to the question of Being, or even to set out on *the* "way" to answering this question.

IV   The Destiny of a Historical People

Heidegger's long Aristotle-Introduction of 1922 had brought to light the fact that all philosophical inquiry, as historical, must understand itself as working within assumptions determined by the present hermeneutic situation. This entails, Heidegger says, that interpretation is always a "reading-in" (*Hineindeuten*) of prior assumptions that determine how things can show up for that interpretation. In his words, "All interpretations . . . which strive . . . not to read anything into the texts must admit that they too commit such reading-into, only they do so without orientation and with conceptual means from the most disparate and uncontrollable sources" (PIRA, 359). The idea that all inquiry is entangled in a "hermeneutic circle" is even more forcefully stated in *Being and Time*:

If, when one is engaged in a particular concrete kind of interpretation, in the sense of exact textual interpretation, one likes to appeal to what "stands there," then one finds that what "stands there" in the first instance is nothing other than the obvious undiscussed assumption of the person who does the interpreting. (*SZ*, 150)

If all interpretive inquiry is inevitably a form of "reading in" the "undiscussed assumptions" of the interpreter, however, what is to keep philosophy from sinking into a pernicious relativism that treats interpretations as totally subjective and incommensurable? In *Being and Time,* where Heidegger discusses this issue in relation to historical inquiry, he says that the "main point," in such research is "the cultivation of the hermeneutic situation" of the one who does the research. Cultivating the hermeneutic situation of the historian is possible only if the inquirer first achieves resoluteness (in order to understand the temporality and "historicity" of the human condition), and then makes a decisive commitment to interpreting what has come before in a "repetitive disclosure of what-has-been-there." Genuine historical inquiry is therefore said to be based on "the *authentic disclosedness* ('truth') of *historical existence"* (*SZ,* 397).

Heidegger's account of the authentic disclosedness of historical existence starts out from the assumption that authentic historiography, like the temporality of Dasein itself, is fundamentally *futural.* This claim had already been made in the 1924 lecture, *The Concept of Time,* where Heidegger introduces what he calls *"the first principle of all hermeneutics."*[29] The aim of this principle is to overcome "the dangerous threat of relativism" by clarifying the "ground" of historiography. It states: *"The possibility of access to history is grounded in the possibility according to which a particular present understands what it is to be futural".*[30] In other words, the understanding of the present hermeneutic situation needs to understand the course of events as directed toward realizing possibilities. Put into concrete, "ontic" terms, this principle seems to demand that we see that the particular present in question gains its sense from a projected image of where the course of events of which it is a part is headed as a whole. Only on the basis of such an anticipated vision of the outcome of events, Heidegger says, is the *"'selection'* of what is to become a possible object for historiography" possible (*SZ,* 395). The point here is that, just as in reading a story we understand the events described only in terms of some anticipation about where the story is going overall—the story's upshot or point or culmination—so historical interpretation is possible only in the light of an "assumption" about the direction of historical events: the projected fulfillment or realization of history.

Authentic historical understanding must therefore begin from an understanding of what Heidegger calls our *destiny,* an understanding of the point or direction of history which the historian shares with the "people" (*Volk*) whose history he seeks to understand. What prevents a vicious relativism from creeping into our interpretations is this shared understanding of the *future* a "community," a "people," formulates together in their "communicating and struggling" (*SZ*, 384). This shared vision of where things are headed then provides a basis for selecting what counts as *relevant* for the historical story and for knitting events into a cohesive, coherent whole.

The notion of a people's history, seemingly an afterthought at the end of *Being and Time*, becomes central to *The Origin of the Work of Art*. In this essay, the work of art plays the role of galvanizing and orienting a community, giving them a shared sense of what is at stake in life. Like the object of "infinite passion" in Kierkegaard, it provides a positive content that integrates human existence by providing a focus and direction. But unlike Kierkegaard's defining relation, the artwork provides a sense of what is important in life not just for the individual, but for an entire community.

The picture of "authenticity" as a *communal* project is apparent in Heidegger's description of the role of *decision* in relation to the artwork. According to Heidegger, the artwork opens a "world" for a people, and in doing so "it submits to the decision of an historical humanity the question of victory and defeat, blessing and curse, mastery and slavery" (OWA, 63). The tragedies of Aeschylus and Sophocles, for example, sketch out the possible ways of understanding victory and defeat, blessing and curse, and they thereby call for a choice from the people as to how they will understand their lives in the light of these works. The world opened by the work is therefore described as "the clearing of the paths of the essential guiding directions with which all *decision* complies" (OWA, 55, my emphasis).

As we have seen, however, the work does not just lay out directions and standards that dictate how people must act. Insofar as the work also sets forth the earth, it makes manifest that which cannot be mastered and comprehended within the world. It is precisely because of this concealment set forth by the work that decision is necessary: "Every decision," Heidegger writes, "bases itself on something not mastered, something concealed, confusing; else it would never be a decision" (OWA, 55). A work that dictates how one *must* live is not art; it is a propaganda or didacticism. What is distinctive about an authentic work of art is that it leaves its own significance open-ended, and therefore demands a response from its audience as to what it means. As Heidegger says, "The dawning world brings out what is as yet undecided and measureless, and thus discloses the hidden necessity of measure and decisiveness" (OWA, 63). Seeing the *Antigone*, for example, the Athenians must decide which path they will follow: the old way of the *oikos* or family, or the new way of the *polis*. What this tragedy *means*—its *point* and, indeed, its *being* as the tragedy it *is*—is to a large extent determined by the choice future generations make on this issue.

Thus, the meaning of an artwork is determined by the decisions made by a community in response to the questions it poses. For this reason, Heidegger can say that the work is created not just by its creator, but also by the *preservers* who realize the work's being through their ways of carrying it forward into the future. A work "is in actual effect as a work only when we . . . move into what is disclosed by the work, so as to bring our own nature itself to take a stand in the truth of what is" (OWA, 74–75). Understood in this way, preserving has nothing to do with "aesthetic appreciation": "Preserving the work does not reduce people to their private experiences," Heidegger says. Instead, preserving gives people a common task and binds them together into a community with a shared vision of their own "sending." Preserving aligns people with the truth that happens in the work, and it thereby "grounds being for and with one another as the historical standing-out of human existence in reference to unconcealedness" (OWA, 68).

Because the artwork sets truth to work for a community, Heidegger can say that with the appearance of a crucial world-defining work, history begins. "Whenever art happens . . . a thrust enters history, history either begins or starts over again. History means here not a sequence in time of events. . . . [Instead,] history is the transporting of a people into its appointed task. . . ." (OWA, 77). With this transformed picture of temporality and disclosure, Heidegger reverses the order of dependence of individual and community. Where the earlier writings had focused on the individual philosopher and derived history from the individual's temporality, *The Origin of the*

Work of Art treats a people's temporal unfolding as primary, and sees the individual's task as a matter of complying with the wider context of "decisions" being made in the social arena.

The art essay leaves us with the idea that philosophy must depart from the realm of quiet thinking and step out into the "appointed task" of decisively *acting* in the public realm. The aim is not to *discover* a truth about Being, but to *create* such a truth by inaugurating a "new beginning" in the history of Being. After Heidegger's disgraceful experiment with political activism, however, a new, more quietist interpretation of the stance of the philosopher evolved in the late thirties, as is evident in the *Beiträge*. But certain fundamental themes articulated in *The Origin of the Work of Art* will remain even in these later works, in particular, the recognition that inquiry is historically embedded, and the sensitivity toward the finitude of philosophy and humanity's dependence on and answerability to something greater than itself.[31]

II

Modernity, Self, and World

5

Kierkegaard's Present Age and Ours

Alastair Hannay

To a modern reader Kierkegaard's account of his own culture in *A Literary Review* can sound startlingly topical. Scandinavians in particular will recognize themselves in Kierkegaard's description of a culture given to the discussion of matters of principle at the cost of what he thinks are principles in the true sense, initiatives that first emerge in the form of enthusiasm for a personally engaging idea.[1] His was a society of the kind in which, had the expressions been coined at the time, calculating risks, sharing responsibility, and consulting public opinion would have been familiar democratic virtues. For Kierkegaard, however, the virtuous appearance would belie a weakness of the spirit. Hierarchical distinctions once lived out in relationships of honor, professional pride, and personal accountability, were now topics for reflection and negotiation. There was a prevailing tendency to disparage any kind of exceptionality.

The term Kierkegaard uses for this tendency is "levelling." It is not an easy term to interpret, and this essay in honor of Hubert Dreyfus is an attempt to locate the specific sense in which Kierkegaard uses it in a text to which, over the years, Dreyfus has devoted considerable attention. Dreyfus claims that we can pick out a distinctive feature of our own culture as what Kierkegaard means by levelling. He calls it "modern nihilism" and defines this as the difficulty the individual has in giving his or her life a sense of meaning. I have to agree that many of the portraits Kierkegaard gives in his early works seem to anticipate nihilism as Dreyfus presents it; Kierkegaard may himself have been an example. But I shall argue that levelling in Kierkegaard's account is first and foremost a process at which people more or less consciously connive in order to avoid exactly any sense of there being a difficulty of the kind Dreyfus describes.

There seems something not quite right about calling Kierkegaard's time a nihilistic one. Danes for the most part led lives in which what counted for them and each other were the positions they held in their society. The very complacency of a society, many of whose elite had self-consciously seen their careers vindicated by the thought that they were living examples of Hegel's objective spirit, was part of what Kierkegaard saw as its most obvious failing. True, the transition from monarchical to democratic government then under way left those whose sense of the unity of political and social life depended on the establishment with an anxious sense of impending disintegration. But 1848 was still two years away and Kierkegaard's analysis of his culture in the *Review* is focused less on disintegrating tendencies than on the ways currently proposed for reconstituting society, ways which he thought evaded the real human issues to which modern society was leaving people increasingly exposed. This is not to say that there was nothing that might be called nihilistic in the culture of the time, nor that Kierkegaard did not see it. There are clear expressions of a nihilistic attitude in his aesthetic writings, and these may well be personal rather than just vicarious. But, or so I shall argue, for all the light that Dreyfus has cast on that part of the *Review* that deals with the "present age," the disparagement of exceptionality that Kierkegaard calls levelling, and which forms the main motif of that part of the *Review*, has no obvious connection with modern nihilism as Dreyfus describes it.

Dreyfus's view that Kierkegaard was addressing a problem that can be identified as modern nihilism is presented in the Appendix, co-authored by Jane Rubin, to Dreyfus's *Being-in-the-World*.[2] More recently, it is both presented and illustrated in their "Kierkegaard on the Nihilism of the Present Age: The Case of Commitment as Addiction."[3] There Dreyfus and Rubin (henceforth Dreyfus/Rubin) see Kierkegaard and Heidegger as criticizing a common feature of culture, a feature our own culture shares with theirs. They see

Kierkegaard and Heidegger as grasping this feature from two interestingly different perspectives.

While thinkers such as Heidegger are primarily interested with the consequences of modern nihilism for Western culture as a whole, Kierkegaard is concerned about the implications of this situation for individuals in our culture. If nothing makes any difference to our culture, it is difficult to see how anything can make any difference to the individuals in it. To say that nothing makes any difference to an individual is to say that his or her life is meaningless. Kierkegaard's interest, and ours in an increasingly nihilistic age, is in how we can recover the sense that our lives are meaningful.[4]

As noted, Dreyfus/Rubin take the nihilism of our age and Kierkegaard's to be what the latter refers to as "levelling." Uncontroversially enough, since it is little more than to rephrase the metaphor, they read this initially as an erosion of qualitative distinctions: "Kierkegaard defines nihilism—or, as he calls it, 'levelling'— as a situation in which 'qualitative distinctions are weakened by a gnawing reflection'."[5] And it is true that Kierkegaard sees reflection as the medium, as it were, in which levelling occurs, or perhaps as the form that levelling takes in his society. Indeed, the work in which the section they draw on, called "The Present Age," is an extended comment on the contrast between the recent revolutionary past and Kierkegaard's present, a time in which the revolutionary ideals of equality and freedom (and fraternity) had lost their initial power to inspire individuals into collective action and had become excuses for letting public opinion upstage individual conscience. The novel Kierkegaard is ostensibly reviewing, *Two Ages* (*To tidsaldre*), is in fact a portrayal of the contrast from the perspectives of two interlocking generations. It is also true that the levelling Kierkegaard talks about, and which has to do with his culture being a reflective one in ways not unlike our own, is something which he saw would lead to a crisis of the kind Dreyfus/Rubin call nihilistic, where the problem is one of "commitment" and the ability to give one's life a distinctive meaning. But again, as I shall argue, the problem of commitment is not one that Kierkegaard saw as characteristic of his age.

What does it mean to say that "the present age has levelled qualitative distinctions"?[6] Dreyfus/Rubin understand what they call

Alastair Hannay

modern nihilism in something like the following way. Since in our culture no one thing is more important that any other, each person must define his or her own world. By choosing a definition, a person carves out a value for—and in—himself or herself, some value that is not already established or validated by cultural norms, because the "present age" validates no specific set of norms. On a less heroic scale, the same problem could be put by saying that it is, quite generally, that of making life seem worth living at all, given that no *ways* of living are given as having any more value than any others. Put in this way, the problem appears as one of motivation: how to make things matter, but also, since no one thing matters more than any other, where to begin. Underlying that problem, however, is the question of meaning itself, what sense there can be to a human life at all.

Since the context of Dreyfus/Rubin's claims about nihilism and levelling is Dreyfus's influential but also controversial interpretation of Heidegger, it is interesting to see how this model compares with Heidegger's own brief references to levelling (*Einebnung*) in *Being and Time* and in the lectures on the *Concept of the History of Time*. Heidegger talks famously of a mode of Dasein which he calls "das Man," a mode that grounds the "polished averageness of the everyday interpretation of Dasein." Along with an averageness of "the assessment of the world" and a "similar averageness of customs and manners," this polished averageness of the everyday interpretation of Dasein "watches over every exception which thrusts itself to the fore," so that "[e]very exception is short-lived and quietly suppressed . . . [a]nything original . . . smoothed out overnight into something which is available to Everyman and no longer barred to anyone." This "absorption in the world," a way in which people (or to put it in the philosophical parlance Heidegger thought so misleading, subjects of experience) originally share a world into which they are "thrown," Heidegger calls a "*levelling* of being-with-one-another" and "the levelling of all differences."[7]

Dreyfus/Rubin's words are almost exactly similar, and Heidegger's idea too may at first glance seem to be essentially theirs. The task Heidegger is addressing is that of "being oneself" in a world that cannot help but possess a significant degree of conformity. To be themselves, in a sense that recognizes the particularity of Dasein in each of its instances, a feature of human being equally inescapable as the basic conformity just referred to, people have to struggle against an innate tendency to blend smoothly into a cultural landscape in which an everyday averageness, carried to its extreme, leaves no foothold for the individual as such. The more the *das Man* mode becomes dominant in a culture, the more difficult it is to "be oneself." But the levelling Heidegger is referring to is inherent in Dasein itself, and not, as Dreyfus/Rubin present it, one that *confronts* Dasein as a problem of establishing a sense of its particularity. On the contrary, Dasein "goes along" with the tendency, "using" it, one might say, to lose sight of this other task. To a culture marked by the dominance of this tendency, a culture in which the originary *das Man* mode has more or less taken over, there will be no sense of a difficulty of commitment of the kind Dreyfus/Rubin refer to. Or if there is, it will arise only in the outsider, for instance Kierkegaard. As for the typical denizens of the culture, these will be marked by what to the outsider will appear to be a complacent willingness to go along with what a common world, what Heidegger following Kierkegaard calls a "public" world, has already decided. But not really decided, since decisions are made by individuals, individually or in association, and in confrontation with choices, whereas the public world the typical denizens comply with is one in which everything has been "talked about" but nothing has been "gone into." As Heidegger says, it is a world in which there is an "insensitivity to all distinctions in level and genuineness."[8]

It was just such a world that Kierkegaard criticized in the *Review*. But in dealing with Kierkegaard's notion of levelling we have to make a clear distinction between the phenomenon that he saw at work in his society and the place that levelling has in Kierkegaard's version of what Heidegger calls authenticity. In the latter it plays a positive role, but in the former it is analogous to, or perhaps even a case of, what Heidegger talks about as Dasein's failure to emerge from absorption in everydayness.

The first occurrence in the published works of the verb "to level" is in Kierkegaard's dissertation on irony. What marks out irony, says Kierkegaard, is the "abstract criterion by which it levels everything"

and "controls every excessive emotion"; instead of having enthusiasm overcome the fear of death, total extinction seems to it just a
"curious thought."[9] The contrast that levelling makes with enthusiasm is common to both contexts (irony and reflection are both
enthusiasm quenchers), but in the case of irony levelling is something required for the emergence of selfhood in what Kierkegaard
later calls the category of spirit. The role of irony, as Kierkegaard
sees it, is to create a distance from the everyday as such, so as to leave
room for the thought of oneself as poised in some sense to take on
the finite world afresh and as such, that is to say from a position in
which the distinction between finite and infinite has been brought
to the individual consciousness and the infinite can be applied
actively (ethically) to the finite world, instead of being considered
(fantastically, as in traditional metaphysics, romanticism, and "speculative" idealism) to be discoverable through thought, or in immediate experience, within it. As Kierkegaard has Climacus say in the
Postscript, irony is "the making [*Dannelse*] of spirit."[10] Roughly speaking, levelling the qualitative distinctions that confront a person in a
state of what Kierkegaard calls immediacy leaves that person in a
position to grasp another set of qualitative distinctions, namely those
that correspond to the values embodied in an ethical way of life. For
irony, as the *Postscript* also tells us, "is the boundary between the aesthetic and the ethical."[11]

In this context, Kierkegaard's levelling both compares and contrasts with Heidegger's. There is the shared theme of authenticity.
But while levelling in Heidegger is a levelling of distinctions that
Dasein must counter in order to have its "own world," in Kierkegaard, in the context of irony and distancing, levelling is a necessary step on the path to an authentic path of living *with* qualitative
distinctions in *the* world. As Dreyfus/Rubin point out, it is not clear
that Heidegger can justify the normativity invested in his notion of
authenticity, and indeed Dreyfus prefers to think that we can ignore
this notion in Heidegger. But Heidegger does struggle to extract
some such notion in spite of his insistence that Dasein never escapes
its "originary" *das Man* mode. Presumably authenticity must be something like putting a personal stamp on Dasein's exemplification of

its everydayness, "owning" up to it perhaps, in the sense of accepting responsibility for the particular and finitely enframed mix of common practices that form one's self. For Kierkegaard, however, there is a clear sense in which authenticity of the self requires the individual to hold the finite features that form *das Man* at a distance; it being only in the space provided by this distance that authentic selfhood can emerge.

In the case of the cultural phenomenon Kierkegaard calls levelling and criticizes in the *Review*, levelling is not a cultivation of, but, on the contrary, a flight from, authentic selfhood. Here there is a closer resemblance to Heidegger. Just as Heidegger sees the disposition to remain levelled as something Dasein must overcome if it is to be in any way or to any degree (at any level) genuine or authentic, so for Kierkegaard there is a pressure that keeps people from facing any problem of genuine selfhood. There is of course the difference that Heidegger is offering a structural account and so focuses on the claim that the pressures are endemic to Dasein itself, while what Kierkegaard offers is a diagnosis of how the pressures are at work in a particular society. Yet there is no reason to suppose that Kierkegaard might not have underwritten some such structural account had he placed any importance in arriving at one. His immediate interest, however, was his own society.

As noted above, it was a society undergoing political change. Since his student days Kierkegaard had been critical of the political movements of the time, not least the way in which the transition was being made from monarchical to constitutional government. The cultured elite in Copenhagen had taken sides, in the end many sides, and the first seeds of liberal reform were sown by the liberal press in its campaign for freedom from censorship. The process of levelling which Kierkegaard deplored had its core in the collective discourse produced in the public debate surrounding liberal politics and carried on energetically in coffeehouses and the press. As Kierkegaard had predicted in his first public speech ten years earlier, the liberal "movement" quickly shattered into a multitude of shades of variously radical and conservative opinion. The ensuing discussions between the competing liberal wings and between these and the conservatives

produced an explosion of discussion which in the end reduced to
what Kierkegaard looked upon as an endless "chatter" in which
themes which had once been a call to arms ("freedom and equality") inherited from the French Revolution were lost in debates on
the form of the relationships that constitute a society, relationships
that had to be discussed, and the discussing of which became more
important than living them.[12]

Is such a society, or its culture, nihilistic? Not if by nihilism one
means straightforwardly a culture in which people in general have
difficulty giving their lives meaning. Kierkegaard's culture was not
nihilistic in that sense. But there is another sense in which a culture,
including the one just described, can indeed be nihilistic. It is one
that Heidegger discusses in connection with Nietzsche. Heidegger
sees the core of Nietzschean nihilism to be the merely habitual and
self-serving hold on us of norms we no longer adhere to or appropriate personally. This is not the more radical nihilism often associated with Nietzsche, the nihilism consequent upon the death of God
and a belief in the sheer contingency of everything, including ourselves. If the less radical nihilism leaves no values in place, at least it
leaves a place for values, those values that would be there if we could
appropriate them personally. There is much to be said for viewing
Kierkegaard's sense of his own mission in a Nietzschean light, as that
of infusing new value into customs and practices that were becoming just empty habits. Nor is this incompatible with what I have
suggested, namely that in the case of Kierkegaard's culture the qualitative distinctions Dreyfus/Rubin speak of as having been levelled
were still largely in place. However, we can suppose that Kierkegaard
was someone who, by virtue of his own situation, was prone, or
perhaps even privileged, to see others in a light other than that in
which they saw themselves. Maybe—and it is a very complex matter
to decide—there is a hint of self-deception in the degree to which
he did so. But even if Kierkegaard's perception of the emptiness of
the lives of his colleagues was to some extent a product or projection
of his own sense of exclusion, the very fact that he had some sense
of their refusing opportunities to be what human beings could
become, and as he sometimes says in his pseudonymous works, are
programmed to become, allows us the thought that he saw his con-

temporaries as leading nihilistic lives. So, even if the primary task, the propaedeutic so to speak, was to get them to relinquish the false and, in a Nietzschean sense, empty meanings Kierkegaard thought that they did attach to their lives, once these lives had been deprived of their specious senses of value the task ahead would indeed be to put some properly fulfilling value back in place. In this attenuated sense, the characterization of the problem of the age as that of making life meaningful might well apply.

It would be interesting to consider how to place an attempt like Kierkegaard's to bring Christianity out of what he presents as though it were a *das Man* condition of spiritual torpor within, or in relation to, Heidegger's *Daseinanalyse*. Heidegger describes his account of Dasein as structural and as for that reason deliberately eschewing theology,[13] but as we noted, being structural it cannot predetermine the forms *das Man* might take and Heidegger says quite explicitly that his kind of account "precedes" any considerations of a theological kind.[14] It may be rather hasty therefore to refer, as Dreyfus/Rubin do, to Heidegger's account or any of its parts as a secularization of Kierkegaard. It all depends on what a Heideggerian can allow to come *after* an analysis of Dasein.

What about Dreyfus/Rubin's claim that a levelled "present age" presented individuals in Kierkegaard's society with the problem of how to be "committed to anything"?[15] The claim implies two things. First, it assumes a felt need to be committed to something, and second, that there are no commitments on hand to choose between. As for the first, as hinted earlier, it is surely closer to the truth regarding Kierkegaard to say that what he thought was wrong with his own age was not that it gave no scope for what Heidegger calls Dasein's having its "own world," but that it shunned the very idea of having to view the world from a perspective of contingency and finitude at all. From a Heideggerian point of view you could say that the problem both Kierkegaard and Heidegger envision is not that *das Man* offers no personal footholds, but that individuals delude themselves into thinking they can get along without having to conceive of such a foothold. And as for there being footholds, there were plenty of opportunities for commitment in Kierkegaard's time, indeed opportunities were proliferating in proportion to increasing enfranchisement and access to positions of influence and power. Politics itself offered ever-increasing chances to make a personal mark, to say nothing of journalism and the press.

Dreyfus/Rubin relate Kierkegaard's remarks on the malaise of his time interestingly to recent debates in the United States about education and core curricula. They quote the following passage as indicative of the kind of situation that has been brought into focus by authors such as Allan Bloom:

More and more people renounce the quiet and modest tasks of life . . . in order to achieve something greater; in order to think over the relationships of life in a higher relationship till in the end the whole generation has become a representation, who represent . . . it is difficult to say *who*, and who think about these relationships . . . for *whose* sake it is not easy to discover.[16]

I shall later offer a slightly different context for what Kierkegaard says here, but we can note here how closely the claim that the whole generation becomes a higher-level representation of no one in particular mirrors Heidegger's talk of "levelling" in Dasein's *das Man* mode. The latter, being "original," cannot of course be the product of Dasein's own powers of reflection; whatever produces the mode, Dasein simply finds itself in it. We saw that Heidegger describes it as talk rather than thought: what Dasein begins with is a world in which everything has been "talked about" but not "gone into," and Heidegger attributes this talking to the "public world" itself, not to Dasein.[17] The higher-level representation that Kierkegaard talks about and which represents everybody, and so no one in particular, is really not very different, though, again, Kierkegaard sees it as a feature of his time, a time of reflection and much talk, rather than as an inescapable part of the lasting structure of Dasein. Levelling, for Kierkegaard, is a contingent malady of his age, not an inescapable feature of human being as such.

To help identify the precise nature of the malady as Kierkegaard sees it, we can take another passage. He says:

The individual does not belong to God, to himself, to the loved one, to his art, to his research; no, just as a serf belongs to an estate, so the individual becomes conscious of belonging part and parcel to an abstraction under which reflection subordinates him.[18]

What is meant by belonging to an abstraction, in the sense Kierkegaard intends, can be grasped if we see the malady of the time as illustrating the logician's fallacy of division: the error of assuming that what goes for the group goes for the individuals forming it. Kierkegaard illustrates this with the case of members of a group deciding to give away all their fortunes to some charity. He thinks it unlikely that the members would have done that individually and it was precisely the malady of the age that they would not, but more to the point, that the reason they would have given was fear, not of poverty, but of the "judgment of reflection."[19]

Historically, the authority of reflection may be seen to derive from the influence of Hegelianism, and the same goes of course for the importance attached to group membership, which Kierkegaard specifically refers to in the *Review*. Although Hegel's direct influence on culture was on the wane at the time Kierkegaard wrote the *Review*, in the discussions centered on liberal reform there were other, nearer, and more forward-looking, sources of the gathering prestige of reflection and its judgments. The unreflected and traditional bases of group membership were being eagerly criticized and revised according to progressive ideals. It was possible for a person of Kierkegaard's prescience, therefore, to foresee a society composed of practices, guidelines, by-laws, and rules for revising these, a society in which abstract considerations of justice and equality reigned supreme and left no foothold for individual initiative. Though this was not yet the levelled society Kierkegaard lived in, it was the state of affairs he saw coming.

The most dangerous abstraction diagnosed by Kierkegaard in his time, however, is not that of group membership per se, with fear of the judgment of reflection as the individual's main source of motivation for social action. What he feared was the kind of group membership that levelling tends toward in which the group itself no longer displays any of the marks of integrated individuality. As so often, here too there is a parallel with Hegel. For Hegel abstraction occurs when there is an erosion of the link between a person's politically relevant actions and his or her situation in society. The ultimately levelled individual for Hegel would be a mere atom, a political abstraction, abstract because considered in isolation from any actual role played in society. For Hegel that spelled the importance of political representation at the level of what he saw as organically interrelated groupings in society. Anything more individual would be a dangerous abstraction. There is an analogy here with Kierkegaard's fear of the "public." The public is an abstraction whose members, to the extent that they become it, drop whatever organic relationships their social and political affiliations bestow on them. The group itself is then no longer really a group at all, not a "concretion," and obliterates the very notion of there being parts to play in a greater whole.

The real leveller then, for Kierkegaard, is this public. Since the public possesses none of the characteristics that belong to individuality, neither in its parts nor in the whole, the levelling it brings about is unaccountable. Levelling is a process, not an activity. There is no one in charge, no person or group to contact or influence in any attempt to stop it, no representative or spokesperson upon whom to vent one's moral indignation. As Kierkegaard says, no one, not even any *organized* body of individuals, can stop it.[20] Although a real factor in culture, in the sense that it is a force to be reckoned with, the public is also just a fiction created by the press.[21] In his student days Kierkegaard had shown great interest in the press and taken an active part in newspaper polemics. But even then he was criticizing the press for failing to take initiatives, and the newspapers for lacking any consistent or recognizable point of view.[22] Now, eleven years later, and himself soon to become a victim of popularist journalism, Kierkegaard saw the press itself as a faceless representative of its own monstrous creation: "A newspaper, a journal is no political concretion and an individual only in an abstract sense."[23]

It is clear that Kierkegaard took the way the press was about to treat him in the *Corsair* affair as an example of the lowest or basest form of levelling (*Nivelleringens laveste*).[24] The text provides what is for all intents and purposes an allegoric account of what was to be a personal experience. The public is personified by a bored Roman Emperor who has a dog let loose just for amusement, knowing he can then blame the dog (by common consent a mere cur) for whatever harm is done.[25] The public levels by bringing down the better and the stronger. Kierkegaard remarks that if anyone on the periphery of the public nevertheless entertained a sympathetic thought for the person abused, he or she would be wrong to sympathize. For those who really deserve sympathy are those weaker ones who show it by their weeping.[26]

This helps us to capture something of the special sense Kierkegaard attaches to levelling. Any sympathy emerging from the "public" would be due to a misperception about what it means to be distinguished from the "mere" public. The distinction is not that, unlike most, one is able to show sympathy; it is the ability to suffer at the public's hand and feel oneself the stronger for it. This highlights a crucial component in Kierkegaard's thought, namely that it is one's distance from the public that counts for selfhood. Levelling is not just the phenomenon that "one [*Man*] wants to drag down the great";[27] from a higher point of view any exceptionality defined in merely finite terms has to be "levelled" by being placed in the shadow cast by an absolute idea in respect of which everything worldly becomes indifferent. The exceptional person has to derive strength not from any sense of toughness that might count in his favor in the eyes of *das Man* itself, or of those who stand on the edge, but from a recognition that suffering in this way counts as directing oneself toward the absolute and acting on *its* terms. In conforming, as he says, to "what one [*Man*] wants" (and we see how easily the frequent use of the form "one" in this context could become encapsulated in the Heideggerian *das Man*), what Kierkegaard saw as his own acceptance of the general demand that he be reduced to the ranks was a position of strength rather than weakness. It was a cultivation of spirit. Summarizing his own life in the *Corsair* affair and its aftermath, Kierkegaard remarks:

I posed ... the problem the whole generation understands: equality between man and man. I posed it executively in Copenhagen. That's more than writing a few words about it; I expressed it approximately in my life. I have levelled in a *Christian* sense, but not in the rebellious sense against power and worth which I have with all my might upheld.[28]

The fact that there can be a Christian way of levelling may be seen in the light of the point made in the passage quoted above, in which Kierkegaard observes that "[m]ore and more people renounce the quiet and modest tasks of life . . . in order to achieve something greater." The Christian as such has no special tasks beyond those confronting the Christian locally; even in a Christian context Dasein has no possibilities exceeding the range of *das Man*. Kierkegaard could very well agree with Heidegger's insistence that Dasein is unable ever "really [to] extricate" itself from the original mode of *das Man*.[29]

In a properly Christian world no outer distinction would count for your worth; that is what it would mean to answer as well as to pose the problem of equality between man and man in practice, the problem Kierkegaard says he expressed approximately in his life. But it is important to note the corollary. Without belief in the Christian basis for the world, to measure one's worth in a way in which nothing external counted would leave you with no distinguishing marks at all. This is the inexorable logic of levelling as Kierkegaard presents it in the *Review*. The common topic of levelling, we can say, is human equality; but levelling in its uncontrollable form is a consequence of the "superiority of the category of the generation over that of the individual" in modern culture.[30] The kind of claim Kierkegaard makes here is analogous to that made by Heidegger in the *Letter on Humanism* where he says that the "public realm" is currently typified by the "dominance of subjectivity."[31] In cases of comprehensive background influences of this kind there is no way to change or reverse the categories:

No single man (the eminent person in terms of superiority and the dialectic of fate) will be able to stop levelling's abstraction, for that is a negative aim and the time of heroes is over. No congregation [a reference to the Grundtvigian movement] could stop levelling's abstraction, because the congregation is itself through the context of reflection in the service of levelling. Not even the individualities of nations will be able to stop it, for the abstraction of levelling reflects on a higher negativity: pure humanity.[32]

Pure humanity, as a totally empty way of defining selfhood, is what you are left with after the elimination of external measures of distinction. At its extreme, therefore, levelling leaves you with a clear choice: God or nothing. So, in extension of the original thought of irony's potentially edifying levelling being in the service of spirit by making room for it, the levelling that has arisen from the cult of reflection, and is now driven by its own momentum, has one mitigating benefit in prospect. Though initially motivated by a fear of individuality, the very process through which people prone to reflection efface their individuality by claiming group membership will, if carried to the limit, force them to face the very thing they are trying to escape. They will see that they must either "perish" in the "abstract vertigo of the infinite" or be "saved infinitely" in the "essentiality of religiousness."[33]

On the model of levelling presented by Dreyfus/Rubin, what they call "modern nihilism," levelling is a levelling of the cultural landscape, an equalization of all options. The individual is then faced with the huge task of introducing contours singlehandedly. Their model allows them to present the Kierkegaardian "stages" (though we should bear in mind that Kierkegaard himself presents these in the pseudonymous works while the *Review* is a signed work) as variously contoured worlds in which the individual seeks (though unsuccessfully until the final stage) to make life meaningful *ab initio*. This assumes that the "natural" way to begin is to start with the aesthetic. And indeed what could be more natural for people lacking any cultural inducements than to start off by defining the world in terms of the pursuit of pleasure?

If we look at the account Kierkegaard gives of the aesthetic stage, however, we see that it is this very stage that brings about the levelling Dreyfus/Rubin refer to. The seduction recorded in the famous "Diary" responds to a boredom (expressed most tellingly in the preceding essay which proposes the method of crop rotation) which the aesthetic life is bound to end in. Far from being a response to levelling, the aesthetic life-view is a symptom of it, a symptom that in the end brings it to an awareness of what it is and the respects in which it is limited. It is interesting that Dreyfus/Rubin take Kierkegaard to be analyzing not only modern nihilism but also "the way individuals attempt to escape it."[34] What they mean by escaping nihilism is the individual's defining of a world for itself. Now it is true that the aesthetic stage is presented as a refuge, or so at least it is made to appear from the alternative provided, the ethical perspective. But neither the aesthetic nor the ethical is presented as a response to nihilism; rather, together with the succeeding religious stages, these two are presented as successively more adequate ways of appreciating the problem of selfhood. It is here that irony and *its* levelling play their positive role. The levelling Kierkegaard talks about in the *Review* is not one from which his age was trying to escape; on the contrary, levelling was itself the *means* of escape. It was a flight from the project of individuality into reflection and, with it, connivance at the cult of the generation. In the end, however, levelling would confront people with a bleak disjunction: God or nothing.

Although the levelling Kierkegaard criticizes in his time is not structural to human being in the way Heidegger's levelling is, there is something "structural" about it all the same. What is structural is the human being's natural tendency to escape the disjunction. Of course, if you begin by believing in God, the difficulty is to sustain the belief when you realize that God is not in the world. But if you believe that the world is all there is, then the realization that it lacks what is needed for your fulfillment leaves you with another difficulty, that of having to live within what you take to be your means. Either way, the prospect is intimidating. Rather than face it, one tends, as the pseudonym Vigilius Haufniensis so tellingly puts it, to turn back toward the world, clutching at "finiteness" to prevent losing one's balance.[35] One overcomes one's dizziness by turning one's gaze fixedly at the familiar and placing one's hopes for a kind of fulfillment in the finite world.

This might be a way of grasping the problem of our own age. It would be a Kierkegaardian way. But it is not the way that Dreyfus/Rubin lead us to grasp it. Instead, they see the problem facing individuals as "Sartrean." It is a world in which "our capacity to choose anything makes no choice compelling."[36] Clearly there is a vast difference between asking "What among all these things can be made to matter?" and asking "But what if nothing matters?"

It is the former question that allows Dreyfus/Rubin to introduce their claims for the superior ability of Kierkegaard's analysis of nihilism to explain the popular appeal of the "addiction model." These claims are based on a subtle and interesting analysis of the stage Kierkegaard's Climacus calls "Religiousness A." In brief, they see in Religiousness A an analogue to the way in which self-defined addicts who subject themselves to recovery programs are able to satisfy the combined requirements of identity and lasting commitment but without reaching the level of a true personal commitment.

The recoverer's world contains the important but never-ending task of achieving indifference to the temptation to give in to a dominant desire. We see here an echo of the role Kierkegaard attributes to irony as giving room for a goal that puts all finite achievements in the shade. However, Dreyfus/Rubin see the recovery-program maneuver and Religiousness A as both containing a fatal flaw as attempts at commitment. An ideal state of perfect indifference is envisioned though permanently postponed. But the levelling of perfect indifference aimed at is precisely the nihilism from which Religiousness A (and joining the programs) is an attempt to escape.[37]

I have no space here to discuss or judge the insightful claims their claimed analogy embraces. I shall simply repeat that Religiousness A cannot reasonably, any more than the stages that precede it, be interpreted as an attempt to escape nihilism. The levelling that Dreyfus/Rubin see as causing Religiousness A's downfall, as an attempt to define a world, is simply the levelling that Kierkegaard sees as a preliminary to being able to accept or recover the finite world but on God's terms, levelling in a Christian sense. In a way, for Kierkegaard, any activity that does not have this latter levelling as its point of departure is itself addictive, it represents an addiction to the shared world as the arena in which to measure one's worth, in terms of one's difference from, inferiority or superiority to, others, what Heidegger calls *Abständigkeit*,[38] a concern with difference which can just as well take the form of a concern to eliminate difference, which is exactly what Kierkegaard thought had gone wrong with the ideal of equality. Instead of the false picture of human equality that *Abständigkeit* projects, an equality in externals, Kierkegaard's "true" picture is one that requires the cultivation of an indifference to difference, or in a manner of speaking that frames Heidegger's concept in the way he intends, a distancing from *Abständigkeit* itself.[39] It is also worth noting, as Dreyfus/Rubin would certainly agree, that the notion of religiosity Kierkegaard presents is far removed from the irrational escapisms that can substitute for addiction as flawed forms of commitment. It is easy to see how the dizzying prospect that pure levelling leaves you with can have you clutching at the handrail and trying desperately to make meaning out of what for all we know has none. Dreyfus/

Rubin's very plausible claim that the choice of addiction and recovery can be seen as a way of securing something as near as possible to an absolute that substitutes for the real thing fits in well with Kierkegaard's concept of despair, according to which human activities *in general* tend to answer to that description. But then *The Sickness unto Death*, the main source for Kierkegaard's concept of despair, leaves us with yet one more indication that Kierkegaard, even if, against my argument, he had seen his own work in the *Review* or elsewhere as providing any kind of analysis of modern nihilism, would never have recommended an escape from it in the form of a definition of one's own world, a self-definition "from scratch," as Dreyfus/Rubin's notion of genuine commitment seems to require. As is made quite clear in *The Sickness unto Death*, to define one's *own* world (or self) is despair's most blatant form. It is *the* world we have to find our place in and reveal ourselves to. If there is anything like commitment in Kierkegaard (and there is no precisely corresponding Danish word for it), we should probably say it is a prior commitment to the belief that the world does indeed have a meaning. But given the kind of commitment it is, it is inconsequential what our own selves are, how they are defined, and what they are in terms of socio-political categories; we are committed only to being what we ourselves are, ethically speaking, and the terms of such definitions specify only our places in the world, not our worth. This is the direction in which Kierkegaard thinks equality should be understood, the very opposite of that in which he thinks the tendency to level, with its focus on externals, is taking us. In other words, the answer Kierkegaard presupposes to the question "Does life have a meaning?" renders the other question redundant. You don't have to ask "What among all these things can be made to matter?" Looking ethically at the options, that is, as Judge Wilhelm would put it, having chosen good and evil, they all matter; and what commitment then amounts to is staying with what you have.[40]

6

The End of Authentic Selfhood in the Postmodern Age?

Michael E. Zimmerman

In the late nineteenth century, Marxists complained that industrialism was dehumanizing, because it alienated laborers from essential aspects of their being. Some contemporary social critics are concerned with a form of dehumanization that affects not industrial laborers, but rather affluent people for whom goods and services intertwine with the electronic technology of the workplace in ways that blur the line between home and office, private and public, personal and professional. Many people find themselves confronted with captivating, seductive, and expansive options that allow people readily to exchange one identity for another, such as Internet chat rooms. That people relish the freedom to explore new technologically generated options and alternative personal identities is evidenced by the vast sums of money being spent on them. Yet, despite all the excitement, some people report feeling disintegrated, superficial, even dehumanized. If selfhood were transformed into a kaleidoscope of transient social roles to which one lacks serious commitment, this development would mean the end of "authenticity," as early Heidegger defined it. In my view, elements of the phenomenon of authenticity remain valid, even though later Heidegger not only developed a rather different concept of authenticity, but also contributed to postmodern hype about the end of humanism and the erasure of the subject.

In this chapter, I will explore some of the complex relationships among decentered selfhood, modern technology, and the possibility of authenticity, as articulated in recent work by Hubert Dreyfus and Charles Spinosa (henceforth, Dreyfus/Spinosa). In connection with postmodern selfhood, social psychologist Kenneth Gergen has raised two questions: How can one practice being a "self" at a time in which constant change, vastly increased possibilities for relationship, transitory commitments, and social fragmentation displace the rational sincerity, integrity, and continuity idealized by the *modern* self? What does it mean to be a "self" at a time in which appearances, shifting perspectives, and the infinitely expanding horizontal network of the Web supplant the passionate depths of the *romantic* self? Although in the digitally dominated postmodern age, the once-venerated romantic and modern ideals of authentic selfhood are being displaced by the "saturated self," Gergen argues that postmodern, decentered, relational selfhood has positive traits worth encouraging.[1]

Agreeing with aspects of Gergen's contention that human selfhood is dramatically changing in the technological era, Dreyfus/Spinosa also seek constructively to deal with the potentially dehumanizing consequences of those changes. Unlike Gergen, however, Dreyfus/Spinosa interpret the emergence of modern technology in accordance with Heidegger's view that the West's productionist metaphysics inevitably ends in the era of technological nihilism, when the human subject and its object alike are transformed into flexible raw material for the technological system. Drawing on Heidegger's notion of the "gathering of the fourfold" (earth and sky, gods and mortals), Dreyfus/Spinosa suggest how contemporary people may achieve a level of integration that avoids dehumanizing dispersal into countless and often unrelated social practices. The trick is to engage in practices made possible by modern technology, *without* thereby being dehumanized in the sense of being transformed into flexible raw material.[2] For Dreyfus/Spinosa, again following Heidegger, such "integration" seems to be all that "authenticity" can mean in the postmodern age.

Dreyfus/Spinosa's account of how to cope with modern technology assumes the validity of Heidegger's claim that in the technological age, both subject and object have vanished. Arguably, however, early Heidegger's concept of authentic selfhood as anxious being-towards-death retains considerable force today, when millions of technologically advanced people report being plagued by anxiety, panic attacks, and other "disorders" linked to perceived threats to egoic subjectivity. The ideal of authenticity, defined by early Heidegger as owning one's finitude so as to choose *one* possibility, retains importance, despite talk of "morphing" or identity-shifting. Postmodernists criticize the modern egoic subject for overstating the possibility (and desirability) of *unity* of self, but the totally heterogeneous, splintered postmodern self overstates the possibility of *differentiation* of self.

After suggesting that Dreyfus/Spinosa's account of postmodern "dwelling" in the fourfold would be strengthened by discussing the need for personal narratives to make sense of the numerous possibilities confronting a person, I examine how Ken Wilber's metanarrative of the progressive development of human consciousness provides not only a warning about the personal and socially regressive possibilities involved in the postmodernism's surrender of the achievement of personal integrity, but also an account of authentic post-egoic selfhood as *transpersonal* existence, which is related in some ways to Heidegger's early view of authenticity. Sustaining a transpersonal mode of existence requires that a person succeed first in being an integrated person, something like the modernist self described by Gergen. Transpersonal existence also discloses that romantics were right in seeking to recover the self's depths, which were eclipsed by modern rationalism. For Wilber, however, these depths are constituted not by inchoate feelings and passions, but rather by spirituality, which both includes and transcends the planes of material body and rational mind.

I   Dreyfus and Spinosa on Personal Identity in the Technological Age

Dreyfus/Spinosa's essay, "Highway Bridges and Feasts: Heidegger and [Albert] Borgmann on How to Affirm Technology" seeks to address the problem of existing in the technological age without being reduced to flexible raw material. Dreyfus/Spinosa argue that new technologies make possible new practices and identities. Unlike those who believe that modern technology results from unpredictable cultural differentiation, Dreyfus/Spinosa follow Heidegger in arguing that modern technology is the inevitable outcome of the historical process by which the Being of entities has hidden itself. Dreyfus/Spinosa examine Heidegger's account of an affirmative relation to modern technology without once mentioning *Gelassenheit* ("releasement"), an overworked term that has yielded few insights about what Heidegger meant by "letting technology be". Dreyfus/Spinosa remind us that later Heidegger envisioned modern technology not in anthropocentric-instrumental terms, but rather as a process of *"endless* disaggregation, redistribution, and reaggregation *for its own sake,"* as best exemplified by computer technology, which reduces all phenomena to digital code.[3] Just as this process annihilates the object once dominated by the modern subject, it supposedly also vaporizes the human subject itself. For Heidegger, the simultaneous elimination of subject and object defines the peculiar mode of human existence that characterizes the technological age, which for the purposes of this essay is equivalent with postmodernity.

Dreyfus/Spinosa maintain that the extraordinary interconnectivity of the Internet best exemplifies the radical transformation of the traditional fixed subject position, which has been displaced by rapidly growing possibilities of identity-shifting and has been transformed by technologically assisted multi-perspectivalism. Sherry Turkle describes such identity-shifting as "morphing" in connection with her discussion of an Internet social phenomenon known as MUDs, multi-user dungeons, a term taken from "Dungeons and Dragons," the role-playing game popular with adolescents. Dreyfus/Spinosa quote Turkle as saying that, "In MUDs you can write and revise your character's self-description whenever you wish. On some MUDs you can even create a character that 'morphs' into another with the command '@morph'."[4] Seemingly enthusiastic about the "age of the Net," Dreyfus/Spinosa write that "we shall have many different skills for identity construction, and we shall move around virtual spaces and real spaces seeking ways to exercise these skills, powers, and passions as best as we can." Net-surfers will assume an identity "for as long as the identity and activity are exhilarating and then mov[e] on to new identities and activities. Such people would thrive on having no home community and no home sense of self." As opposed to what Gergen calls the modern's quest for sincerity and integrity, and the romantic's quest for depth and commitment, the Net-surfer's society will be governed by a style that "would be one of intense, but short, involvements, and everything would be done to maintain and develop the flexible disaggregation and reaggregation of various skills and faculties. Desires and their satisfaction would give way to having the thrill of the moment."[5]

Faced with today's technological revolution, one can understand Heidegger's concern that postmodern humanity is being reduced to flexible standing reserve, without enduring essence or identity. As standing reserve, human behavior would become totally coordinated with whatever technological devices happen to be available in a given situation. In other words, instead of using this or that device in accordance with a plan developed by oneself as an autonomous subject, the post-subject human would almost immediately begin engaging in whatever (more or less) skillful practice is elicited and required by the technological device that presents itself. Humans as self-conscious agents would virtually vanish into an ever more tightly coupled relationship with the electronic technology involved in the planetary-wide processes of production and consumption. Despite being concerned that humans are on the verge of becoming dehumanized raw material, Dreyfus/Spinosa argue that, if we take Heidegger seriously, people *can* adopt attitudes toward modern technology that avoid dehumanization. In the Heideggerian context, "dehumanization" means for people to lose their understanding of human *Dasein*'s world-disclosive capacity and thus to become nothing but clever animals, that is, particularly flexible raw material useful for increasing the power of the self-sustaining technological system. According to Dreyfus/Spinosa, successful coping with the new technological opportunities and requirements would involve learning how to be attuned to oneself as a flexible resource, while not understanding oneself as such a resource at all times and places.

Drawing on Heidegger's notion of "things" that gather together, focus, or appropriate earth and sky, gods and mortals, Dreyfus/ Spinosa describe how such adaptation might occur. At first, in view of Heidegger's allegedly retro-romantic attitude toward the lifestyle of the German peasant, one might suppose that he would deny that modern technological devices could serve as "things" that can focus, gather, or appropriate the fourfold. Dreyfus/Spinosa point out, however, that in addition to speaking of how the jug and the stone bridge gather the fourfold in local practices, Heidegger once suggested that even a modern highway bridge could gather together the fourfold in a way that enables a driver both to appreciate the freedom of zooming across the bridge, and to acknowledge that such freedom is not infinite for mortals. In the fourfold gathered together by the highway bridge, the *gods* have been pushed aside, the *sky* has been reduced to the manifestation of multiple technological possibilities or options, and the *earth* refers to the fact that such possibilities somehow still matter. Regarding the fourth ingredient of the fourfold, *mortals*, Dreyfus/Spinosa write:

To understand oneself as mortal means to understands one's identity and world as fragile and temporary and requiring one's active engagement. In the case of the highway bridge, it means that, even while getting in tune with being a flexible resource, one does not understand oneself as being a resource all the time and everywhere. . . . Rather, as one speeds along the overpass, one senses one's mortality, namely *that one has other skills for bringing out other sorts of things, and therefore one is never wholly a resource.* [Such alternative skills enable one] to relate to the highway bridge not just as a transparent device but in its specificity as a way of bringing the technological ordering out in its ownmost. But that is to say that the highway bridge can be affirmed as a possible kind of focal thing that calls to us as mortals, only if there are other focal things around that preserve styles in which things can thing.[6]

Only insofar as the technological understanding of Being has *not* achieved complete domination can the bridge play the role of a "thing" that gathers the fourfold. Were such domination complete, there would be no alternative ways of disclosing things other than as flexible raw material. Hence, there could be no recognition, however dim, of the fact that human *Dasein contributes* in some way to the disclosure process. According to Dreyfus/Spinosa, local styles and practices—those that have not yet been co-opted by the technological disclosure of entities—remind us that we *are* disclosive beings, precisely because things show up differently in accordance with differing practices and styles. Learning to bring into harmony a host of such practices, skills, roles, and styles is what provides "disclosers with a sense of integrity or centeredness."[7] Hence, although contemporary technological things typically distribute people into disaggregated skills with a style of flexible dispersion, nevertheless such things can gather "the skills for treating ourselves as disaggregated skills and the world as a series of open possibilities are what are drawn together so that various dispersed skillful performances become possible."[8]

According to Dreyfus/Spinosa, in the electronically published version of their essay, the differentiating, interconnecting, and dynamic character of current technological practices will not satisfy the desire for single-authorship or centered selfhood, but such practices can open up possibilities "for new ways of conceiving ourselves."[9] Further, "The point of technological things is not to satisfy our desires transparently but rather to stimulate us to reaggregate our tastes, interests, skills, and so forth so that we can transform ourselves and thereby our desires."[10] The "saving power" of technology, then, involves freeing ourselves from a "total fixed identity so that we may experience ourselves as multiple identities disclosing multiple worlds."[11]

As Dreyfus/Spinosa rightly point out, engaging in the metapractice of partaking in multiple local practices would seem to pose obstacles to the ideal of achieving that measure of centeredness or integrity presumably required for a "crisp" performance of various practices, whether local or technological. Dreyfus/Spinosa ask how can we overcome such obstacles. First, they tell us, one could try to control the sequence or constellation of practices, so as to maximize their number, but doing so would encourage constant anticipation of the next move (or simultaneous ones), rather than full engagement in the local focal practice now before one. Without such engagement, crisp performance is not possible, as anyone knows who is thinking about the next step while supposedly attempting to accomplish the previous step. Moreover, as Dreyfus/Spinosa observe, this control-orientation is characteristic of the desiring egoic subject whose era is waning, rather than of the postmodern, post-subjective "self" whose era is apparently waxing.

Second, one could become completely absorbed in each particular local focal practice and move sequentially from one practice to the next as opportunities presented themselves, or one could engage in multiple local practices simultaneously. Insofar as such practices may be totally unrelated to one another, and insofar as a person may simply have responded semiautomatically to the availability of the practice, this approach gives rise not to a "gathering" or a sense of coherence, but instead to the experiences of fragmentation, dispersion, incoherence, and lack of autonomy which are symptomatic of people on the verge of becoming nothing but nodes in the totally interconnected network. Losing any sense of coherent identity, "one will exist either as a collection of unrelated selves or as no self at all, drifting in a disoriented way among worlds."[12] Avoiding such unwelcome outcomes requires a life in which practice flows coherently from one to the next, thereby giving one "a sort of poly-identity that is neither the identity of an arbitrary desiring subject nor the rudderless adaptability of a resource."[13] Dreyfus/Spinosa conclude that "as mortal disclosers of worlds in the plural, the only integrity we can hope to achieve is our openness to dwelling in many worlds and the capacity to move among them."[14] Clearly, however, as Dreyfus/Spinosa imply, to achieve such relative integrity, one must limit oneself to inhabiting a determinate number of worlds, rather than immersing oneself in one unrelated world after the next.

Albert Borgmann, whose reflections on Heidegger's philosophy of technology inspired the Dreyfus/Spinosa essay, would be sympathetic to Dreyfus/Spinosa's effort to salvage something worthwhile from the options made possible by contemporary technological innovations. He believes that postmoderns are mature enough to tolerate and even to welcome many different communities and to develop a life of coherently flowing alternative practices. Such openness to and celebration of alterity and plurality, so Borgmann hopes, may eventually give rise to a "community of communities," a "hidden center" that might unite the manifold local practices in "communal celebration, namely religion. People feel a deep desire for comprehensive and comprehending orientation."[15] Through much of his career, Heidegger's own yearning for a comprehensive understanding is reflected in his notion that each historical epoch is governed by a single, all-pervasive understanding of the Being of entities.

Dreyfus/Spinosa maintain, however, that toward the end of his life, Heidegger abandoned the notion of such a unifying understanding, just as he gave up privileging the ancient Greeks as the one true "origin" of the Western understanding of Being. He also concluded that the gathering of local worlds by things cannot adequately be understood in terms of the "ontological difference" between Being and entities. Instead, he emphasized the importance of local understandings and practices, which retain their capacity for gathering only insofar as they retain their own coherence. Noting that for Heidegger local practices are always at risk of being eclipsed by the dominant practice, Dreyfus/Spinosa argue that the dominant practice itself *needs* local practices in order to be able to disclose entities most effectively in its *own* particular way. In other words, full appreciation of the possibilities of technological disclosure of entities requires alternative disclosures that *contrast* with it. At the same time, without local practices, however marginal, there would be no way for people to notice that the technological disclosure of entities is *not* eternal and universal, but historical and particular.

Taking into account the late turn in Heidegger's thought, Dreyfus/Spinosa suggest that a positive relationship to technology is possible because the technological understanding of Being is not and could never be fully monolithic in the first place, since there is no univocal "history of Being" shaping Western history. While intriguing, this approach leaves open the question of why and whether people should concern themselves with Heidegger's concerns about modern technology's dehumanizing potential. In view of Heidegger's late shift, can one even speak of the technological era? Were dehumanization to occur, would it merely be an ontical matter, that is, would technological devices simply outstrip human cognitive and behavioral capacities to such an extent that a dystopian future would emerge, in which humans would be enslaved by the descendents of devices that previous humans had once created? In other words, how does Heidegger's very late shift beyond both the history of Being and ontological difference enable us to make sense of his previous admonitions and reflections about modern technology? Answers to such questions will have to be postponed for another occasion.

II   Contributions to a Dialogue on Postmodern Selfhood

Dreyfus/Spinosa have made an ingenious effort to show that Heidegger's thought can provide a constructive account of how to take advantage of the opportunities afforded by the (allegedly) postsubjective technological era, without in the process becoming reduced to flexible raw material. Their essay forms part of a broader effort to provide a contemporary interpretation of what Heidegger meant by the "gods." In effect, Dreyfus/Spinosa are seeking to understand the cultural implications of widely reported sightings of angels and other phenomena that are irreconcilable with the materialist ontology of modern technology. In what follows, I hope to add to their constructive exploration of issues that have such important implications for human existence. Here, I should also like to acknowledge Hubert Dreyfus for his pioneering and highly influential attempt to interpret Heidegger's view of the "understanding of Being" in terms of the *practices* that embody such understanding. Although not fully sharing that interpretation, I can now scarcely imagine approaching Heidegger's complex writings without the benefit of it.[16]

In their analysis of Heidegger, Dreyfus/Spinosa suggest that local practices can somehow provide resistance to the totalizing technological understanding of Being. If all non-"high tech" social practices, styles, and modes of understanding were eliminated, humankind would lose its essence as world-discloser in Heidegger's sense. In such a case, authenticity would be impossible, if authenticity (*Eigentlichkeit*) meant "owning" one's mortal openness for the Being of entities. Although later Heidegger redefined authenticity to mean being appropriated (*vereignet*) by the fourfold, he retained a profound concern for human mortality. Moreover, I would argue that his early views on authenticity retain considerable validity today, despite Heidegger-inspired talk of the disappearance of the subject. In effect, Dreyfus/Spinosa may either be overstating the case for the alleged disintegration of the modern subject, or may be interpreting the transformation of subjectivity in terms of problematic conceptual categories. Before turning to these issues, however, let us consider Dreyfus/Spinosa's contention that the highway bridge may appropriate the fourfold in a way that gives rise to a saving sense that there are alternative practices to those generated by the technological understanding of Being.

In regard to the fourfold, how are we to understand the driver's sense of good fortune in having access to the flexibility and excitement of the all-encompassing interstate highway system? Does this correspond to the spontaneous sense of grace shared by friends gathered together by the wine with which they give toasts at a meal? Heidegger himself suggests that the highway bridge can "gather," but in a way that is attenuated at best. Conceding that the elements of the fourfold gathered by the bridge are feeble in comparison with Heidegger's accounts of the fourfold appropriated by more traditional "things," such as the wine-filled goblet, or for that matter a wooden bridge of a bygone era, Dreyfus/Spinosa suggest that the sense of "good fortune" is a vestige of being blessed by a god.[17]

Having spent considerable time in the San Francisco Bay area, where Dreyfus and Spinosa are fortunate enough to reside, I myself have felt an undeniable sense of good fortune when driving across either the Bay Bridge or the Golden Gate Bridge, with the San Francisco skyline, the hills of Marin County, or the Berkeley hills lying ahead, and with the sparkling waters of San Francisco Bay lying on either side. These bridges, magnificent technological achievements built during the 1930s when Heidegger was focusing on the problem of modern technology, still "gather" in a way not usually associated with modern technological phenomena. Hurtling along a typical interstate highway in the middle of California or Iowa, however, a driver is often oblivious to bridges, many of which are virtually identical and thus call little attention to their work of gathering. Recalling that one is mortal, according to Dreyfus/Spinosa, can bring a person back from such oblivion and can trigger off the mood that lets the bridge do its gathering work. Understanding one's mortality, we are told, involves understanding not only how fragile and temporary are the world and one's own identity in that world, but also how limited are one's capacities for taking advantage of endlessly proliferating possibilities.

Further questions arise here, however. For openers, how and why should mortality even arise as issues for a postsubjective morpher lacking an integrated sense of identity? In what way can driving across an interstate highway bridge elicit a sense of mortality sufficient to counter technological culture's drive to attain immortality, either by dominating the forces of nature (thus continuing modernity's project by using ever more powerful digital technology), or else by "downloading" human consciousness into virtually indestructible silicon chips? Contemporary cyberpunk fiction, such as *Neuromancer*, describes how futuristic morphers refer to the organic body as "the meat" to be left behind as they "jack in" to the extraordinary flexible and infinite vastness of silicon-based cyberspace. Plugged in to the infinite interconnectivity of the wired world, a morpher would presumably experience a kind of ersatz immortality that would scarcely invite reflection about finitude and mortality.

For a postmodern morpher, would recognition of finitude amount to anything more than acknowledging that space, time, and energy constrain the number of practices that he or she can adopt? In other words, just as a desktop computer's CPU can only process so much information at any time, so too at any given moment a contemporary morpher may be able to adopt only so many temporary identities and engage in only so many unrelated practices. If human brains are complex parallel processors (as some people suggest), in other words, the issue for postmodern morphing culture becomes how to deal with the inherent limits of the brain's processing capacity. If one regards the human capacity for engaging in intelligible practices as a function of the computational brain, one could begin to devise ways to increase dramatically the brain's flexibility and power by linking brains to computers, in ways envisioned both in current science fiction as well as in science research. If efforts to create human-technological "cyborgs" are successful, and steps have already been taken in this direction, would not humankind be well on its way to becoming nothing more than flexible raw material in a system whose aims are no longer commensurate with merely "human" affairs?

To be sure, someone driving on the interstate is not inhabiting the "consensual hallucination" of cyberspace, although she may be simultaneously watching traffic on the road, receiving a fax, talking on her cell phone, listening to a talk show, keeping an eye on her two-year-old in the back seat, glancing at roadside advertising, and taking in a sunset whose brilliant colors result from a toxic brew of petrochemicals. It is possible that at this very moment, she would recognize that not everything is possible and that her best efforts are finite. However poignant this moment of reflection might be, and there is reason to believe that such moments *do* occur, it seems removed from the extraordinary decisional epiphany involved in resolute being-towards-death as described in *Sein und Zeit*.

Early Heidegger has an explanation for the unexpected onset of mortality-awareness, or *Angst. Dasein*'s ontological structure, care, cares for a Dasein lost in the routine practices and tempting distractions of everyday life by generating the mood of *Angst*. This ontologically self-corrective intervention reveals in a dramatic, transformational manner that Dasein is not a thing, but rather finite/mortal openness for Being. Nothing so wrenching, however, seems to be required of the postmodernist driving across a six-lane bridge connecting two river banks in a city that can scarcely be differentiated from any other postmodern urban center. Supposedly, even though bombarded with distractions and opportunities undreamed of in the 1920s, today's driver must simply recall that no matter how accessible opportunities become, one cannot take advantage of *all* of them. "So many options," she might muse to herself, "so little time." Awareness of such limits, according to Dreyfus/ Spinosa, invites the driver to remind herself that she has *other* skills and practices for disclosing things, skills and practices that do not involve optimizing one's technologically oriented possibilities in the ways made possible by highway bridges and the Internet. Here, she might appreciate her capacity for moving skillfully between and within rather different worlds, but it is by no means obvious that such appreciative insight would be triggered off by the mood of *Angst*.

Let us dwell for a moment on early Heidegger's notion of the relation between *Angst*, mortality, and authenticity.[18] Even though he later concluded that *Sein und Zeit*'s account of human existence was tainted with a residual subjectivism, later Heidegger remained concerned with human mortality and finitude, which he described in very different ways than do Dreyfus/Spinosa in their account of the driver zooming across the highway bridge. Commenting on Rilke's observation that we live in destitute times, for example, later Heidegger wrote:

The time remains destitute not only because God is dead [and the gods have fled—MZ], but because mortals are hardly aware and capable even of their own mortality. Mortals have not yet come into ownership of their own nature. Death withdraws into the enigmatic. The mystery of pain remains veiled. Love has not been learned.[19]

In his essay, "The Thing," in which he discusses the fourfold in detail, Heidegger describes mortals in the following way:

The mortals are human beings. They are called mortals because they can die. To die means to be capable of death as death. Only man dies. The animal perishes. It has death neither ahead of itself nor behind it. Death is the shrine of Nothing, that is, of that which in every respect is never something that merely exists, but which nevertheless presences, even as the mystery of Being itself. As the shrine of Nothing, death harbors within itself the presencing of Being. As the shrine of Nothing, death is the shelter of Being.[20]

In envisioning the postsubjective *Dasein* capable of singing the song of the coming gods, Heidegger contemplated someone capable not only of experiencing mortality, but also of understanding the profound relationship between mortality and the nothingness that makes world-disclosure possible. For Heidegger, death refers not to an approaching event, but rather to the mortal nothingness that always already enables human *Dasein* to encounter entities *as* entities. This conception of mortality would seem to differ rather significantly from that ascribed to the postmodern morpher.

Up to this point, I have been intentionally emphasizing problematic aspects of postmodern morphing of which Dreyfus/Spinosa themselves are critical. As a result, my account of the driver does not offer a sufficiently charitable view of a point they are trying to make. If a driver returning home from a week-long hike into the Sierra Nevada were to have an epiphany regarding the finitude (and thus the impermanence) of worlds, she might experience a startling contrast between the world of camping in relatively uncivilized nature, on the one hand, and the world of driving in advanced cars on interstate highways, on the other. She might appreciate both the efficiency of freeway driving (if not snarled in traffic) and the skills needed to make a week-long hiking trip enjoyable. The driver can encounter the technological in its extraordinary character (including its threatening as well as beneficial dimensions) only in contrast with the other world that she has recently left behind or to which she is heading. Even in an age dominated by ostensibly death-defying technological achievements, then, some "things" and "practices" may be able to reveal the difference between and thus the finitude of worlds. In crossing the interstate bridge, then, the driver might for a moment experience the residue of the gathering of the fourfold, in the form of the blessing of high-speed travel networks, even as she recognizes how different networks are from footpaths in the mountains.

In speaking of the fourfold of earth and sky, gods and mortals, rather than the twofold of *Dasein* and Being, later Heidegger was trying to move beyond the problematic dualism involved in the duality of the ontological difference between beings and Being. Though later Heidegger spoke of the event of appropriation (*Ereignis*), whereby mortal *Dasein* is appropriated (*vereignet*) as one of the interdependent elements in the fourfold, early Heidegger spoke of authenticity quite differently. In *Sein und Zeit*, he defined authenticity in terms of individual *Dasein*'s resolve to own (*eignen*) its own mortal openness. For the most part, *Dasein* is absorbed in they-self's inauthentic and/or everyday understanding of Being. I say "and/or" because there are at least two aspects to the they-self, the everyday aspect and the inauthentic aspect, between which Heidegger himself never adequately distinguishes.[21] The everyday aspect involves a culture's taken-for-granted way of understanding humanity, nature, society, and the meaning of life, as well as the practices that both manifest and help to shape such understanding. In heeding the call of conscience, *Dasein* surrenders to its radical finitude and to the world-collapsing experience of *Angst*. Although authentic *Dasein* becomes profoundly aware of the limits of such practices and modes of understanding, authenticity cannot involve total abandonment of them, but instead renewed and deepened appropriation of them. This becomes clear in the chapters on historicality and destiny, in which Heidegger asserts that authentic *Dasein* does not make arbitrary choices, but rather chooses to reappropriate (*wiederholen*) the possibilities of its *own* heritage, understood as the destiny that establishes from the very beginning the possibilities for the future.

For modern *Dasein*, one of these practices includes interpreting oneself as an egoic personality to be distinguished sharply from others, precisely because there is so little difference among individuals. Heidegger suggests that most cultural practices serve to guarantee survival, not only by making possible the production and distribution of material goods, but also by making possible a façade that conceals the truth about each *Dasein's* mortality. Hence, *Dasein* says to itself, "one" (*das Man*) dies, not I myself. In referring to Leo Tolstoy's short story, "The Death of Ivan Ilych," however, Heidegger meant to underline the experiential, not-to-be-outstripped, individual dimension of mortality.[22] When the mood of *Angst* arises, it offers *Dasein* the opportunity to experience its mortal openness in a way unimpeded by the seductive attitudes of "the they." Surrendering to *Angst* involves undergoing a virtual death experience, involving the annihilation of one's possibilities as well as the ordinary egoic self to whom such possibilities seem to belong. Temporarily obliterating egoic subjectivity, *Angst* reveals that *Dasein* cannot be reduced to the status of thing, rational animal, or person, but instead exists as what I will call the *transpersonal* clearing in which entities can be manifest. In the clarity afforded by such transpersonal experience, *Dasein* can choose the possibilities that matter most, rather than allowing itself to be ensnared by distractions, including the postmodern kind which seem to be high tech variants of the distractions that Kierkegaard described in *The Present Age* (a work to which *Sein und Zeit* is profoundly indebted).

Criticizing Kierkegaard and Rilke because their talk of cultivating "inwardness" was linked to metaphysical subjectivism, Heidegger nevertheless appreciated the *phenomenon* toward which "inwardness" was pointing. The phenomenon involves that which is of ultimate worth, namely, the finite clearing or openness in which things can manifest themselves and thus "be." The loss of this clearing would be greater—according to Heidegger—than the destruction of the planet by nuclear war. Dim remnants of this extraordinary phenomenon are discernible in the driver's insight into the difference between worlds while driving across the interstate bridge. Instead of a startling epiphany that reveals the extent to which one's mortal openness has been dispersed in the multiple affairs of *das Man*, however, the driver recognizes that not every technological option can be pursued, and that each world is finite, despite its pretensions to the contrary. For resolute *Dasein*, in contrast, disclosure of mortality reveals an essential truth about human existence, a truth that alters one's experience, even if not its specific *contents*. Resolute *Dasein* affirms its own mortal openness, takes a stand upon its own nothingness, thereby requiring *Dasein* to choose one possibility rather than another.

For the driver on the interstate highway, recognition of limits may lead her to appreciate the importance and fragility of local practices, although no insight about human existence necessarily follows from this. In the technological age, the gods have departed, the sky has been effaced, the earth has been exposed to ruin, and the mortals have forgotten who they are; in short, the world has become an unworld. In such an age, perhaps even the slightest recollection of mortality is to be acknowledged and encouraged, especially insofar as it helps to reveal that the hegemonic technological disclosure of entities is not the *only* possible disclosure. Moreover, in such a world, perhaps authenticity could amount to little more than the integrity needed to make successful transitions from one world to the next, especially in worlds that involve overlapping practices. If this is what "authenticity" amounts to in the postmodern age, however, it is a faded image of early Heidegger's robust conception of authenticity, and Kierkegaard's notion that "purity of heart" meant choosing *one* thing. Indeed, one could argue that some versions of postmodern poly-identity resemble the "rotation method" used by the aesthete in Kierkegaard's pseudonymous work, *Either/Or*, to avoid being a specific individual and thus to evade the overarching question of the meaning of his mortal existence.

In one of the widely circulated *samizdat* versions of the text that he later published as *Being-in-the-World*, Dreyfus pointed out that

Kierkegaard would have looked askance at someone pursuing a multitude of practices such as Zen, yoga, martial arts, Christian silent prayer, Hindu meditation, and so on. For Kierkegaard, as well as for Dreyfus several years ago, such a "person" would be dispersing himself or herself in ways that would have made authentic existence impossible. Likewise, early Heidegger would probably have said that someone existing as a poly-identity was falling into inauthenticity, seized by ambiguity and curiosity which conceal the individual's finitude and mortality. In contrast, authentic *Dasein* resolves upon, that is, becomes attuned to the limited possibilities of, its own situation.

To be sure, later Heidegger distanced himself from his earlier account of authenticity, in part because of its voluntarism and subjectivism. Indeed, critics have sometimes argued that *Sein und Zeit*'s account of subjectivity and its attendant anxiety described bourgeois, individualistic subjectivity. I would interpret the matter rather differently. As an "unpolitical" (that is, antiliberal) German, early Heidegger was already a critic of bourgeois subjectivity. Nevertheless, he implicitly recognized that death-anxiety can assume its characteristic force only because each *Dasein* is capable of recognizing that it cannot be totally reduced to being a member of the family or cultural herd. Everyday life practices have the disburdening and soothing effect of covering up the unwelcome awareness of personal separateness, the fact of which reminds individuals of their mortality. The role played by *Angst* is to remove the concealments that prevent one from seeing *not* that one is an ego-subject (for "everyone" already knows that oneself is an ego!), but rather from seeing that one is this particular, finite, mortal openness that includes but *transcends* the ego-subject. In other words, were one not always already something like an ego-subject, an individual, a rational agent, a competent adult, death anxiety could not occur in a way that could make possible the choice for authenticity. One must first *be* an ordinary egoic subject before existing authentically as the transpersonal clearing, within which something like "personhood" can manifest itself. In other words, before one can become "no one," one must first be "some one." Recognizing the constructed nature of the egoic subject is possible only insofar as such a subject has been *constructed* in the first place.

Sein und Zeit's depiction of authentic *Dasein* combines certain elements of Gergen's modernist and romantic sense of selfhood. Authentic *Dasein* seeks to recover the forgotten dimension of human existence as the clearing, but also seeks to become integrated (whole, owned) by standing within and existing as the truth of its own mortal openness, rather than allowing itself to be dispersed endlessly into the distracting affairs of everyday life. Although authenticity involves self-integration characterized by choosing one possibility while forsaking others, the integrity of authenticity transcends the integrity achieved by the normal bourgeois individual, whose sense of personhood is largely defined by taken-for-granted cultural assumptions. Early Heidegger's concept of authenticity may be best understood as transpersonal existence, that is, a mode of openness that includes but goes beyond the limits of personal existence. As we shall see, the phenomenon of transpersonal existence may shed light on contemporary changes in human existence.

Dreyfus/Spinosa, however, turn to later Heidegger for help in understanding what authenticity/integrity might be like for a postmodern human who ostensibly no longer identifies with any particular metaphysical foundation, nation state, religion, ethnicity, or personal attributes, but instead inhabits a number of competing and even contradictory positions, while recognizing some value in each. In contrast with some celebrants of postmodern poly-identities, however, Dreyfus/Spinosa recognize the *drawbacks* involved in efforts to engage in virtually infinite self-morphing. Struggling with the issues posed by the "death of the subject," Dreyfus/Spinosa rightly recognize that some measure of integrity, coherence, or congruity is necessary on the part of individuals engaged in a multitude of diverse roles and practices. In my opinion, however, the gathering accomplished by "things" is insufficient to provide such congruity. Even in the ancient Greek world, encounters with gods were experienced in terms of complex *narratives* that explained the origins of, relations among, capacities/personalities of, and human duties to the gods. Such narratives, in other words, enabled a person to situate himself and others within the cosmos and to interpret in a relatively coherent manner all sorts of experiences and events. The meanings of events, in other words, were made explicit through narratives with cosmological import. It seems doubtful to me that Heidegger's narrative of the fourfold can orient people in today's increasingly complex world.

In *The Self after Postmodernity*, which addresses some of the same issues of disintegration of self that are discussed by Gergen and Dreyfus/Spinosa, Calvin Schrag offers some useful suggestions for understanding how narrative can help to provide coherence, orientation, and relative integration for the contemporary "self." Instead of the metaphor of practices preferred by Dreyfus/Spinosa, however, Schrag uses metaphors of discourse, narrative, and language games. Anticipating postmodernist concerns that talk of presence or integrity indicates onto-logo-egocentrism, Shrag insists that the "who" of discourse is not a thing, zero point, ghost in the machine, or foundational substratum, but instead

an achievement, an accomplishment, a performance, whose presence to itself is admittedly fragile, subject to forgetfulness and semantic ambiguities. But in all this there is still a unity and a species of self-identity, secured not by an abiding substratum but rather by an achieved self-identity, acquired through a transversal extending over and lying across the multiple forms of speech and language games without coincidence with any one of them. This transversal dynamics, effecting a convergence without coincidence, defines the unity, presence, and identity of the self. And they are a unity, presence, and identity that are concretely manifest in narration, in the telling of the story by the who of discourse, emplotting the multiple and changing episodes of her or his communicative endeavors.[23]

Schrag maintains that a narratival agency is needed to make sense of the manifold practices in which one is engaged. Making sense involves, at least in part, assigning priorities both to one's daily affairs and to long-term plans. A person can navigate in and between many different worlds, in part because she has already made some important decisions about her "identity," even if such decisions are not fixed. For example, even an allegedly postmodern morpher will presumably assign special importance to practices associated with earning a living. Noted authors who proclaim the end of the subject do not hesitate to affix their names to their own writings, nor do they decline to accept royalty checks made out to the person named as the author of those writings. Even someone thoroughly conversant with modern technological practices and opportunities may identify himself primarily as a father, as a corporate leader, as a lover, or as an artist, even while taking on identities in worlds that may overlap very little with the world in which the primary identification is found. One does not have to conceive of oneself *exclusively* as playing a role or as having a particular identity, but without some provisional identifications and without narratives that can provide orientation while moving between and through various worlds, people would either not be able to function very well socially, would report feeling confused or pointless, or would regress to a pre-egoic state with its attendant problems.

Arguably, those who effectively and satisfyingly inhabit different worlds have developed a workable narrative of personal connectivity made possible by their having *already* developed a relatively stable and integrated egoic subjectivity concerned with sincerity, truthfulness, and integrity. Such a narrative would need to transform the modern egoic ideal of integrity in a way that recognizes new opportunities for individual achievement and social contribution made possible by technologies that enable one to inhabit more subject positions than possible in the past. Though perhaps now recognizing the limitations of terms such as integrity, truthfulness, and sincerity, and thus resorting to locutions like "virtual" integrity, the competent postmodern would recognize the value—and perhaps even the necessity—of having been raised with the ideal of *attempting* to be truthful and sincere, before subsequently moving on to a more ironic mode of existence, characterized by inhabiting perspectives that are not always reconcilable with one another.

Here, I wish to observe that leaving behind egoic subjectivity can involve moving in one of two very different directions. On the one hand, a person may *regress* to the level of pre-egoic subjectivity, in which case he or she may become completely opportunistic, scheming, pathologically lying, always seeking to maximize possibilities for satisfying desire, at the expense of others. Some postmodern morphers may well be prone to such regression. Moreover, the malaise reported by some people exploring multiple worlds may have something to do with a perceived loss of ordinary integrity, truthfulness, and personal reality. On the other hand, a person may progress to the level of transpersonal existence, which involves *incorporating* the constructive achievements of personal subjectivity, including integrity and sincerity, while *transcending* its limitations, including being overly identified with one's personality, possessions, race, gender, national origins, and so on. Expanding that with which one identifies, an expansion made possible by acknowledging that one is mortal openness or nothingness, usually brings with it an increase in compassion and thus a growing concern to participate in improving social conditions of one's various communities.

Using the term the "pre/trans fallacy," Ken Wilber has very usefully described the difference between regressing to prepersonal existence, on the one hand, and progressing to transpersonal existence, on the other.[24] Calling on the work of a number of developmental and social psychologists, Wilber argues that the emergence of something akin to egoic subjectivity (not necessarily of the Anglo-American variety, to be sure) is the culminating point of normal adulthood in recent societies.[25] He goes on to argue, however, that there are higher, more integrated, *transpersonal* modes of awareness that lie beyond the stage of egoic personhood. Sustained practice of these stages is difficult, just as attaining and sustaining responsible adulthood proves to be difficult for adolescents. In Wilber's view, increasing numbers of people are exploring transpersonal awareness that both builds on and transcends the achievements of egoic selfhood, but new information technologies and multiple cultural options—in and of themselves—cannot generate transpersonal awareness of this kind. Engaging in many different practices is not evidence for transpersonal existence, either in Wilber's sense or in the relatively "integrated" mode of selfhood described by Dreyfus/Spinosa. As Scott Bukataman and Claudia Springer have noted, even postmodern writers and filmmakers find it difficult to describe the "virtual subject" or "morpher" without referring to the gendered, egoic personality structure.[26] On the other hand, far from generating a more inclusive, robust, and satisfying way of life, contemporary exaggeration about post-egoic subjectivity, the end of authenticity, and personality morphing, may encourage some people to regress to pre-egoic personality states, and may prevent others from ever attaining an adequate egoic personality in the first place (in the case of children and adolescents growing up in a world in which integrity, sincerity, and self-consistency are not fostered). How could such half-baked egos *avoid* becoming flexible raw material, precisely in the way warned against by Heidegger? Could they *really* be expected to make the far-seeing differentiation between "serious" local practices and the more all-encompassing technological practices of (post)modern morphing? Dreyfus/Spinosa are aware of the seriousness of such questions.

In addition to integrative personal narratives that orient a person attempting to navigate through different worlds, I am convinced that people need cultural narratives that attempt to make sense of humanity's origins and destiny. In my view, however, cultural narrative drawing on Heidegger's talk of the fourfold and the return of the gods is not adequate to the contemporary situation. For one thing, he was such a staunch adversary of modernity that he could not appreciate its positive political achievements, many aspects of which deserve to be defended even as changes in human practices and modes of awareness arise in postmodernity. Moreover, I am concerned about the political implications of the notion that a polytheistic world, like that of the ancient Greeks, would simply be *different* from that of the modern world, not inferior to it. I am more sympathetic toward Wilber's developmental narrative, according to which modernity's ideal of rational autonomy is an important achievement, despite its several unfortunate consequences, including ecological crisis, marginalization of difference, denial of "interior depth" or "subjectivity," overreliance on scientific modes of truth, and so on.

Wilber emphasizes the difficulties facing those who try practicing a genuinely multicultural, "aperspectival" mode of awareness, that is, those who adopt various identities while recognizing the limitations of each of them.[27] Not everyone is prepared to undertake successfully such a practice, which requires suspension of the notion of a substantial ego. Existentialists reported experiencing *Angst* and nihilism when confronted both with their own mortality, and with the meaninglessness of any particular cultural position, including their native one. Anxiety remains a widely reported phenomenon, perhaps especially among those coping with proliferating possibilities of moving among personal identities. Although asserting that anxiety cannot be avoided, indeed, must be embraced, Wilber maintains that nihilism can be averted through a developmental narrative. According to this narrative, the postsubjective, aperspectival, transpersonal mode of awareness does not render null and void egoic consciousness and its supporting institutions, but rather represents a *further* stage in the development of humankind, a stage that builds on and presupposes the achievements of the prior stage, that is, egoic subjectivity.

Wilber's narrative, then, unlike a number of alternative accounts of postmodernity, emphasizes the *dignity* of modernity.[28] He notes that only by taking seriously the claims of modernity, namely, that all persons are of equal worth, can once-oppressed peoples today assert their own validity and worth, both as individual persons and as members of once-despised peoples. Moreover, only by taking seriously the claims of modernity did First World intellectuals finally listen to Third World peoples and engage in a searching examination of the extent to which colonialism represented oppression of others in the name of their liberation. Postmodernity, then, must include the practical truth of "universal worth of the individual person," even while questioning both the foundationalism on which such universality is "grounded," and the nature of personhood itself.

Following Weber, Habermas, and others, Wilber argues that one of modernity's crucial achievements was the separation of the spheres of morality, science, and art in a way that made possible such achievements as democratic politics and free scientific inquiry. Just as modernity goes too far by *dissociating* rationality from the body/emotions rather than *differentiating* between them, however, postmodernity goes too far by dissociating spirit from the cosmos rather than by differentiating among the levels of matter-energy, rational consciousness, and spirit. Most postmodernists have declined to acknowledge spirit, much less reintegrate it into the cosmos, even though they affirm the importance of reintegrating other domains that have been marginalized and/or dissociated by modernists, including the body, females, emotions, peoples of non-European descent, and even nature itself. Dreyfus/Spinosa, however, at least mention that the quiet interior of a church can "solicit meditativeness," thereby enabling us to "manifest and become centered in whatever reverential practices remain in our post-Christian way of life."[29] Moreover, Dreyfus/Spinosa's spiritual interests are discernible in their effort to make contemporary sense of Heidegger's notion of blessings, grace, and gods. They are concerned, however, that Albert Borgmann's interest in religion involves a problematic yearning for unifying diverse perspectives and local practices. Clearly, then, Dreyfus/Spinosa would have reservations about Wilber's grand narrative, which attempts to provide a coherent narrative of much of human existence, past and future.

There is not time here to explain in detail Wilber's effort to describe Spirit not only as the cosmic and social evolutionary processes through which Spirit comes to self-awareness, but also as the all-pervasive, nondual, infinite context in which can occur both the process of constructing metaphysical foundations and the process of deconstructing them. The evolutionary conception of Spirit makes sense of and endorses a progressive account of human history, while simultaneously making possible a criticism of the totalizing claims of such accounts. Hence, deconstructionists are right in saying that they have discovered a larger context which undermines the foundational claims of Enlightenment modernity, but according to Wilber, Spirit constitutes the *infinite* context beyond which no deconstructive scheme can get. Whether Hegel would be right in describing this as a "bad infinity" is a question well worth examining, but not in this essay. Wilber's point, however successfully he can defend it, is that postmodernism does not have to lead to despair and nihilism, but instead can affirm that the death of the meta-physical God makes way for recognition of Spirit as groundless ground, as the infinite context in which the play of all phenomena occurs. According to Buddhism, recognition that all phenomena are empty of self or substance, that is, realization that all phenomena are totally interdependent and arise simultaneously in an infinite context, leads to compassion for all beings, rather than to despair and nihilism.

Whether or not one adopts Wilber's narrative, analogous narratives are needed to help people integrate their personal lives, and to interpret human history and destiny.[30] Wilber helps to make sense of what Gergen describes as "serious play," that is, engaging in practices that today have been "outcontextualized." Cultural practices and narratives that foster responsible, sincere, passionate people aware of spiritual depth are "serious" not because those practices and narratives are "true" or "ultimate," but rather because without them people cannot move on to a transpersonal mode of being-in-the-world. Encouraging relatively individuating, truth-telling, depth-conscious practices and narratives on the part of young people enables them (a) to develop an egoic self that can be sublated when a more comprehensive, transpersonal mode of awareness arises, and (b) to avoid regression when faced with multiple options in multiple worlds.

Arguably, then, there is an end—a goal, a purpose—to authenticity even in the postmodern age, even though many postmodernists proclaim the end—the termination, the vacuity—of such authenticity. The experience of mortal openness made possible by surrender to anxiety characterizes genuine transpersonal awareness, as opposed to aimless postmodern morphing. Achieving and consolidating such transpersonal awareness are difficult matters, as is evidenced by those who engage in a performative contradiction by using multiculturalism as a club with which to beat those who do not share the multicultural perspective! People should be encouraged to aspire to post-egoic, postmodern, multicultural, aperspectival awareness, but only with the proviso that they *first* master the difficult task of being responsible agents and egoic subjects, for whom *there is* something like "truth," something like "sincerity," something like "subjective depth," something like "integrity," something like "Spirit," something like "Nature." If postmodern morphing occurs on a wide scale outside of contexts in which sincerity, subjective depth, and authenticity are encouraged and achieved, I believe there is reason to be concerned about the outcome for individuals and society. People may indeed become nothing but flexible raw material drawn into the interconnective matrix of all-consuming technological systems, the perimeters of which are scarcely even imaginable.[31]

7

"The End of Metaphysics" and "A New Beginning"

Michel Haar

Translated by David E. Bohn

In a brilliant essay on nihilism according to Heidegger, Hubert Dreyfus writes: "Our technological clearing is the cause of our distress. . . . [The] transformation in our understanding of being . . . would take place in a sudden gestalt switch."[1] But how could our epoch change entirely and give place to a new *Geschick*? On the contrary, "the absence of distress (*die Notlosigkeit*) is the highest and most hidden distress."[2] If the major principles of metaphysics (identity, noncontradiction, etc.) and of rationality have now become actual and all-encompassing in technological reality, then it is also the case that a project of unlimited-calculation, led by nobody in particular, has come to encompass the entire planet. It seems, then, that the "end of metaphysics" consists not in its disappearance, but in its complete dominance.

The notion of "the end of metaphysics" occupies a rather cardinal position in Heidegger's thought on history. Actually, it serves as a hinge or linchpin for interpreting the passage from the era dominated by metaphysics to the epoch where metaphysics fades away as doctrine at the same time as its principles are concretely realized, that is to say, the epoch of technology. Such a realization is yet to come, because if technology is "metaphysics completed," the concrete effect of this completion, that is, the passage from principles to their practical realization, is not reducible to the principles themselves. It is new, unforeseeable, and has nothing to do with déjà vu. We still do not know what the completion of the metaphysics of tech-

nology has in store for us. We can hardly imagine what "unconditioned domination" or "total mobilization" will bring about. It is only
beginning. It belongs to the future.[66] The epoch of completed metaphysics stands before its beginning."[3] All we know is that its deployment will be powerful, irresistible, and that it will assume the
metaphysical form of the "will to will" that governs the essence of
technology and permits the giving of accounts of numerous phenomena that we have already before our eyes. Now, to orient ourselves, a completion of facts requires a completion of principles. This
completion that is retrospective by contrast to that of the technical
which is prospective, functions in Nietzsche's philosophy by recapit-
ulating, completing and perfecting all previous major metaphysical
positions. We know that Heidegger read Nietzsche as "the last metaphysician."[4] He is the last one in the sense that he removes from the
metaphysical all new possibilities of development and mutation, and
does so by submitting it to a final triple reversal. For it is true that
Nietzsche not only overturns Platonism, but also Cartesianism and
Hegelianism. These three reversals not only present the same structure, but the same content. In each case, the body and the sensible
take the place of the intelligible in Plato, Descartes, and Hegel. What
is then the specific contribution of each of these three reversals? We
shall try to define them more precisely. In any case, Heidegger's
essential argument is that this inversion does not sustain the metaphysical difference that it reverses from inside out. It inserts in each
case, an *ontological indifference*, a *levelling*. It is this equalizing that
will, in turn, make possible the unleashing of the will to will. These
reversals carried out by Nietzsche would produce the new nihilism
that constitutes the end of metaphysics in which the traditional
fundamental distinctions: essence/existence, soul/body, universal/
singular are erased, neutralized and equalized. The equalization
or levelling that results from the abolition of these distinctions—the
ideological nihilism—would serve more exactly as a basis for a technological nihilism.

I Reversal and Levelling: How Nihilism Gets Included in the Logic of Overthrowal

For the young Nietzsche, inverting Platonism first signifies a mere inversion of the *relation* of the true to the apparent world. The true world is to be escaped, pushed aside. Appearance is to be pursued. A famous although rarely fully cited aphorism attests that: "My philosophy is *Platonism reversed.* The more one removes oneself from true being (*wahrhaft Seiende*), having life in appearance as end, the purer, the more beautiful, the better it will be."[5] At first glance, the doctrine of two worlds is thus conserved intact. The sensible is exalted, the intelligible, the ideal, depreciated. However, as Nietzsche pursues his reflection as much on the level of the ideal as the sensible and "appearance," it seems increasingly clear that this famous dichotomy cannot issue intact from the reversal. Appearance rethought is no longer the opposite of an essence, nor is it the contrary of anything at all: "I do not pit 'appearance' up against 'reality.' To the contrary, I consider that appearance is reality: that which resists all transformations toward an imaginary 'true world.' "[6] But this imaginary true world is itself an appearance. Thus all being, everything, every idea is appearance in the sense of an imposition of meaning produced by the will to power. Appearance is a thing seen from a certain point of view. This is why it is necessary to eliminate all dualisms and affirm the unicity of the world. There is this world here and no other. "The antinomy of the true and apparent worlds, noted in a fragment of 1888, leads to the antinomy of 'world' and *nothingness.*" "The word 'appearance,' " the later Nietzsche will also state, "is an unhappy— 'fatal' (*verhängnisvoll*)—word."[7] "Ultimately," he says, "there is no longer here the slightest reason to speak again of appearance." The theme of "generalized appearance" is, nevertheless, often developed as for example in "Consciousness of Appearance" in *The Gay Science* §54.

Does this theme as Heidegger asserts correspond to a *nihilistic equalization,* preparing the way for technological nihilism? Such would be the unthought of the reversal. However, if one holds to what Nietzsche explicitly states, there is nothing to it, since for him, there is doubtlessly a hierarchy of *appearances* established by the will to power; hence artistic appearance, the most "stimulating" for life, will be preferred to another appearance, that which is everywhere the same for everyone, that of science. Still, Heidegger struggles to show that even if the Nietzschean reversal does not establish, it at least prefers, the "blindly inflexible and superficial."[8] Moreover, he considers that this levelling or making superficial has already been acquired in the last philosophical works of Nietzsche. He writes: "*All that is left is the solitary superficies of a 'life' that empowers itself to itself for its own sake.* If metaphysics begins as an explicit interpretation of beingness as *idea*, it achieves its uttermost end in the 'revaluation of all values.' The solitary superficies is what *remains after* the abolition of the 'true' *and* the 'semblant' worlds. It appears as the selfsame of eternal recurrence of the same and will to power."[9]

In this there is a sort of sophism on the part of Heidegger. The fact that all phenomena get reduced to will to power and that all being gets thought of in terms of values does not mean that there is but one sole level. Nevertheless, in Heidegger's lecture the consequence of the reversal is the elimination of the distinction between essence and existence—being and becoming. Thus, when he defines the Eternal Return as "the most extreme reconciliation of a world of becoming with that of being," or as the act of " inscribing the mark of being on the becoming," Nietzsche obviously takes advantage of this distinction while attempting to attenuate it to the maximum. The Eternal Return should make the becoming as solid and consistent as being. It seems difficult to accept Heidegger's analysis according to which the Nietzschean reversal "extinguish[es] . . . the opposition of Being and Becoming,"[10] or again "the very distinction between what-being and that-being is shunted aside."[11] By affirming that the Eternal Return is but a perspective, Nietzsche in fact affirms that the point of view of being about becoming—its constancy—is but an appearance. In any case, he obviously maintains categories. Yet Heidegger considers that the elimination of the distinction has been acquired, and this annulling of the metaphysical difference leaves the field free to "the complete absence of meaning," since everything finds itself equalized, declared to conform equally to life.

Is the analysis of Descartes, extensively developed in chapter V of "The Eternal Recurrence of the Same and the Will to Power,"[12] any more convincing? Nietzsche deliberately reverses Descartes's position when he writes: "Belief in the *body* is more fundamental than belief in the soul,"[13] or again: "the phenomenon of the body is the richer, clearer, more tangible phenomenon; to be discussed first, methodologically, without coming to any decision about its ultimate significance."[14] In this reversal, the Cartesian primacy of method is maintained. Yet Heidegger points out that a double and coordinated process of levelling is at work: the suppression of the distinction of true and false and the reduction of ideas to affects. Rather than certainty bearing on the evident and true, humankind becomes absolute master of *every perspective*, with the only condition that they want it and that it corresponds with their feelings and desires. Nietzsche eliminates the agreement of knowledge with things and the real to replace it with an agreement with *the growth of power*. Heidegger cites and analyzes numerous fragments that move in this direction: "Objectivity is . . . the faculty to hold in our power the *for* and the *against*."[15] Objectivity is replaced by absolute subjectivity: "The more affects, the more perspectives on a thing . . . the more integrated . . . will be our objectivity."[16] The will to truth, the Cartesian will not to be deceived comes back to a will to power that provides itself a feeling of self-assurance: "I do not want to be deceived" means "I want to be convinced and affirmed."[17] What counts for Heidegger here is the equalization of true and false that appears, for instance, in the famous fragment: "Truth is the kind of error without which a certain species of life could not live."[18] The distinction of the truth and the non-true gets erased in the play of perspectives of power. There is a reversal of Descartes in the measure that the assurance of the false, in other words, of any appearance however useful or advantageous, becomes the only rule. Now there is a levelling for Nietzsche in the sense that the essence of the truth becomes "justice" itself, thought as *agreement* among perspectives and values on the one hand and the sustaining and growth of power on the other. There is levelling and nihilism in the sense that all evaluations are "just," that is to say, express an advantage for the will to power. Here too, it would seem that we can make the same criticism as earlier: is there truly a levelling, since for Nietzsche "justice" is the principle that serves to establish a new hierarchy?

In any case, the body as source and site of affects becomes the unique measure, unique plane, where meaning is decided: there are no longer facts or ideas, Heidegger writes, "'but only our world of desires and passions' as the only definitive 'reality.'"[19] In effect, Nietzsche interprets thoughts as *signs* of the play and combat of affects. Heidegger endeavors to show that this return to the body as the site of unconditioned power secures for Nietzschean subjectivity the absolute mastery of itself as well as of the world in the same way as in the Cartesian project to the degree that the world is redefined and reconstructed in the image of our needs, of our desires, and of our affects. If there is, however, a relativizing of ideas in relationship to affects, and even a complete dependence of ideas in relationship to feelings ("Thoughts are the shadows of our feelings—always darker, emptier, and simpler."[20]), like the true in relation to the false, it does seem exaggerated to say that such distinctions are purely and simply *abolished* by the reversal.

It is in his analysis of the *Overman* that Heidegger develops the idea of an inversion of Hegel. Such a reversal by contrast to the previous two is not thematized by Nietzsche, who rarely speaks of Hegel and not always disapprovingly. The *Overman* would be a new form of absolute subjectivity, no more of reason but of body or as Heidegger curiously says, of *animality*: "the nihilistic negation of reason does not exclude thought (*ratio*); rather, it relegates thought to the service of animality (*animalitas*)."[21] This primacy of the animality of the *Overman* is strange in this interpretation since the *Overman* is above all defined by Nietzsche as the man who is capable of reuniting in itself all of the traits previously separated from the poet, the savant, the lover, the thinker. Also, it is curious that Heidegger prefers to speak of *animality* rather than corporeality, and he will go as far as to say that what characterizes the *Overman* is "brutality" and even "bestiality"![22] "Caesar with the soul of Christ": bestial? In any case, the *Overman* introduces a subjectivity just as absolute as that of Hegel's absolute knowledge, a subjectivity entirely revalued beginning with the body thought as "high reason." The absolute subject of Hegel would still be "incomplete" because it is content to sublimate sensible certainty in the universal, while the will to power affirms unconditionally the drives as tamed and organized chaos. To this point, one does not see what the inversion of Hegel adds to that of Descartes, other than in regard to the reversal of Descartes, Heidegger only describes the preferencing of the body and not animality. Here he writes: "The firm metaphysical definition of man as animal signifies the nihilistic affirmation of overman."[23] He explains by demonstrating that the *Overman* implies a "dehumanization," through which one comes back to a "naked nature," "chaos" and thus an animality that produces an outstripping of existing humankind. The original dimension that an inversed Hegel adds is that of totality.[66] "The mastery of chaos by the new valuation is brought under the law of the totality through the valuation itself, every human role in establishing the new order must in itself bear the mark of distinction of totality."[24] The inversion of the totality of the subject conceived as world history is the totality of the subject conceived as the singular. This singularity of the *Overman* is, however, a collective singularity, that is a type. "Nihilistically inverted man *is* for the first time man as *type.*"[25] The *Overman* is not an individual, but a new type that should extend to all humanity! "The greatness of the overman, who does not know the fruitless isolation of one who is a mere exception."[26] Of course, this interpretation is in contradiction with the letter and spirit of Nietzsche's texts since for him the *Overman* is above all an exceptionally creative individual, while the great majority of humanity remains locked in the stage of The Last Man whose breed he says cannot be eradicated. To create a false opening for this triple overturning, Heidegger Hegelianizes Nietzsche by universalizing the idea of the *Overman* and affirming it to be the *particular casting* that would mark, henceforth, all of humanity. "The overman is the casting of that mankind which first of all *wills* itself *as* a casting and even casts itself as such casting."[27] This "casting" would be the prefiguration of the type (or category) of technocrat. However, in the idea of the casting of a type, the distinction of the individual and the universal would vanish. This would be both a particular model and an altogether new humanity.

In this way one would have successively erased the three major oppositions of metaphysics: essence/existence, soul/body, and individual/universal. This erasure initiates the decline of metaphysics as doctrine, while bringing it into effect in reality, in the measure that technology will be able to function in the speculative mode of the absence of an end or in a circular way. The functioning of technology demands, in effect, a turning back on itself, in the absence of attainable ideals or idealities. Its principle is: *what is doable ought to be done for the sole reason that it is doable. Or: all of the real is doable-makeable.* The important principle derived from the unthought of Nietzsche that rules technology, we already know, is *the will to will.* Now, for this principle to function as perfectly circularity, in the tautology that it articulates, that being as totality would have already been levelled and reduced to metaphysical indifference. Paradoxically, the completion of metaphysics happens on the basis of this indifference.

II The Effective Structures of the Will to Will: Nihilism in Action in the World of Technology

The will to will is not the will to power that continuously projects values, advances the arts, and invents the *Overman.* It is the unthought of the will to power, that is, its implicitly circular and tautological structure. This is because beyond the values it advances what the will to power unconditionally wants is its own conservation and growth. Indeed, it only advances values for this reason. It will "cynically" abandon this or that value if it can obtain its objective more easily, more completely or in another way. The true end is not values, but will that wants itself as will in preference to every value. There is the circularity, an absence of ends that remains unthought. Heidegger shows how this self-affirmation of will as pure form independent of all content is already present in Kant. "Pure will is the sole content for itself as form."[28] In "Nietzsche's Metaphysics" (*Nietzsche* vol. 3, 185–251), Heidegger describes the will to power, surrounded by the calculated circle of its values, as pure self-positioning, detached from all horizons and all rootedness. The will to power is already a sort of purely self-referring and self-regulating cybernetic machine. "In reckoning with values and in estimating according to relations of value, will to power reckons with itself."[29] This idea of a calculation that only counts with itself characterizes the unthought of the Nietzschean will.

But the will to will is not reducible to this unthought of the will to power. The exclusion of every end in itself is but another of its still most important characteristics. The absence of ends makes all apparent ends nothing more than means in view of the pure exercise of force in the framework of a calculation that is in reality but a game. To hide the emptiness and the cynicism of this game in which planetary humans are always played by the will to will, they invent "missions" with most often noble and clearly "humanitarian" objectives.

In the very remarkable chapter in *Vorträge und Aufsätze* entitled "Overcoming Metaphysics," Heidegger describes the principles characteristic of the will to will. These characteristics that are the temporary form of nihilism that is the errancy (or the retrieval of the forgottenness of being) are three in number: *the planning* or equipment, *use*, and *uniformity* to which can be added *the absence of distress* or "the distress of the absence of distress" that marks the general climate or *Stimmung* (mood) of the epoch and consists of an incapacity to gain access to genuine questions. (It is the "no problem" generalized, here everything is "bathing in oil.")

Planning is only the most obvious form of the *equipment* of reality. "Equipment" (*Rüstung* which also means armaments) consists in the systematic organization of all the domains of Being, "objectified nature, the business of culture, manufactured politics, and the gloss of ideals overlying everything."[30] Planning applies to all sectors of collective activity: science, production, consumption, commerce, and demography, and necessitates in its turn a bureaucracy, the establishment of state control and state management. It involves cutting the real up into sectors susceptible of being ordered and regulated with an eye toward what only seems to obey a rational organizational imperative. To the contrary, it obeys out of fear of the void, out of the horror of the emptiness of circumstance. Whatever the case, the landscape must be occupied, exploited, and circumstance already filled. In all totalitarian regimes, planning has not spared the domain of culture. For Heidegger, totalitarian regimes are a consequence of planning, and not the inverse. "The 'Führers' are the decisive suppliers who oversee all the sectors of the consumption of beings because they understand the *whole of those sectors* and thus master erring in its calculability."[31] This notion of circle, of circularity, is indispensable for characterizing the will to will. Here, it is the circle of the sectors of economic activity. Elsewhere, it is the circle of production and consumption that belongs to the essence of the *Gestelle*—the untranslatable word: "the hailing," the "apparatus," the "con-sumption." The energy is unflaggingly produced, accumulated, distributed, transformed, and consumed. There is growth in the speed and means of communication, the speed of production, and the speed of research for speed, itself, is a symptom of nihilism.

Consumption is a phenomenon determined by *equipment*. It characterizes the entire epoch that Heidegger calls "the age of consumption." Consumption has a very precise definition: it is the application of technology in the absence of any end. Consumption is not simply the use of raw materials which implies the exploitation of nature, or the utilization of objects, tools or items of consumption. It is a metaphysical process that applies as well to humankind and could be defined more precisely again as the pure imperative for industrial production and consumption. Likewise, humankind itself is a raw material that one ends up producing: "Since man is the most important raw material, one can reckon with the fact that some day factories will be built for the artificial breeding of human material, based on present-day chemical research."[32] Consumption is but a particular case of production and is inseparable from it. Both are marked by incessant quantitative growth. Mass consumption demands mass production, always increasing because "needs are always and everywhere less and less satisfied." This is not because in effect they are growing quantitatively, but because the will to will itself turns *aimlessly* faster and faster on itself. The augmentation of consumption takes its point of departure from the activism of the "movement of affairs" (*Betrieb*) created by the *emptiness of Being*, rather than by an insufficiency of products or raw materials in relationship to an overpopulation. It is not an objective poverty, but the lack that the generalization of planning itself produces, in the absence of any fundamental project on behalf of humanity. This lack gets translated into the absence of events, the absence of history—the uniformalization of all political, economic, and social processes. Heidegger writes, "This circularity of consumption for the sake of consumption is the sole procedure which distinctively characterizes the history of a world which has become an unworld."[33] The imperative of consumption for consumption is beyond the range of the decisions of individuals or political leaders. It is a trait of the being of beings. "The unconditional pressing of beings toward being used up in consumption."[34] We believe näively in humankind's power over nature, while actually it (humankind) is delivered over irresistibly to power, that is, to the absolute demands of production and consumption. It is "the epoch where power is alone powerful." Consumers have the impression of not being passive in consuming. It is because they participate in the absolute manufacturability that is the essence of consumption. They collaborate not only in the production, but in the producibility of all things, including that of humankind itself. This emptiness, this acceleration, this agitation, this absence of the experience of Being (which goes hand in hand with the inflation of the domain of lived experiences, cf. *Beiträge* §66: *Machenshaft und Erlebnis*) ends up by producing *uniformity*.

It is necessary to understand *uniformity* as more than a levelling of tastes, of tendencies, of opinions or ideas. In a way, it is the applied practice of suppressing metaphysical distinctions. This indifference extends to humankind and the world. Anthropologically, it is the suppression of the difference between drive and reason. This equalization between the most animal trait, that of instinct, and the most human trait, as we have noted—the unthought of the *Overman*— instinct and reason are the modes of calculation of that which is useful and detrimental. "The drive of animality and the *ratio* of humanity become *identical.*"[35] The technical human would be distinguished by the immediate driving character of its reason and the rational character of its instincts: a new Socratism! Another neutralization: no longer any difference between war and peace. Both are varieties of the consumption of being. Suppression also of differences in political regimes: "all forms of government are only one instrument of leadership among others."[36] We could add: suppression of the difference between public and private and of the boundary between rich and poor, employed and unemployed. This description of equalization brings to mind Nietzsche's description of the Last Man. "All will want the same thing, all will be equal. . . .

In the past, everyone was crazy. . . . Whoever will hold a different opinion will voluntarily enter an insane asylum." Heidegger seeks to show that uniformization is not the simple levelling of hierarchies. "The lack of differentiation of total consumption arises from a positive refusal of an order of rank in accordance with the guardianship of the emptiness of all goal-positing."[37] In other words, an order is no longer overturned to modify it, but because one no longer believes in any order. It is not that ancient hierarchies crumble, it is that we refuse to establish new ones.

III   The Problematic Character of the New Beginning

The idea of a "new beginning" and of an "other history" is in one sense evident and quasi-tautological. Completed metaphysics—no longer apparent as doctrine—will not be resurrected. "Metaphysics has become impossible."[38] Unless history stops, unless thought itself disappears (catastrophic hypothesis that Heidegger envisages occasionally as "the death of the essence of humanity"), there must certainly be a beyond to completion, another form of thought. Nevertheless, in another sense, the idea of a "new beginning" is anything but obvious. First because history completed in principle and having become a technological reality can continue *as such* indefinitely. Can there then be another thought in the future than that of the thought of being? It is unthinkable that it not consist of being, and if it always consists again of being, it is the History of Being that continues and that attaches itself to its past. How can we conceive of this new beginning? *Where* would it happen? In what space? Is it not "utopian," since the heritage of the first beginning, the Greek beginning, the technical, cannot be cleared away, evacuated, or made to quickly disappear? The hypothesis of a new beginning that would coincide with a world catastrophe is envisioned only one single time in the work of Heidegger. He still writes in *Overcoming Metaphysics*: "Before Being can occur in its primal truth, Being as the will must be broken, the world must be forced to collapse and the earth must be driven to desolation, and man to mere labor. Only after this decline does the abrupt dwelling of the Origin take place [*ereignet sich*] for a long span of time."[39] And, he adds that in the decline "everything ends," "the whole of the truth of metaphysics approaches its end."

In this extreme hypothesis, the other history would effectively be chronologically posterior. Most of the texts leave one to think that, on the contrary, the other history would be a *secret history, parallel* to that of the technical world which would follow its path without one being able to assign to it visible external events. This would be the secret history of the *Ereignis* that is rather outside of history, non-historical, or in any case outside of the epoch. The *Ereignis* is this event of thought by which such an elementary *constatation* appears as a momentary glimpse that humankind belongs to Being and Being belongs to humankind, that there is a coappropriation which is older than history and rules over all of its phases. It appears that the emergence of the *Ereignis* and of the new beginning depend on our own initiative, or at least in the texts of 1936–38 they arise out of a human decision: "We are standing before the decision between the end (and its running out, which may still take centuries) and *another beginning*, one which can only be a *moment*, but whose preparation requires the patience 'optimists' are no more capable of than 'pessimists.' "[40]

The essential term in this passage, a *moment*, belongs to the vocabulary of *Being and Time* where the moment (*Augenblick*) is, in contrast to a given now (*jetzt*), the moment of the resolute decision where temporality, reassembled into a project, both anticipates the extreme finitude of the future and takes up again the constancy of a possible past. A decision is possible only if we are authentically open to an extreme future and capable of repeating an essential past. Here the essential past is the first beginning, that of the Greeks. We must, says Heidegger, appropriate it for ourselves to put it behind ourselves, and prepare for the second beginning. One sees only at the level of choice that there is no rupture between the first and second beginning, but then how can we talk of another history? If the second beginning is a *choice*, as the *Beiträge* often says,[41] then for the person who chooses there had been a first beginning. The end and the new commencement coexist—are contemporary. In a passage of the *Beiträge*, this is the choice between perpetuating metaphysics completed and preparing another way that exists from the moment it is postulated. The choice is therefore between "either to remain prisoner of the end and its unfolding, that is, new metamorphoses of metaphysics that will become more and more crude and deprived of foundation and objective (the new biologism for example), or then, to begin the new beginning, in other words to be resolved to its long preparation."[42] The new beginning will only be after a rupture; it requires a leap (*Sprung*) toward something radically other that is not yet or has not yet place. At present, we are in the *passage* (*Übergang*) in the transition toward this—new—that he says is already acquired, but must be conquered, notably in the course of the long task of the destruction of metaphysics.

Posed otherwise, the problem is again the following: how can the technological era that is so deeply entrenched come to an end? As Heidegger's meditation deepens, in particular during the after-war years, the idea of a voluntarist passage (transition), the idea of this decisive leap, is more and more clearly rejected. No human decision can produce such a gigantic change as a movement beyond the technological. Nevertheless, this does not mean that humankind has no role in a possible planetary mutation. Thought can make itself attentive to the essence of technology, and from there hear and wait for some other dimension. "[W]hen we once open ourselves expressly to the *essence* of technology we find ourselves unexpectedly taken into a freeing call."[43] Note the passivity: we find ourselves claimed. A turning, the Turning certainly seems to be taking place at present through thought on the essence of technology rather than because of it. The turning situates itself here and now, and at the same time it belongs to a faraway future. "In-turning, as the bringing to pass of the turning about of oblivion, turns in into that which now is the epoch of Being."[44] It is given, and at the same time it is uncertain (the technological can last indefinitely), and in any case finds itself in an undetermined future.

Another of the new beginning's difficulties is the unforgettable character of the History of Being and the first beginning. In fact, Heidegger writes: "The leap into the other beginning is a return to the first and vice-versa."[45] It would seem to be then a direct tie between the two histories through the theme of the repetition and deconstruction of the history of metaphysics. Moreover, Heidegger writes: "The other beginning is not the opposing movement of the first, but situates itself *as other* outside of opposition and all possible immediate comparison."[46] There is a contradiction between the same and the other, between continuity and discontinuity that explains perhaps why the *Beiträge* has not been published and why Heidegger has always talked more about the Turning than an other history and a new beginning. And, if one finds several comments about the other beginning in the *Nietzsche* lectures (published in 1961 and essentially edited in 1941), it is with some ambiguity since it is thought here as *relatively other* as a taking up of and deepening of the first Greek beginning, sometimes *infinitely distant* in the future in relationship to our epoch.[47] Whatever the critical distance taken in regard to Nietzsche, it is striking to state that this theme of "another history" and the expression itself are borrowed from him whom Heidegger names as his "most intimate adversary" and with whom he expressly admits a *profound kinship*.[48] In *Ecce Homo*, Nietzsche says, in effect, that he wants "to break in two the history of humanity," or he writes, "[W]hat I relate is the history of the next two centuries"[49]; or again "from the moment where this thought is present, all colors change and it is an *other history* that begins."[50]

This *fracturing of history* is the necessary antidote to Hegel's idea and the metaphysics of history as the unconditioned and all encompassing totality of thought and "facts." By saying "fracturing of history" we imply that the "other history" cannot be completely other. The history is wounded, altered, but not abolished. It is suspended, in waiting, suffering in a more radical way than in other epochs. Is a completely different ordering conceivable, one where everything that comes to pass has absolutely no rapport with the previous ordering? In this case, it would be necessary in Heidegger's words that "everything" come to an end, that the previous horizon in its entirety be erased without leaving a trace. It would be necessary that every moment of the first history, the archives, the documents, the works of art, the texts, the languages themselves (each word of which incloses the condensed memory of a multitude of ways of being, of practices, of referrals to other beings and a multitude of other determined entities), it would be necessary that the totality of cultural signs, of technical apparatus, of indeed "everything" have disappeared. Such a catastrophe is not in fact inconceivable. It is easy to imagine for example that following massive hydrogen bomb explosions, all organic life might disappear from the surface of the planet. However, in such an instant, the "other history" would no longer be possible either. Thus it is preferable to speak of the Turning and mutation of history.

Still, the idea of a break is required of us to indicate the appearance of a stronger discontinuity than at any other epoch. History continues, but its momentum is broken, or rather what is broken about it is its very epochality and more precisely its periodicity, its capacity to produce new periods or possible new regimes. History congeals, becomes immobile in this present epoch, sealing itself off into one self-same eschatological form. The West has known a number of epochs: the Pre-Socratics, Classical Greece, the Hellenistic period, the Roman era, the Middle Ages, the invention of subjectivity, the conquest of objectivity, the establishment of the techno-scientific apparatus. What would history be without epochs? The break or present discontinuity might be just such a bogged down, stagnant, and paradoxical history.

8

Nietzsche and the "Masters of Truth": The Pre-Socratics and Christ

Béatrice Han

When I first met Hubert Dreyfus, I already was extremely impressed by his work on Foucault, which in my view remains the most exciting and illuminating book I've read on the subject so far. Yet if reading Hubert is interesting for its own sake, talking with him is an even more humbling and stimulating experience. This chapter is the result of one of the many sets of conversations that I've had with him over the last few years, during which his unfailing guidance and support have proved invaluable to me, both as a scholar and as a person. To my knowledge, Hubert has never written on Nietzsche and truth, yet I owe him so much in terms of my intellectual development that although he would no doubt have done better, this chapter is in a way his too.

Among the major themes of Nietzsche's philosophy, his criticism of truth is one of the most ubiquitous and best known. Just as well-known is the paradox that derives from its radicality: unless one accepts the (essentially non-Nietzschean) idea that all statements should be treated as equivalent, this criticism seems to cancel itself insofar as it presupposes an implicit claim to truth.[1] Therefore, Nietzsche's position would be threatened either by a nihilistic and generalized levelling of all values, or by the argument used against the Skeptics from Antiquity: any proposition that denies the existence of truth reasserts by definition the reality of what is negated by it—either a universal relativism, or a contradiction between the propositional content and the very existence of the proposition. In that case, how could Nietzsche justify his own claim to truth?

The usual strategy used by most commentators to save Nietzsche from this quandary consists in distinguishing between different understandings of truth: it is clear that among the three traditional conceptions of the concept (internal consistency, *adequatio rei et intellectus*, practical efficiency), the first cannot be held to, since Nietzsche praised contradiction and rejected the primacy of logic in thought. However, the status of the two remaining understandings, metaphysical (*adequatio*) and pragmatist (efficacy) is more complicated.

Heidegger is the only commentator that, instead of seeing in Nietzsche the self-declared adversary of metaphysics, understands his work as its hidden point of completion. Yet the Heideggerian thesis—which I shall not discuss here for lack of time—agrees *a contrario* with those of other exegetes insofar as it confirms indirectly the existence of an unbreakable bond between metaphysics and the adequationist conception of truth: for Heidegger, the ultimate reason why Nietzsche still belongs to the horizon of metaphysics is that he implicitly reactivates the traditional definition of truth as *homoiosis*.[2]

Although they oppose Heidegger on the question of Nietzsche's relationship to metaphysics, most commentators[3] accept this connection and agree that Nietzsche's criticism of the traditional metaphysical concepts is accompanied by the rejection of the notion of *adequatio* itself. In this view, the denial of the in-itself expressed by *Human, All Too Human* and mostly by the *Gay Science* indicates the impossibility to regard as an ideal the notion of a correspondence with reality[4]: "What is 'appearance' for me now? Certainly not the opposite of some essence! . . . Certainly not a mask that one could place on an unknown X or remove from it."[5] The reason our truths are "false" is not, as in *Truth and Lies*, that they do not encapsulate the essence of things, but that things themselves should be thought of as fictitious; we have to renounce the very possibility of correspondence. According to well-known claims, our truths must be understood as schematizing fictions which crystallize the flux of reality in logical categories (such as identity) that allow us to orient ourselves within the world[6]: a "true" proposition would thus be one

which is useful to life. However, it is essential to note that this pragmatist definition has a mostly *polemic* purport. In fact, the real
meaning of genealogy is to *denounce* the unconscious pragmatism of
science and of metaphysics, precisely by unveiling its original occul-
tation by the adequationist understanding of truth: what we see as
(adequationally) true is, to take up William James's favorite expression, what "works." But the fact that a proposition works is no guarantee of its veracity: "A belief, however necessary it may be for the
preservation of a species, has nothing to do with truth,"[7] the possibility of playing a proposition's efficiency *against* its truth value being
in itself proof of the distance that separates Nietzsche from a pragmatism which remains for him merely a critical tool.[8] Yet if—contrary to what Danto or Rorty think[9]—the pragmatist understanding
of truth cannot be taken to replace its much criticized metaphysical
counterpart in Nietzsche's thought, how will the latter ever be able
to justify his own claims to truth-speaking?

My hypothesis is that the answer to this question lies in the
Nietzschean analysis of the birth of metaphysics and of the adequationist conception of truth. The texts that Nietzsche wrote about the
pre-Socratics and the apparition of Platonism have been studied
many times, but usually with regards to their "downstream" effects,
that is, in order to identify the consequences of the apparition of
Western nihilism.[10] By contrast, my aim here is go "upstream," from
the history of metaphysics to what might be called its *prehistory*: such
a journey seeks to uncover the archaic understanding of truth that
was buried by the joint invention of the intelligible world as ultimate
reality on the one hand, and of truth itself as *adequatio* on the other.
What did speaking the truth mean to the thinkers of the "epoch of
Greek Tragedy"? How different from its metaphysical counterpart
was the understanding of truth presupposed by their discourse? The
first part of this chapter establishes that the latter rests upon two
assumptions: first, the idea that the truth-content of a proposition
does not depend on its adequation with an objective referent (the
notion of which had not appeared yet), but on its link to the living
singularity of its author: as expressed by the notion of an archaic
"tyranny of truth,"[11] a true claim is one that is asserted by someone
truthful (the Master). The second assumption is that truth must not

be understood from an epistemological, but from an *ethical* perspective, a point which I shall elucidate by using Marcel Détienne's famous analysis in *The Masters of Truth in Archaic Greece.*[12] The second step of my chapter will consist in using these results to reinterpret the two major turning points in Nietzsche's genealogy of the West—the birth of metaphysics and that of Christianity—the common thread being that both cases are instances of the archaic understanding of truth being overthrown by an impersonal and highly abstract conception. The final part of this chapter will deal with more contemporary concerns by establishing that Nietzsche's own existential practice of philosophy seeks to revive the magisterial understanding of truth. How is it possible for us Moderns to tell (and recognize) the truth? Given the Nietzschean attack on the metaphysical conception of truth as *adequatio*, authenticity (as a revival of the archaic form of "Mastery of Truth") seems to be the only acceptable precondition to truth-saying—perhaps not a sufficient condition, but a necessary one. Therefore the question of what should count as true for Modernity becomes: what did the Greeks (and Christ) have that we have lost? How can we recapture the ethical state that allows us to ground the truth of our discourse in ourselves? The answer is the aesthetic reconstruction of the self—as we shall see, "becoming what one is" remains the only way left for us Moderns to recover, via the artistic stylization of the self, the integrity that was immediately granted by nature to the pre-Socratics. Having lost the (Schillerian) naïveté of the Greek Golden Age, we must first create ourselves in order to regain the authority to speak the truth.

The late preface (1879) to Nietzsche's writings on the pre-Socratics takes as its guiding principle the impossibility of understanding "early Greek philosophy" without referring it to the individuals that it originates in:

I have selected those doctrines which sound most clearly the personality of the individual philosopher, whereas the complete enumeration of all the transmitted doctrines, as it is the custom of the ordinary handbooks to give, has but one sure result: the complete silencing of personality.[13]

Nietzsche's original intuition is that any true philosophical doctrine owes its authenticity to the singularity of its author (the "personality of the individual philosopher") rather than to its objective content. The correct hermeneutic principle will therefore consist in restoring the organic link that tied the archaic Greek philosopher to his own thought. Viewed in this light, the current depersonalization operated by our "ordinary handbooks" is not only a moral flaw, but also an epistemological mistake: as specified later by the text, each philosophical system is a "tribute" to the "great human individualities," and must be seen from their point of view. Contrary to the positivist dogmas that were prominent at his time, Nietzsche regards objectivity as an enemy to truth. Just as "the worth of an action depends on who accomplishes it and on whether it stems from the depth or the surface of the individual, i.e. on its *individuality*,"[14] the truth-value of a discourse will vary with the speaker's identity: it does not depend on gnoseological, but on ethical criteria. Thus, Nietzsche describes Heraclitus's doctrine as the philosophical transposition of the thinker's virtues—solitude and independence, strength, courage, breadth of view—that allow him to identify justice and harmony behind the universal struggle of life. The reason why the "doctrine of becoming is true" is that the Ephesian "has the truth"[15] because of what he *is*. There is no impersonal access to truth: *aletheia* depends on *ethos*.

In the case of the pre-Socratics, this deep-rootedness of thought in the thinker is seen as *apodictic*: it is caused by the existence of a "*severe necessity between their thinking and their character*,"[16] this internal necessity being explained by the fact that "the early Greek masters . . . all those men are *integral, entire and self contained*, and hewn out of stone."[17] This integrity itself is accounted for by Nietzsche's analysis of the body and its instincts: like the Homeric Greeks described in the first chapters of the *Birth of Tragedy*, the pre-Socratics are still governed by an instinctual hierarchy through which the multiple forces that compose the individual are harmonized.[18] This process results in the emergence and stabilization of a dominant tendency (the "character"), from which the individual's words and deeds will naturally stem. Whereas the hallmark of modernity is reflection—the "sentimental" described by Schiller in *Naïve and Sentimental Poetry*— the pre-Socratics' most distinctive feature is the *naïveté* through which an indissoluble continuity is *naturally* established between what a man is, on the one hand, and his ability to speak the truth on the other. This contrasts starkly with the contemporary "scholar" (*der Gelehrte*), whose loss of unity results in an inconsistent and arbitrary relationship between his being and his thinking:

> Whatever remains to him of his "own person" seems to him *accidental*, often *capricious*, more often disturbing. . . . He finds it an effort to think about "himself," and not infrequently he thinks about himself mistakenly: he can easily confuse himself with another, he fails to understand his own needs and is in this respect alone unsubtle and negligent.[19]

"'Je' est un autre," as Rimbaud said.[20] Concave, almost eviscerated, the modern subject is nothing but a "passage way, the *reflection* of foreign beings and events."[21] Having lost all sense of selfhood, he is unable to distinguish between interiority and exteriority, and therefore to establish a coherent perspective. In this, he is the very antithesis of the strong individual described in the *Genealogy of Morals*, whose multiplication of identities is voluntary, plurality being always controlled by a care for synthesis that enriches his understanding of himself and of the world. Yet the deepest meaning of this modern shattering of the self is not merely psychological: its most fundamental consequence is the impossibility for the Moderns to ground their own discourse in truth, a point to which I shall come back.

By contrast, the distinctive feature of the "real philosophers" is that they achieve a perfect isomorphism between their word and their nature. The man is the incarnation of what he thinks, and his thought, the necessary expression of his character:

> The real philosophers of Greece are those before Socrates (with Socrates something changes). They are all noble persons. . . . They anticipate all the great conceptions of things: *they themselves represent these conceptions, they bring themselves into a system.* (*WP*, §437, 240, emphasis supplied)

The notion of "representation" is not to be taken here in its Classical, Cartesian sense, and does not refer to the conscious thematization of a perceptual or imaginary content. On the contrary, it indicates the *symbolical* movement through which the individual's *ethos* naturally transposes his thought—it is an *embodied* representation, just as the Dionysian man is said to become the incarnation of the dithyramb in the *Birth of Tragedy*. Correlatively, the system loses its metaphysical meaning and ceases to be seen as the theoretical web in which ideas can be caught and fixed[22] (as expressed by Nietzsche's criticism of Spinoza, the "spider"—a pun on the German word "*Spinne*"). Far from being abstract, the systematization now becomes organic, its totalizing aspect being referred to the individual as a living, concrete totality (they "bring themselves into a system"). The pre-Socratics achieved the "individual system" that the Jena Romantics longed for—"aren't all systems individuals just as individuals are systems at least in embryo and tendency"[23]—an ideal the existential possibility of which has been lost by Modernity, to Nietzsche's own regret: "Let us confess how utterly our Modern world lacks the whole type of a Heraclitus . . . Empedocles, and whatever other names these royal and magnificent hermits of the spirit had" (*BGE*, §204, 123).

Having systematized themselves, the original Greek Masters will be "*tyrants of truth*": each great thinker (the text cites Parmenides, Pythagoras, Empedocles, Anaximander), with the belief that he was possessor of absolute truth, became a tyrant (*HH*, §261, 123). Because of its immediacy, the natural balance of the pre-Socratics' instincts prevents the apparition of the reflective element that doubt thrives upon—hence the possibility of the "belief" in oneself and the "*involuntary* way to build all the possibilities of the philosophical ideal."[24] The same process begets that "joy" that Winckelmann deemed characteristic of pre-Platonic Greece: "Perhaps happiness in the belief that one was in possession of the truth has never been greater in the history of the world" (*HH*, §261, 123). As indicated by another text, the presence of this unconditional faith in one's "personal excellence" (*WP* §430, 234) is precisely what defines the noble spirit: "What is noble? . . . It is the *faith* which is decisive here . . . : some fundamental certainty which a noble soul possesses in regard to itself, something which may not be sought or found and perhaps may not be lost either" (*BGE*, §287, 203). This is why, contrary to that which Socrates will establish, the archaic tyranny of truth is not nefarious: in this case, the imposition of truth is not a reactive phenomenon, but a purely active one, the natural consequence of the "severity" and "arrogance"[25] of the pre-Socratics. Conversely,

Nietzsche attributes the decadence of Ancient Greece to the progressive decline of these great tyrants, suddenly overcome by the "quarrelsome and talkative hordes of the Socratic schools" (*HH*, §261, 123). In a highly significant manner, Plato is then described as a *failed* tyrant: "[T]he incarnate desire to become the supreme philosophical lawgiver and founder of states: he appears to have suffered terribly from the nonfulfillment of his nature, and towards the end of his life his soul became full of the blackest gall".[26] Plato is the living proof of the disappearance of the archaic structure: the impossibility for him to "fulfill his nature" by imposing his truth outward turns the violence of his instincts against him and causes *a contrario* the dissolution of his internal unity—"the tyrannical element now raged as poison through [his] own body".[27]

Significantly enough, there is a striking similarity between the Nietzschean analyses on one side and, on the other, those elaborated by Marcel Détienne almost a century later in *The Masters of Truth in Archaic Greece*. For Détienne too, the leading question is to know "how the passage . . . was operated to a new intellectual regimen, that of argumentation and of the principle of contradiction, along with the transition to a dialogue with the object and the referent of a statement."[28] Like Nietzsche, Détienne is interested in the birth of the adequationist conception of truth, accordingly defined by "conformity with logical principles on the one hand, and with reality on the other," and thus "impossible to dissociate from the notions of demonstration and verification."[29] Détienne's most interesting point, in this regard, is that the premetaphysical understanding of truth is characterized by its *non*adequationist aspect. It is a magisterial form of truth, the specificity of which is the impossibility to dissociate it from the one who speaks it: "In archaic Greece, [the Masters of Truth] have the privilege of dispensing the truth *simply because they are endowed with the qualities that make them special.*"[30] Thus, "when a poet praises someone, he does so in his own name, through aletheia: his word is *alethes*, like his mind. The poet is . . . a Master of Truth."[31] In the same way, Nereus, the "Old Man of the Sea," can prophesies that he himself is *alethes*, truthful. As Nietzsche already pointed out, archaic thought does not view the truth of a discourse as an objective feature: it depends on the personal ability of the speaker to speak truly. Thus, the King of Justice's sentence cannot be verified by its relationship to reality, nor by the search for "objective" proofs.[32] On the contrary, it is because it is the *King of Justice's* sentence that it can transform reality by freeing the accused from guilt: "*Aletheia* states an assertoric truth: it is an efficient power, it *creates being.*"[33] It is only fair to add, however, that according to Détienne the possibility of speaking the truth depends as much on the (socio-institutional) *function* of the speaker (as a poet, a seer, or a King) as on his personal capacities. Yet notwithstanding this (nonnegligible) divergence, it is clear that the notion that the possibility of speaking the truth cannot be "severed" from "the qualities . . . of a certain type of man, like the idea that the word of the Master of Truth is "*the privilege of an exceptional man,*"[34] both follow the same logic as the Nietzschean interpretation, which thus derives from Détienne's study an unexpected confirmation.

This account of the structures of pre-Platonic thought sheds a new light on the Nietzschean analysis of the birth of metaphysics. At the beginning of the fourth century B.C., the archaic understanding of truth was brought down by the combination of two major events: on the one hand, the creation of a new object (the intelligible world), and on the other, the apparition of an impersonal subject of knowledge (the theoretical man). Because of this dual modification, the very horizon of truth changed:

The great concepts "good" and "just" are severed from the presuppositions to which they belong and, as liberated ideas, become objects of dialectics. One looks for truth in them, one takes them for entities, or signs of entities: one *invents* a world where they are at home, where they originate. (*WP*, §430, 234–235)

What takes place is a three-staged falsification process: first, the "great concepts" seem to benefit from the metaphysical turn in that they are freed from the magisterial relationship (they become "liberated ideas"). But as in the case of the emancipation of women— and as Derrida points out, is not truth, too, "woman"[35]?—such a liberation is nothing but an illusion[36]: just as the "emancipated" woman loses her femininity through the voluntary adoption of virile features, in the same way thought, severed from the living singularity of the individual, acquires a false universality by forgetting its local source (the "presuppositions" of the concepts, which are not theoretical but refer to the particularities of the "Greek soil" in which they are rooted). Second step of this metaphysical trickery: these concepts become *in themselves* the *loci* of truth ("one looks for truth in them"). This phony autonomy is explicitly aimed at the archaic necessity that requires that truth should be grounded in the speaker's integrity—an indirect proof of the *reactive* character of Platonic nihilism. The final stage of this logic of ever-increasing isolation consists in substantiating these abstractions by "inventing a world" for the ideas, an intelligible and distinct world that will retrospectively be identified as their "true" origin. This covering-up dynamic, which insensibly transforms the concrete deep-rootedness of values in the contingency of a spatio-temporal set of conditions (the "soil") into a transcendent foundation, is thus the hallmark of the slowly emerging metaphysics. Interestingly, Détienne describes the same phenomenon in fairly similar terms: "*Aletheia* becomes a power more strictly defined and more abstractedly understood: it symbolizes . . . a plane of reality that takes the form of an atemporal reality, that asserts itself as immutable and stable Being."[37]

This degeneration of the archaic model is accompanied by the birth of a new type of man, the "abstractly perfect man," who is the ethical counterpart of the "theoretical man" already exemplified by Socrates in the *Birth of Tragedy*.[38]

One had need to invent the abstractly perfect man as well—good, just, wise, a dialectician—in short, the *scarecrow of the ancient philosopher*: a plant removed from all soil. . . . The perfectly absurd "*individuum*" in itself! (*WP*, §430, 235, emphasis supplied)

The absurdity of the concept of an "individuum in itself" is due to the impossibility of universalizing specific characteristics without denaturing them: as shown by Kierkegaard, what defines individuality is *singularity*. To try to generalize it, or worse to substantiate it as an in-itself, denotes therefore a fundamental mistake that deprives the magisterial relationship of its idiosyncratic conditions of possibility—the pre-Socratic philosopher is superseded by the scarecrow.

This movement is amplified by the apparition of Socratic dialectics as a new discursive mode. Beyond depriving the strong of the use of their strength—which is Deleuze's main point in his famous exegesis[39]—the true aim of dialectics is to ruin the archaic understanding of truth by claiming that the dissociation of speech from its author is a *necessary precondition* in obtaining truth. In this regard, the way Nietzsche describes the *pre*dialectical times is particularly significant: "Before Socrates, the dialectical manner was repudiated in good society.... Why this display of reasons? Why should one demonstrate? *Against others one possessed authority*" (*WP*, §431, 235).

The archaic understanding of truth could account for this "authority" by rooting it in the speaker's personal "excellence." As indicated by Détienne, "the truth [of the Master] is an assertoric truth: no one discusses it, no one demonstrates it. Fundamentally different from our traditional conception, *aletheia* is neither conformity between a proposition and its object, nor between a judgment and the judgments of others"[40]—in Nietzschean terms: "*One commanded: that sufficed*" (*WP*, §431, 235).

Yet this noble structure (it is typical of "good society") is replaced by the "*cold knife thrust of the syllogism*" (*WP*, §431, 235): a mode of discourse the objectivity of which severs the organic link between the pre-Socratics and their discourse and, by turning the latter into a reasoning articulated through logical structures, emphasizes the depersonalization of the philosopher and makes him "*the embodiment of cool, triumphant reasonableness*" (*WP*, §431, 235). As indicated by Plato himself in the *Cratylus* (385b), to speak the truth will hereafter mean to "say things as they are."

Set within this wider context, the psychology of Socratism finds its true function: to genealogically reveal the way the metaphysical conception of truth has been able to supersede its archaic counterpart. Socrates is identified as a catalyst[41]: as we know, he is depicted by the later Nietzschean texts as a being endowed with "depraved and anarchic instincts," as a "monster" whose physical aspect is the (un)aesthetic reflection of internal disorders. According to the pre-Socratic logic of truth, however, his ugliness[42] would have been *in itself* the refutation of his thought—not a theoretical proof, to be sure, but a judgment from nature that would have revealed Socrates's utter lack of the harmonious *ethos* necessary to found the truth of his discourse. Prevented, as he was, by his unbalanced nature from being a Master, Socrates was forced to develop a hyper-rationalist attitude: "shrewdness, clarity, severity and logicality as weapons against *the ferocity of the drives*. These must be dangerous and threaten destruction: otherwise there would be no sense in developing shrewdness to the point of making it into a tyrant" (*WP*, §433, 237, emphasis supplied). The original "tyranny of truth," which stemmed from the Master's power to impose his own truth on others and was the immediate consequence of his faith in himself, was therefore reversed into a "counter-tyranny"(*TI*, "The Problem of Socrates," §9, 15). Tyrant in spite of himself, Socrates was mostly *tyrannized*.[43] He became moral "not from choice, it was *de rigueur*" (*WP*, §432, 236), and thus succumbed to the "greatest seduction"—"to make oneself abstract: i.e., to detach oneself" (*WP*, §428, 232). Now impersonal, truth can be objectively proven so that everyone can agree on it—it has become a commonplace: just like the Athenian democracy itself, it is nothing but a public matter.[44]

Interestingly enough, this conflict between the two understandings of truth—archaic and metaphysical—is also operative in another famous opposition, that of Christ and Paul. The analogy bears on three points. First, one of the Messiah's most prominent characteristics is the impossibility of dissociating the content of his teaching from his person and from his life: "Christ has *demonstrated and lived* a new way of life."[45] The syncope is explicit: demonstrating does not mean giving theoretical reasons—it is, simply enough, living. Messianic truth is proven neither by nor in discourse: "He no longer required any formulas, any rites for his intercourse with God—not even prayer. . . . [H]e knows that it is only in the *practice* of life that one feels 'divine.' "[46] Conversely, the life of the Redeemer was *nothing other than his practice*, and this is what makes it "a real life, *a life in truth*" (*WP*, §166, 100). Second, Christ is endowed, like the ancient Masters, with the internal harmony that allows him to ground in his personal *ethos* the truthfulness of his words. He possesses "the deep *instinct* for the way one must live in order to feel oneself in heaven, to feel oneself 'eternal' (*AC*, §33, 607): echoing the "severe necessity" characteristic of the pre-Socratics, the intuitive "depth" of this instinct unifies his life and his works. As suggested by the predominance of "feeling" and by the absence of any reflective element (one "*feels* in Heaven," one "*feels* eternal," or again one "*has the feeling* of being divine") Jesus—like the archaic Greeks—is thus defined by a *naïveté*[47] the Christian equivalent of which reveals itself as the Messianic "innocence." Finally, he is no more a Dialectician than the pre-Socratics: "*Dialectic is equally lacking: the very idea is lacking that a faith, a 'truth,' might be proved by reasons*" (*AC*, §32, 606). Christ does not try to convince through objective proofs, neither does he seek to elicit beliefs that are deemed too intellectual: "Christ's faith is not set in formulas—it *lives*, it is diffident of formulas. . . . The *experience of "life*," as he alone knows it, is adverse to any kind of letter, formula, law, faith, tenet" (*AC*, §32, 606, emphasis supplied). Ultimately, Christ's teaching is not theoretical: it is embodied in his life.

In fact, the Messiah is the very *archetype* of the Master of truth in that he gives the notion of an adequation between the man and his word, which is the very core of the magisterial relationship, its strongest meaning. Christ is *by definition* the incarnated Word. The reason why he "does not require any formulas, any rites in his intercourse with God" (*AC*, §33, 607) is that he is the "glad tiding" (*AC*, §35, 609) become Man. In this, he reveals himself as the absolute singularity, the very incarnation of the singular—"*there was only one Christian*, and he died on the Cross" (*AC*, §39, 612), a fact which in turn has two major consequences. First, Christ's incommensurability to anyone but himself gives his discourse absolute credence: spoken by the one who is above all men, the Messianic word will be truer than any other. Second, this singularity is deeply "exemplary" (*WP*, §169, 102) insofar as what it demands from the disciples is not a merely intellectual comprehension, but practice: "Christianity is a *way of life*, not a system of beliefs" (*WP*, §212, 125). Christ does not convince, but converts: he shows us "*how to act, not what we ought to believe*" (*WP*, §212, 125). For this reason, the *imitatio Christi* reveals itself as the hidden horizon and the extreme limit of the magisterial relationship: by imitating Jesus, the disciples will directly partake, through a quasi magical contagion effect, of the Messianic *ethos* itself.

Thus, "only Christian *practice*, a life such as he lived who died on the cross, is Christian" (*AC*, §39, 612).

While the figure of Christ functions as the religious transposition of the pre-Socratic Master of truth, Paul can be interpreted as the Christian analogon of Socrates. Just like the latter, Paul is "passionate," "violent"[48]: he is a "very tormented, very pitiable, very unpleasant man who also found himself unpleasant" (*DB*, §68, 40). The very existence of this torment and the lack of serenity that results from it are in themselves proofs of the loss of the original "innocence" or naïveté: Paul is a Modern in that he is a man of reflection—the rest of the text describes him as preyed upon by internal divisions that create a succession of anarchic cycles, in which exhilarated moments alternate with depressive fits. Moreover, the reason why the Jew is incapable of truth is that, like Socrates himself, he is fighting against his own disorganized nature. "General problem [of the Christian]: what will become of the man who defames the natural, and denies and degrades its practice?" (*WP*, §228, 132). Identical problems call for analogous solutions: "In fact, the Christian proves himself to be an *exaggerated form of self control*: in order to restrain his desires he seems to find it necessary to extirpate and crucify them" (*WP*, §228, 132). Mirroring the Socratic cure, the Paulinian remedy against the "natural drives . . . reinterpreted as vices"[49] will lie in setting up a tyranny whose reactive character is expressed by the fact that—just like in Platonic times—it stems from *need*, not strength.[50]

Incapable of being a Master of Truth, Paul follows in Socrates's steps by turning against the magisterial relationship itself. In this regard, the form of his "torment" is highly significant: "[Paul] suffered from a fixed idea, or more clearly from a fixed question . . . : what is the Jewish *law* really concerned with? And in particular, what is the fulfillment of this *law*?" (*DB*, §68, 40). Here again, the presence of an "obsession" denotes the loss of immediacy; but the fact that it has the *law* as its focus, that is, a theoretical object, a command that is by definition both abstract and universalizing, shows how far Paul has come from the original paradigm of the *imitatio Christi* (which was not grounded in precepts but in the setting of an exemplary model of life). As Socrates did before him, the Jew wants to replace facts by interpretations: "Psychology of [Saint] *Paul.* The given fact is the death of Jesus. This has to be *explained*" (*WP*, §171, 103, emphasis supplied). And since he does not find any explanations in Christ's life, Paul makes them up: "From the facts of Christ's life and death [Paul] made a quite arbitrary selection, *giving everything a new accentuation*" (*WP*, §167, 101, emphasis supplied). This is particularly clear in the case of the Messiah's death: according to the mimetic logic of the magisterial relationship, Jesus' death was nothing more than "one more sign of how one ought to behave. . . . *not to defend oneself.* That had been the lesson" (*WP*, §170, 103). As the martyrs perfectly understood, this death had to be imitated, not explained: "salvation through faith (namely, that there is no means of becoming a son of God *except by following the way of life taught by Christ)*" (*WP*, §170, 102). Yet Paul gave a formal meaning to the Messiah's ending by reinterpreting it in a transcendent way, as a promise of redemption through which the sensible world is deprecated a second time.[51] The essentially immanent notion of *imitatio Christi* was thus reversed "into the faith that one is to believe in some sort of miraculous subtraction of sins" (*WP*, §170, 102), whereas in fact, "it is false to the point of nonsense to find the mark of the Christian in a "faith," for instance in the faith in redemption through Christ" (*AC*, §39, 612).

By giving Christ's death a theoretical meaning, Paul was not only mistaken: he caused others to break away from the magisterial relationship. Like Socrates before him, he proceeds by inventing "counterfeits of true Christianity,"[52] *formal* counterfeits that are best characterized by their impoverished existential content. Thus, "the teaching that the son of man is the 'Son of God,' the *living relationship between God and man*; this is made into the 'second person of the divinity'" (*WP*, §170, 102, emphasis supplied): the concrete, living individual is reinterpreted as an abstract person, a move which in itself is symbolical of the passage from the Greek emphasis on singularity to the formalism of the Roman world.[53] In the same way, "brotherhood on the basis of sharing food and drink together after the Hebrew-Arabic custom, [is seen] as the 'miracle of transubstantiation'" (*WP*, §170, 102): an ordinary practice (the sharing of food) is torn from its local origin (the "Hebrew-Arabic custom") and turned into a dogma, the dramatic consequences of which (during the Reformation) Nietzsche, as a pastor's son, could not be unaware of. The common point between these examples is that they use the same decontextualizing and depersonalizing logic:

> Consider with what degree of freedom Paul treats, indeed almost juggles with, the problem of the person of Jesus: someone who died, who was seen again after his death . . . : a mere *"motif"*: *he then wrote the music to it.* (*WP*, §177, 108, emphasis supplied)

Thus, Paul is the "inventor of Christianity" (*DB*, §68, 41) precisely in that he *betrayed* Christ by turning the embodied "person of Jesus" into a "motif", that is, a decorative element destined to be merged within a wider context (Christianity itself) in which its singularity will disappear. By reversing the former priority of the practical over the theoretical, or more precisely by abolishing the necessity of grounding an individual's ability to speak the truth on his *ethos*, Paul—ironically enough—"annulled primitive Christianity *as a matter of principle*" (*WP*, §167, 101, emphasis supplied).

Yet the most interesting feature of Nietzsche's analyses of the premetaphysical understanding of truth and of its decline may be that they allow us to identify the deep reason for his condemnation of his contemporaries: "Lack of respect for individual philosophers has involuntarily generalized itself into lack of respect for philosophy" (*BGE*, 6, §204, 119). The main evil that Modernity suffers from is *the loss of the magisterial relationship.* Severed from its deep-rootedness in the singularity of the thinker, philosophy has been objectified, "reduced to a theory of knowledge" (*BGE*, 6, §204, 119). The circle of nihilism is now completed: at the very opposite of the positive domination of the "tyrants of truth," philosophy lives "its last throes, an end, an agony, something inspiring pity. How could such a philosophy—*dominate!*" (*BGE*, 6, §204, 110). As could be anticipated from the disappearance of the magisterial structure, such an agony comes from "the exaggerated manner in which *the "unselfing" and depersonalization of the spirit* is being celebrated nowadays as if it were the goal itself and redemption and transfiguration."[54] Attuned to the general—"already his thoughts roam *to a more general case*"

(*BGE*, 6, §207, 122–123)—the German has lost any sense of his own singularity, and reveals himself unable to systematize his being and his thought:

> His habit of meeting everything and experience halfway, the sunny and impartial hospitality with which he accepts everything that comes his way, his type of unscrupulous benevolence, of dangerous concern about Yes and No . . . And as a human being he becomes all too easily the *caput mortuum* of these virtues! (*BGE*, 6, §207, 122–123)

In this reversal of the archaic logic, the individual, instead of being the living proof of the virtues expressed by his discourse, becomes the point in which these virtues, unable to root themselves in his ethical substance, degenerate and perish.

On the contrary, the Nietzschean practice of philosophy can be interpreted as a desperate attempt to revive the ancient understanding of truth. Thus, the philosophers of the future, these "new friends of truth," reject the idea that "their truth [should be] supposed to be a truth for every man, which has hitherto been the secret desire and hidden sense of all dogmatic endeavours" (*BGE*, §43, 53). Against the universalizing assumptions of metaphysics, one must restore the singularity of the magisterial relationship: "In the end it must be as it is and has always been: great things for the great, abysses for the profound, shudders and delicacies for the refined, and, in sum, all rare things for the rare" (*BGE*, §43, 54). This ideal of a scarcity of truth ("all rare things for the rare") is the only way truth can recover its value: the greatness of philosophical conceptions must become again the reflection of the achievements of the individual. Thought has to recover its nontheoretical meaning by being linked anew to the life of the thinker: "Philosophy, *as I have so far understood and lived it*, means living voluntarily among ice and high mountains— seeking out everything strange and questionable in existence."[55] Theoretical comprehension must be rooted in existential experience: understanding something means living it. Another passage is even more explicit: "I have always written my writings with my whole body and life. *I do not know what purely intellectual problems are.*"[56] In this existential context, then, it is hardly surprising that

Nietzsche should take up the magisterial admonition to honesty originally betrayed by Socrates, then by Paul: "Will to truth does not
mean: 'I will not allow myself to be deceived' but—there is no
alternative—'*I will not deceive, not even myself*'; and with this, we stand
on moral ground" (*GS*, §344, 281). After the collapse of the metaphysical "*Hinterwelten,*" the foundation for a cognitive content can
only be ethical: truth is not proven, but endured. Conversely, only
the philosopher's capacity to endure truth can serve as a criterion
to discriminate between philosophies: "How much truth does a spirit
endure, how much truth does it dare? More and more that became
for me the *real measure of value.* Error (faith in the ideal) is not blind-
ness, error is cowardice" (*EH*, Preface, §3, 218, emphasis supplied).
One must reverse the Socratic principle and the idealist tradition
that supports it (the "faith in the ideal"): contrary to Socrates'
famous claim, it is not "enough" to judge well in order to behave
well. One must behave well *prior* to judging well. What really matters,
in the formation of knowledge, is the relationship to the self: "Every
attainment, every step forward in knowledge, follows from courage,
from hardness against oneself, from *cleanliness* in relation to oneself"
(EH, Preface, §3, 218, emphasis supplied).

In this endeavor, however, the major difficulty remains the identification of a *modern* criterion for veracity. The scission characteristic
of the post-Socratic times makes it impossible for us "Sentimentals"
to resurrect the archaic ideal of a natural balance between our
instincts: as A. Schlegel put it, "The Greek ideal of humanity was
perfect concord and symmetry of all powers, natural harmony, but
the Moderns show an awareness of inner dissension which makes
such an ideal impossible." The Hellenic Golden Age has vanished,
and even Goethe, the greatest of all the Europeans, was unable to
retrieve it:

> He felt the profoundest desire to regain the traditional ways of art and to
> bestow upon the ruins and colonnades of the temple that still re-mained
> their ancient wholeness and perfection. . . . His demands were, to be sure,
> having regards to the powers possessed by the Modern age, unfulfillable.[57]

Therefore, the only possibility for us Moderns to tell the truth will
depend on the greatest individuals' ability to shape themselves and

their lives. Once reflection has settled in, the pre-Socratic integrity can only be recovered *via* a work on the self which aims at restoring the internal unity of character, and consequently the possibility of a necessary connection between the individual's *ethos* and the truth he speaks.

In this regard, Pindar's famous admonition, "becoming what one is," can be seen as a testimony to the Nietzschean desire to revive the magisterial relationship: one must become *worthy of truth* in order to be able to found it *as* true. This is the deep purport of the "grand style," of the well-known admonition to "master the chaos that one is" (*WP*, §842, 444), "to become *simple*." The artist has to conquer *through art* what was freely given by *nature* to the pre-Socratics—the integrity of a harmonious *ethos*. Thus, he is haunted by an obligation which is the exact transposition of the archaic ideal—to "turn things into the reflection of our inner plenitude and perfection" (EH, Preface, §3, 218, emphasis supplied): deprived of the instinctive unity of his archaic forerunners, the modern artist must *create himself so as to be able to create*. One may therefore apply to him, although in a very different sense, the famous imperative initially expressed in the *De Profundis*—"to turn one's life into a work of art": yet contrary to what O. Wilde intended in his apology of dandyism, this does not mean that the artist's life might substitute itself for his works as the ultimate, embodied artwork.[58] The true reason why we must turn our lives into works of art is that one's life is the *existential condition of possibility of any claim to authenticity,* while conversely, the value of an individual's art can only be measured by his capacity for style: "The greatness of an artist is not measured by the 'beautiful feelings' that he elicits . . . , but by his aptitude for grand style" (*WP*, §842, 444).

In this regard, Goethe's paradigmatic status and claim to greatness is precisely that he has been able to recover the archaic ideal by satisfying its demand for integrity: "What he wanted was *totality* . . . : he *created himself*" (*TI*, "Raids of an Untimely Man," §49, 123, emphasis supplied). The "man," however, was the product of his epoch insofar as he had internalized even its worst characteristics—"sentimentality, idolatry for nature, the idealistic, unrealistic instincts" (ibid.). Yet unlike his contemporaries, he also possessed the ethical stance necessary for the harmonization of these contradictory qualities— "He was not faint-hearted and took as much as possible upon himself, above himself, *into himself*" (*TI*, §49, 123). Thus, Goethe managed to overcome the dissensions typical of the Christian age: "He fought against the separation of reason, sensation, emotion and will (preached with the most horrifying scholasticism by Kant, the antipodes of Goethe); *he disciplined himself into wholeness*" (Ibid.).

By disciplining himself, Goethe *stylized* himself: he reestablished the archaic harmony between being, doing, and speaking, which is the reason why he can be said to be "strong enough for freedom" (*TI*, §49, 83). Seeing beyond the chimeras of German idealism, that identified freedom with an autonomous faculty the legitimate use of which was to be grounded in rational deliberation, Goethe recovered the *instinctive* sense of freedom: "the *feeling* of freedom, subtlety, full power, of creative placing, disposing, and forming reaches its peak: in short, *necessity and 'freedom of will' then become one*" (*BGE*, §213, 139, emphasis supplied). Contrary to what Spinoza thought, freedom is not necessity well understood: it is necessity well *perceived*, that is, the subjective feeling of strength that results from the perfect harmonization of character achieved either by nature (the pre-Socratics) or *via* art (Goethe himself). In this heroic endeavor, Goethe reached the paradoxical point "when we no longer do something 'voluntarily' but do everything out of necessity" (ibid.). Freedom unveils itself as compatible with destiny, and bestows on the newly unified individual the "faith"—another pre-Socratic theme *par excellence*—that is required to "stand with a glad and trusting fatalism in the midst of the universe" (*TI*, §49, 83). Now able to ground the truth of his word in the newly formed integrity of his character, Goethe can claim as his own the highest of all truths, that is, the Eternal Return—he can endure the knowledge that "as a whole, everything affirms and redeems itself" (*TI*, §49, 83).

Thus, Nietzsche's reconstruction of the pre-Socratic understanding of truth plays an architectonic part in the Nietzschean corpus: going back to the very origins of our history, it enables us to grasp the common point between such diverse events as the invention of metaphysics and of adequationist truth by Socrates, on the one hand, and the reformulation/betrayal of Christ's teaching by Paul on the other. In both cases, the truth-speaking power that the Master derived from his personal excellence is brought down. In both cases, the principal cause of this fall is ressentiment: because they were by definition unable to enter the magisterial relationship, Socrates and Paul turned against it and replaced it by an abstract, impersonal understanding of truth. Moreover, the ideal horizon outlined by the possibility of recovering the archaic conception of truth allows for a better understanding of the importance devoted by Nietzsche to the theme of self-creation and to such heroic figures as Goethe or Zarathustra: for each of these modern heroes of truth, the ultimate stake of the metamorphosis of the self is to recover the unified *ethos* in which the archaic "Tyrant" could ground his own truth, and thus to revive the magisterial relationship.

Finally, this prospect sheds a new light on Nietzsche's relationship to his own thought. Most commentators have underlined the highly personal character of Nietzsche's writings, and the necessity—explicitly expressed in such a text as *Ecce Homo*—to take into account the author's psychology in the interpretation of his work. In this regard, A. Nehamas and L. Thiele have defended apparently opposed theses: according to the former, Nietzsche created himself as a literary character through his writings,[59] while the latter thinks that Nietzsche used his writings to shape his own life.[60] Both interpretations obviously share the same assumption, namely that it is impossible to read Nietzsche's texts without linking them to the self-creating work done by the author on himself.[61] "My judgment is *my* judgment: no one else is so easily entitled to it—that is what such philosophers of the future may perhaps say of themselves" (*BGE*, §43, 53). It is hardly difficult to recognize, in this deep continuity between speaker and spoken word, the main characteristic of the magisterial relationship, that is, the necessary rooting of philosophical truth in the *ethos* of the philosopher. In the light of this, it does not come as a surprise to see Zarathustra, Nietzsche's spokesman, defined by his *truthfulness*: "His doctrine, and his alone, has truthfulness (*Wahrhaftigkeit*) as the highest virtue" (*EH*, "Why I am a Destiny," §3, 328). Because of their lack of ethical substance (they suffer from the "cowardice of the idealist who flees from reality"), the Last Men can only triumph "*at the expense of truth* and at the expense of the future" (ibid.), that is, by renouncing the magisterial relationship and by taking refuge in the intelligible world, a move that also provides them with a criterion for (adequationist) truth. On the contrary, Zarathustra is the living synthesis of the three figures of mastery analyzed by Détienne: at the same time Poet, Seer, and Legislator, and "more truthful (*wahrhaftiger*) than any other thinker," he will be the Master of truth of the future (*EH*, §3, 328).

9

What Is Dwelling? The Homelessness of Modernity and the Worlding of the World

Julian Young

Heidegger remarks that great philosophical classics need to be re-created for each new generation. It was Bert Dreyfus's superb commentary on *Being and Time* that first showed me that Heidegger is profound, exciting, relevant, and, above all, intelligible. Bert's gift for providing modern instances for Heideggerian saws has become a model I try to emulate. His two visits to Auckland have thus been a source of pleasure and excitement to both my students and myself. With characteristically egalitarian generosity, Bert offered, on both occasions, to read through works of mine. On the second, the work was the manuscript of a projected book on Heidegger's philosophy of art. Naturally, it contained a great deal of talk about the topic introduced by my title, dwelling. After a great deal of reading, however, Bert wrote in the margin: "What *is* dwelling?" The question is, of course, raised by Heidegger himself at the beginning of "Building Dwelling Thinking."[1] But his answer—and evidently mine, too—is not without its obscurities. Here, then, is a second attempt to answer Bert's question.

"Dwelling" appears in the title of two of what are, to anglophone readers at least, the most familiar of late[2] Heidegger essays: "Building Dwelling Thinking" and ". . . Poetically Man Dwells . . ."[3] Together with its cognates—homeland (*Heimat*), being/becoming homely (*Heimischwerden/Heimischsein*[4])—and contraries—homelessness, estrangement, alienation (BW 219)—dwelling can plausibly be said to constitute the central topic of the thinking of the late

Heidegger. And it is, in fact, the preoccupation of the last sentence he ever wrote, a few days before his death in 1976: "It requires reflection, whether and how (*ob und wie*) there can still be homeland in the age of the technological equi-formed world-civilization."[5] One of the ways in which one might attempt to capture the contrast between, on the one hand, early and middle Heidegger and, on the other, late Heidegger would be to say that while, at the most fundamental level, the former is concerned (with Nietzsche) with the meaning-nihilism duality, the latter, again at the most fundamental level, is concerned (with Hölderlin) with the dwelling-homelessness duality. But just what, to repeat Bert's question, *is* dwelling?

One approach to trying to answer it would be to begin by focusing on Heidegger's presentation of the *opposite* or *absence* of dwelling—homelessness. Such an account is, I believe, to be found in early Heidegger, in *Being and Time*.[6]

I

A central concept in *Being and Time*—arguably the central concept[7]—is "thrownness." So far as its definition is concerned, thrownness is a technical term which identifies the fact that every person, *as* a person ("Dasein"), finds itself "already in" a cultural tradition which delimits both the range of actions which it makes sense to perform, and of those which it is valuable to perform. But to suppose Heidegger's choice of *Geworfenheit* to designate this technical feature (rather than, let us say, "constructedness") to be an arbitrary one would be naïve. For it would be to ignore the poet in Heidegger, as present in the early as in the late work—though more covertly so. The fact is that "thrownness" belongs to a family of expressions used in *Being and Time*—"abandonment," "being delivered over," "care," "anxiety," "death," and "the nothing"[8]—which have, *inter alia*, the function of expressing a particular mood pertaining to the world in which Dasein finds itself; the mood of expulsion from the homeland (paradise, if we are sensitive to *Being and Time*'s "godless theology"), alienation, homelessness. Homelessness, to use the language of the middle Heidegger, is the *Grundstimmung*, the "fundamental mood" of Dasein's "being-in-the-world" and it is the fundamental mood of *Being and Time* itself—a fact which marks it as (but does not limit it to being) a product of the Weimar Republic. Given this, it is unsurprising that *Being and Time* explicitly acknowledges *Unheimlichkeit*, "uncanniness" but also, as Heidegger emphasises, "not-being-at-homeness" (*Unheimlichkeit*), as an inescapable—"existential"—feature of the human condition. Homelessness is a shadow over our being which we can "dim down" in the inauthentic camaraderie of "the One" but never extinguish (*BT*, 188–189).

What, in *Being and Time*, is the source of our homelessness? The source is "anxiety," anxiety in the face of death, of, that is, "the nothing." Early Heidegger pictures Dasein's world as a "clearing" of light.[9] Since he conceives being as simply "the meaning of being" or, as Bert Dreyfus puts it, the "intelligibility" of beings that show up in the clearing, over and above the clearing there is—nothing: emotionally this is received as, to use a Nietzschean word *Being and Time* indeed deploys, an "abysmal" (*BT*, 152) nothingness, an infinitely dark and absolute emptiness that "threatens" (*BT*, 343) to break into the clearing at any moment in the form of pain and death. At its heart, therefore, Dasein's existence is permeated by radical—as I shall sometimes say, "ontological"—insecurity.

Radical insecurity, however, is always understood by Heidegger as incompatible with, as the opposite of, dwelling. Dwelling, say the *Ister* lectures, is a kind of "rest," a resting in the "steadfastness," the "inviolability" of one's "essence."[10] The essential character of dwelling, Heidegger adds later, is "safety" (*PLT*, 120). It is to be in what Old High German called "the free (*das Frye*)." Otherwise put, it means "to be at peace (*zufrieden sein*) . . . to be protected from harm and threat (*Bedrohung*), safeguarded, . . . that is, cared for and protected (*geschont*)." "The fundamental character of dwelling," Heidegger concludes, "is this caring for and protection (*Schonen*)."[11] Dwelling, then, is ontological security—precisely what is excluded by *Being and Time*.

It is of course true that *Being and Time* is centrally concerned to provide an account of "authentic" life. This is the nearest it comes to providing an account of what it is to, in Aristotelian language, "thrive" or "flourish." Disdaining the evasiveness of inauthenticity, authentic Dasein "anticipates" death, lives a life governed by a squarely faced knowledge of death—of "the nothing"—a life marked by clarity, directedness, vividness, energy, and urgency. Being thus authentic is not, however, a homecoming. It is not a "solution" to, or overcoming of homelessness. It is, rather, a *living with* homelessness. (If it is a solution to anything it is a solution—by way of a *Gestalt*-switch from seeing the clearing as a threatened almost-nothing to seeing it as a fragile and precious wonder—to the "nausea," the Hamlet-like paralysis of action, which, in *The Birth of Tragedy* (section 7), Nietzsche sees as threatening anyone foolish enough to look unflinchingly into the heart of being.) Thus, not dwelling but rather heroic alienation, the courage to carry on in the face of the nihilating pressure of the nothing, is the fundamental character of *Being and Time's* (as Nietzsche would say) "higher type." As many have recognized, "heroic nihilism" is *Being and Time's* fundamental stance to life and the world.

II

It is a mark of the profound changes that occurred in Heidegger's thought between 1927 and 1951 that dwelling, the feature universally, ontologically, absent from human existence in 1927 has become, by the latter date, definitive of the human "essence" (*PLT*, 228). "To be a human being," says "Building Dwelling Thinking" "means ... to dwell," a truth intimated in the fact that the "*bin*" of "*ich bin* (I am)" comes from the Old High German "*buan*," which means "to dwell" (*PLT*, 147). The point is repeated in "Poetically Man Dwells" where it is said that dwelling is not an achievement of some human beings some of the time but belongs to "every man and all of the time" (*PLT*, 213). Clearly, then, there is some ontological transformation which lies at the heart of the passage from early to late Heidegger: ontological insecurity, understood as the heart of human being, has been transformed into ontological security. Why has this sea change occurred? The answer, I would argue, lies in Heidegger's gradual, but radical, reappraisal of the character of "the nothing."

In "Building Dwelling Thinking" and its companion piece "The Thing" Heidegger makes an obscure, but emphatic, connection between dwelling, death, and the nothing. "Mortals dwell," he says, "in that they initiate (*geleiten*) their own nature—their being capable of death as death—into the use and practice of this capacity" (*PLT*, 151). "Death," he continues, "is the shrine of the nothing" (*PLT*, 178); not, however, the "empty nothing" (*PLT*, 151) but rather "the mystery of being itself. As the shrine of the nothing, death harbours within itself the presencing of Being" (*PLT*, 178–179). To understand this, "to initiate mortals into the nature of death," is to become capable of "the good death" (*PLT*, 151).

The meaning of all this is presented much less enigmatically five years earlier in the 1946 Rilke Lecture, "What are Poets For?" This work begins by repeating the thought which led early Heidegger to conclude that dwelling is impossible—this time, however, without valorizing, or even mentioning, the heroic authenticity which faces and accepts the lot of homelessness. In the face of the "abyss (*Abgrund*)," he says, in the "absence (*Ab*) of the "ground (*grund*) which grounds," we cannot dwell. Life lived in the face of the abyss (whether it is heroic or evasive makes no difference) is "destitute" (*PLT*, 92). The reason is that before the abyss we are unable to "read the word 'death' *without* negation" (*PLT*, 125).

But, Heidegger now says,—attributing the insight to Rilke—human life is *not* lived before the abyss. Why not? While warning that the image must not be taken too literally Heidegger answers in terms of Rilke's image of being as, like the moon, a "globe," with the "world" or "clearing" as no more (or less) than its lighted side. Understanding being in this way has, suggests Heidegger, profound implications for the understanding of death. For it lets us see that "death and the realm of the dead," like the dark side of the moon, "belong to the whole of beings as its other side." There are, he adds, "regions and places which, being averted from us, seem to be something negative, but are nothing of the kind if we think of all things as being within the widest orbit of beings" (*PLT*, 124–125).

We can now see the profound difference between late and early Heidegger. In *Being and Time*, we saw, being is nothing other than "the meaning of being," the structure of the clearing, so that beyond the clearing, beyond the "whole of beings," lies only the "empty,"[12] completely "negative,"[13] absolute and abysmal "nothing." Now, however, the structure of the—our—clearing is nothing more than the horizon of disclosure under which being reveals itself to us—for now. That which transcends the clearing is no longer an "emptiness" but has become, rather, its opposite. It is "plenitude" (*PLT*, 124), a "reservoir of the not-yet-uncovered," of the "concealed" (*PLT*, 60).

Being to be sure is not a being. It is not to be confused with any denizen of the clearing or with the totality of such denizens—hence the need not to take the Rilkean image too literally. In a sense, therefore, being is appropriately said to be "nothing" (no-thing): "Seen from the horizon of the ontic, being *is* nothing." But this nothing must not be understood as an absolute or "negative" nothing. The point, rather, of calling it "nothing" is to mark the fact that "being is something (*etwas*) completely and utterly Other (*Anderes*) than beings (*das Seiende*)."[14]

The profound change that separates late from early Heidegger consists, therefore, in a reassessment of the characters of the nothing. In early Heidegger it is an absolute nothing. In late Heidegger it is (to use Schopenhauer's distinction) a relative nothing. In early Heidegger it is emptiness, in late Heidegger it is "plenitude."[15]

What has this to do with the transition from homelessness to dwelling, from ontological insecurity to ontological security? To understand this one needs to understand the paradoxical character of Heidegger's conception of dwelling. In a nutshell, what he holds is that we dwell as human beings only because we simultaneously dwell as more or "other" than human beings. There is a distant echo of Kant in the thought: we can dwell in the realm of the living only on account of our simultaneous membership of the "realm of the dead." We can dwell as mortals only because we also transcend mortality, belong to the realm of immortality. As human beings we belong to the world. But the world is just the lighted side of the "globe of being." It follows that, like every other being, we are a "plenitude of . . . facets" (*PLT*, 124) that transcend the clearing. Death is, of course, the end of the individual ego. But that no more constitutes an annihilation of the self than the onset of day is an annihilation of the moon. Understanding dwelling, understanding our "safety" in the face of death, thus involves understanding that as well as being an "I" we are also a "self."[16]

To understand the meaning of Rilke's image is thus to understand what it is that constitutes our ontological security. If we "initiate our nature" into this understanding we acquire the capacity to "face the word 'death' *without* negation," to die the "good death." We acquire, that is, the capacity to dwell.

III

The transformation of early into late Heidegger is the transformation of the human being from one who is, in essence, homeless into one who, in essence, dwells. What is initially strange, however, is that the motif of homelessness is far more prominent in late than it is in early Heidegger. For late Heidegger, that is, the present age is marked, defined even, by its "plight of dwelling" (*PLT*, 161). The "homelessness of contemporary man" (*BW*, 241) is his constant preoccupation. How, then, can "man" dwell yet "contemporary man" be homeless?

Heidegger elucidates this puzzling conjunction in the "Letter on Humanism." In the "nearness of being," he says, in, "the light of the *Da* [here], man dwells as the ek-sisting one without yet being able properly to experience and take over this dwelling" (*BW*, 241).

"Ek-sistence," standing out and beyond, is what I have been referring to in terms of transcendence. Human beings dwell because they "stand out" beyond the clearing into the nothing of plenitude and are thus ontologically secure. This is the ontological *truth* of the matter. No matter how oblivious we may be of it, we are, in truth, ontologically secure.

Typically, however, and in modernity almost universally, we *are* oblivious of our security. We suffer from *Seinsvergessenheit* (or, as one might also say, *Nichtsvergessenheit*), "oblivion of being," and because of this, experience our world in just the way captured, so expressively, in *Being and Time*. We experience ourselves as essentially insecure and hence fail to experience our world as a place of safety, as a dwelling-place. We fail, as the "Letter on Humanism" puts it, to "experience and take over" our dwelling.

Three points need to be stressed here. First, "contemporary man" is, let us recall, "homeless." In other words he does not dwell. But essentially, ontologically, all men dwell. To avoid contradiction, Heidegger must be understood as operating with two different notions of dwelling; "essential" dwelling, on the one hand, and, as I will say, "ordinary" dwelling on the other.

In the ordinary sense, to dwell is to live a life that is informed by a particular experience—the experience or feeling of being "at home" in one's world. To dwell, ordinarily understood, is to live a life that is informed by the experience of the place in which one lives as a dwelling-place, a homeland. (A life that has this character is, Heidegger explains, a life of caring for: "The fundamental character of dwelling is care and conservation (*Schonen*)" [*PLT*, 149: compare footnote 11 above]). Essential dwelling, on the other hand, is entirely independent of any feeling or experience. It is simply one's "ek-sistence," one's transcendence into the "Other" of beings. This quality one possesses regardless of whether one feels at home or alienated in one's world.

The second point that needs stressing is that essential dwelling, though not sufficient, is a necessary condition of ordinary dwelling. Since ordinary dwelling is a "taking over" into one's experience and life of essential dwelling, one could not dwell ordinarily unless one dwelled essentially.

The final point to stress is that ordinary dwelling consists in *ignorance* of essential dwelling, and that this consists in the fact that the nature of the world, of the "clearing" and of "truth," has not been properly understood, properly "thought": "Homelessness is a symptom of oblivion of being ... [of the fact that] the truth of being remains unthought" (*BW*, 242). It follows from this that the overcoming of homelessness—the achievement of dwelling in the ordinary sense—must consist in the overcoming of ignorance, of "oblivion of being."

IV

What is the source of the ignorance that is "contemporary man"'s failure to dwell? (From now on I shall understand the unmodified "dwell" always to mean "dwell in the ordinary sense.") It is, of course, *Gestell*, the "essence" of modern technology, the horizon of disclosure under which everything shows up as "resource." What is really "dangerous" about *Gestell*, however, is the fact that it is the culmination and most absolute form of what Heidegger calls "metaphysics."

Metaphysics is the absolutizing of some—any—given horizon of disclosure, the treatment of a way in which being shows up as *the*— one and only—way it is.[17] Metaphysics precludes dwelling because it is, as it were, two-dimensional; it precludes "depth." In terms of Rilke's image it is equivalent to taking the moon to be a flat, illuminated disk. By thus reducing being to the clearing it misunderstands "the nothing" as the abysmal nothing and so precludes the possibility of experiencing the "safety" that is dwelling.

It follows that the security of dwelling must consist in the overcoming of metaphysics. How is this to be achieved? It is in the context of this question that the deployment of the most frequent of all Heidegger's quotations—meditational texts—from Hölderlin, "poetically man dwells," is to be understood.

V

"Full of merit, yet poetically, dwells man upon this earth."[18] To dwell, then, is to inhabit "the poetic" (*PLT*, 228), to experience the world poetically: "Poetry is what first causes dwelling to be dwelling. Poetry first lets us dwell" (*PLT*, 225).

Heidegger first discovered poetry in the early 1930s—discovered, that is, its importance for philosophy. In *Being and Time* it is a non-event receiving a total of four lines of discussion. At one point, it is true, "the nature which "stirs and strives"[19] and enthrals us as landscape," the nature of the "springhead in the dales" (*BT*, 70), in other words, the poet's nature, is acknowledged as falling outside *Being and Time*'s analysis of "world" in terms of "equipment." But the significance of this theoretical lacuna receives no further discussion. It seems clear, therefore, that the discovery of poetry is importantly connected with the discovery of dwelling. What, then, is the connection? What is poetry? What, as Heidegger often puts it, is the "essence" of the poetic "word"?

Ordinary language, language used as a tool for the communication of information, is, says Heidegger, "*eindeutig.*" The ordinary "name" is, or at least aspires to be, "unambiguous," an ideal which reaches its culmination in the one-to-one correspondence between word and concept to be found in the artificial language of "cybernetic representation" (*Denkerfahrungen*, 142), "computer information language" (*Denkerfahrungen*, 159). The poetic name, on the other hand, is "*vieldeutig*." If we were interested only in information transference we might understand this expression in terms of its everyday, pejorative, meaning: "ambiguous." But information transference is not the point of poetry. If we are to use it to understand poetry we must, says Heidegger, deconstruct the term into its literal meaning—"possessed of a 'multiplicity' or 'richness of meaning.'" For to every genuinely poetic word there corresponds an "inexhaustibly" large "space of [semantic] vibration (*Schwingungsraum*)," from which it follows that, unlike the word of (at least ideal) information exchange, the poetic word has no "definition."[20] It says, means, more than can even be captured in words.

Eindeutig language is the language of "metaphysics." In *eindeutig* world-experience the richness of many-faceted being is shut out by the cage of language, by an absolutized horizon of disclosure. When poetry "works," on the other hand, when, under the "power" of, for example, Trakl's "A Winter Evening"—

Window with falling snow is arrayed,
Long tolls the vesper bell,
The house is provided well,
The table is for many laid . . .

—we are brought to experience the world poetically, then beings start, as Heidegger puts it, to "thing" (*PLT*, 199–200), to sing with the song of being, ring with the "inexhaustible" and "unfathomable" (*PLT*, 180) "richness" of being itself. Beings which, in the *eindeutig* representations of metaphysics are "opaque" (*PLT*, 108) become, in poetry, as Heidegger sometimes puts it, "transparent" to being, to, as Hölderlin calls it, in virtue of its awesome, but also gift-giving might, "the holy." Poets are those who, in naming, bringing forth, the unnameable, in bringing being to presence in beings, the transcendent in the immanent, "name," "ground" or "found" the holy.[21]

Poets, then, let us dwell because they allow us to "experience and take over" our "ek-sistence." Rilke, for example, by allowing us to experience our world and lives as the lighted side of the "globe of being," allows us to experience our "standing-forth" into the nothing of plenitude, which is what makes him a poet for our "needy," metaphysical, times. And Hölderlin does the same by, as "Poetically Man Dwells" puts it, bringing "God" to presence in the "familiar" sights of sky and earth—not of course the "God" of Christianity but the "unknown" God of Hölderlin's poetry (*PLT*, 224–225). Poetry lets us dwell because it renders the ordinary extraordinary (compare *PLT*, 54).

VI

"Poetically man dwells." But Heidegger also says that we dwell insofar as we "belong . . . within the fourfold of sky, earth, mortals and divinities."[22] How are these two descriptions of dwelling related? Clearly there is intended to be a strong connection, an equivalence, even an identity between "the poetic" and "the fourfold." But how is this connection to be understood? What is the fourfold?

So far, I have been concerned to emphasize the discontinuity between *Being and Time* and late Heidegger. Let me now, however, turn to a continuity. This consists in the fact that late, like early, Heidegger understands human "being-in-the-world" to be a *structural* concept, a concept to be elucidated by an elucidation of the elements of the structure in question. In *Being and Time* these elements are described as the "existentials" of human being. Though not the same set of existentials, late Heidegger, too, understands being-in-the-world in terms of a structure of existentials.

In *Being and Time* Dasein's being-in-the-world is said to consist in "care." And care is defined in terms of the three-part structure of "temporality": it consists in "involvement" in a present world of "equipment" and other Dasein, an involvement that is conditioned by the legacy of a cultural past which Heidegger calls "heritage" and which provides Dasein with the outline of the proper projection of its life into the future. Late Heidegger defines being-in-the-world as a matter of being "on the earth," "under the sky," "among men," and "before the divinities" (*PLT*, 149). How, I want now to ask, does this fourfold structure map onto the threefold structure of "care"?

"Earth" and "sky," in some sense, nature, map onto, that is replace, "equipment." *Being and Time*'s highly abstract, denatured, almost disembodied, conception of the essentials of human existence has been replaced by a clear recognition that human beings are, inter alia, natural beings, *Erdsöhne* (sons of the earth), to use the Hölderlinian term Heidegger takes over in his discussions of the poet. "Poetically man dwells *on this earth*" runs the key text.

"Mortals," clearly, correspond to the (by definition mortal) "Dasein" of early Heidegger. As *Being and Time* identifies being among Dasein, "being-with-others (*Mitsein*)," so late Heidegger identifies "belonging to men's being with one another (*gehörend in das miteinander der menschen*)" (*PLT*, 149) as an existential of being-in-the-world. (Notice, again, that the abstractedness of "Dasein" has been replaced by the naturalness of "man.")

The element in late Heidegger's understanding of being-in-the-world that is most difficult to comprehend is "the gods."[23] Who are Heidegger's gods?

In "Building Dwelling Thinking" and "The Thing" the divinities are described as "messengers" (*PLT*, 150, 178), a point made in the Hölderlin discussions by calling them "angels": "The angel is the essence of what we otherwise call 'the gods' more purely expressed."[24] What, however, is the "message" that they bring?

Heidegger associates the gods with, above all, what he variously calls the "divine destinings" (*QCT*, 34), "laws"[25] or "edicts."[26] He says, for example, that Greek tragedy "brought the presence of the gods, brought the dialogue of divine and human destinings, to radiance" (*QCT*, 34). The divine laws of a community, its "simple and essential decisions" (*PLT*, 48), are what we may call its fundamental *ethos*. They provide the standard against which state law is ultimately to be judged. Antigone's resistance to the merely "human statutes" of Creon's state, for example, is grounded in and justified by, in Sophocles's words, "the immutable, unwritten edict divine."[27] Divine law also provides the basis for a critique of current public opinion. They "tend both towards and away from," in the title of one of Hölderlin's poems, "The Voice of the People" (HE, 288). Generalizing, then, we may say that divine law constitutes the basis for a critical assessment of current practice.

Though occasionally inclining to the view that the divine laws are "of the gods" in the sense of being *sanctioned* by them (at, for example, *GA* 4, 126), Heidegger's final (and certainly best) view is that they are "of the gods" in the sense of being brought to us, given "voice," by the gods (*GA* 4, 169). Since, however, the laws are "unwritten," the gods, unlike Moses, cannot articulate the laws verbally. They communicate them by, rather, being embodiments, incarnations, paradigm *exemplars* of the laws. They communicate them not, or not primarily, by saying them but by being, rather, the beings who they are.

In *Being and Time* Heidegger speaks of the "existence possibilities" embodied in "heritage" as the "sole authority" acknowledged by a "free" being, the authority that provides the basis for a critical assessment of the practices of the current "One" (*das Man*), the practices validated by current public opinion (*BT*, 391). He also holds that these "existence possibilities" are embodied in the figures of "heroes," memorialized in the collective memory of a culture. Hence, living autonomously is a matter of Dasein's "choosing its hero" (*BT*, 385) and following "loyally" in its footsteps (*BT*, 391).

These parallels make it clear, I think, that the "divine laws" of late Heidegger correspond to the "existence possibilities" preserved as heritage of early Heidegger, and that "the gods" are principally late Heidegger's way of talking about early Heidegger's "heroes." If this is correct then the important point to notice is that since heritage (as a part of "thrownness" in Heidegger's technical sense) is an *existential* feature of human being so, too, are the gods. Living "before the divinities" (*PLT*, 149) is something we *always* do—as long, at least, as we remain *human* beings.

Late Heidegger makes this point hard to grasp by defining modernity as the age of the "default" (*PLT*, 91) or "absence" (*PLT*, 184) of the gods, talk which one is inclined to equate with Nietzsche's talk of the "death of God," the extermination of the divine from modern culture. In fact, however, "default" is clearly not to be equated with "death" since, for example, "Building Dwelling Thinking" speaks of that paradigm of modernity, the highway bridge (*Autobahnbrücke*), as "a passage which crosses before the divinities." The gods, then, are *present* in modernity even though, as in the case of the bridge, "their presence is obstructed . . . even pushed wholly aside" (*PLT*, 153). Gods, in modernity, are not dead, merely "withdraw[n] into concealment" (*PLT*, 150). Heidegger makes this relatively explicit in the following passage:

The default of God and the divinities is absence. But absence is not nothing[28] rather it is precisely the presence, which must be first be appropriated, of the hidden fullness and wealth of what has been and what, thus gathered, is presencing, of the divine in the world of the Greeks, in prophetic Judaism, in the preaching of Jesus (*PLT*, 184).

In modernity, then, the gods remain with us. They are, however, not "appropriated" in our lives, do not "dispose the world's history" (*PLT*, 91), fail to make a difference to what actually happens in the world.

What is the difference between dead gods and concealed gods? Presumably, so long as we retain the capacity to respond to the "default" of the gods—the "darkening of the earth" as the *Introduction to Metaphysics* calls it—*as* a default, then no matter how ineffectual the gods may be in our lives, we remain in possession of our heritage. This is why Heidegger says that the time in which a culture "can no longer discern the default of God as a default" (*PLT*, 91) is "much grimmer" than the default of God itself. Such an intimation of a possible postmodernity is Heidegger's ultimate nightmare because (like Nietzsche's vision of the "last man," incapable any more of "giving birth to a star") it is a vision of the end of man as an ethical being, for Heidegger that is, a vision of the "death of man."

Why are the gods absent, concealed, in modernity? Concealment in general Heidegger understands as lack of illumination, lack of light. The concealed, dark side of the "globe of being," for example, is that which is unilluminated. Similarly, the concealment of the gods is due to the absence of the "divine radiance" (*PLT*, 91), of, that is, "the holy" which is the "ether" in which alone gods can appear as gods (*PLT*, 94). The gods, when they appear, appear "out of the holy sway" (*PLT*, 150) so as to be "remove[d] from any comparison" with all other beings (*PLT*, 178). Gods, in other words, are not just the "messengers" of the divine laws but are messengers possessed of *authority*. And it is the nature of ultimate ethical authority that it is charismatic.[29]

VII

The gods of late Heidegger correspond, then, to the heroes of *Being and Time*. They embody, are, heritage, and as such are existential features of our lives, our being-in-the-world. As human beings, whatever we do, whatever bridges we construct, we do and construct "before the divinities." It seems, then, that late Heidegger's account of being-in-the-world is given in terms of four existential elements: we live our lives on (a part of) the planet ("earth"), in a particular climate ("sky"), among human beings ("mortals"), and under the (appropriated or unappropriated) guidance of a given cultural tradition.

What, however, of "the fourfold," and what of dwelling? Habitation of the fourfold cannot be simply equivalent to this four-aspected being-in-the-world for, since this is a universal structure, *all* men would then (in the ordinary as well as essential sense) dwell and the homelessness of contemporary life would be impossible. There must be more to the fourfold than has so far been brought to light.

Here is Heidegger's description of the elements of the fourfold:

Earth is the serving bearer blossoming and fruiting, spreading out in rock and water, rising up in plant and animal. . . . The sky is the vaulting path of the sun, the course of the changing moon, the wandering glitter of the stars, the year's seasons and their changes, the light and dusk of day, the gloom and glow of night, the clemency and inclemency of the weather, the drifting clouds and blue depth of the ether. . . . The divinities are the beckoning messengers of the godhead. . . . The mortals are the human beings. They are called mortals because they . . . are capable of the death as death. (*PLT*, 149–150)

To say that mortals are capable of death as death is to say that they are capable of death as "the shrine of the nothing" (*PLT*, 178). The difference between this and my prosaic description of the fourfold being-in-the-world is surely obvious. Whereas I employed the *eindeutig* words of astronomy, meteorology, biology and sociology, Heidegger employs the *vieldeutig* words of poetry. And he does so, not as casual literary hyperbole, but rather to show something. What he shows, in his saying of the fourfold, is what it is to dwell. To dwell, Heidegger shows, is to inhabit the poetic: it is for the existential structure of being-in-the-world, to be lit up poetically, for it to become transparent to "the holy," for the "unknown" God to come to presence in the sight of familiar things. What Heidegger shows is that "poetically man dwells."

One dwells when one's world shows up poetically, when, as Heidegger sometimes puts it, things "shine." (More accurately, one dwells when one lives a life informed by such an experience, the life of care and conservation.) But one's world is a fourfold structure. So one dwells when the fourfold structure shines, when the planet becomes "earth," when sky becomes "the heavens" (*Himmel*, in German, covers both words), when men become "shrines of the nothing," and when the existence possibilities of heritage become radiant divinities. This is the connection between the two descriptions of dwelling with which this discussion began. "Dwelling is belonging within the fourfold" is the fully established meaning, the elucidation (*Erläuterung*) of "Poetically man dwells."

VIII

Heidegger calls the shining of things the "world's worlding." (He also describes it as its becoming a "site" for the fourfold (*PLT*, 154).) I should like to end this discussion by commenting on an aspect of "worlding" not yet mentioned. This is the thought that worlding is a "mirror-play," a "ring" or "round dance" of earth, sky, mortals, and divinities (*PLT*, 179–180). The fourfold is, says Heidegger, a "simple oneness" such that the thought of any one element immediately passes one on to the others. The picture presented is thus a dynamic one: the experience, for instance, of earth, of *poetic* earth, passes one onto that of sky and so on round the ring of the dance and back to earth.

I think that what Heidegger's conception of the mirror-play and ring dance points to is what Jeff Malpas, in *Place and Experience*,[30] calls "the complexity of place." Place, dwelling place, is not land nor people, not space nor time, not past nor present nor future. It is, rather, all of these together. If I try to think of the "essence" of England, for example, I think, perhaps, of the bare arms of winter oaks, of the Malvern hills imperceptibly shading into the dove-gray sky, of Elgar walking them to the sound of the singing of distant, Welsh voices, of the particular Englishness, the melancholic dignity of Elgar's *nobilmente*, of the funeral of Edward VII, of the proud heroes of a noble past, and of the Thatcherized present in relation to those heroes and that past. And so on, without end. Each of the elements of the fourfold is inextricably connected with all of the others and receives its being from that connection. Those particular hills are unthinkable without that particular sky, English melancholy, and hence the quality of English dignity, is unthinkable without the damp obscurity of the English winter, one's stance to the social present is unthinkable without one's preservation of the nobilities of the English past, and so on. Heidegger makes this point in *Hölderlins Erde und Himmel* by calling the fourfold "the un-ending (*un-entliche*) relationship." He explains that

None of the four stands and goes one-sidedly for itself. None is in this sense ending (*entlich*). None is without the others. *Un*-endingly they hold themselves towards each other, and are, what they are, out of the un-ending relationship, are this whole itself. (*GA* 4, 170)

10

Uncovering the Space of Disclosedness: Heidegger, Technology, and the Problem of Spatiality in *Being and Time*

Jeff Malpas

I

Of all the ways in which modern technology has brought about a transformation in the world and our experience of it, it is in our relation to space—and thereby also time—that its effects have been most striking and pervasive. Indeed, technological development has often taken as its icons images of speed and power that are representative of precisely the technological mastery of space—the locomotive, the aeroplane, the automobile. Moreover, many of the technologies that have been most significant in their impact on everyday life have been those that enable the overcoming of distance through new forms, not only of transportation, but of communication as well. In 1950, Heidegger took television to represent what he then called "the peak of this abolition of every possibility of remoteness"[1]; in the 1990s the Internet achieved an even more radical abolition of "remoteness," allowing us not merely to see and hear, but also to act in relation to things far removed from us in physical space.[2]

It is easy to think of the technological "conquest" of space as having vastly increased the accessibility and availability of things, yet Heidegger claims that in its seeming "abolition of remoteness," technology actually brings about a profound "distancing" of ourselves from the things around us and from the world.[3] Indeed, although technology is, as Heidegger acknowledges, a *mode* of disclosedness or revealing, its particular "en-framing" of things also entails a covering-over of things as they extend beyond the technological frame: within the domain of the technological, things are disclosed, not as *things*, but as *resource, material* or *"stock"* (*"Bestand"*—often translated as "standing-reserve"[4])—as "commodities" to be transformed, stored, and consumed in a way that obliterates difference and renders everything in a one-dimensional sameness. Thus Heidegger writes of the essence of technology that it "conceals that revealing which, in the sense of *poiesis*, lets what presences come forth into appearance. . . . The coming to presence of technology threatens revealing, threatens it with the possibility that all revealing will be consumed by ordering and that everything will present itself only in the unconcealedness of standing-reserve."[5] Appearing only as resource, the thing is stripped of its complex and multiple connections with the world—reduced to a single "aspect"—and, in this way, the very fact of disclosedness is itself covered over—within the technological frame, there is nothing to disclose other than what appears and what appears is just resource. Disclosedness, understood as the bringing to appearance of what would otherwise remain hidden (and so as an unconcealing that always presupposes hidden-ness), is itself covered over by technological revealing.

In the face of technology, disclosedness still occurs, but such disclosedness remains hidden, just as both the thing disclosed, and the world wherein disclosedness takes place, are also hidden—the thing appears only as resource and not as thing, while the world is reduced to a uniform system of transformable, consumable such resources. Disclosedness as more than this—disclosedness that allows the appearance of thing and world in their unitary complexity (which is the form of disclosedness that will be the focus throughout my discussion here) and which therefore allows disclosedness itself to come into view—is only possible, according to Heidegger, on the basis of a certain form of involved being-in-the-world which, even in the early work, he associates with "dwelling"[6] (although little is made of this concept in *Being and Time*). As Heidegger writes in "The Thing": "Men alone, as mortals, by dwelling attain to the world as world. Only what conjoins itself out of world becomes a thing."[7] The thing is a thing through being embedded in the world in a complex but integrated fashion—through its conjoining, its "gathering together," of such elements of world as earth and sky, mortals and gods. Inasmuch as technology threatens the possibility of such conjoining, it also threatens the disclosedness of the world and the possibility of mortal dwelling.

Moreover, just as the technological en-framing of things is associated with a certain transformation of spatiality and place, so too is dwelling, and the disclosedness of things to which dwelling is tied, associated with a form of space and place of its own (though the space at issue here is not that of mere physical extension). Dwelling is always "in" place, it opens up a space—it "gives room" for things and thereby allows things to stand forth and be disclosed as the complex but unitary things that they are. It is the disclosedness that arises in relation to the space and place of dwelling that Heidegger also refers to as "nearness"[8] and it is precisely such nearness that technology obliterates, according to Heidegger, through its en-framing of things as mere resource and its corresponding transformation of spatiality and place.

It is clear that spatiality plays an important role both in the Heideggerian critique of technology and in Heidegger's account of that being-in-the-world which we can also refer to as dwelling. But why should space play any role here at all—and why should it have anything to do with the structure of disclosededness? Or, to put the point in a way that brings out more clearly what might be at stake: exactly why should the technological transformation of space be connected with the obliteration of the possibility of that form of disclosedness that enables both thing and world to appear?

It will not be sufficient, in trying to answer such questions, simply to restate the Heideggerian claims concerning the concepts at issue. What we need is something that, within the framework of his own thinking (particularly of the later thinking in which these issues become explicitly thematized), Heidegger does not, and perhaps could not, provide. What is needed is an argument to show that the mode of disclosedness in which both thing and world are revealed is, in fact, only possible in relation to the involved being-in-the-world that is *dwelling*; an argument that thereby also demonstrates why the technological transformation of space and its obliteration of nearness renders such dwelling, and the possibility of disclosedness, in the sense at issue here, impossible. The presentation of such an argument, at least in outline, is just what will be attempted in the pages that follow. The basic strategy is to take up the issue of spatiality in more detail and, in particular, to pursue Heidegger's own analysis of that concept as it is set out in *Being and Time*. Through the analysis of spatiality, and of the relation between spatiality and disclosedness, the dependence that obtains between dwelling and disclosedness, and the role of the concrete thing in relation to these, should also be clarified.[9]

Spatiality occupies a problematic role in Heidegger's masterwork: on the one hand, many central concepts seem clearly to have strong spatial connotations[10] and yet, on the other hand, spatiality is explicitly seen as secondary to temporality. An investigation of these problems is significant, not only in illuminating certain difficulties in *Being and Time* itself, but also because it enables us to see why spatiality must indeed play a central role in relation to the concepts of disclosedness, dwelling and place, that are already taken up, even if only implicitly, in *Being and Time* and that come to center stage in Heidegger's later thinking. Hubert Dreyfus writes that "The discussion of spatiality is one of the most difficult in *Being and Time*, not because it is deeper than any other discussion but because it is fundamentally confused."[11] I agree with Dreyfus that the discussion is indeed "confused," but, as my comments above should already have indicated, I also think that the problems at stake in that discussion are quite fundamental to the issues that Heidegger pursues, not only in *Being and Time*, but along the entire course of his thinking.

Dreyfus's work will be an important source in the discussion that follows, and the account set out here might even be seen as something of a continuation of the investigation of the problem of spatiality that Dreyfus begins in his invaluable commentary. Yet this account also tries to push matters rather further than Dreyfus takes them in *Being-in-the-World*—Dreyfus's discussion there does indeed provide an entry into the problems at issue, but is not, I think, brought to a wholly satisfactory conclusion. This is not, of course, intended as any diminution in the achievement that *Being-in-the-World* represents. Dreyfus's work in that book—and not only there, but also in his teaching and in his many other writings—has shed new light on Heidegger's own thinking while also extending and elaborating Heideggerian ideas in new and original ways. Few other contemporary philosophers have done as much as Dreyfus in bridging the gulf between so-called continental thought and its "analytic" counterpart and few other philosophers can compare with Dreyfus in their commitment and dedication to the discipline. On a more personal note, I will always be grateful for Bert's friendship—for what I have learned from him, for the pleasure of his company, and for his loyalty and support. This chapter must stand as a small and very inadequate repayment for so much.

II

The problematic character of spatiality in *Being and Time* emerges as soon as Heidegger attempts, in §12 of the work, to clarify the notion of "being-in" (*In-sein*)—a notion that is clearly a central component in the structure of Dasein understood as being-in-the-world. "Being-in" has, on the Heideggerian account, two distinct senses. The first is that which involves spatial or physical containment and designates, as Heidegger puts it, "the kind of Being which an entity has when it is 'in' another one, as the water is 'in' the glass, or the garment is 'in' the cupboard".[12] The second sense of "being-in"—the sense that Heidegger takes to be proper to the structure of "being-in-the-world"—is that associated with residing or *dwelling* ("wohnen, habitare, sich aufhalten"[13]) and is presented by Heidegger as not primarily a matter of being "in space" at all, but rather of "familiarity with" and of "looking after." In this sense, "being-in" seems to be primarily a matter of a certain sort of engagement or involvement and, indeed, Dreyfus characterizes the contrast between the senses of "being-in" at issue here in terms of a contrast between "two senses of 'in': a spatial sense ('in the box') and an existential sense ('in the army', 'in love'). The first use expresses inclusion, the second conveys involvement."[14]

The sense of "being-in" that is explicated in terms of what Dreyfus calls "inclusion," and that might also be understood in terms of "containment," is essentially a conception tied to a particular understanding of space—a characteristically modern understanding that is based in the idea of bodily extension and is exemplified, in an especially significant form, in the writings of Descartes.[15] In Albert Einstein's characterization, the modern idea of "an independent (absolute) space, unlimited in extent, in which all material objects are contained" is arrived at by "natural extension" from the concept of the particular space that exists within any particular enclosing or "containing" body.[16]

Of those entities whose being is simply a matter of their being "in space"—of their being "contained" in relation to some other such entity or in relation to "world-space"—Heidegger says that they all possess a characteristic sameness: "All entities whose Being 'in' one another can thus be described have the same kind of Being—that of being-present-at-hand—as Things occurring 'within' the world."[17] Thus Heidegger connects the modern or "Cartesian" understanding of spatiality directly with the other important "Cartesian" idea— central to much of Heidegger's critical analysis in *Being and Time*— that understands things as theoretical or epistemic "objects" that are merely "present" or "occurrent" (*Vorhanden*) rather than "available" for use.[18] We might say, then, that grasping things as spatial, in the modern understanding of the term, is also to grasp those things as "objects" and so as "objective."

The sense in which merely "occurrent" entities are "within" the world is, in fact, a somewhat derivative sense—with respect to all such entities, they are "in" the world only in the sense in which they are "contained within" other such entities or in which all such entities may be said to be contained, within the space of the world or, better, of the physical universe. This point is given a special emphasis inasmuch as merely "occurrent" entities that have their being "in space" cannot, according to Heidegger, stand in any essential relation of involvement or contact with one another—such entities "can never 'touch' each other, nor can either of them 'be' 'alongside' the other."[19] Here Heidegger essentially reiterates the contrast between the "being-in" of "inclusion" or "containment" and that of "involvement," but in a way that puts additional emphasis on the "merely occurrent" character of entities as they are "in space." Entities can only be brought into any real contact—and so, one might say, be properly grasped from "within" the world—inasmuch as they are taken up within Dasein's own context of involvement. Dasein itself, however, brings its world with it through its involvement in that world. As Heidegger notes: "Being-in . . . is a state of Dasein's Being; it is an existentiale. So one cannot think of it as the Being-present-at-hand [occurrentness] of some corporeal Thing (such as a human body) 'in' an entity which is present-at-hand."[20]

At this point it becomes very clear, if it were not already so, the way in which the concept of space is, on the Heideggerian approach, intimately bound up with an ontology to which the account developed in *Being and Time* is fundamentally opposed. Thus Heidegger writes that "[i]n ontology . . . an attempt has been made to start with spatiality and then to Interpret the Being of the 'world' as *res extensa*. In Descartes we find the most extreme tendency towards such an ontology of the 'world'."[21] This passage is particularly significant, not only in foregrounding the contrast between Heidegger's approach and that which takes the being of things "in" space as its starting point, but also inasmuch as it indicates something of the tension in Heidegger's approach to the question of spatiality: the account of Dasein cannot begin with spatiality even though it does begin with a set of concepts that seem to carry spatial connotations—Dasein cannot be properly understood on the basis of spatiality conceived in terms of the notions of containment, extension, and "occurrentness" and yet Dasein does have a spatiality of its own. Not only can these tensions be seen as part of the internal problematic of *Being and Time*, and important for that alone, but they also have an obvious relevance to the broader question within which the present inquiry is framed concerning the role of spatiality in the disclosedness of things and the structure of such disclosedness itself.

Of course, the solution to these tensions, at least as Heidegger presents matters in *Being and Time*, seems clear enough: Dasein's own spatiality ("existential spatiality") is explicated through the structure of Dasein's involvement within the equipmental ordering of things which, as we shall see below, is itself grounded specifically in temporality; the broader sense of spatiality that might seem already to be implicated in the discussion of Dasein as "being-in-the-world" (but which tends to remain implicit in Heidegger's discussion) is in fact to be understood in terms of the "being-in" of involvement which receives its full explication in terms of the notions of care (*Sorge*), of "being-towards-death" and so, ultimately, of temporality also. It thus turns out that the spatiality that is proper to Dasein, whether understood in terms of the particular spatiality proper to Dasein or in terms of the apparently spatial character of Dasein's being as such—a spatiality which, in either sense, is distinct from the spatiality associated with merely occurrent entities—is actually to be understood as fundamentally temporal.

Heidegger's determination to exclude spatiality from any fundamental role in the understanding of the structure of Dasein is evident, not only in passages such as that concerning the nature of "being-in," but, most explicitly and directly, in the discussion of the priority of temporality in §70 of *Being and Time*—the section titled "The Temporality of the Spatiality that is characteristic of Dasein" ("Die Zeitlichkeit des daseinmässigen Räumlichkeit").[22] Here the primary aim is the establishment of the derivative character of Dasein's own existential spatiality,[23] but it can also be taken as indicative of the derivative character of spatiality as such—something that is, of course, also evident as part of the larger argument that gives priority to the being-in of involvement over that of inclusion and to availableness over occurrentness.

The argument that Heidegger sketches out here (and it is really the barest of outlines) focuses on the character of existential spatiality (already set out, as I noted above, in §§22–24) as based in the referential ordering of things within a "region" (*Gegend*) of activity, that is, in the ordering of things (as "available" or "ready-to-hand"—*Zuhanden*) within an equipmental totality. Hammer, saw, and other tools thus each have a "place" (*Platz*) within the interconnected network of places that is the region of activity established through the work of carpentry, and only through being ordered within this region, and so in relation to the overarching activity with respect to which it is constituted, are they available as the tools that they are. Each tool thus "refers" to the larger structure and framework of activity within which it is "placed" and thereby made available. While the ways in which we read the details of Heidegger's analysis may vary, it is this equipmental ordering that is the basis for Dasein's oriented spatiality—a spatiality elaborated further through the notions of "orientation" or "directionality" ("*Ausrichtung*") and "distance" or "de-severance" ("*Ent-fernung*"). Heidegger argues that this equipmental ordering, and the referentiality that is characteristic of it, derives from the directionality of temporality. To put matters slightly differently, since the ordering of equipmentality in which spatiality is based is tied to activity and since activity is always projective—presently oriented toward a set of future possibilities on the basis of a past actuality—so it is temporality that enables the opening up of the spatial ordering of Dasein's world.

If it were indeed the case that a derivation of spatiality from temporality could be shown to be possible, then it would clearly demonstrate the untenability of the idea that spatiality has any special role in the structure of disclosedness. The direction suggested by my comments in the opening discussion above would thereby have been shown to lead to a dead end—or to a dead end whose only exit was through time. Yet while the centrality of concepts of activity, and so of temporality, to the problems at issue here cannot be doubted,[24] the idea that one can indeed achieve a derivation of the spatial, in any significant sense, from the purely temporal is certainly a dubious one. In fact, if we consider the issues at stake here more closely, it soon becomes evident that such a derivation, as Heidegger himself came to recognize,[25] is impossible. Moreover, not only is the failure of the attempt to show the derivative character of space important in coming to an understanding of the problematic of *Being and Time*, but the reasons behind the impossibility of such a derivation provide a means to understanding the way in which spatiality might after all have a role to play in the disclosedness of things.

One of the first points to note in relation to the supposed derivation of spatiality from temporality is that, taken on its own, temporality lacks the resources to establish any sense of simultaneous dimensionality, and with it the sense of *externality*, that is necessary, not only for spatiality, but also for the possibility of distinguishing between different entities or between oneself and entities other than oneself. Thus, when Heidegger considers the structure of equipmentality, the impression one is given is of a network of interrelated entities whose spatial arrangement is wholly dependent on their belonging within a system of referential ordering that derives from the directionality and referentiality of the temporal. Already, however, in the very assumption that there are indeed a set of distinct entities involved here, some notion of spatiality has been assumed, since only within a spatial domain—that is, within a realm of simultaneous dimensionality—is it possible for entities to be arrayed in such a way that they can indeed accord with a certain equipmental ordering.[26]

It might seem, of course, as if this is already to treat the entities at issue here as if they were merely occurrent rather than available. But this would be, in part, simply to assume that the only model of spatiality that is available here, other than the "temporalised" model that Heidegger advances as the basis of existential spatiality, is that of Cartesian spatiality. Certainly, the account of spatiality found in Descartes and in modern thinking generally, does represent a particular way of trying to articulate what is involved in the idea of space, but it need not be supposed that it represents the only, or, indeed, a fully adequate and exhaustive articulation of the concept of space as such. Heidegger, at least in *Being and Time*, seems to assume that it is, and so it is not surprising that he is led to insist on treating spatiality, as it is relevant to the existential structure of Dasein, as derivable from temporality.

There is, however, an alternative here, and that is to view the Cartesian idea of spatiality as expressing what is already a particular and somewhat narrow appropriation of the idea of the spatial. Spatiality, in its more basic sense, could then be seen as identical with the notion of simultaneous dimensionality that is an irreducible element in the experience of movement and is presupposed by the capacity to distinguish between ourselves and the things around us, both available and occurrent. Understood in this way, spatiality is only partially grasped in the "objective" terms of Cartesian thinking, since such thinking leaves no room for space as it is a feature of our own locatedness—or our own place-ing—in the world (which is not, I should emphasize, merely a matter of our own subjectivity) nor even, in an important sense, of the locatedness of things. From this perspective, Heidegger must be viewed as actually overestimating the resources of Cartesian spatiality and so misconstruing the nature of spatiality almost from the start.

The "being-in" of spatial containment—supposedly identical with Cartesian spatiality—is exemplified, so Heidegger claims, in the mode of being of merely occurrent or present-at-hand entities. Heidegger also observes that such entities cannot stand in any essential relation of contact with one another—they can neither be said to "touch" nor to be "alongside" each other. The difficulty is to make sense of the notion of containment at work in the account of the being-in of occurrent entities in the absence of any such notion of contact between the entities at issue. It is instructive, at this point, to consider Aristotle's analysis of the being-in associated with *topos* (often translated as "space," though the translation is a problematic one) in *Physics* IV. This analysis, while not explicitly referred to by Heidegger, seems nevertheless to stand in the background of his discussion.[27] Aristotle defines *topos* explicitly in relation to a notion of containment (indeed containment seems to play an important role in the development of all spatial thinking) and in terms of the point at which an enclosed body "touches" the body that surrounds it. *Topos* is thus "the limit of the enclosing body, at which it is in contact with that which is enclosed."[28]

It is worth noting that the example of containment to which Heidegger first turns in his discussion in §12 of *Being and Time*—the example of the water in the glass is a prime example of containment, and of *topos*, in the Aristotelian sense in which the water is "contained" and so has a place through being enclosed by another body (in fact by two bodies, we might say, the glass around, and the air above, the surface of the water). Perhaps even more noteworthy is the role played by the consideration of containment in "The Thing." There the thing that is the focus for Heidegger's discussion is a jug and it is precisely through thoughtful consideration of the jug *as container* that Heidegger leads us to an account of the jug as gathering together and so disclosing the world.[29]

Now we can always choose to define the notion of containment so as to fit whatever spatial framework we prefer and so we can certainly construct a notion of containment—as tied, for instance, to a notion of coordinate position—that will fit within a Cartesian view of space. But when defined in such a way, containment becomes a wholly derivative rather than a basic concept. In this respect the development of the modern conception of space, while it certainly has its origins in notions of containment (as containment plays a role in the development of all spatial thinking), actually consists in a gradual separation of the concept of spatiality away from the notion of containment. And, in fact, the so-called "container" view of space associated with Descartes and with Newton involves only a very attenuated notion of containment. With post-Newtonian physics, and the development of the idea of a space-time "field," the idea of containment is finally expunged from the concept of spatiality altogether.[30]

Although, as the history of philosophy shows, the Aristotelian notion of *topos* faces a number of problems, that account is nevertheless significant in suggesting an important connection between the concepts of space and place and the notion of containment. Inasmuch as our basic grasp of spatiality, which is not separable from our grasp of place, involves a notion of containment that gradually disappears from the concept of space as it is developed in physical theory, so space as physics conceives of it cannot be treated as identical with the concept of space that is already part of our ordinary conceptual repertoire or that is evident to us in our everyday experience of the world. Moreover, inasmuch as the idea of containment, while historically and genetically important to the modern conception of space, cannot be theoretically basic to that conception, so containment must be treated as merely a derivative notion within physical theory—as the idea of place must also be treated.[31] In that case, Heidegger makes a serious error when he takes the "being-in" of inclusion or containment to be basic to Cartesian spatiality and to the spatiality associated with the merely occurrent—he must be viewed as similarly mistaken in taking the spatiality of containment as having no relevance to the being-in of being-in-the-world.

One particularly important consideration in this regard, one that is explicit in Aristotle, concerns the connection between containment and boundedness. Indeed, this is especially clear when we come to consider the nature of space as it relates to place—the opening up of a space in place is essentially a space that is opened up as it is also bounded and only though such bounded are the determinate spaces of place and region even possible. In his later thinking, through both an emphasis on the necessary connection of spatiality with place and on the centrality of place to the possibility of things being revealed (dwelling is itself to be understood only in connection with place), this error is avoided—although at the same time, the structure of spatiality as such, and the exact details of its connection with place and dwelling, is never properly filled out.

Notions of region and place already carry within them, and require for their proper articulation, the very notion of containment or enclosedness that Heidegger seems, in *Being and Time*, to consign to the realm of Cartesian spatiality. Containment—which must be understood in terms of the constraining or limiting of one thing by some larger structure—is what makes for the possibility of the sort of ordered and bounded spaces and places that are evident even in the structure of spatiality as tied to the ordering of equipment. The "nesting" of places that Heidegger notes, in §12, as a feature of the spatiality of "occurrentness," turns out to be a feature of equipmental space also—tools are found "within" particular equipmental regions, which regions are themselves located within other such regions and in being involved in some activity Dasein is itself directed and constrained by that framework of regionality essentially, though this requires further explication, through being located within it. Spatiality thus provides a structure within which things are differentiated from each other and from Dasein through their externality to one another and to Dasein; while the possibility of a certain structure of equipmental ordering depends on a certain bounded space within which that ordering is opened up. And such a space cannot be derived from equipmentality nor from temporality, even though its ordering is not independent of them, for these structures themselves depend on some form of spatiality for their articulation. Once again, what emerges here is an overall structure in which both spatial and temporal notions (tied, in the first instance, to equipmentality) are joined together in their mutual articulation and in the articulation of a structure that we may well, following later Heidegger, speak of in terms of the structure of place (*topos, Ort*).

The role of spatiality as already presupposed (although not recognized as such) by the structure that Heidegger attempts to lay out in *Being and Time,* and so as being also presupposed by the structure of disclosedness as such, is especially evident in connection with the analysis of "dis-tance" (*Ent-fernung*). And it is here that the various issues at stake come properly into focus. Indeed, although what has been shown up to this point has indicated some of the difficulty in deriving spatiality from temporality, and this has also resulted in certain features of spatiality itself being uncovered, the central question as to how, and in what sense, spatiality might be connected to disclosedness has still to be answered. In the discussion of the problem of dis-tance (and to some extent, also, with respect to the related issue of "orientation" or "directionality"—*Ausrichtung*) the elements of such an answer come together and the argument for the necessity of a certain form of spatiality (and so also of dwelling and place) to disclosedness can be made more explicit.

The account of existential spatiality in relation to the concept of dis-tance is, in fact, the focus for Dreyfus's claim, already encountered above, that Heidegger's discussion of spatiality is "fundamentally confused." The source of this confusion, according to Dreyfus, concerns Heidegger's failure to distinguish "*public* space in which entities show up for human beings, from the centered spatiality of each *individual* human being"[32] More specifically, Dreyfus claims that "Heidegger fails to distinguish the general opening up of space as the field of presence (dis-stance) that is the condition for things being near and far, from Dasein's pragmatic bringing things near by taking them up and using them. Such pragmatic bringing near as Heidegger uses the term can only be near to *me*, it is not a dimension of public space."[33] The establishing of things as ordered within a spatial field in which they show up as near or far actually depends, argues Dreyfus, on the ordering of the public structure of equipmentality. Heidegger, however, remains unclear on this point, treating dis-tance as apparently a matter both of the field of presence given in equipmentality and of Dasein's own capacity to "bring things near" through its active engagement in the world. As Dreyfus points out, this seems to threaten an incipient subjectivism in Heidegger's account, since dis-tance seems to be something established by the individual activities of Dasein rather than being already given in the public space of equipmentality. Moreover, if dependent on each individual Dasein, then dis-tance, and the field of spatiality, would be primarily subjective structures, from which public spatiality would need somehow to be derived.[34] Yet although Dreyfus is mostly correct in his identification of the problems here, it is not merely some general confusion on Heidegger's part that explains the difficulties that arise in the discussion of spatiality. Instead those difficulties derive directly from Heidegger's inadequate conception of spatiality and his insistence on deriving spatiality from temporality.

I noted above the way in which the structure of equipmentality, although viewed by Heidegger as the basis for spatiality, itself depends on some notion of spatial dimensionality and externality in order to be possible. In addition, it should now be evident that this need not imply that equipmentality is thereby grounded in some form of Cartesian spatiality. Spatiality, including the idea of spatiality as connected with the notions of containment, boundedness and externality, is conceptually more basic than the idea of spatiality as formulated in physical theory. The structure of equipmentality can thus be viewed, as I indicated above, as both based in the structure of spatiality, while also articulating that structure in a specific form that derives from a certain public and communal mode of "engagement" in the world (a structure that in this respect, drawing on the language of the later Heidegger, derives from human "building"). It is the exact nature of this engagement, however, that turns out to be crucial.

The structure of equipmentality is, as Dreyfus emphasises, a publicly available structure[35] that is also based in communal interaction and articulation (dependent, therefore, on a "history" and "tradition"). The engagement of Dasein in the world that makes for such interaction and articulation is not a mode of engagement that pertains to Dasein in some generalized sense—Dasein, in its generality, is not capable of concrete engagement at all, no more than the *concept* of Dasein is capable of using a hammer. The engagement of Dasein in the world must thus be a matter of the engagement of *individuals* (though it is *not* dependent on the engagement of any *particular* individual) and this is simply because engagement is always *with* some particular thing or things, *within* some ordered region, *from* a particular location (it requires the locatedness of the individual actor, as well as of the things interacted with, both of which stand within the same framework of a single "place" of engagement). Without Dasein, of course, there is no equipmentality—a workbench, for instance, with all its various tools in "place," but removed from the context of the Dasein (that is, the human community) with whom it belongs, no longer carries any equipmental ordering, and so no spatial ordering beyond that of the merely occurrent. Yet for an equipmental structure to stand in proper relation to the Dasein with whom it belongs is just for there to be a community of individuals who are themselves engaged within that equipmental structure. The opening up of what Dreyfus calls "the field of presence"— dis-tance—thus has to be understood as based in both the equipmental ordering of space *and* in the ordering that derives from individual locatedness within that ordering.

Dreyfus's claim that Heidegger confuses the way in which dis-tance is already opened up in the public space of equipmentality with the capacity of individual Dasein to bring things close in using them can now be seen as indicative of what may be a more basic confusion concerning the way in which equipmental ordering and concrete locatedness are involved here. Yet the role of locatedness as a prerequisite for the possibility of Dasein's engagement in its world has still to be properly filled out. Clearly the idea of locatedness is tied to the connection between the notions of containment, boundedness, and place that have already been sketched out above—locatedness, in the sense relevant to engagement, necessarily entails a certain positioning within a particular and constraining set of possibilities. For such positioning to be possible, however, it must involve more than the simple location of an undifferentiated, dimensionless "point." Such simple location—the sort of location associated with Cartesian spatiality—would not carry any orientation or directionality with it of the sort that would either open up any differential ordering amongst entities or that would enable an entity such as Dasein to be differently positioned in relation to the things around it. In short, Dasein must be oriented with respect to the particular "places" and regions around it, and such orientation is first and foremost a matter of those places and regions being related back to differences in

Dasein itself—which must here mean, to differences in Dasein's own body, since it is only by means of its body that Dasein is located in respect of, and so capable of engagement with, things.[36] Dasein's locatedness must thus be a matter of its engagement in the world on the basis of a differentiated and extended body. Heidegger's failure to take proper account of locatedness—and so of dis-tance and orientation—is directly tied, therefore, to his inadequate treatment of the body. While the issue of embodiment is something that Heidegger recognizes, he seems effectively to consign the body (perhaps not surprisingly given the framework of his account) to the realm of Cartesian spatiality.[37] The body is thereby denied any significant role in Heidegger's account and the issue of locatedness as it relates to engagement cannot be adequately addressed.

Not only is individual Dasein necessarily located and oriented in the world, but so are the things with which Dasein engages inasmuch as both "fit" into space in different ways that are appropriate to them. Grasping the nature of the object is, in large part, a matter of grasping that fit. In this respect, the ordering of equipmental region, and the grasping of that ordering, is not just a matter of the way in which the things that make up that region are geared in relation to one another, and to the activities proper to the region, in terms of role or function, but is also necessarily tied to their spatial "fit," that is, to the way they are oriented in relation to each other and to any engaged individual Dasein.

Both the equipmental structure, as I noted earlier, and the structure of spatial locatedness are part of a single public structure—even though it is a structure with which Dasein engages through the engagement of individuals. As a public structure, it is a structure that, with respect to any particular individual Dasein, is always given prior to any such individual—individual Dasein thus always finds itself already within an ordered public space. Moreover, inasmuch as Dasein's being "within" such a space is always a matter of its oriented, embodied location in that space, Dasein is always situated in a public space with respect to which, as a consequence of its concrete, embodied location, it already has a certain orientation. It is precisely on the basis of this structure, in which both equipmentality and embodied locatedness play equally essential roles, that distance—

the disclosedness of things as near and far—is itself made possible. In sitting at a dinner table, for instance, I am thereby situated bodily, and so in certain concrete spatial relations, with respect to other people, table and chairs, cutlery, dishes, food, drink, and the room in which all are contained. On this basis, a certain orientation and dis-tance is "automatically" and immediately opened up to me with the opening up of a particular place that is structured in terms of both equipmentality and embodied locatedness (which are themselves, in certain important senses, mutually dependent).[38]

The dis-tance that is involved here is, of course, opened up to me with respect to my particular perspective, but it is not thereby subjectively based. The structure of dis-tance derives from my particular situatedness within a public space and a publicly accessible equipmental structure; it involves my particular relatedness to things and other persons that are themselves concretely located in a public space. Furthermore, the exact manner in which things are given to me here, although dependent on my bodily location, is, in principle, open to almost any one who is disposed, in terms of her spatial and equipmental orientation, in the same way. I say "almost," because what I have left out here is the one thing that Heidegger leaves in—namely temporality. In fact, spatial and bodily locatedness has to be complemented (or perhaps "elaborated") in relation to a temporal orientation also. But that temporal orientation is itself partly dependent on the public orientation of the equipmental structure (a structure that turns out to involve both spatial and temporal elements) and partly dependent on a past history of bodily orientation and activity. For these reasons, among others, there are important advantages in talking, not simply of spatiality alone here, but rather of *place* as a structure that encompasses (though in no simple fashion) both spatial and temporal structures as well as structures deriving from the equipmental and the social.

The problem Heidegger faces should be clear, within the framework of *Being and Time*, in taking adequate account of the considerations at issue here. Since Heidegger is already committed to the founding role of temporality alone, and, in any case, allows no room for spatiality other than in terms of the choice between the impoverished spatiality of "inclusion" or the temporalized spatiality of "involvement," so he cannot take adequate account of either embodiment or spatial locatedness. But if the latter are refused admission to the discussion (or are allowed entry in only a secondary role), then one is left with no choice but to try and understand dis-tance and orientation as based in some subjective capacity to "orient" oneself and to "bring things near" that must be somehow derived from temporal projection (although even in *Being and Time* it remains obscure as to how this could possibly be achieved). Moreover Heidegger's hermeneutical orientation in his earlier thinking, and the accompanying focus on the problem of meaning, also seems to be a source of misdirection. If it is the meaningfulness of Dasein's being-in-the-world that has to be explained, then focusing on the referentiality of the equipmental structure, and so on temporality, will indeed look like a plausible path to take in looking for some way to ground such meaningfulness. Yet since meaning is essentially based in relations between *kinds* of entities, rather than between entities in their *particularity*, so the emphasis on meaningfulness will likely be accompanied by a de-emphasis of the particular, the concrete, and the located. It will also tend, as a consequence, to reinforce any existing tendency to neglect the spatial and to prioritize the temporal. It is perhaps no accident, then, to find the shift away from a purely temporal analysis to be accompanied by a shift, as Heidegger describes it in the Le Thor seminar, away from meaning, in the first instance to truth, and then to place.[39]

If we shift our considerations to a broader perspective, then we can begin to see why it is that disclosedness, which can be seen as already implicitly at issue in the discussion of dis-tance, might indeed be tied to spatiality, to place, and thence, of course, to dwelling. Heidegger understands the disclosedness that is at issue here in terms of the disclosedness of things *as* things, that is, in their complex but unitary embeddedness in the world. Such embeddedness can be understood as just a matter of the concrete locatedness of things within a particular, bounded place—only thus is the thing enabled to stand forth as the focus for the multiplicity of different aspects and interconnections that are also part of the structure of the world. Such disclosedness—understood now just as the possibility of "nearness"—is itself possible only on the basis of human engagement in the world (engagement which is necessarily the engagement of a community rather than merely a single individual) which is also tied to the concrete locatedness of Dasein within a particular, bounded place (and so with respect to particular things within that place) and by means of which a form of ordered spatiality is opened up. Although there is, of course, much more that needs to be said here to fill out this account in its entirety, it is essentially inasmuch as Dasein finds itself in the world in terms of this sort of oriented, located engagement that Dasein can be said to dwell and it is thus, to cut matters all too short, that disclosedness must rest in the possibility of dwelling and in the possibility of the particular form of spatiality with which dwelling turns out to be associated.

Since the structure of disclosedness as here set out cannot be viewed as founded in any single element—one cannot take the locatedness of Dasein or the things with which it is engaged as that which constitutes the underlying ground for the structure of disclosedness as a whole (in the manner, for instance, in which *Being and Time* attempts to treat temporality as providing such a ground[40])—so an important methodological point emerges as a crucial element in this account. Dasein's located, embodied engagement opens up a space within which things can also be located, but such opening up of a space is itself already dependent on the character of things in their worldly embeddedness. We might say, therefore, that the methodology that becomes evident here is a methodology that reflects the structure of disclosedness itself. The structure at issue is one that is made up of a number of interrelated components that jointly provide an articulation, and so a grounding, for the structure of disclosedness as a whole. It is only on the basis of the structure of disclosedness as such, however, that any element within that structure can be exhibited. In this respect, the task of providing an account of the structure of disclosedness is not only an account that must attend to the concepts of space and place as they play a role in the structure at issue, but the elaboration of that structure can also be understood as essentially a matter of the mapping out of a space, or better a place, within which a multiplicity of interrelated elements appear and which are mutually constitutive of that very space or place.[41] Such an approach is characteristic of Heidegger's later thinking and is reflected in his emphasis on the importance of "topology" and his frequent use of ideas and images of space and place.[42] It is strikingly evident in the structure of the Fourfold (*Das Geviert*) which, as a gathering together, in relation to the thing, of earth and sky, mortals and divinities, is itself constituted through the elements it unifies, while those elements are themselves revealed through that very unity.[43]

III

If the discussions in the previous section have even partially achieved their goal, then we should now be in a better position to explain exactly why it is that the technological transformation of space presents a problem for the possibility of the sort of disclosedness of thing and world that seems so to preoccupy Heidegger. Technology clearly does not change the basic physical disposition of things in the world—both persons and things are still located within physical space much as they were before. But within the reign of technological modernity, space no longer separates things as it might have previously—distance is no longer a barrier to access or availability—and consequently the difference between what is near and what is far is immensely reduced if not obliterated. This is most dramatically the case in relation to media and computer technology. Seated before my computer I may find that something physically far removed from me is actually closer, through its electronic accessibility, than something in my immediate environment—an electronic text held on a web server two thousand miles away may actually be closer than the hard copy of the same text that sits on the shelf in the next room.

The result of this obliteration of the difference between near and far is a corresponding obliteration or covering over of the differences in the spatial ordering of things, not merely in my immediate vicinity, but throughout the world as a whole. Now given the way in which, as the previous analysis has indicated, the disclosedness of things *as* things is fundamentally dependent on the concrete locatedness of both individual human actor (Dasein) and thing, so the very concreteness and particularity of things tends to be covered over by this obliteration of difference. Of course, it is still the case that human engagement in the world is indeed dependent on engaged location with particular objects, but the fact of such concrete engagement is covered over and hidden as technology takes up both human actor and thing within a framework removed from such concreteness.

One way of describing the particular covering over of things that is characteristic of technological revealing is to say that it replaces the *things* themselves with images or *representations* (*Vorstellungen*)[44] of things—that is, it re-presents things within a particular "frame" and in a way that is abstracted from their original locatedness. Moreover, in re-presenting things in this way, and in covering over things in their concrete particularity, so technology also obscures the character of such re-presented things *as* re-presented. When the representation refers us to nothing beyond the representation or system of representations as such—when the mode of disclosure is such that what is revealed is shown as nothing beyond what is actually given in that particular mode of disclosedness—then the representation comes to be all that there is. Within the technological frame, then, the revealing of things as resource or "standing-reserve" blocks off the possibility of things as anything more than just resource and it does this precisely through removing things from their full, three-dimensional locatedness and representing them in an abstracted and reduced form. Just as a photograph reveals things from only one perspective, in only one pose, so does technology disclose things in a similarly one-dimensional fashion. Moreover, unlike the photograph, which itself appears *as* a photograph with its frame clearly in view, the technological representation of things is not self-evidently a mode of representation at all—instead technology presents its representations of things as identical with the things themselves.

The technological shift from locatedness to dislocation, from things to "representations," brings with it a number of problematic consequences. Inasmuch as technology covers over the concrete locatedness of both human being and worldly object, it covers over the nature of both the human and the thing. As a result, technology leads us to misunderstand the character of our own being-in-the-world as well as the mode of being of the things with which we are engaged. In this respect, inasmuch as technology removes us from our proper place, obliterating any proper sense of place, it also covers over our own mortality—a mortality that can itself be viewed as essentially connected to the place-bound character of our being.[45] This covering over of mortality is in turn associated with a covering over of human boundedness, with an overestimation of human capacities and an inability to recognize the proper scope of human activity—it is thus that technological revealing gives rise to the appearance of technology as something that is always amenable to human direction and control, while, at the same time, the human is itself brought increasingly within the frame of resource. At the same time, the technological transformation of the world transforms the character of human experience of the world: such experience becomes a matter of re-presentation, of a narrowed-down sensitivity (often focused on only a narrow range of sensory and interactive modalities—in the case of the television, and the computer, primarily those of sound and vision), rather than of the engagement of the body in its entirety.[46] As the thing is no longer present to us in its concrete locatedness under the sky and upon the earth, so the sky is no longer "seen" nor is the earth "touched"—we no longer find ourselves in the world, we no longer engage with things, we no longer encounter ourselves.

Heidegger writes: "Unless man first establishes himself beforehand in the space proper to his essence and there takes up his dwelling, he will not be capable of anything essential within the destining now holding sway."[47] Such a prior "establishing," or perhaps we should say "recovering," of our own place and space is inseparable from a recovery of the place and space proper to things—it is only in relation to things, and in the space of place, that we ourselves are brought into view. Recovering such a space and place for things, and for ourselves, cannot, however, be a matter of simply deciding for or against technology. Technology, as a mode of revealing, is that on the basis of which decision is possible rather than being established through any such decision. The recovery of a proper space for human dwelling in the face of technological en-framing has thus to be worked out in relation to technology itself, even though it cannot be achieved by any purely technological means. Exactly how that is to be possible must remain in question (it is, according to Heidegger, something we can only await)—what is clear, however, is that such a recovery of the possibility of dwelling must involve a recovery of that space of nearness in which not only thing and world, but also disclosed-ness itself (and so technology as a *mode* of disclosedness), can be uncovered.

III

Heideggerian Encounters

The Primacy of Practice and Assertoric Truth: Dewey and Heidegger

William D. Blattner

I Introduction

Richard Rorty and Mark Okrent have offered us a reading of *Being and Time*[1] that portrays Heidegger's early thought as essentially pragmatist. Rorty writes, "With Okrent, I read Division One of *Being and Time* as a recapitulation of the standard pragmatist arguments against Plato and Descartes."[2]

What is the essence of this pragmatism? Rorty clarifies:

Once understanding is de-intellectualized in the way in which both Dewey and Heidegger wanted to de-intellectualize it—by viewing the so-called "quest for disinterested theoretical truth" as a continuation of practice by other means—most of the standard pragmatist doctrines follow.[3]

According to Rorty, Dewey and Heidegger share the same basic, anti-intellectualist move: they both deny that understanding is an autonomous, intellectual endeavor, aiming in the first instance at theoretical truth. Rather, understanding is primarily a sort of practice, or as Heidegger says, a sort of competence or ability, and theoretical knowing is a special case of this. This is the essential, anti-Cartesian, antitraditionalist move made by both authors.

Dewey and Heidegger are both clearly anti-Cartesian, and both do "de-intellectualize" the understanding. Rorty is apt to mislead us, however, by suggesting that Dewey and Heidegger "de-intellectualize" understanding in the same way.[4] In fact, as I shall argue, Dewey and

Heidegger de-intellectualize the understanding in conflicting ways. If so, the question inevitably then becomes, how important are these conflicts? The standard that I shall use in assessing their importance is one suggested by the passage from Rorty: do the "standard pragmatist doctrines" follow from both philosophers' conceptions of understanding? They do not. In particular, the pragmatist account of truth does not follow from Heidegger's vision of understanding.[5] Dewey motivates the pragmatist account of truth by appeal to an essentially biological and organic conception of understanding. Heidegger does not share Dewey's biologism, and therefore, his work does not provide a fertile ground for the pragmatic conception of truth.

II The Primacy of Practice

Dewey's biologism and Heidegger's near total avoidance of biology are glaring features of their philosophical writings. Rorty and Okrent are certainly not unaware of it. So, what has led them to focus on the similarities between the authors? Here Rorty's phraseology proves insightful. Both philosophers do think of theory, indeed cognition, "as a continuation of practice by other means." Cognition arises in the context of ongoing practice and is an alternative means whereby we achieve the pretheoretical goals of that practice. Why do we try to achieve the goals of practice "by other means," through cognition? Because sometimes unmodified practice confronts obstacles to its habitual ways and proves unable to surmount these obstacles without the aid of the explicit attention afforded by cognition. Cognition's purpose is to return us to precognitive practice by overcoming the obstacles. Cognition is not an autonomous enterprise with its own goals and aspirations, with methods and foundations freed from the concerns of practice. Cognition is an episode within our practical activity.

Dewey develops this theme colorfully in his 1908 "Does Reality Possess Practical Character?"[6]:

The brain, the last physical organ of thought, is a part of the same practical machinery for bringing about adaptation of the environment to the life requirements of the organism, to which belong legs and hand and eye. . . . That the organ of thinking, of knowledge, was at least originally an organ of conduct, few, I imagine, will deny. And even if we try to believe that the cognitive function has supervened as a different operation, it is difficult to believe that the transfiguration has been so radical that knowing has lost all traces of its connection with vital impulse. (*RPPC*, 132–133)

Cognition is an organic process, and its function is tied intimately to the functions of the less theoretical side of our being. The point and purpose of cognition is to bring about "adaptation of the environment to the life requirements of the organism." Cognition is part of what Dewey calls our "practical machinery."

Dewey writes further, "Awareness means *attention*, and attention means a crisis of some sort in an existent situation" (*RPPC*, 138). Consciousness or cognition, attention, arises only when a difficulty emerges in a situation, when practice confronts an obstacle. Dewey deploys a central pragmatist distinction to spell this out: that between flowing, coordinated activity and halting, uncertain activity. He first works with this distinction in his seminal, psychological essay from 1896, "The Reflex Arc Concept in Psychology,"[7] where he contends with William James's theory of perception. There he takes over and redescribes James's example of the child who reaches out for the flame of a candle (which I shall replace with a similar one that brings more developed human capacities into focus). Normally, when confronted by a box of chocolate candies, Jones's "seeing-grasping coordination" goes into effect, as her hand reaches out for a chocolate and pops it in the mouth. This coordination is exercised for some purpose, in this case, satisfying a sweet tooth. It is typically a flowing activity of seeing and grasping. It is only when this coordination encounters a difficulty that Jones explicitly attends to her visual stimuli, focuses on them, and settles on a response. If Jones has lately been fooled by a box of plastic chocolates, for example, she hesitates before grasping one. She examines the chocolates more carefully, perhaps touches one, all in the interest of determining whether they are the genuine article. If she is satisfied they are, she will reach out, grab one, and eat it.

From this example and from the passages quoted above from RPPC we learn two things about Dewey's approach to cognition: first, that Dewey understands cognition as explicit awareness or attention; second, that the function of cognition is to overcome some obstacle that arises in the ongoing flow of practical activity. Jones's first impulse to reach out and grab a chocolate is inhibited by her memory of being deceived by the plastic chocolates. "It is the initiated activities of reaching, which, inhibited by the conflict in the co-ordination, turn round, as it were, upon the seeing, and hold it from passing over into further act until its quality is determined" (*RA*, 107). Once activity has been brought to a halt, cognition jumps in to find a solution to the obstacle and get precognitive, practical activity back under way. The function of an idea is to overcome an obstacle to practice.

"Intelligence" too is a term that has its most basic application in the domain of practice. Intelligence is not in the first instance a feature of autonomous theorizing, but rather:

Intelligence, in its ordinary use, is a practical term; ability to size up matters with respect to the needs and possibilities of the various situations in which one is called to do something; capacity to envisage things in terms of the adjustments and adaptations they make possible or hinder. (*RPPC*, 130)

Intelligence or understanding is one's comprehensive, practical grasp of the environment. It is "what the Yankee calls gumption[8]— acknowledgment of things in their belongings and uses . . . horse sense" (*RPPC*, 129–130). Understanding is not a systematically arranged set of beliefs, linked together by logical relations. Rather, it is a fluid mastery of the environment.

Heidegger too argues that the term "understanding" picks out a fundamentally practical capacity, and he also endorses the two theses located above in Dewey, viz., that cognition should be understood as explicit consciousness, and that the function of cognition within normal activity is to get that activity back under way again, once it has been disrupted.[9] In his 1927 *Being and Time* Heidegger explicitly distances himself from a cognitive interpretation of understanding, when he writes:

By the term understanding, . . . we mean neither a *sort of cognition*, distinguished in some way from explaining and conceiving, nor even cognition in general in the sense of thematically grasping [something]. (*SZ*, 336)[10]

He fills out what he does mean by "understanding" in a passage strikingly similar to the one quoted before last from Dewey, one in which he too relies on the everyday usage of the word:

In ontical [everyday] discourse we often use the expression "to understand something" to mean "to be able to manage a thing," "to be equal to it," "to be capable of something." In understanding, as an existentiale,[11] that of which one is capable is not a What, but rather being as existing. (*SZ*, 143)

Heidegger, like Dewey, does not cash out understanding in terms of having a systematic set of autonomous representations of reality. Rather, he identifies understanding with ongoing mastery. In §13 (*SZ*, 61–62) Heidegger describes cognition (*Erkennen*) and taking-as (*Vernehmen*) as forms of interpretation (*Auslegung*), which he then later (§32) identifies with the "explicitness of what is understood" (149). Furthermore, interpretation in general, and therefore cognition as well, is a "development [*Ausbildung*] of understanding" (148), that is, one way in which understanding achieves its goals.

Heidegger makes it entirely clear that he regards cognitive understanding as derivative of skilled activity:

If we Interpret [understanding] as a fundamental existentiale, we thereby indicate that this phenomenon is conceived as a fundamental mode of the *being* of Dasein.[12] Whereas "understanding," in the sense of *one* possible sort of cognition among others, perhaps distinguished from "explaining," must thereby be Interpreted as an existential derivative of primary understanding. (*SZ*, 143)

Heidegger does not, unfortunately, carry all the way through with the project of spelling this out: in an infamous footnote late in the treatise (*SZ*, 363), Heidegger concedes that he has not yet explained "how the intentionality of 'consciousness' is *grounded* in the ecstatic temporality of Dasein," and that this explanation would be offered in the (alas, never written) third division of the first part of *Being and Time*. Although he never produces this account, he does give us some guidance concerning how we should understand the relationship phenomenologically.

In §16 of *Being and Time*, he outlines phenomenologically the way in which the typically transparent character of our precognitive comportment changes over into explicit awareness during a breakdown in ongoing practice. We are primarily and usually immersed in the routine of daily life, unaware of the paraphernalia we use in going about our business. When our activity "breaks down," to use Dreyfus's words, or when there is a "disturbance in reference" (*Störung der Verweisung, SZ*, 74),[13] in Heidegger's words, then the paraphernalia of our precognitive activity shows up for us for the first time. In §§16, 31, 32, and 69b of *Being and Time* Heidegger botanizes the various sorts of explicit awareness, ranging from momentary attention to clear up a minor difficulty or malfunction, all the way to deliberation and theorizing.

Thus, both Heidegger and Dewey locate cognition as a phase within practice, a phase that restores ongoing practice, resolves its difficulties. Cognition is here understood as explicit, conscious awareness. Both also take "understanding" to have a basic application to our ongoing activity, an application prior to any reference to theory or cognition. Understanding is one's ongoing, fluid coping with the situation in which one lives. Ideas, cognition, theory, the "quest for disinterested theoretical truth" are a "continuation of practice by other means," because they are all derivative of the more basic phenomenon of understanding. They are ways in which practice can cope with situations that otherwise would confound it.

Let us call this thesis—that cognition is derivative of practice— "the primacy of practice."[14] One might think that the primacy of practice defines pragmatism the movement. It is Heidegger's commitment to it that inspires Rorty and Okrent to classify him as a pragmatist. How are we to decide whether Heidegger ought really to be counted among the pragmatists? Rorty has shown us the way: we must ask whether the "standard pragmatist doctrines" follow from his account of understanding. This is another way of asking whether the primacy of practice itself entails "the standard pragmatist doctrines." We shall see that it does not, that in this sense Heidegger is not a pragmatist. Heidegger does not share the pragmatist theory of truth.

III   Dewey's Biologism and the Pragmatist Theory of Truth

I have proposed as the test of Rorty's and Okrent's pragmatizing interpretation of Heidegger the question whether the pragmatist theory of truth follows from Heidegger's manner of "de-intellectualizing" the understanding. In order to address this question, we must first get clear about what the pragmatist theory of truth is. And here we face a morass of difficulty. There is no generally accepted formulation of "the" pragmatist theory of truth. There are (at least) four candidate, pragmatist theories of truth:

1. The verificationist account of truth as warranted assertibility (Dewey and maybe James).

2. The ideal-consensus, verificationist account of truth as warranted assertibility at the ideal limit of inquiry (Peirce, Sellars, Putnam, and maybe James).

3. The deflationary account of truth as a word of commendation (Rorty and maybe James).

4. The prosentential theory of the predicate ". . . is true" as a pro-sentence forming operator that reasserts sentences anaphorically referred to by the prosentence (Grover, Camp, Belnap, and Brandom).[15]

(1) and (2) are variations on a verificationist theme, (3) and (4) on a deflationary theme.

There are as many, indeed more, arguments in favor of pragmatist accounts of truth as there are authors selling such accounts. In order to maintain our focus on Heidegger and Dewey, I shall not consider the deflationary theme (theories 3 and 4).[16] In James and Dewey's writings on truth, we find essentially two different sorts of argument in favor of a pragmatist account of truth.

We find an *analytic* argument to the effect that if we analyze what we *mean*, when we say of a sentence or idea that it is true, we find that we mean. . . .

We also find an *ontological* argument to the effect that if we understand what ideas and assertions *are*, we will see that their truth must be. . . .

The analytic arguments have not fared well over time. Robert Brandom[17] has traced the careers and vicissitudes of these arguments and urged that the only conclusion they may be able to reach is a prosentential theory of truth as embedded within a project of reconstructing linguistic practice along the lines he offers in his later work, *Making It Explicit.*[18]

The line of argumentation that has not been nearly so well discussed, but really lies at the heart of at least *Dewey's* move from the primacy of practice to a pragmatist account of truth, is his ontological, biologistic reconception of ideas. Dewey uses a biologistic reconceptualization of ideas and thought in order to motivate a warranted assertibility account of truth (1 above). It is to this argument that I want now to turn.

Dewey "de-intellectualizes" understanding in an essentially biologistic way. The controlling metaphor throughout Dewey's pragmatic writings is that of *organism*. His principal aim in treating any particular human phenomenon is to ask what its *function* is. The function of some human phenomenon, such as understanding, is always stated in terms of the role that it plays in the overall operation of the human organism. This is evident as early as his "Reflex Arc" essay. It enframes his entire discussion of ideas, intelligence, and truth.

As we have already seen, ideas play a definite role within the economy of our everyday, precognitive practice: they get activity back under way, after it has been confronted by some obstacle that brings it to a halt. Of the example above (Jones and her box of chocolates) Dewey writes, "The question of whether to reach or to abstain from reaching is the question what sort of a [chocolate] we have here" (*RA*, 106). Here Dewey *identifies* the question, "What sort of a chocolate do we have here, real or fake?" with the question, "Should I reach for one or not?" The answers to the first question, "Yes, they're real," and "No, they are fake," *mean* the intentions to reach or to abstain from reaching, which are the answers to the second question. Dewey analyzes the ideas that arise in the context of solving the problem Jones confronts with the plans of action and intentions aimed at resolving the problem. *If* we view practice as the functioning of the human organism, and we view cognition as a derivative, organic phase of this functioning, then it is appropriate to *define* cognition in terms of the role it plays in that functioning. An idea *is essentially* the function it performs in organic activity. Specifically, an idea is the intention to get activity back under way in some definite fashion. This is Dewey's argument for the classical pragmatist thesis that ideas are "plans" or "rules" of action. In his 1908 "What Pragmatism Means by Practical,"[19] Dewey joins James and Peirce in accepting that "ideas are essentially intentions (plans and methods), and that what they, as ideas, ultimately intend is *prospective*—certain changes in prior existing things" (*WPMP*, 99).[20]

Since it is the function of an idea to get precognitive activity back under way, ideas should be evaluated by the degree to which they contribute to solving the problems that confront practice. Dewey recommends that truth and falsity be thought of as success and failure at fulfilling the function of knowing. He suggests that we may view classical, correspondence conceptions of truth as likewise taking this for granted; they simply specify the office of knowledge differently.

> The issue is no longer an ideally necessary but actually impossible copying, *versus* an improper but unavoidable modification of reality through organic inhibitions and stimulations: but it is the right, the economical, the effective, and, if one may venture, the useful and satisfactory reaction *versus* the wasteful, the enslaving, the misleading, and the confusing reaction. (*RPPC*, 134)

> Hence the appropriate subject-matter of awareness is not reality at large, a metaphysical heaven to be mimeographed at many removes upon a badly constructed mental carbon paper which yields at best only fragmentary, blurred, and erroneous copies. Its proper and legitimate object is that relationship of organism and environment in which functioning is most amply and effectively attained; or by which, in case of obstruction and consequent needed experimentation, its later eventual free course is most facilitated. (*RPPC*, 136)

If the point of knowing were to copy reality or to settle upon a consistent mental life, then correspondence or coherence would be the form of truth. But since the purpose of knowing is to assist in controlling the environment, success at it (truth) is effective control. Ideas are plans or intentions, not representations. Consequently, good ideas are successful plans or intentions, not accurate representations.

Dewey's line of thought gathers considerable strength, furthermore, when we consider that a classical, correspondence theory of truth *does not even make sense on the biologistic conception of cognition*. It does not make sense to ask of a plan whether it accurately represents reality. To use language deployed by John Searle, plans and intentions have world-to-word direction of fit, while representations have word-to-world direction of fit.[21] In this way, ideas are like directives, not like photocopies.[22] If ideas or cognitions are not representations, but rather plans or intentions, then they should be evaluated not by their accuracy, but rather by their success in molding the world to their purposes. Indeed, it is meaningless to talk about the accuracy of a directive or intention to act. In the case of understanding, once we have conceived it as a form of ability or competence, it becomes incoherent to ask whether it "corresponds" with, or accurately represents, reality. Of abilities we may only ask whether they effectively control the domain to which they are relevant. Hence, the pragmatic conception of truth: truth is what works.

In his 1941 "Propositions, Warranted Assertibility, and Truth",[23] Dewey does characterize his own view as a "correspondence" theory of truth, but it is important to see that his intention there is provocative, not classificatory. He co-opts the term "correspondence" and rereads to suit his own intentions:

In contrast with this view [i.e., a traditional one], my own view takes correspondence in the operational sense it bears in all cases except the unique epistemological case of an alleged relation between a "subject" and an "object"; the meaning, namely, of *answering*, as a key answers to conditions imposed by a lock, or as two correspondents "answer" each other; or, in general, as a reply is an adequate answer to a question or criticism—as, in short, a *solution* answers the requirements of a *problem*. (PWAT, 179)

This is a "problem-solving" conception of truth. Whether we call it "a correspondence theory of truth" is far less important than that we understand how it differs from traditional conceptions of truth as correspondence. For Dewey, ideas (judgments, assertions) are true, if they solve the problems they are designed to solve, not if they match reality.[24]

So, we may summarize Dewey's ontological argument for his version of the pragmatist theory of truth thus:

1. The *thesis* of the primacy of practice: cognition is a derivative phase and development of practice. It arises, when precognitive practice confronts obstacles that it cannot overcome on its own.

2. A biologistic *conception* of practice: practice is the ongoing, intelligent struggle of the organism to bring "about adaptation of the

environment to the life requirements of the organism" (*RPPC*, 132). Cognition, as a derivative of practice, shares this function.

3. The *proposal* that since cognition is a form of problem solving, true cognition should be understood to be successful problem solving.

Conclusion: True ideas are those whose proposals for altering the environment work. A true idea is one that works.

So, the meaning of an idea or belief is spelled out prospectively in terms of how it proposes to overcome the obstacle to practice that gave rise to idea in the first place. If those changes are successful—where success is measured by their ability to solve the problem confronted— then the idea is warranted assertible, and hence, true. This view of ideas and meaning issues from Dewey's biologistic approach to cognition and practice (developed in penetrating detail by Burke[25]). In his overlong 1938 *Logic: The Theory of Inquiry*[26] Dewey works out an elaborate, biologistic conception of inquiry, and his notions of warranted assertibility and truth are defined in terms of that conception. His pragmatist theory of truth, therefore, flows from his biologism.

IV Why Heidegger Does Not Subscribe to the Pragmatist Theory of Truth

Heidegger's thinking is anything but biologistic. But does this make a difference to his theory of truth? That is, one might well grant that Dewey is a biologistic thinker, and Heidegger not, but urge that this does not influence Heidegger's choice of a theory of truth. One might read Rorty (in the quote with which I opened this paper) to be suggesting that a pragmatist account of truth flows from the primacy of practice, and thus, that the ontological disagreements between Dewey and Heidegger are irrelevant to our concerns here. Indeed, one might be emboldened to take this stance by the work not only of Mark Okrent, but also of Carl Friedrich Gethmann, both of whom offer pragmatist readings of Heidegger's account of truth.[27]

Okrent has argued that Heidegger's conception of truth is verificationist, and if he is right, then this much at least Heidegger and the classical pragmatists have in common.

The being-true of an assertion thus amounts to the being-uncovering of the assertion in the sense that the assertion successfully *reveals* how the thing it refers to is. Being true is being uncovering. (*Heidegger's Pragmatism*, 102, my emphasis)

Okrent's explanation here is closely based on Heidegger's original language:

The entity meant [*gemeinte*][28] shows itself *just as* [*so, wie*] it is in itself, that is, that *it* in its sameness is just as *it* is pointed out, uncovered in the assertion as being.... The assertion *is true* means: it uncovers the entity [its object] in itself. It asserts [*sagt aus*] the entity in its uncoveredness, it points it out [*zeigt auf*], it "lets it be seen" (*apophansis*). *The being-true* (*truth*) of an assertion must be understood as *being-uncovering*. (*SZ*, 218)

An assertion means an entity as being thus and so. When we seek to prove the assertion true, Heidegger asks, what do we seek to show? We aim to demonstrate that the entity shows itself to us just as the assertion means it. Heidegger's example from the beginning of the paragraph with which we are working here is this: Jones stands with her back to the wall and says, "The picture on the wall is crooked." Suppose that she now seeks to confirm her assertion. What would she do? She would turn to the wall and look at the picture. If the picture shows itself to her as crooked—that is, in this case, if she perceives it as crooked—then the assertion has proven itself to be true. Heidegger concludes: when we confirm an assertion, we demonstrate that the assertion uncovers its object just as it is. Thus, for an assertion to be true is for it to uncover its object just as it is.[29]

To decide whether this formulation amounts to verificationism requires that we determine in turn what Heidegger means by "uncovering" (*entdecken*). The example that Heidegger offers (of Jones and the picture), if not read carefully, might well obscure his point. In *confirming* an assertion we seek to reveal the object of the assertion to be just as it is meant in the assertion. But that does not settle the question whether uncovering the entity—as opposed to confirming the assertion—requires that the entity show itself to us, in person, as it were. What does Heidegger mean by the "uncovering" that takes place in assertion?

In order to describe the work of the assertion, Heidegger uses not merely "uncovering," but also (almost tautologically) "asserting" (*aussagen*) and (more helpfully) "pointing out" (*aufzeigen*).[30] In order to avoid verificationism in the very definition of "assertion," we must show that Heidegger does not intend the term "uncovering" to require that the assertion actually reveal its object to us. Heidegger endorses this implication and thereby confirms the weaker interpretation for which I aim, when he writes:

> Also, if this entity [the object of the assertion] is not within reach or sight, the pointing-out means the entity itself and not anything like a mere representation of it, neither "something merely represented" nor even a psychical state of the asserter, its representing of this entity. (*SZ*, 154)

Heidegger uses the term "pointing out" to cover not just drawing attention to an entity so that it may reveal itself to us, but also to include the case of meaning an entity that is not currently available to the senses or to practical activity, one that "is not within reach or sight." Therefore, I conclude, the "pointing out" that takes place in assertion does not require revealing the object, at least in the sense of "revealing" in which we mean showing itself in person to cognitive or practical activity.

One might fear that I am ascribing to Heidegger a traditional theory of reference, one namely, according to which assertions have some autonomous, almost magical, power to point to entities independently of how things show themselves to Dasein. But this I certainly do not want to do. Heidegger argues that an assertion can only point something out—or also in the more extended case, in which the assertion does not directly reveal an object to us, can only point to an object—if the object is already more basically uncovered and available to be pointed out. Heidegger's notion of pointing out is not much like a traditional conception of reference, because he does not think of pointing out as a direct relation between either the assertion or some abstract sense or meaning associated with it, on the one hand, and an object or referent, on the other. Assertions can only point objects out in terms of or on the background of a more basic, practical disclosure of the world around us:

> The pointing-out of the assertion is carried out on the basis of what has already been disclosed in understanding, or better, circumspectively uncovered. Assertion is no free-floating comportment, which could on its own

primarily disclose an entity in the first place [*überhaupt*]; rather, it maintains itself always on the basis of being-in-the-world. What was indicated earlier in connection with cognizing the world [*Welterkennens*] applies just as well to assertion. Assertion requires a fore-having of what is disclosed in the first place, which it points out in the manner of determining. (*SZ*, 156–157)

Assertion points out objects within a field of data provided to it by a more basic phenomenon: the pragmatic disclosedness of the world in engaged action. The world is articulated and organized at a basic, practical level, and assertion points out or to something within the world only in terms of the more basic achievement.[31] Given this more basic achievement, however, assertion is able to point objects out without directly revealing them to us, either cognitively or practically.[32]

Now we may return to the theme of assertoric truth. We have seen that Heidegger defines the truth of an assertion as its "being-uncovering." And we have just seen that Heidegger does not require of uncovering that it actually reveal the object of the assertion in person. So, if the truth of an assertion is not its successfully revealing an object to us, what then is it? Heidegger approaches the truth of an assertion as what we try to establish in confirming the assertion. And that, he says, is the identity of the entity as it is with the entity as it is meant in the assertion. "And what is shown through perception [that confirms an assertion]? Nothing other than *that* it is this entity itself that is meant in the assertion" (*SZ*, 218). Further down on the same page Heidegger writes of confirmation that it means "the entity showing itself in its sameness." This implies, if we let the confirmation-theoretic reference to "showing itself" drop out, that truth is the entity in its sameness, by which he means that the entity as it is is identical with the entity as it is meant in the assertion.[33]

One might be inclined to characterize this account as a theory of truth as the "correspondence" of the entity as it is with the entity as it is meant in the assertion. This inclination finds aid and comfort in Heidegger's 1930 "On the Essence of Truth,"[34] where he describes assertoric truth as "correspondence" (*Übereinstimmung*). But in *Being and Time* Heidegger meticulously avoids the term "correspondence" (both "*Übereinstimmung*" and "*Korrespondenz*"). His reason appears to be that in *Being and Time* he regards the concept of correspondence as connected with the traditional idea of an ontologically unclarified relation between an ideal judgmental content and a real object. (*SZ,* 215–216, 223–225)

Beyond this semantic association, however, there are two further reasons why it is appropriate to withhold the term "correspondence" when describing Heidegger's theory of truth. First, Heidegger insists, as we have seen, that truth is grounded in a more basic, practical disclosure of the world. This more basic, practical disclosure of the world makes up what he refers to, in the passage above from *SZ,* 156–157, as the "fore-having" (*Vorhabe*) of the assertion. It is what we must have in advance, what we must have mastered beforehand, in order that the assertion can do its work. The assertion must point out or to an entity on which we have a prior, practical grasp, and must do so in terms of a predicate that does or can aim our attention at some feature of the object that we have "sighted" in advance (the "fore-sight," *Vorsicht*).[35] Traditional accounts, which just assume that either an assertion or its sense can point out an object, without clarifying how this is achieved, rely on mysterious, ontologically unclarified, linguistic powers.

Second, Heidegger understands the identity or matching that lies at the heart of truth to be identity between the object as meant and the object as it is. Traditionally, truth as correspondence was understood as a relation that obtains between either the assertion or its sense on the one hand, and the object on the other. If the object is just like—in some hard to define, relevant sense—either the assertion or its sense, then the assertion is true. For Heidegger, however, the "correspondence" is between an entity *as meant* and the same entity *as it is in itself*. Both of the "corresponding" items are on the side of the object.[36] The traditional view, in contrast to Heidegger's, assumes a mysterious relation of matching that holds between two items that are ontologically quite *unlike* each other, a problem pointed out long ago by Berkeley. Heidegger's account, however, has the identity subsist between a thing and itself, a kind of self-identity, which is a far less mysterious concept.

These two points of divergence, however powerful they may be in moving us to withhold the classification "correspondence theory of truth" from the theory of *Being and Time*, are nonetheless not of the right kind to assimilate Heidegger's view to Dewey's. To say that assertoric truth is grounded in a more basic, practical disclosure of the world is simply not to say that assertoric truth is to be understood as itself a practical relation. Moreover, neither is it to say that assertoric truth is a relation that is modeled on that between a plan and its execution, or a problem and its solution. And these are the sorts of distinctively pragmatist ideas that set Dewey's thinking apart from the tradition. And it is upon this distinction that I want to insist.

Potentially spoiling my plans, Gethmann has argued that, "Heidegger, more implicitly than explicitly, carries out a fundamental *shift in the model of truth*," a shift from a propositional model, in which truth is conceived as a form of correspondence (*Übereinstimmung*), to an "operational model of truth," in which truth is a success term (*Dasein: Erkennen und Handeln*, 156–157). In particular,

According to the operational model of truth, truth is related to the assertion not as redness is to the table, but rather, as the key is related to the lock. The correspondence is not that between a photograph and an original, but rather, that of a key to a lock. Whether the key "corresponds" to the lock reveals itself in the locking, thus in its use, not in talking about it. (*Dasein: Erkennen und Handeln*, 157)

But what reason does Gethmann have to attribute such a conception to Heidegger? Gethmann's argument for reading Heidegger this way is as follows:

"Correspondence" [between a true assertion and an object] describes a relation of fitting [*ein Passungsverhältnis*] between a plan and its fulfillment. Husserl's conception of truth already in its fundamental notion heads in this direction. The terms "empty meaning"[37] and "fulfilling meaning" are sufficiently clear: the fulfillment is as it were the cognitive success of an expectation that is built into the empty meaning. By referring to this operative usage [presumably of "correspondence"], Heidegger strengthens his fundamental, pragmatic bent, which Husserl had already introduced into his conception of truth. (*Dasein: Erkennen und Handeln*, 156)

In Husserl's framework, an empty meaning is the sort of mental act one lives through, when one means an object without its being present to one's senses. When the object is present to the senses, the sensory experience fulfills the empty meaning. When one thinks about a cat, for example, one anticipates that if one were present, it would look thus and so. When it is present and does look thus and so, one's empty meaning of the cat is fulfilled by a sensory experience.

It is true that the pragmatists emphasize the way in which, when an idea or assertion is confirmed, an expectation built into the idea or assertion is fulfilled. Peirce recurred most directly to such a way of looking at confirmation.[38] But it is important to see that this is as such insufficient to underwrite the strongly "operational" or pragmatist language that Dewey pioneers and that Gethmann wants to ascribe to Heidegger.

According to Husserl and Heidegger, the success that attends expectation in favorable circumstances can be defined as a form of identity. For Husserl, when an empty intention is fulfilled by a fulfilling intention, the conceptual contents of the two states (the anticipation and the visual experience) are identical. Heidegger uses precisely such an example of confirmation in his exposition of assertoric truth (Jones says the picture is crooked; she turns around to see that it is), and he, following Husserl, characterizes truth as an identity. For Husserl, then, the question is whether the conceptual contents of two mental acts match each other or are identical. In Heidegger's formulation, the question is whether the entity as meant is identical with the entity as it is. Again, the issue is whether one item matches or is identical with another.

But the rubric of identity or matching does not apply to the relationship between a lock and a key, or a problem and a solution. According to Dewey, a solution to a problem is a way of *transforming* a problematic situation so that the obstacles to fluid action are removed; it is not a sort of identity or matching. That is the central thrust of Dewey's colorful argumentation in the passages, quoted above, in which he dismisses the metaphors of picturing or copying. If a judgment proposes a solution to a problem, it suggests a way of modifying the conditions described in the problem, so that action may be freed up once again.[39] Modification is, by definition, not a form of matching or identity. Therefore, the identity that lies at the heart of truth and confirmation for Heidegger is in its essence a very different sort of phenomenon than the transformation or

modification that defines, for Dewey, a solution to a problem. Gethmann conflates the two very different models of "fitting" (*Passung*),
viz., that found in the satisfaction of expectations and that embodied in the relation between a problem and a solution, when he writes,

> In contrast, in the "operational model of truth" "true" or "false" is predi-
> cated [of an assertion], if an intention has found its realization, if a problem
> has found its solution. (*Dasein: Erkennen und Handeln*, 156)

Heidegger "operationalizes" neither truth nor confirmation,
because he conceives neither on the model of a problem and a solution. Confirmation takes place, when an entity reveals itself to be just
as it was meant (asserted) to be. Likewise, truth is the identity of an
entity as meant (asserted) with an entity as it is in itself. But a
problem and a solution are in no recognizable sense an identity of
any kind.

V   Conclusion

Heidegger does endorse the primacy of practice. In the context of
the theory of truth, this is expressed in his attempt to ground assertoric truth in a more basic, practical phenomenon of disclosedness.[40]
*But Heidegger does not "operationalize," or pragmatize, his conception of
assertoric truth.* Heidegger does not conceive the relation between an
assertion and its object, or between the object as meant (asserted)
and the object as it is in itself, to be the pragmatic relation of problem
to solution. Why not? Because he does not conceive assertion as
problem solving. Assertion does play the role of getting action back
under way; it is, at least in the first instance,[41] part of a strategy
for coping with felt difficulty. But it is not internally defined by this
function.

*We learn from this that the primacy of practice leads one to a pragmatic
view of truth, only if one takes the problem-solving function of ideas and
assertions to define what ideas and assertions most basically are.* Dewey does
so, because he conceives ideas and assertions biologistically, that is,
in terms of their functional role in the overall economy of the human
organism's interaction with its environment. Heidegger is not a biologistic thinker. He conceives of assertions and ideas as "existential

derivatives" of originary disclosure, but not as functionally defined phases of organic activity. This difference makes all the difference in the world, for on it hangs the answer to the question whether the primacy of practice implies a pragmatist or operational theory of truth.

Rorty overlooks this difference, or perhaps disregards it, in his attempt to line up the support of not just Dewey and Heidegger, but also Wittgenstein and Davidson, behind his rejection of epistemology. My suggestion, then, is that Rorty has moved too quickly, that he is trying to house fundamentally incompatible philosophies under one roof, that the primacy of practice does not without further ado imply the standard, pragmatist doctrines. Two tasks that now stand before those of us who are committed to the primacy of practice, as well as those of us who would like to bring Heideggerians and Deweyans into one conversation, are to trace out the consequences of the conflict between Deweyan biologism and Heideggerian existentialism, and to evaluate the comparative virtues of the two approaches.[42]

Absorbed Coping, Husserl, and Heidegger

Dagfinn Føllesdal

Hubert Dreyfus's *Being-in-the-World: A Commentary on Heidegger's Being and Time, Division I,* (henceforth cited as *BW*) has been highly praised for "its philosophical grasp and clarity of detail" (Charles Taylor) and for bringing out Heidegger's radical criticisms of Husserl, in particular of the "doctrines which Husserl shared with Descartes" (Richard Rorty).

The book has several attractive features: it is lively and well written, it ties the interpretation of Heidegger to key issues in contemporary cognitive science, and above all: it has a dramatic build-up, there is the traditional, cognitivist view of Descartes and Husserl where a subject relates to objects through the intermediaries of representations, and there is Heidegger, who splits the darkness and makes us see things right.

The book has become a major influence on Heidegger interpretation on the North American continent. And—unfortunately—it has given many of its readers an excuse for not reading Husserl. Its depiction of Husserl's philosophy has spread to other books and articles whose authors have not bothered to check their picture against Husserl's texts.

Dreyfus and I have been discussing Husserl and Heidegger for more than forty years. We disagree on the interpretation of both thinkers, but, fortunately, our disagreement has not hurt our friendship. Just after the book came out I presented some of my objections in a panel discussion with him, Izchak Miller, and Richard Tieszen.

In the following, I will concentrate on the interpretation of Husserl and not go into Heidegger.

Husserl started out as a philosopher of mathematics, and most of his philosophical writings focus on cognition and the mind. However, there are many manuscripts by Husserl that contain discussions of the body and of practical activity and how they relate to our theoretical and constitutive activity. The earliest of these date from 1908. Dreyfus comments in his book on an article I wrote in 1979, in which I discuss some particularly important manuscripts and lectures which date from 1917–18.[1] Husserl's main work, the *Ideas*, was planned as a three-volume work with the second volume devoted mainly to the body and the constitution of the social world. A manuscript for this volume was written in 1912, before the first volume had appeared in print. Husserl there stresses that "the 'nature' and the organism (*Leib*), and in combination with it, the soul, become constituted in interrelation with each other, in unity with each other."[2]

Husserl became quite absorbed by this sphere of problems and also with issues connected with values and practical activity and reworked parts of the manuscript several times. He never published it, but discussed it with his students and assistants and gave a copy to Heidegger early in 1925. Merleau-Ponty studied the manuscript in Louvain in 1939, even before the Husserl archive was officially opened, and expressed his indebtedness to Husserl's insights. In 1952, the manuscript was finally published in *Husserliana* (Vol. IV), and in 1989 Kluwer published an English translation by Richard Rojcewicz and André Schuwer.

Husserl takes up a number of issues that are not dealt with by Heidegger nor by Dreyfus, such as problems of freedom, rationality, responsibility, values, and so forth. However, I shall quote a few passages that illustrate how he deals with what Dreyfus calls "absorbed coping."

Before turning to these passages, I shall briefly explain Husserl's notion of "motivation," which plays an important role in his discussion. For Husserl, motivation is a label for the intentional connections, the connections of sense or meaning that structure our experience. Husserl contrasts motivation with the causal connections of nature, and says that his notion of motivation is "a generalization of the concept of motivation in accordance with which we can say, for example, that the willing of the end motivates the willing of the means" (*Ideen* I, 89, *Husserliana* III,1.101.n). Husserl says in *Ideen* II that motivations are "intentional" connections or tendencies (*Husserliana* IV.225.24), and points out how "the mode of givenness of one part supports that of the other" (*Husserliana* IV.226.23–24). This complex web of motivations ('Motivationsgeflechte' *Husserliana* IV.224.38) is worlds apart from Dreyfus's simpleminded notion of a rule of computation, which is one of his main objects of attack in his book, and which he attributes to Husserl and to Searle.

Now to the passages on "absorbed coping." According to Husserl, motivation is something that we seldom are aware of and that is only rarely brought into relief: "In most cases, however, the motivation is indeed actually present in consciousness, but it does not stand out; it is unnoticed or unnoticable ('unconscious')" *Husserliana* IV.222.36–223.2. "From an Objective-physical standpoint, obviously a material state comes first, although I know nothing about it and do not have to" (*Husserliana* IV.259.32–34). We have "a background that is prior to all comportment and instead is presupposed by all comportment" (*Husserliana* IV.279.7–9). Also in many other places, for example, on page 189 of *Ideen* II, Husserl talks about this background, which is normally unnoticed, but which we can turn toward and, for example, relate to theoretically, esthetically, or ethically (*Husserliana* IV.189.24–31).

Particularly illuminating is the following passage:

Now, the proper behavior is, in the background consciousness, not an expecting in the proper sense but a protention directed toward the future occurrence, a protention which can become an expectation with a shift of the attention of the Ego. (*Husserliana* IV.256.11–15)

Husserl does not think that this background is brought about through judgments, on the contrary: "Even without our performing acts of belief, they enter into motivations" (*Husserliana* IV.224.32–33). This is an important point in Husserl's view on evidence and justification. In an earlier paper, "Husserl on Evidence and Justification,"[3] I argued for a number of theses concerning Husserl's view on evidence. One of these was that evidence is not confined to acts of judgment; an object can be evidently given without having to be judged about in a predicative judgment. One piece of evidence I gave for this, was the following passage:

> An object, as the possible substrate of a judgment, can be given with evidence without having to be judged about in a predicative judgment. On the other hand, an evident predicative judgment concerning this object is not possible unless the object itself is given with evidence.[4]

Another thesis I set forth is the following:

> Evidence is not yielded just by sensory filling, but also by practical activity and by feeling.

One passage I quoted in support of this is the following, which also is highly pertinent to Dreyfus's interpretation of Husserl:

> However, in its orientation on scientific determination and its tendency toward science and scientific theory, this traditional logic has never brought into question the *entwinement of cognitive behavior with the practical and the evaluative* and has never investigated how a judgment is produced which does not serve purely cognitive interest in this way but rather serves the practical in the most general sense of the word; nor has it investigated how predicative self-evidence is built on *this* domain of the prepredicative, on practical evidence and the evidence of feeling. It is indisputable that these are original sources of the giving of existents themselves, of the disclosure of determinations which, by their nature, can take place only in practical activity itself and not in mere contemplation. But it is precisely about these modes of giving a thing itself that we do not ask; we do not ask how it is possible to construct a judicative act of objectification *on them*; rather, we create the fiction that the ego, in a purely contemplative activity without any purpose or interest other than that of contemplation, turns immediately toward what exists as it is passively and affectively given to us. In other words, we create the fiction of a subject that behaves in a purely contemplative way and which is not aroused to any practical activity by the existent by which it is affected environmentally.[5] (*Erfahrung und Urteil*, 14, pp. 68–69; Churchill & Ameriks, pp. 65–66. My emphasis.)

In his manuscript for *Ideen* II, Husserl discusses how such determinations are brought about by practical activity. As we could guess, the answer is fairly trivial, practice and training are the key:

> The Ego exercises itself, it habituates itself, it is determined in its latter behavior by its earlier behavior, the power of certain motives increases, etc. The Ego "acquires" capacities, posts goals, and, in attaining these goals

acquires practical skills. It not only acts, but activities themselves become goals, and likewise do systems of activities (e.g., I want to be able to play a piece on the piano with ease) and the corresponding skills and faculties. (*Husserliana* IV.253.27–34)

Such activities can be carried out while we are thinking of something else. Husserl often uses the following cigar example:

However, mere nature is the entirety of the "mechanical I-do." There arises some sensuous drive, for example the urge to smoke. I reach for a cigar and light it up, whereas my attention, my Ego-activities, indeed my being affected consciously, are entirely somewhere else: thoughts are stimulating me, I am following them up, comporting myself to them as actively verifying them, approving them, disapproving of them, etc. (*Husserliana* IV.338.22–27, see also 258)

One could go on and on discussing Husserl's view on the practical and on the development of skills. For further discussion of some of the issues I refer to, see Thomas Nenon and Lester Embree's volume on Husserl's *Ideen* II, notably Kristiana Arp's excellent contribution to that collection.[6]

One wonders, however, whether more detailed discussion and more textual evidence is what is called for. *Ideen* II and the quotations from unpublished manuscripts that I have given above have been available for years. And the disagreements concerning the interpretation of Husserl begin at a far more elementary level. Here are some points where Dreyfus and I interpret Husserl differently. Since I have presented my interpretation at length in several papers from 1958 on, I shall not here repeat the arguments and textual evidence for my interpretation.

1. "Heidegger seeks to demonstrate that what is thus revealed is exactly the opposite of what Descartes and Husserl claim. Rather than first perceiving perspectives, then synthesizing the perspectives into objects, and finally assigning these objects a function on the basis of their physical properties, we already manipulate tools that already have a meaning in a world that is organized in terms of purposes." (*BW*, 46–47)

The second sentence of this passage could have been taken straight out of Husserl, who also discusses tools and the "infinite chain of goals, aims and tasks" that make tools what they are. It is, indeed, a key point in Husserl's phenomenology that we relate to objects of all kinds, including tools, directly, not via intermediaries. We do not perceive sense data and then synthesize them into things, nor do we perceive perspectives and then synthesize them into objects. Similarly, we do not perceive physical objects and synthesize them into tools, we do not perceive bodies and synthesize them into persons, nor do we perceive movements and synthesize them into actions. Husserl, more than any other philosopher I know, stressed the directness of our relations to all these entities. And Heidegger followed in his footsteps.

Also, the following passages are supposed by Dreyfus to be points where Heidegger has seen the light, while Husserl remained in darkness:

2. "Heidegger, however, is trying not to explicate our commonsense concept of action but to make a place for a sort of comportment, as he calls it, that has been overlooked both by common sense and *a fortiori* by the philosophical tradition" (*BW*, 57).

3. "In opposition to the tradition, Heidegger wants to show that we are not normally thematically conscious of our ongoing everyday activity" (*BW*, 58).

4. According to Dreyfus, I (and presumably Husserl) have overlooked that "Being-in is something quite different from a mere confrontation, whether by way of observation or by way of action; that is, it is not the being-occurrent-together of a subject and an object" (*BW*, 49, quotation from *Sein und Zeit*, 221).

5. "Intentionality is not an occurrent relation between an occurrent subject and an occurrent object but is constitutive for the relational character of the subject's comportment as such" (*BW*, 76, quoting *Basic Problems of Phenomenology*, 313–314). Similar points are made by Husserl repeatedly, for example in *Husserliana* IV.146.16–24.

6. "The idea of a subject which has intentional experiences merely inside its own sphere and is . . . encapsulated within itself is an absurdity" (*BW*, 51).

7. According to Dreyfus, for Husserl, "an 'I' or subject is primarily given" (*BW*, 13). No reference to Husserl's text is given to back up

this. The evidence for attributing the view to Husserl is that Heidegger criticizes the view. I can think of various philosophers Heidegger could have in mind here. However, Husserl is not among them.

Rather than continuing this enumeration, I will end on a methodological note. In reading Heidegger, I am struck by the great similarities between his philosophy and that of Husserl. This holds even for the points where, according to Dreyfus, Heidegger made the greatest advances over Husserl, and which Dreyfus emphasizes in his book. The points listed above are only a sample. By misrepresenting Husserl, Dreyfus makes Heidegger come out more original and makes his book more dramatic to read. However, while I blame Heidegger for not giving enough credit to Husserl, Dreyfus tacitly assumes that Heidegger had an even greater moral flaw: Heidegger dedicated *Being and Time* to Husserl "in friendship and admiration" and professed to be doing phenomenology in the book. However, instead, according to Dreyfus, the book was a subversive attack on Husserl: *Being and Time* can be understood as "a systematic critique of Husserl's phenomenology, even though Husserl and his basic concept, intentionality, are hardly mentioned in the book" (*BW*, ix).

Husserl complains in his comments in the margin of his copy of *Being and Time* that "The whole problematic is translation, to the ego corresponds Dasein, etc.", and "What is said here is my own theory, but without a deeper justification". Husserl does not even get the idea that the views that Heidegger criticizes and often attributes to Descartes, are supposed to be his own. Dreyfus may be right that Heidegger behind Husserl's back presented an image of Husserl that made Heidegger's own work appear highly original. However, given that both Dreyfus and I regard Heidegger as exceptionally dishonest, it becomes urgent to check Husserl's writings rather than uncritically promulgating the picture of Husserl that Heidegger surreptitiously tried to create.

I trust that Dreyfus will present a fairer picture of Husserl in the next edition of the book. It will make the book duller, but definitely better.

13

Proofs and Presuppositions: Heidegger, Searle, and the "Reality" of the "External" World

David R. Cerbone

I Introduction

Prominent among the interlocutors who have shaped Hubert Dreyfus's reading of Heidegger has been John Searle, his colleague of many years. Searle's views on intentionality, meaning, and human agency have provided fruitful points of contrast and commonality, in terms of which the nature and significance of Heidegger's contribution to modern philosophy might be better understood.[1] Thus, it does not seem unfitting in a volume celebrating the work of Dreyfus to devote considerable attention to Searle's views as a means for clarifying Heidegger's.

My interest in this chapter lies in understanding a feature common to both Heidegger's and Searle's philosophical positions: the rejection of the demand for a proof of the existence of the external world. In particular, my interest lies in understanding how their views diverge, despite this common feature. In *Being and Time*, Heidegger's rejection of the demand for a proof is framed in terms of a response to Kant's famous "scandal to philosophy," namely "that the existence of things outside of us . . . must be accepted merely on *faith*, and that if anyone thinks good to doubt their existence, we are unable to counter his doubts by any satisfactory proof."[2] Heidegger's rejoinder is encapsulated in the following remark: "The 'scandal of philosophy' is not that this proof has yet to be given, but that *such proofs are expected and attempted again and again*."[3] Though unequivocal in his condemning of Kant's demand, his reasons for doing so can be more difficult to discern. This is so in part because the chapters of Division I of *Being and Time* which precede his rejoinder to Kant might very well be construed as mounting a somewhat different response, more along the lines of an actual proof, rather than an emphatic rejection. That is, Heidegger's "phenomenology of everydayness," with its appeal to engaged agency, appears to provide the resources necessary to meet the demand for a proof of the external world in a manner similar to G. E. Moore's. Heidegger is, however, emphatic in his claim *not* to be trafficking in any such proofs. Though the identification of Heidegger and Moore is *prima facie* problematic, several questions still need to be addressed: What, from Heidegger's perspective, is wrong with Moore's proof? What is it about Heidegger's project that signals a rejection of the demand for a proof, rather than a direct response in the manner of Moore?

That Heidegger both appeals to the priority of engaged agency over detached reflection and, in doing so, rejects the demand for a proof of the external world appears to bring his position into alignment with Searle. In numerous writings, Searle has argued vigorously for what he calls the hypothesis of the Background, which is meant to be the aggregate of skills and capacities against which, or on the basis of which, a human being's intentional states operate. In elaborating his hypothesis, Searle claims that realism is "part of" the Background. That this is so undermines the possibility of a proof, since any demand for a proof already *presupposes* what the proof would try to prove. According to Searle, we are always already *committed* to the existence of an external world, and so no proof can be given. While Searle's response does seem to be remarkably close to Heidegger's, there are features of it that would elicit Heidegger's dissatisfaction. In particular, Searle's talk of *presupposing* the existence of an external world is something Heidegger explicitly rejects in *Being and Time*. Moreover, Searle's continuing to talk of the *external* world preserves the basic outlook of the epistemological tradition Heidegger wants to circumvent. In doing so, Searle's view continues to beg the question against the skeptic who demands a proof, whereas Heidegger wants to subvert the epistemological tradition altogether by reasserting the priority of ontology. A demand for proof exhibits, from Heidegger's perspective, a distortion, and ultimately a disowning, of the understanding of *being*. Heidegger's rejection of the demand for a "proof of an external world" is thus an illustration of the importance of ontological difference.

II If I Had a Hammer

In his 1939 "Proof of an External World," G. E. Moore confronts head-on Kant's famous "scandal of philosophy." The aim of Moore's essay is to provide such a "satisfactory proof," and so bring to an end the scandal of which Kant complains. Moore's proof is surprisingly simple, requiring only two premises and no further intermediate steps prior to the conclusion: to prove "the existence of things outside of us," Moore simply displays the first two "things" he happens upon, in this case his two hands. The premises of the argument are thus the assertion, by Moore, of the existence of each of his own hands, that is, "Here is one hand," and "Here is another," accompanied by the appropriate gestures. These assertions are sufficient to prove what Moore sees as needing proof: "By doing this, I have proved ipso facto the existence of external things."[4]

The opening chapters of the existential analytic of Dasein in Division I of *Being and Time* might be understood as confronting Kant's scandal in a roughly Moore-like fashion. That is, Heidegger insists that a proper understanding of what it is to be a human being must *begin* from the standpoint of what he calls Dasein's "everydayness," where that means our day-to-day, pretheoretical mode of activity. Central to Heidegger's development of that standpoint is a characterization of those *entities* which we encounter in our everyday dealings, namely what Heidegger calls equipment, or the "ready-to-hand." Equipment, for Heidegger, consists of "those entities which we encounter as closest to us," (*BT*, 95) and our encounter with, and skillful handling of, such entities marks "the way in which everyday Dasein always *is*" (*BT*, 96). That is, "[t]he kind of dealing which is closest to us is . . . not a bare perceptual cognition, but rather that kind of concern which manipulates things and puts them to use" (*BT*, 95).

While Heidegger is careful to underscore many of the ways in which the entities we encounter and manipulate in our day-to-day lives differ from mere things, they nonetheless appear to count as

David R. Cerbone

"things to be met with in space" in Moore's sense of the term. Things like hammers and nails are not "internal" like thoughts, nor are they like "things" such as after-images, which *appear* as though in space, but cannot be met there. In other words, they have the requisite features to make them appropriate starting points for a proof like Moore's. In response to the demand for proof, Heidegger's existential analytic thus appears to provide a seemingly unlimited stock of Moore-type sentences to use as premises for such a "proof."

Were this Heidegger's response to the demand for a proof of the external world, were he, that is, more or less like Moore, his position would be open to the same kinds of complaints as can be raised against Moore's. That is, we are apt to feel that Moore's "proof" comes too late, in the sense that if one has, by means of skeptical arguments, found reasons to call the existence of the world into question, then those reasons suffice to call into question the premises of the argument Moore constructs. Moore is entitled to the premises of his argument only to the extent to which the existence of the external world has already been established: one needs, that is, to have secured the *conclusion* of the argument before one can be entitled to assert the premises.[5]

Despite the tone of some of Heidegger's remarks, that he is not proceeding in a Moore-like fashion can seen by considering more carefully the opening chapters of the existential analytic. Early in Division I, Heidegger notes at one point:

The world itself is not an entity within-the-world; and yet it is so determinative for such entities that only in so far as 'there is' a world can they be encountered and show themselves, in their Being, as entities which have been discovered.[6]

Recall that Moore, in constructing his proof of an external *world*, takes as a satisfactory demonstration of *this* conclusion the demonstration of the existence of a plurality of *things*. Heidegger's claim that "The world itself is not an entity within the world" (*BT*, 102), helps to underscore what, from his perspective, is problematic with Moore's line of reasoning: if the world is not one more entity, then pointing to objects or entities "within the world" will never suffice to demonstrate that there is a world.

That the world is "determinative" for entities (and so pointing to entities is itself dependent on the *prior* givenness of the world) suggests that the world operates as a kind of *background* for these pointings; it is what gives them the sense they have. As such, no proof for the existence of the world can be furnished, since, as the background to any "foregrounded" activities like pointing to objects or making assertions, it has already been presupposed. Such talk of the world as a background and as something whose existence is, and must be, presupposed permeates Searle's philosophy of mind and language. Working through Searle's position, then, might be fruitful for understanding Heidegger's, even if the two do not ultimately coincide.

III Searle and the Background of Realism

For Searle, the Background plays an integral role in his conception of intentionality, although many of his arguments for the Background emerge out of his account of literal meaning. The fixing of literal meaning is something that happens for Searle only against a Background of embodied skills and cultural practices. To use one of his examples, in the sentences "Sally cut the cake" and "Sally cut the lawn," the word "cut" is in each case to be understood literally, that is, in neither case is "cut" being used metaphorically or figuratively. Nonetheless, if Sally were to run the cake over with a lawnmower or were to sever each blade of grass individually with a kitchen utensil, we would say that "cut" has not been properly understood in these two sentences. What "cut" literally means in each case (slicing with a knife in the first case, and mowing with a lawnmower in the second) is not something which can be determined by means of the individual sentences alone: that "cut" means one rather than the other is something which depends upon our taken-for-granted understanding of things like cakes, knives, lawns, and lawnmowers. That is, only given our shared understanding of what counts as cutting a cake or cutting the grass can the words in the sentences function in their literal sense.

What holds for literal meaning holds equally in the case of intentional states like beliefs and desires, since these states have propositional contents which are equally in need of fixation. When I *believe* that Sally cut the cake, or when I *want* Sally to cut the grass, *what* I believe or want cannot be specified independently or in isolation. Searle's rejection of the possibility of independently specifying the contents of intentional states has two levels, the first of which remains at the level of the intentional: this is Searle's notion of the Network. That a subject has intentional states (beliefs, desires, intentions, fears, etc.) is not something which can be understood purely atomistically: in order to have, or be in, one state, one must have, or be in, many. Every intentional state refers to others, and thus any state "can only be the [state] that it is, because it is located in a Network of other beliefs and desires."[7] There is, however, no saying just what else must be in the Network in order for any particular intentional state to be possible.

Indeed, it is by attempting to enumerate all of the members of the Network that one inevitably, according to Searle, finds oneself driven toward the Background: eventually, Searle maintains, "we would soon find ourselves formulating a set of propositions which would look fishy" (*Intentionality*, 142). What Searle means by "fishy" here is that these propositions "are in a sense too fundamental to qualify as *beliefs*, even as unconscious beliefs," and so cannot be construed as further elements of the Network: such "fundamental" propositions are signs that one has reached the Background. If, however, this were the only argument, one could always maintain that those "fishy" propositions are present as unconscious beliefs just like many other elements of the Network, only they are rarely brought to the level of consciousness because of their pervasiveness and generality. Searle does try to differentiate between unconscious elements of the Network, such as a person's unconsciously believing that larger states have more electoral votes than smaller states, and supposedly "fishy" propositions, such as "Tables offer resistance to touch," by contending that in the latter case there is no belief of this sort about tables, unconscious or otherwise. Instead, "I use a table as a work bench, and so on. And as I do each of these things I do not in addition think unconsciously to myself, 'it offers resistance to touch'" (*Intentionality*, 142). But Searle's talking of "thinking unconsciously to oneself" is misleading here, since one can ask whether a person intending to run for president "thinks unconsciously" to himself, "Larger states have more electoral votes than smaller ones," even though he surely believes such a thing. If a negative answer here does not thereby rule out the presence of an unconscious belief with that content, then it seems that Searle's not "thinking unconsciously" that tables offer resistance to touch does not preclude the presence of a belief with that content either.

Fishiness, then, cannot be the only criterion for when one has reached the Background: once one allows for the presence of unconscious beliefs, it will always be debatable whether any proposition is too odd-sounding to count as one. The task of enumerating the elements of the Network leads to the Background, not ultimately by the questionable appeal to something's being too fishy to count as even an unconscious belief, but by reflection on the fact that all of the elements of the Network have *content*, that is, they all have conditions of satisfaction. That this is so, for Searle, cannot be accounted for by the continued listing of beliefs and other intentional states, since every new intentional state is going to have a determinate content which needs to be accounted for, and a regress quickly ensues unless one posits a pre- or non-intentional Background, for which the question of content or conditions of satisfaction does not arise.[8]

Searle contends that "Many philosophical problems arise from the failure to understand the nature and operation of the Background" (*Intentionality*, 158). One source of this failure, Searle thinks, is our lack of a suitable vocabulary for talking about the elements of the Background, since "when it comes to examining the conditions of the possibility of the functioning of the mind, we simply have very little vocabulary to hand except the vocabulary of first-order Intentional states" (*Intentionality*, 157). As a result of this limitation, we have a tendency to talk about elements of the Background in intentional terms. As an example, Searle describes a case where, upon lifting a mug of beer that is made of plastic rather than glass, he is surprised by its lightness. Of this case, Searle states that "We would naturally say I *believed* that the mug was made of glass, and I *expected* it to be heavy," but, he notes, "that is wrong." He continues: "In the sense in which I really do believe without ever having explicitly thought about it that interest rates will go down and I really do expect a break in the current heat wave, I had no such expectations and beliefs about the mug; I simply acted" (*Intention-ality*, 157). The lesson of this example, according to Searle, is that "From the fact that it is possible to treat an element of the Background as a representation, it does not follow that, when it is functioning, it is functioning as a representation" (*Intentionality*, 158). In the case of the mug of beer, the "element" which was "functioning" as part of the Background was not an unconscious belief or other representational state, but instead something more along the lines of a taken-for-granted skill or stance with respect to the handling and composition of beer mugs.

The failure to appreciate the lesson illustrated by the beer mug example is what allows the question of the reality of the external world to get a grip. That is, we are apt to reason about the existence of the world in the same manner as we (incorrectly) reason about the mug of beer, namely by treating it as one more belief or hypothesis in need of justification. Searle thinks this line of reasoning is incorrect. Instead, what Searle calls his "commitment to 'realism'" is "part of the Background."[9] That realism is part of the Background is shown, Searle thinks, by the very bewilderment that attends any demand for a proof of the external world:

It seems that I could never show or demonstrate that there existed a real world independent of my representations of it. But of course I could never show or demonstrate that, since any *showing* or *demonstrating* presupposes the Background, and the Background is the embodiment of my commitment to realism. (*Intentionality*, 159)

If Searle is right, then, that realism is part of the Background, that would help to explain why the demand for proof seems both unintelligible and unsatisfiable.

In recent writings, Searle has raised explicitly the issue of the relation between his view and Moore's attempt at a proof of an external world, as well as Kant's famous "scandal" to which Moore responds. Searle expresses sympathy for Moore's attempt at a proof: it seems to be undeniable that Moore has two hands, and his displaying them for all to see seems to be ample demonstration of their existence, and so an ample demonstration of the conclusions which follow logically. To continue this line of reasoning, since the existence of the external world is part of the truth conditions of the claim that Moore (or anyone else) has two hands, then the truth of that claim shows that the conditions of its truth have been fulfilled: we are thus permitted to infer the obtaining of one of the truth conditions from the claim whose truth has already been demonstrated.

Searle, however, recognizes that the pattern of reasoning Moore deploys is ultimately question-begging. For Searle, the mistake in Moore's proof consists in a failure to distinguish between the truth conditions of a particular claim or belief, and the conditions for that claim's or belief's intelligibility. That is, Searle wants to resist the idea that the existence of the external world is a deductive consequence of Moore's assertion of the existence of his two hands, which it would be were it construed as one of the truth conditions for those assertions. Instead, the existence of the external world is something that is taken for granted in the very *understanding* of Moore's premises. It is thus one of the conditions that we "take for granted" in making claims of that sort, or in having beliefs and other intentional states with that content, and if we did not, "We could not understand utterances the way we do or even have the intentional states with conditions of satisfaction that we have."[10] This leads Searle to reiterate a claim made in *Intentionality*, to the effect that "ER [External Realism] functions as a taken-for-granted part of the Background," (*CSR*, 181–182) and that, moreover, it is an indispensable part. Searle thinks that "[u]nless we take ER for granted, we cannot understand utterances the way we normally do" (*CSR*, 182). Thus, Searle concludes that ER is "a *necessary* presupposition for a large chunk of thought and language. We can't give it up as, for example, centuries ago we gave up our presupposition that the earth is flat" (*CSR*, 182).

Now, what does it mean to say that we must "presuppose" External Realism on pain of forfeiting our understanding of large regions of our discourse? Searle offers some examples which are designed to underscore this point. He asks us to consider the following pair of sentences:

(A) You owe me five dollars.
(B) Mt. Everest has snow and ice near the summit.

David R. Cerbone

These are both sentences we understand, but what distinguishes our understanding of (A) from (B) is the effect of embedding them in certain counterfactual contexts. That is, when we conjoin (A) and (B) to the counterfactual, "In a world that is like ours, except that representations have never existed in it. . . .", very different things happen to our understanding of (A) and (B). In the case of (A), the resulting sentence:

(A′) In a world that is like ours, except that representations have never existed in it, you owe me five dollars

has what we might call an attenuated sense: we're inclined to say that (A′) is simply false, but that cannot be the whole of the matter, because the sentence, "In a world that is like ours, except that representations have never existed in it, you *don't* owe me five dollars" is also false. What's going on here, according to Searle, is that we're imagining a situation in which the conditions for the possibility of there being things like money and debts are absent, and as a result, the *sense* of claims couched in those terms disappears. But what about (B)? Here, Searle claims, the case is quite different, since the following sentence:

(B′) In a world that is like ours, except that representations have never existed in it, Mt. Everest has snow and ice near the summit

makes perfect sense, as does the related sentence in which the negation of (B) is embedded in the same counterfactual context. What this shows, for Searle, is that it is part of our ordinary understanding of claims like (B) (but not [A]) that there is a world which is a certain way independently of any of our representations of it. Were we in some way to deny or disown that conception of the world, we could not make the sense we do of large portions of our language.

Now, it might seem that Searle's theory of the Background gives us something like the proof that Moore is seeking in the following way: since the words, or again the thought expressed by the words, "Here is one hand" *do* have content, do have a literal meaning (or, in the language of *Intentionality*, have determinate conditions of satisfaction), the conditions of their having a meaning (or conditions of satisfaction) *are* in place, and so, at least implicitly, one has *shown* that the external world exists. Searle, however, is careful to emphasize that he does not take the indispensability of our commitment to, or presupposition of, external realism to be tantamount to proving its truth. Indeed, Searle does not believe that "there could be a non-question-begging argument for ER" (*CSR*, 184).

That the indispensability of our commitment to realism does not establish its truth can be seen in another feature of Searle's conception of the Background: that it consists only of what he calls "mental phenomena." Nothing therefore follows about the existence of a real world given the insight that there must be a Background against which intentional states function, even if part of that Background is a commitment to the existence of the external world. All of Searle's remarks about the Background are, he claims, compatible with the idea of one's being a brain-in-a-vat, and since a brain-in-a-vat presumably still has various mental states with intentional content, then such a brain-in-a-vat would likewise have a commitment to realism to the same degree as Searle does when he skis his mountains.[11] The coherence for Searle of the brain-in-a-vat scenario helps to underscore why his hypothesis of the Background disallows any substantive conclusions about the character of the real world or the success of our relation to it.

IV The Recovery of Being

Just as there are aspects of Heidegger's phenomenology of everydayness that appear to correspond to Moore's endeavor, so too are there affinities between his position and Searle's. Like Searle, Heidegger finds problematic the idea that located somewhere in our psychic economy is a *belief* in the existence of the external world. For instance, in *The History of the Concept of Time*, Heidegger declares:

[N]othing exists in our relationship to the world which provides a basis for the phenomenon of belief in the world. I have not yet been able to find this phenomenon of belief. Rather, the peculiar thing is just that the world is "there" *before* all belief. The world is never experienced as something which is believed any more than it is guaranteed by knowledge. Inherent in the being of the world is that its existence *needs no guarantee in regard to a subject*.[12]

Heidegger's talk here of the world being there "before all belief" appears to correspond to Searle's insistence that our commitment to the existence of the external world precedes, and indeed makes possible, our having beliefs about particular states of affairs in the world: a commitment to the existence of the external world is part of the Background, and so among the *preconditions* of intentionality.

Furthermore, Heidegger, like Searle, rejects the demand for proof. Of this demand, Searle, as we have seen, remarks that "we are embarrassed to try to prove what our attempts at proof already presuppose" (*CSR*, 196). In a similar vein, Heidegger, in *Being and Time*, writes that Dasein "defies such proofs, because, in its Being, it already *is* what subsequent proofs deem necessary to demonstrate for it" (*BT*, 249), and, shortly thereafter:

The "problem of Reality" in the sense of the question whether an external world is present-at-hand and whether such a world can be proved, turns out to be an impossible one, not because its consequences lead to inextricable impasses, but because the very entity which serves as its theme, is one which, as it were, repudiates any such formulation of the question. (*BT*, 250)

Despite the Searlian ring to these passages, there are also differences which are important to note.

Most prominently, in *Being and Time*, Heidegger explicitly takes issue with any talk of our having to *presuppose* the existence of the external world. He writes:

Even if one should invoke the doctrine that the subject must *presuppose* and indeed always does unconsciously *presuppose* the presence-at-hand of the "external world", one would still be starting with the construct of an isolated subject. (*BT*, 249—my emphasis)

And, later in the same paragraph, he writes that "'earlier' than any presupposition which Dasein makes, or any of its ways of behaving, is the '*a priori*' character of its state of Being as one whose kind of Being is care" (*BT*, 249). Searle's position appears to fall clearly within the scope of such remarks, since, as we have seen, talk of presupposition permeates Searle's engagement with the demand for a proof: "The presupposition of ER is thus a *necessary* presupposition for a large chunk of thought and language" (*CSR*, 182); "when we attempt to communicate to achieve normal understanding with these sorts of utterance we must presuppose external realism" (*CSR*,

184); and "External Realism is a Background presupposition on the normal understanding of a very large class of utterances" (*CSR*, 185).

Given Searle's understanding of the Background as consisting of pre- or non-intentional states, his talk of presupposition is rather murky, since to talk of something's being presupposed has, at the very least, the connotations of an attitude (viz. an intentional attitude) taken by an agent or subject. But Searle denies that realism, as part of the Background, is "a matter of any intentional states at all" (*CSR*, 195). The question, though, is whether any positive characterization can be given of just what it is for it to be "part of" the Background. The following passage, which continues the remark just cited, helps, I think, to display the difficulties that arise here:

> One of the keys to understanding the Background is this: One can be committed to the truth of a proposition without having any beliefs, thoughts, assumptions, hypotheses, or other "propositional attitudes" regarding the proposition at all. *"Taking something for granted" need not name a psychological state.*[13]

The difficulty is this: if, as Searle consistently maintains, the Background consists of "mental phenomena," and external realism, that is, a commitment to the existence of a mind-independent world, is *part of* the Background, then that commitment, or presupposition, ought to be a mental phenomenon. However, according to the above passage, this commitment need not be a "psychological state" at all, nor, as he also says, need it involve any "assumptions" on the part of the one who is committed. Despite the absence of both explicit thoughts and unconscious beliefs, I have, according to Searle, presupposed that a proposition to the effect that there is an external world independent of my (and all other human beings') attitudes is true. The problem, for Searle's account, is understanding this talk of presupposing.

Heidegger takes issue with the idea of presupposition as it carries connotations of an *act* that is performed by an isolated (or "worldless") *subject*. He thus detects an intimate connection between the very idea of something's being presupposed in this context and describing what's presupposed as *External* Realism. If this is right, it helps to underscore a further disagreement between Heidegger and Searle, despite their common ground of rejecting the demand for a proof of the external world: on Searle's account, the conception of the world in play is the same conception held by the one who demands a proof, and Searle is saying that *that* world is already presupposed by *my* meaningful use of language, and so cannot be proven by means of meaningful language (and so cannot be proven full-stop).[14] Heidegger, by contrast, focuses his attention on the very dichotomy between internal and external upon which traditional epistemological problems rely, and which, in this instance, frames the demand for proof. As cited above, from Heidegger's perspective, those who talk of presupposing the world still take for granted the standpoint of "a subject which is proximally *worldless* or unsure of its world, and which must, at bottom, first assure itself of a world" (*BT*, 250), and it is precisely the legitimacy of this standpoint which Heidegger challenges.

Searle's continuing to talk of our having presupposed the existence of the *external* world, or describing our commitment to an independent reality as External Realism, suggests, from Heidegger's point of view, that Searle remains trapped within the traditional epistemological picture marked by the dichotomy of inner and outer, subject and object. As seen before, especially in the discussion in *Intentionality*, Searle continues to take seriously certain skeptical fantasies such as brains in vats. Such fantasies are, for Searle, fully compatible with what he describes as a commitment to realism: we can never take seriously, or get ourselves into the position of believing, such fantasies, since our continuing to make sense of ourselves and one another depends upon our continued commitment to realism. At the same time, Searle maintains that this commitment to realism is fully compatible with the falsity of *all* of a subject's beliefs. To be sure, from that subject's standpoint, it will not *feel* that way, because that subject, as a subject with contentful intentional states, will continue to have among his mental phenomena the commitment to the reality of the external world.

Searle's continued allegiance to the intelligibility of certain sorts of skeptical fantasies suggests that, even with his talk of realism's being part of the Background, he operates with a more or less traditional picture of the subject's relation to the world. To put it in Heidegger's terms, Searle continues to employ a particular model of "transcendence." The model Heidegger has in mind is especially well developed in *The Metaphysical Foundations of Logic*, in those sections where he explicitly returns to the problematic of *Being and Time*.[15] In philosophy, the problem of transcendence, according to Heidegger, involves a particular conception of the subject, articulated largely in spatial terms, such that it is "thought of as a sort of box with an interior, with the walls of a box, and with an exterior" (*MFL*, 160). Intrinsic to this conception, then, is the notion of a barrier which must first be crossed: the problem of transcendence thus depends on the idea that "the inner is, first of all, really restricted by the barrier," and so one must explain how it is that the subject can "break through" the barrier or "*remove the restrictions*" (*MFL*, 160).

The confinement envisaged here thus serves as the point of departure for a philosophical account of how, for example, knowledge (of objects, other minds, etc.) is possible, and so what stands in need of explanation is how, if at all, the subject manages to *transcend* the interior, how it gets outside the "box." To the extent that Searle takes seriously talk of an external world (or External Realism), this kind of picture of consciousness as an "interior," as a "box," filled with representations still seems to be present. To be sure, Searle, with his notion of the Background, has supplemented representations (or intentional phenomena) with something else (skills, stances, capacities), but insofar as these supplements are just more mental phenomena, the account of a subject's commitment to realism is fully compatible with that subject's confinement to the "interior."

For Heidegger, the problem of transcendence needs to be radically reconsidered from an ontological, rather than an epistemological, point of view. What Heidegger calls "the acclaimed pseudoproblem of the reality of the external world" (*MFL*, 151) gets a grip precisely because of insufficient ontological investigation: "The problem of transcendence depends on how one defines the subjectivity of the subject, the basic constitution of Dasein. Does this boxnotion have any *a priori* validity at all or not? If not, however, why does it arise with such persistence?" (*MFL*, 161). The "subjectivity of the subject," for Heidegger, is what that stands in need of clarification with respect to the concept of transcendence: the epistemological conception, with its "box-like" picture of subjectivity, cannot simply

David R. Cerbone

be taken for granted. Heidegger can, in this way, be understood to be asking what makes something, some particular being, a subject in the first place? What does it mean to say that Dasein *is* a subject? Heidegger's answer to these questions does not rest on the notion of intentionality in the sense of the possession of mental states whose content is directed toward objects. Instead, for Heidegger it is this notion of intentionality itself that stands in need of explication.

The ontological basis of subjectivity, what Heidegger calls "primal transcendence," is the understanding of being, which is not a matter of the fulfillment of any particular intentional states. We have seen that for Searle, there is something prior to the subject, understood in terms of intentional states, and that something is the Background: "Without the Background" intentional states "could not determine conditions of satisfaction" (*Intentionality*, 151). But again, since the Background is just a matter of more "mental phenomena," one has only filled the "box" of consciousness with further items. From Heidegger's perspective, then, Searle's talk of presupposition still begins with the notion of a subject as the performer of the act of presupposing. As he puts it in *Being and Time*, "in so far as it does this presupposing as an entity (and otherwise this would be impossible), it is, *as an entity*, already in a world" (*BT*, 249).

Heidegger's appeal here to "already in" registers the idea that the act of presupposing does not, and cannot, have the founding role Searle takes it to have. The act of presupposing itself has presuppositions, namely that the entity doing the presupposing is "already in a world," where "in" means not mere spatial containment, but involvement of familiarity.[16] However, if this is correct, Searle's appeal to presupposition becomes superfluous: Dasein always already is what this presupposition is meant to secure. Thus, any talk of presupposition, as something that a subject has done or as a commitment that has been incurred, cannot do justice to what Heidegger calls primal transcendence, or the understanding of being. The latter are not a matter of commitments or acts, but name how an entity (Dasein) is, as a being "already in a world."

The point might be put like this: Heidegger and Searle both reject what might be called the autonomy of the intentional, in the sense that the content of intentional states like beliefs and desires cannot be understood except on the background of something else. For Searle, that something else is the Background which includes, as we have seen, a presupposition to the effect that there is an external world. For Heidegger, by contrast, the something else just is being-in-the-world, where this is not a collection of (non-intentional) mental phenomena. Indeed, being-in-the-world is a kind of intentionality that Heidegger sometimes calls "primordial intentionality." Were it not, the connection between it and intentional states like beliefs and desires would be hard to make out. From Heidegger's perspective, then, Searle's account of there being a presupposition which serves as a "condition of intelligibility" faces a dilemma: either this presupposition on the part of a subject is intelligible, in which case it too stands in need of a condition for *its* intelligibility, or it is itself unintelligible, in which case it's difficult to see how it can be picked out *as* "a commitment to the existence of the external world." This dilemma is, I take it, one way of spelling out Heidegger's complaint that talk of a subject's making a presupposition itself presupposes that there is an entity doing the presupposing, and the being of such of entity is what needs to be investigated.

Central to such an investigation is the idea that transcendence is part of Dasein's "primordial constitution." This should not be construed as a claim about a range of mental phenomena, but about Dasein's way of being, what Heidegger calls its comportment. Comportment here does not designate dealings with any particular object or range of objects: "That 'toward-which' the subject, as subject, transcends is not an object, not at all this or that being" (*MFL*, 166). Instead, "that toward which the subject transcends is what we call *world*" (*MFL*, 166). These remarks underscore the importance of the difference, for Heidegger, between being and beings, understood here as the difference between the world and entities within the world: transcendence, as transcendence toward the world, is an ontological, rather than an epistemological, notion, equivalent to what Heidegger in other contexts would call an understanding of being.

Given Heidegger's conception of ontological or primal transcendence, one can begin to understand his dissatisfaction with the demand for proofs of an external world: "The question of whether there is a world at all and whether its Being can be proved, makes

David R. Cerbone

no sense if it is raised by *Dasein* as Being-in-the-world; and who else would raise it?" (*BT*, 246–247). Now it is important to notice that Heidegger says here that the question "makes no sense," rather than that, say, it is one which is easily answered. Thus, when he writes that "If Dasein is understood correctly, it defies such proofs, because, in its Being, it already *is* what subsequent proofs deem necessary to demonstrate for it" (*BT*, 249), he must be carefully understood. That is, saying that Dasein "already is what subsequent proofs deem necessary to demonstrate for it" appears to concede too much to the picture of human beings Heidegger is opposing: what "subsequent" proofs" try to demonstrate is that the confines of the "box" of consciousness have been transcended, but for Heidegger there is no "box" in the first place: "What we mean by transcendence cannot be made compatible with the previous formulations of it and is very difficult to see, in light of the usual deadlocked version of the problem" (*MFL*, 167).

At one point in *Being and Time*, shortly after Heidegger has rejected the demand for proof and has turned his attention to the concept of truth, he remarks:

A sceptic can no more be refuted than the Being of truth can be 'proved'. And if any sceptic of the kind who denies the truth, factically *is*, he does *not* even *need* to be refuted. In so far as he *is*, and has understood himself in this Being, he has obliterated Dasein in the desperation of suicide; and in doing so, he has also obliterated truth. (*BT*, 271)

It may be unclear just why Heidegger concedes that the skeptic cannot be refuted: after all, if Heidegger is right that being-in-the-world is the basic state of Dasein, and that this precludes the raising of the demand for proof, that ought to be enough to constitute a refutation of skepticism. For Searle, that skepticism is not refuted seems to follow from the claim that the Background consists of mental phenomena: the necessity of presupposing the existence of the external world is fully compatible with the truth of skepticism. Heidegger's refusal to identify the understanding of being with any set of mental phenomena appears to point to a more robust position against skepticism than one finds in Searle: we are always already in a world, and not just committed to conceiving of ourselves in that way.

The mistake in this line of reasoning comes from reading Heidegger's remarks about being-in-the-world as a kind of epistemological guarantee: that we are, as beings with an understanding of being, always already in a world means that the world is an ever present *object* of knowledge. On the contrary, Heidegger's remarks must be understood as ontological, not epistemological: his point is not one about knowledge, but about intelligibility. For this reason, no proof can be given: since again any premises would have to be intelligible, they would have to be understood.[17] But there is no understanding without an understanding of being, and the latter notion, for Heidegger, just is being-in-the-world. "What" is being presupposed here is not a thing or the existence of any particular entity, but instead the being of beings. A skeptic who demands a proof of the external world at the same time denies his own capacity to make sense, to be the kind of being whose being is an issue. Someone who denies his own intelligibility, his own understanding of being, is not so much in need of an argument as of reminders. Indeed, Heidegger's suggestion is that no argument, in the form of a proof, can be given: the skeptic, if there ever is such a person, needs to recollect the being of beings, or rediscover his own understanding of being.

Within his discussion of the problem of transcendence in *The Metaphysical Foundations of Logic*, Heidegger invokes Plato's doctrine of recollection as a way of understanding the primacy of being.[18] Using deliberately Platonic language, he writes:

Being is what we recall, what we accept as something we immediately understand as such, what is always already given to us; being is never alien but always familiar, "ours." Being is, accordingly, what we always already understand, and we only need to recall it once again to grasp it as such. In grasping being we do not conceive anything new, but something basically familiar; we always already exist in an understanding-of-being, insofar as we relate to what we now call "beings". (*MFL*, 147)

The skeptic, the one who demands proof, is someone who suffers from a failure to recollect his own understanding of being, or who willfully denies possession of that understanding. Shortly after the

David R. Cerbone

above passage, Heidegger refers, approvingly, to Plato's claim in the *Phaedrus* (249b–c) that "a living thing that has never seen the truth can never take on the shape of a human" (*MFL*, 148). A human being "must understand and know in such a way that he thereby addresses what he knows with regard to its being" (*MFL*, 148). A skeptic who denies that understanding, who demands proof of its legitimacy, denies his own human form, and it is for this reason that Heidegger likens the demand for proof to the act of suicide.[19]

Intending the Intender
(Or, Why Heidegger Isn't Davidson)

Mark Okrent

For several years I have been attempting to convince Hubert Dreyfus that the early Heidegger can be profitably compared with Donald Davidson. In this chapter I take up this challenge yet again, but with a twist. I start by pointing out what have come to seem to me obvious points of similarity between Davidson and Heidegger concerning the nature of intentionality. But, I then ask, if Heidegger and Davidson are so similar, why do they appear so different? The answer is that Heidegger *seems* to give a certain priority to first person approaches to intentionality that Davidson denies, but that this seeming emphasis is merely apparent. Having said this, I go on to suggest that Heidegger does have a unique view of the relation between self-directed intentions and intentions directed toward other entities that distinguishes him not only from Davidson, but also from everyone else.

My positive thesis regarding the difference between Heidegger and Davidson has three parts. First, Heidegger holds with much of the Continental tradition, but against Davidson, that there are two intentional aspects of every intentional state: an intention directed toward the object of that state and an intention directed toward the one who has that state. On this view, part of what it is for me to intend a hammer, for example, is for me to intend myself. This thesis crucially distinguishes Heidegger from Davidson. But, second, virtually the entire Continental tradition interprets this supposed constraint on intentionality in terms of self-presence. And it is easy to interpret

Heidegger as accepting this view, while Davidson rejects it, thus severing the tie between intentionality and consciousness. I argue, however, that Heidegger also rejects this understanding of the relation between self-directed intentions and intentionality in general. Instead, I argue that for Heidegger, all intentionality involves intending an entity as an entity of one sort or another, and, given the distinctive normative character that Heidegger holds is central to the intentionality of Dasein, to intend an entity as having some specific determination is also to intend oneself as a Dasein of some particular sort. The intention of self that is involved in all intentionality does not, for Heidegger, involve any consciousness or presentation of self, even in the form of "what it is like" to be Dasein. Rather, the very intention that is correctly describable as a taking of something as a shoe, for example, is always necessarily also correctly describable as a taking of the intender as a certain sort of Dasein:

The shoemaker is not the shoe; but shoe gear, belonging to the equipmental contexture of his environing world, is intelligible as the piece of equipment that it is only by way of the particular world that belongs to the existential constitution of the Dasein as being-in-the-world. In understanding itself by way of *things*, the Dasein understands itself as being-in-the-world by way of its world. The shoemaker is not the shoe but, existing, he is his world.[1]

The third part of my thesis is that when we properly understand this dark saying, we also understand what is distinctive, and important, about Heidegger.

I   Intentionality, Representation, and Consciousness

Let us begin with Davidson's and Heidegger's common enemy: Rene Descartes. Here is the central Cartesian picture. The mind is a substance whose essential attribute is thinking. This claim has two parts. First, to be a substance is to be an entity whose being is logically independent of the being of any other entity. So, even though it may be true that entity A is causally dependent on entity B, as long as what it is for A to be is specifiable independently of any relation which A might have to B or anything else, then A counts as a substance. Second, all of the attributes of the substance which is the mind are modifications of thought, where the extension of the term "thought" includes "everything that is within us in such a way that we are immediately aware of it."[2] That is, to be a thinking thing is to be a substance such that it is essential to the substance's attributes that the substance is aware of those attributes. For a Cartesian, nothing belongs to me which is not *conscious*; or, as Descartes himself puts it: "We cannot have any thought of which we are not aware at the very moment when it is in us."[3] Although a thinking substance might have some determinations which are not conscious, all of these are modifications of consciousness, in the sense that they are dispositions to think, or possible thoughts, or abilities to think, and so forth.

The other pillar of the Cartesian view of the mental is that all thoughts involve ideas, where an idea is "the form of any given thought, immediate perception of which makes me aware of the thought."[4] The Cartesian asserts that every conscious event, and thus every thought, has a form, and these events are typed and identified according to their form. It is by the "immediate perception" of this form that the thinker is "immediately aware" of her thought. The form of a thought, by which it is typed and of which the thinker is immediately aware, is also the *content* of the thought, in the sense that this thought, in virtue of its form, amounts to a representation of some object. In virtue of that representational relation with that object, it is intentionally directed toward that object. Finally, since thoughts are the thoughts they are in virtue of their form, which is immediately perceived by the thinker, the nature of her thoughts and what they represent are transparently presented to the thinker.

Cartesians thus believe: (1) The mind is a substance; (2) All mental states are conscious; (3) A state has intentional content just in case it is conscious; (4) A conscious mental state is intentional in virtue of its character as a representation; (5) What is represented in a mental state is transparent to the thinker.

So, how is Donald Davidson similar to the early Heidegger? They both reject all of 1–5. Moreover, they both reject 1–5 for the same reasons and in the same way.

Let's start with proposition (1), that the mind is a substance. The mind, or self, is not a substance for either Heidegger or Davidson, if "by *substance* we can understand nothing other than a thing which exists in such a way as to depend on no other thing for its existence."[5]

For Davidson, a person is simply an entity which has mental states. Davidson follows Brentano in identifying mental states with intentional states ("the distinguishing feature of the mental is not that it is private, subjective, or immaterial, but that it exhibits what Brentano called intentionality"[6]), but distinguishes himself by insisting that if we use the criterion of intentionality to distinguish the mental, then *actions* must also be seen as "mental". "[I]ntentional actions are clearly included in the realm of the mental along with thoughts, hopes, and regrets."[7] Indeed, for Davidson, that non-action mental states are intentional depends upon their role in the rational explanation of behavior, teleologically or intentionally described, and the specific intentional content of any given state is a function of the specific role of that state in the explanation of behavior. "Adverting to beliefs and desires to explain action is therefore a way of fitting an action into a pattern of behavior made coherent by the theory. . . . there is a clear sense in which attributions of belief and desire, and hence teleological explanations of belief and desire, are supervenient on behavior more broadly described."[8]

Rational explanations are distinctive in that they appeal to *reasons.* Reasons are themselves distinctive in several ways. For a state of an individual to count as a reason it must be so related to a set of other possible states of that individual that if the person has the first state, (and perhaps some others), then the entity *should* have some of the others. If I believe that Gray is between Portland and Lewiston, and that Portland and Lewiston are thirty-five miles apart, then I *should* also believe that Gray is less than thirty-five miles from Portland. Similarly, if I want to go to Gray, and believe that Route 26 is the best way to get there, then all things equal, I *should* take Route 26. That is, it is essential to reasons as reasons that they belong to a system which stands under norms which specify the manner in which the states in the system should be related. An entity has reasons for what it does only if it stands under the inferential norms of rationality.

But when does an entity have states that stand under the normative constraints of rationality? Reasons not only specify what an agent ought to do, as reasons they also explain what the agent in fact does.

And, Davidson thinks, a being can count as standing under the normative constraints of rationality just to the extent that its reasons explain its behavior, and reasons explain behavior only to the extent that the entity in facts acts as it ought given its reasons. So, I stand under the constraints of rationality if my reasons explain most of my acts, and my reasons explain most of my acts if I tend to act rationally.

My beliefs and desires ought to be related to each other rationally. And, insofar as my acts can in fact be rationally explained, they *must* by and large be related to those beliefs and desires as they ought to be. So my acts being rationally explicable entails that my acts are generally coherent with each other and that my other mental states, my beliefs and desires, are generally consistent with each other and with my acts.

If to be a person is to be a being with mental states, and for a state to be mental is for it to be intentional, and a state is intentional only if it is an act or potentially involved in the rational explanation of acts, then an entity has intentional states only if she acts, and the conditions on being a person include whatever conditions there are on correctly describing a being as acting intentionally. It is a condition on acting intentionally that one act coherently, and for Davidson an entity can count as acting coherently and thus having mental states at all just in case it is possible to interpret it in such a way that most of what it does is successful and most of what it believes is true, (the doctrine which is called the "principle of charity"). Since these conditions involve specific relations between the entity and her environment, it follows that nothing can be a person, and nothing can count as a mental state, unless they are related in the right way to beings other than themselves.

This directly implies that no person can be a substance, if by a substance one means a being which needs no other being in order to be. For if a person must have mental states, and to be a mental state involves a relation between the person and some other thing, then what it is to be a person is only specifiable in terms of those relations, and nothing can be a person unless other things exist.

In *Being and Time*, Heidegger quotes the Cartesian definition of substance which I cited above, and states that the categories of the extant, such as substance, can not be used to articulate the self. But why not? In discussing this issue, Heidegger typically first reaffirms the Kantian point that the subject as thinker and agent can never be represented as such. Any such representation would present the self as if it were merely one object among others. And, since substance is a category which applies to and organizes representations, it never applies to the subject. As Kant says, "Consciousness in itself is not a representation . . . but a form of representation in general."[9]

Heidegger does not think that this critical stance toward Descartes is critical enough, however. And he is right. If to be a substance is to be a being such that it needs nothing else in order to be, then the subject as described is a substance. It is a substance because it is conceived as *consciousness*, and the notion of consciousness is essentially Cartesian. For Descartes, the paradigm acts of the subject, or mind, are conscious and self conscious; they are presentations of the self to the self which present beings other than the self. But since these presentations are conceived as *representations* it is thought that it is possible for the self and its representations to be even if what is represented is not. Perhaps, as Kant thinks, the subject must *think* objects in order to think itself, but what it is to be a subject (the form of representation of objects) can be specified independently of other beings, so, according to the definition, the subject is *ontologically* conceived as substance.

To complete the criticism of the conscious substance which Kant started, Heidegger reminds us that even for Kant, the I think is the I think something. To think something is to intend something. And, Heidegger believes, there is a necessary condition on the possibility of intending something, being-in-the-world. Since, as we shall see, being in the world demands the being of beings other than Dasein, Dasein cannot be without other beings: it is not a substance.

But what of the Cartesian claim that all mental states are conscious? Let us recall the central components of the Cartesian notion of consciousness. First, a thought is typed and identified by its form, which fixes its content by specifying what object the thought is about. Second, it is essential to a thought that it is immediately and completely known by the thinker. That it is so known is a function of the Cartesian claim that the form of the thought, the idea which the thought embodies, is an object of "immediate perception". Since the content of a thought is essential to it, and it is necessary that a thought be completely known by its thinker, it follows that the person who thinks a thought has a complete knowledge of the form of that thought, in virtue of which knowledge she also has complete knowledge of what is intended in the thought and the manner in which it is intended.

For Davidson, thoughts so understood are simply impossible:

> If a thought is constituted the thought it is by the mind's knowledge of the identifying object, then someone knows what thought she is thinking only if she knows what object she has in mind. Yet there seems to be no clear meaning to the idea of knowing which object one has in mind. The trouble is that ignorance of even one property of an object can, under appropriate circumstances, count as not knowing which object it is. This is the reason philosophers who have wanted to found knowledge on infallible identification of objects have sought objects that, like Hume's impressions and ideas, "Are they seem and seem what they are"—that is, have all and only the properties we think they have. Alas, there are no such objects. . . . Not even appearances are everything we think they are.[10]

We can understand *why* Davidson thinks this if we recall his views on what thoughts *are*. Thoughts are states of agents which can be appealed to in the course of giving rational explanations of intentional action. Such states are intentional and have content solely in virtue of their roles in such explanations. So "what a thought is about" which identifies the thought as the thought which it is, is solely a function of its relations to other mental states, thoughts and actions. And there is no reason to think that the person who has a thought has any special access to *those* relations. So even though we can monitor our own states in ways in which others cannot monitor them, it does not follow from this that we can know *the intentional content of our thoughts* in ways in which others cannot. Nor does it follow that if we do not monitor one of our states in this way, that it is not a thought.

For a Cartesian, a state is intentional in virtue of its representing its object. This claim amounts to the thesis that it is in virtue of the state which is intentional, I, standing in the representation relation R to object O that I intends O. It is because the Cartesian thinks that

I stands in this relation R to O in virtue of the form of I, and this form is transparent to the thinker, that she thinks that the content of I is transparent to the thinker. But Davidson rejects the notion that the content of I is fixed by its transparently available form. Rather, Davidson thinks that the intentional content of a mental item is a function of its role in the rational explanation of the pattern of an agent's behavior, and since there is no reason to think that this relation, E, is in any way similar to R, there is no reason to think that intentional states are representations. "Beliefs are true and false, but they represent nothing. It is good to be rid of representations."[11]

So Davidson rejects 2–5 just as completely as he rejects 1. For Davidson, agents are not Cartesian substances, mental states, though intentional, need not be conscious, their intentional content is not transparent to the thinker, and mental states represent nothing. But where does the early Heidegger stand on consciousness, representation, and intentionality?

These issues are complicated in Heidegger by his Husserlian upbringing. As Husserl clearly rejected the notion that intentionality was a matter of representation, it was easy for the early Heidegger to reject this view as well. For Heidegger the key point was that any intentional act is directed toward its object, not a representation of an object. When I see a chair it is the chair itself which I am intending, not any ghostly mental object. "When I look, I am not intent upon seeing a representation of something, but the chair."[12] "To say that I am in the first place oriented toward sensations is all just pure theory. In conformity with its sense of direction, perception is directed toward the extant being itself. It intends this precisely as extant and knows nothing at all about sensations that it is apprehending."[13]

What leads us to think that there must be representations immediately present to the mind through which we are related to an object is the relational character of intentions and intentional discourse. When I see the chair it seems that there is *something* which I see, as the verb "to see" here takes an object. But *the chair* itself need not be there, or be at all, as the fact of hallucination makes clear. So the relation cannot be a real relation between me and the chair, as real relations presuppose the existence of both relata. This suggests that there must be another object, distinct from me and the chair, to which I am related and through which I might perhaps be related to the chair. The problem Heidegger sees with this, however, is that seeing the chair, for example, is an activity which takes *the chair* itself as object, not any chair representation.

Thus, we have a puzzle. Intentional states are typed and identified by the object toward which they are directed. But the intentional character of these states cannot be understood as a relation between these states and the actual object toward which they are directed, nor can it be understood as a relation between the intentional states and some mental representation of the real object. Heidegger's solution to this puzzle is to take the directedness toward, which is the defining property of the intentional, as an intrinsic, nonrelational property of the intentional comportment itself. Thought transcends itself towards its object in virtue of its own essential character as directedness toward, so the thought need not involve a real relation with its object, whether that object is conceived as actual or merely mental. Thoughts are about their objects; they do not represent those objects.

This solution to the puzzle raises as many problems as it solves. For, what is it for an intentional comportment to be open to or directed toward its object in its very nature? What must a state *be* to be intentional? What must a person *be* if she is to have intentional states? The properties of substances are either intrinsic properties, in which case they characterize the substance apart from any relations that substance has to any other entity, or the properties are relational, in which case the property involves a relation between the substance with the property and some other existing being. It is impossible for the properties of classically conceived substances to involve relations to something else *in-themselves*.

In the lecture courses prior to the composition of *Being and Time*, Heidegger frequently assumes the orthodox Cartesian position that the realm of intentionality is coextensive with the realm of consciousness. Nevertheless, by the time we get to the text of *Being and Time*, the word "Bewusstsein" has virtually disappeared from Heidegger's lexicon. Why is this? There are strong programmatic considerations undermining Heidegger's adherence to Cartesian orthodoxy. Heidegger needs to answer the question regarding what sort of being can have states which relate to others, even though those others need not exist. And in response to this question he asserts that only an entity whose being is characterized as being-in-the-world can count as having such states. But what is it to be in the world and what sort of states are paradigmatic of entities which are in such a way as to be in the world?

Heidegger gives the following list of "modes of in-being belonging to everydayness", and the list remains pretty constant throughout the period of *Being and Time*: "Working on something with something, producing something, cultivating and caring for something, putting something to use, employing something for something, holding something in trust, giving up, letting something get lost, interrogating, discussing, accomplishing, exploring, considering, determining something."[14]

Heidegger characterizes the common denominator of these states as "concern", but from the standpoint provided by the puzzle of intentionality, another aspect of this list jumps out at you. All of these states involve overt behavior of embodied persons, overt behavior which is described in intentional terms. And, from the standpoint of the intentionality puzzle, what is striking is that each of these states demands *some* relation between an agent and its environment, but need not involve a relation between the agent and the object which is mentioned in the characterization of the act itself. When I am doing something which is correctly characterized as attempting to produce a widget, I must interact with my environment in some definite way, but as yet there is no widget for me to enter into relationship with. So, when I am in the state of producing a widget, I am both directed toward the widget, and in no real relationship with any widget.

But this is just what is required for a solution to the puzzle of intentionality. The intentional act of producing a widget is directed toward there being a widget, and in that sense directed toward the widget. But this being directed toward the widget of the production involves no relation to any widget. Thus insofar as Heidegger holds that the being-in-the-world of an agent is the necessary condition of all intentionality, we can say of the early Heidegger precisely what we said of

Intending the Intender (Or, Why Heidegger Isn't Davidson)

Davidson, that an entity has intentional states only if she acts, and the conditions on being a person include whatever conditions there are on correctly describing a being as acting intentionally.

The act centered answer to the puzzle of intentionality, an answer which suggests that intentional acts can be directed toward their objects without those acts being in a real relation to those objects, but only if the act involves a relation between the agent and other actual entities, demands that being conscious of oneself as attempting to produce something is not *sufficient* to guarantee that one is really attempting to produce. But is consciousness of one's attempt *necessary* for production, as Descartes thinks, or is it unnecessary, as Davidson thinks? Since each of these types of intentional activity are fundamentally overt doings, even if they are described in intentional terms, there does not seem any particular necessity that the agent *knows* what she is doing while she is doing it. In everydayness Dasein does not find herself by reflecting on the state she is in while she is performing an act: there is no moment of self-reflective consciousness built in to the act itself. Rather, we find ourselves, as ourselves, precisely in our everyday activities, and not in any conscious reflection on them: "Each one of us is what he pursues and cares for. In everyday terms, we understand ourselves and our existence by way of the activities we pursue and the things we take care of."[15]

But does this Heideggerean specific lack of focal knowledge of ourselves as agent amount to the claim that self-consciousness in an act is unnecessary for the intentionality of that act? There are two things which should arrest us about the entirely typical passage I just quoted from the early Heidegger. First, the Cartesian analysis of intentionality in terms of consciousness, the claim that every intentional state directed toward an object is in addition an immediate transparent presentation of the self to itself, is rejected. For Heidegger there is something *deeply* wrong with the Cartesian conception of intentionality as consciousness. But second, for Heidegger there is also something *deeply* right in the claim that every intentional state in *some* way involves a self reference:

But the question remains, *In what way is the self given?* Not . . . in such a way that an "I think" accompanies all representations and goes along with the acts directed at extant beings, which thus would be a reflective act directed at the first act. Formally, it is unassailable to speak of the ego as consciousness of something that is at the same time conscious of *itself,* and the description of the res cogitans as cogito me cogitare, or self-consciousness, is correct. But these formal determinations, which provide the framework for idealism's dialectic of consciousness, are nevertheless very far from an interpretation of the phenomenal circumstances of the Dasein. . . . We must first of all see this one thing clearly: the Dasein, as existing, is there for itself, even when the ego does not expressly direct itself to itself in the manner of its own peculiar turning around and turning back, which in phenomenology is called inner perception as contrasted with outer. The self is there for the Dasein itself without reflection and without inner perception, *before* all reflection."[16]

So, we are left with the following attitude of Heidegger toward the Cartesian claim that all intentional states are conscious. If by this claim it is meant that every intentional state involves, in addition to its directedness toward an object, a self-referential intention directed toward the person with that state, then Heidegger is willing to grant that Descartes was right. If, on the other hand, it is claimed that this self-reference involves an immediate specific awareness of one's own intentional state as one's own intentional state, then Heidegger claims that the Cartesian tradition is wrong. And, as the notion of consciousness is usually taken to involve the latter determination as well as the first, we must conclude that Heidegger agrees with Davidson in denying that all intentional states must be conscious.

The strong emphasis on the necessarily self-referential character of all intentionality serves to sharply distinguish Heidegger from Davidson, however. Davidson believes that nothing can have beliefs and desires which is incapable of having beliefs and desires about itself, as he holds that only linguistic beings have beliefs and desires, and that intentions of the third order are necessary for language. Further, for Davidson all intentional states are and must be states of some person; as mental states only come as a holistic package, and that package amounts to a teleological theory of a person, if there is a mental state, then it is necessarily the state of a person. But, following the German tradition to which he is the heir, Heidegger also holds that the intentionality of *each intentional state* requires an intentional directedness toward the being which has this state, and there is nothing in Davidson which is analogous to this condition.

II Self-reference, Consciousness, and Action

How are we to understand the element of self-reference which Heidegger thinks is essential to all overt intentional action? The paradigm case of intentions directed toward the self are to be discerned in practical intentions which are primarily directed toward entities other than the self. So when it is said that one finds oneself in what one pursues and cares for, what this implies is that while one is working on a pair of shoes, the primary intentional object is the shoes, and not oneself. But nevertheless, insofar as one intends the shoes as products to be produced, the hammer and nails as tools to be used in that productive act, and another person as the customer for whom the shoes are to be made, one is also intending oneself as *shoemaker*. But what is it to intend oneself in that way?

There is a temptation in Heidegger himself to think of the self-reference which he holds to be essential to each intentional state as if it were just like consciousness, except that our self-awareness is horizonal rather than focal, as ordinary objects of consciousness have traditionally been taken to be. Such an understanding of the self-reference of intentionality is a development of the Kantian notion that self-consciousness is to be found in the form of representation rather than as a representation. On this view, for me to be working on the shoes is for me to be consciously *focused* on the shoes, but, given the form of intentionality involved, this focus is only possible if I am aware of myself as well as an aspect of the horizon in which the shoes are focal.

Were we to interpret him in this way, Heidegger would reject Cartesian principles (1), (4), and (5): the mind is not a substance; mental states are not intentional in virtue of being representations; and the content of mental states need not be transparent to the thinker. Heidegger would remain committed, however, to two central aspects of Cartesianism. He would hold that all mental states are conscious and that a state is intentional just in case it is conscious, even though he would have reinterpreted the nature of consciousness. Such an interpretation of Heidegger, in which intentionality remains associated with a nonfocal conscious presence of self to self, cannot be maintained, however.

To see that this interpretation of Heidegger is incoherent we need to go back and look once again at what could be meant by the suggestion that the intentional activity of, for example, producing a widget, is a paradigmatic case of being-in-the-world, and that being-in-the-world is necessary for all intentionality. There are two ways to understand what is meant when one says that someone is attempting to produce a widget. The traditional interpretation is that when one produces a widget one has a representation of a widget in mind and that this representation of the widget guides the act of production. On this view, an act of production is an act of production if it is guided in the right way by an internal widget representation. This view is highly congenial to the Cartesian understanding of the relation between consciousness and intentionality. If an overt act has the intentional directedness it does only if it is related to a certain sort of representation, it is natural to think that that representation must be a conscious one, and that whatever intentionality actions have must be parasitic on the intentionality of conscious thought. So on the traditional view, there is no formal necessity that (attempting to) produce involves the agent actually engaging with entities other than herself. Even if I am in thrall to an evil demon, I can have widget representations which are related to other conscious intentional states of mine in such a way that I can count as attempting to build a widget. But on the traditional view it is formally impossible that I could attempt to produce a widget and not be conscious of that fact.

Alternatively, one can think that a certain behavior is directed in the way it is in virtue of its relations with other behavior. On this view, "Adverting to [mental intentions] to explain action is . . . a way of fitting an action into a [coherent] pattern of behavior."[17] According to this second model, it is not the case that overt behavior counts as directed toward producing a widget in virtue of its relation with some mental representation. Rather, one has internal mental intentions only insofar as they are related in the right way with overt behavior which is rationally coherent in attempting to attain a goal.

Which of these understandings of "producing something" does Heidegger have in mind when he says that being in the world is a necessary condition of intentionality, and that producing something is a paradigm case of being in? Well, it cannot be the first model. If attempting to produce a widget demands that one has an internal intention that would be intentional even if there were no things other than the thinker for her to act on, then it would be incoherent to say that attempting to produce a widget is a paradigm of being in and there are no intentional states without being in. For in that case there would be such states without being in, precisely those intentional states which are necessary for an overt act to count as an attempt to produce a widget. That is to say, the intentional character of overt acts cannot be explained by appealing to the intentionality of internal mental states if one maintains, as Heidegger does, that those internal states could not be intentional unless there were intentional action. To do so would be to privilege the intentionality of internal mental states at the same time that one is asserting the priority in regard to intentionality of action. So, for Heidegger, the intentionality of overt action cannot be grounded in the intentionality of internal mental states. But it is only for such internal states that one is tempted to link intentionality with consciousness, focal or nonfocal. So one cannot coherently interpret the Heideggerean requirement that every intention directed toward an object is also an intention directed toward the intender as an assertion that every intention involves a nonfocal self presentation.

Thus it is wrong to think that Heidegger is different from Davidson in virtue of his holding that there is a lived experience involved in every intentional state, and that determinate intentionality demands self-presence. Heidegger does indeed think that every intentional state also implicitly intends its intender. It is, however, a mistake to think that Heidegger believes that we should understand this intention of the self in terms derived from the notion of self-consciousness.

III Self Reference and Practical Explanation

Davidson thinks that a state has intentional content just in case it is an act, could play a role in the rational explanation of acts, or is rationally related to states which could play a role in such explanation. Heidegger thinks that only an entity which is in the world in such a way as to act could have intentional states. On either of these views, the ability of an entity to act is a necessary condition on that entity having any intentional states whatsoever, and what it is for a state to have any intentional content and the content which it has is determined by its relations with actions.

Actions are intentional, in the sense of being directed toward. What they are directed toward is the goal of the act. Most things in nature have no telos, they simply occur. Acts have a point, and that point is their end. For both Heidegger and Davidson one event can have a goal only if it is related in the right way to other events which have a goal. Indeed, for both of them, it is not only the case that there cannot be a single act, it is also the case that there can be no acts unless these acts are related in the right way to other intentional states which are not act events. Both Heidegger and Davidson are holists regarding action: a single act has a goal only if it is properly related to other events that have goals, and to the intentional states of an agent, and an agent has such intentional states only if it is related in the right way to acts which have goals.

But the devil is in the details. What way of being related is the "right" way of being related for events to count as acts? And what sorts of ends do these relations bestow? Davidson's answer to this question adverts to the familiar homilies of belief/desire psychology and instrumental reason. Heidegger, however, thinks that only agents who are in the world act, that the paradigmatic acts of such agents involve tool use, in which the agent intends the tool as a tool, and that all such tool use involves an intention by the agent toward herself, an intention which intends the agent as an agent of some definite sort. Indeed, for Heidegger it is proper to say that action not only involves an intention directed toward the agent's own person, it is also correct to say that the act has a dual end; it is both in order to realize some definite state of affairs within the world and, in addition, for the sake of constituting the agent as an agent of a certain sort. It is this difference in the understanding of action which lies at the center of the important difference between Heidegger and Davidson regarding intentionality. For Davidson, one acts if one has some coherent set of beliefs and desires. But for

Heidegger every act involves in addition an interpretation and constitution of oneself as an agent of some definite type. Let me expand on this difference.

For Davidson, an event is an act if it is part of a pattern of events which are coherent in the sense that they are integrated into a system in which, by and large, the agent does what she should do, given her reasons for action. Those reasons, in turn, are understood in terms of the agent's beliefs and desires. An individual act is rational, in the shallowest sense, if it is an act which the agent should perform given the belief and desire of the agent which explain that act. So it is rational for me to flip the switch if I believe that doing so will turn on the light and I want the light to be on. Conversely, the content of a given state is partially fixed by the normative role of that state in the system of the agent's acts. Roughly, for a state to be the belief that flipping the switch will turn on the light is for it to be a state such that, given that one is in that state, if one also had the desire to turn on the light, then, ceteris paribus, one should flip the switch. These relations suggest that one interpret the goal or telos of an act as the realization of a state of affairs which satisfies the desire which rationalizes the act. I believe that flipping the switch will turn on the light, and I want the light to be on, so I should flip the switch. I should flip the switch insofar as the flipping of the switch is an act which is toward the light being on. Thus the content of the desire which is ingredient in the explanation of the act is covariant with the direction or goal of the act itself. The telos or goal of my flipping the switch is that the light be on. That is, the telos of an act is just that the state of affairs which the agent desires be actual.

Understood in this way, it is clear that for Davidson the telos of activity involves a specification of some type of state of affairs which is to be made actual. If acts are events which fit into a pattern which is made coherent in part by specifying the desires which are part of their causes, then the end of the act is typically going to be that some state of affairs obtain that satisfies the desire that motivates the act. The content of the belief which is relevant to an act's explanation would then be that state of affairs, which, if it were actual, would make it rational for the agent to do as she does, given her desire.

The normativity involved in this sort of instrumental rationality ultimately derives from the ends which are specified by the desire of the agent and the means which are sufficient to realize those ends under a variety of possible circumstances. I should do that which in the actual circumstances would realize my desire. And, given the minimal conditions on rationality, I most often do that. But not always. One of the jobs of the concept of belief is to help fill in this gap. Often when I do what I should not, given my ends and the actual situation, I do what I should given my ends and my beliefs. So the content of my belief specifies the state of affairs under which I should have done what I in fact did do in order to realize my end.

From the perspective of the contrast between Davidson and Heidegger, what is striking about this account of the character of rational explanation and the goals of acts is the way in which it specifies those goals, and articulates the nature of reasons, in ways in which intentions directed toward the agent herself do not appear. The end of an act is that some state of affairs obtain; and there is no necessity that that state of affairs involve the agent. It is the case that the goal of the act covaries with the agent's desire, but what is desired may very well be that something other than the agent have some property. So Davidson does not emphasize that "The self is there for Dasein itself without reflection and without inner perception."[18] And it is this claim which distinguishes Heidegger from Davidson.

But just *how* is the self there for Dasein itself? As in Davidson, so in Heidegger, the character of intentional comportments must be understood through the character of intentional action, and the character of intentional action must be understood by way of the reasons for that action. In the place where a Heideggerean theory of action should stand, however, we find an articulation of the being of tools and the being of the world in which these tools, and we ourselves, have our being. Why is this the case?

Action which involves equipment displays a characteristic type of normativity which is different in kind from that displayed by non-equipmental action. If I want water in the desert and believe that water is at the oasis then I should walk in the direction of the oasis; if I believe the oasis is west I should walk west; and if I believe that the sun sets in the west, the sun is setting over there, and that the oasis is in the west, then I should also believe that water is over there. If I do or believe something which I should not, that I should not depends on the relation between what I believe or do and what I want. The only sense in which I should not do or believe something which is instrumental to one of my ends is that realizing that end might be incompatible with some further end of my own. There is a sense, however, in which a tool can be used incorrectly, even when it is used successfully to achieve some end of the agent. A hammer can be used successfully as a paperweight, but insofar as it is indeed a hammer, to use it in this way is to fail to use it as it should be used. It is to miss the fact that it *is* a hammer and not a paperweight; or, as Heidegger would put it, it is to fail to understand the being of the hammer. So, insofar as human action involves using tools as tools, that is, as to be used in certain characteristic ways, human action involves a kind of normativity which is foreign to the nontool using animal kingdom.

What is it for something to be a tool? Characteristically, Heidegger approaches this ontological question by way of a discussion of the related issue of what it is to intend something as a tool. And, for Heidegger, the primary manner in which we intend equipment as equipment is through using it as equipment: "The less we just stare at the hammer-Thing, and the more we seize hold of it and use it, the more primordial does our relationship to it become, and the more unveiledly is it encountered as that which it is—as equipment."[19]

But what is it to use something *as a tool*? One might think that to use, for example, a hammer as a hammer is to act out of a desire to make a nail fast and a belief that the nail could be made fast if one moves this object in just this, hammering, way. But Heidegger thinks that this is too simple. Tools are not merely things which *can* be used so as to achieve certain ends in certain circumstances. In fact, defective tools can be tools even if they are not capable of being used to achieve their characteristic ends: something is a defective x only insofar as it is to be used as an x. And objects which are capable of being so used need not be tools. Rather, tools are things which are to be used in certain ways, or should be used in certain ways. To intend something as a hammer is to intend it as an entity which *it is correct to use* in certain normatively described situations, with certain other types of tools to achieve certain normatively described types of ends.

This "to be used" character of equipment cannot be derived from the ends of the agent. Indeed, this normative character of tools is rooted in the distinction between the ends for which the tool can be used and the ends for which it is to be used.

This distinction between merely instrumental and humanly equipmental types of normativity opens up two questions: (1) How, in practice, is genuine tool use, which involves taking something as equipment by using it as a thing which it is correct to use in a certain way, different from merely using an object instrumentally to achieve some desired actual state of affairs? (2) How do intentions directed toward a single tool involve intentions directed toward that tool's normative relations with other tools, and with Dasein itself, and thereby involve intentions directed toward Dasein?

While the first question is certainly important, in the present context it is more important to remind ourselves of Heidegger's answer to the second question:

The specific *thisness* of a piece of equipment, its *individuation*, if we take the word in a completely formal sense, is not determined primarily by space and time in the sense that it appears in a determinate space- and time-position. Instead, what determines a piece of equipment as an individual is in each instance its equipmental character and equipmental contexture. What then is it that constitutes the specific equipmental character of a piece of equipment? Equipmental character is constituted by what we call *Bewandtnis, functionality*. The being of something we use, for instance a hammer or a door, is characterized by a specific way of being put to use, of functioning. This entity is "in order to hammer", "in order to make leaving, entering, and closing possible". Equipment is "in order to".[20]

But the "in order to" of a hammer, which is constitutive of its being a hammer, involves a necessary reference to other "in order tos", other normative tool types which together form a functionality whole, and I can treat this thing as a hammer, as something which it is appropriate to use in some definite way, only if I somehow intend the context of functional relations in which *anything* can count as a hammer. "The contexture of the what-for and in-order-to is a whole of functionality relations. . . . The functionality whole, narrower or broader . . . is the prius, within which specific beings, as beings of this or that character, are as they are and exhibit themselves correspondingly. . . . A specific functionality whole is *pre*-understood."[21]

So for Heidegger I act in a human fashion insofar as I use tools as tools; I use tools as tools only if I use them as having characteristic ways in which it is correct or appropriate to use them; I intend a tool as having a correct way to be used only if I also intend the functional whole in which this normative characterization occurs. But Heidegger also holds that insofar as one intends such a functionality contexture, one also intends oneself as a certain *kind* of person. "In understanding a context of relations such as we have mentioned, Dasein has assigned itself to an 'in-order-to', and it has done so in terms of a potentiality-for-Being for the sake of which it itself is."[22]

For Heidegger, when one of us uses a tool as the tool which it is, and thereby intends it to be correctly used in a certain way, we also intend ourselves as a certain type of person. When the shoemaker uses his equipment as shoemaker equipment he interprets himself *as* a shoemaker, for to be a shoemaker is to act as shoemakers are supposed to act, and shoemakers are supposed to act as they do when they use their tools as to be appropriately used in the correct situation along with other correctly used tools to achieve the appropriate ends of shoemaker activity. When I treat the shoemaker's equipment as to be used as shoemakers are supposed to use it, I acknowledge the norms which establish the being of shoemakers. Since shoemakers are nothing but agents who act as shoemakers act, for the reasons they act, every time I act as a shoemaker, that is, acknowledge the shoemaker's tool kit as to be used in the way shoemakers should use it, I also make myself *be* a shoemaker. It is not *my* ends which fix the manner in which the shoemakerly equipment is to be used, it is the ends which are definitive for being a shoemaker which do that. And when I treat those tools as having a correctness of use which is constituted by the shoemakerly ends, I identify myself as a shoemaker, for things have for me the significance which they have for those of us who are shoemakers. Thus my act, while it is correctly described as having the end of realizing some shoemakerly state of affairs, such as there being a new pair of shoes, also has the telos of making me be a shoemaker; it is for the sake of some possibility of my human being:

> The shoemaker is not the shoe; but shoe gear, belonging to the equipmental contexture of his environing world, is intelligible as the piece of equipment that it is only by way of the particular world that belongs to the existential constitution of the Dasein as being in the world. In understanding itself by way of things, the Dasein understands itself as being in the world by way of the world. The shoemaker is not the shoe but, existing, he is his world.[23]

IV Conclusion

And this is why Heidegger is not Davidson, and why he offers something unique to the tradition. What Heidegger has to offer philosophy are two important insights having to do with the normative character of intentionality. The first is the insight that the normativity of human intentionality is different in kind from merely teleological action. Human action is tool using action, a tool is an object which is a tool insofar as it is appropriate to use it in some definite way, and one can use it as a tool only if one can use it as having some appropriate use. From this insight and the further premise that human action is the necessary foundation of human intentionality it follows that all human intentionality rests on a normative foundation of appropriate action. This first insight is not exclusive to Heidegger, however. One can surely find it in both Wittgenstein and Sellars, for example.

What is unique to Heidegger is the second insight. Tool using action is action which involves accepting proprieties of action, and acceptance of such proprieties at the same time is an acceptance of a certain style of human being. So to use an object as it is appropriate to use it according to a certain style of norm is also to choose, intend, and constitute oneself as one of those who accept that style of norm. The end of my act is at once that the environment come to be in some definite way and that I be a certain definite kind of person. My acting in a professorial manner has the dual telos of realizing an external end and constituting me a professor. I write this chapter in order to publish it, but for the sake of my being a philosopher.

From this insight, together with the premise that all intentionality is rooted in relations with intentional action it follows that every intention involves a self-referential component, although this component need not be conscious. It is this appreciation of the essentially self-referential character of human intentionality which explains why it is that Heidegger isn't just Davidson in deep disguise.

IV

Responses

15

Responses

Hubert L. Dreyfus

Reading through these chapters made me extremely happy. Not just because I saw that my teaching and philosophical concerns have been successfully carried further by many thinkers in many domains, but because I found I wanted to say so much to each author. I felt that many chapters were either the next move in a dialogue already begun or the beginning of a dialogue that should have begun already. Since space is limited, most of this ongoing discussion will have to take place outside the confines of this book. Still, I cannot resist saying something to each contributor who has taken the time to think and write about the issues that concern me most.

I have not gone into equal detail in all my responses, however. As I read each chapter I mostly wanted simply to write "good" in the margin again and again. But, in anticipation of future dialogue, I have spent the most time and ink on those chapters that got under my skin by disagreeing with me, and comparably little on those chapters that delighted me by developing my arguments further. With the understanding, then, that unequal treatment does not betoken unequal gratitude, here goes.

Responses to Part I

Authenticity must be a phenomenon whose time has come. The next SPEP meeting will have a panel devoted to Heidegger's account of authenticity in *Being and Time* and the pressure has been building up

for me to complete my *Commentary*, *Being-in-the-World*, by including a full-fledged interpretation of Division II. Since I have agreed
to both these jobs, I consider it good luck that there are four chapters on authenticity is this volume (five counting Hannay's). I can
begin writing the second edition of my *Commentary* by learning from
these four contributors, all former students from whom I have gained
a great deal already, and then marking off my position from theirs.

Reply to Taylor Carman

As usual, I have learned a lot from reading Taylor's work. He accepts
the account of Heidegger's relation to Kierkegaard that Jane Rubin
and I spell out in the Appendix to my *Commentary*, but, in reading
his presentation of my view, I realize I no longer hold it. I still think
that both the person in Kierkegaard's Religiousness A and Heidegger's authentic Dasein embrace their nullity, but, I now see more
clearly that, unlike Kierkegaard's selfless receptive Christian, Dasein
has to take a stand on its nothingness and give itself an identity by
taking over a social role and the skills and responsibilities that that
role entails. Furthermore, Dasein, unlike the person in Religiousness
A, has to take up its cultural past and make a "reciprocative rejoinder" to it. In so doing, it both preserves and transforms its cultural
heritage, thereby revealing that its nullity is not that of an empty
receiver of God's grace, but that of an entity actively involved in
world-disclosing.

The question Carman forces me to face is my own: Why does Heidegger claim that resolute (i.e., authentic) Dasein must be constantly
ready to fall back into irresoluteness? I find helpful Carman's idea
that irresoluteness involves falling away from what he calls Dasein's
"finite particularity" and that the pull toward this falling, a kind of
existential gravity, is the result of the functioning of discourse. I can
understand the phenomenon behind Carman's proposal once I
correct a serious mistake I made in my commentary on Division I.
I said there that there could be no higher intelligibility than the
average intelligibility provided by the one for, as I asked in a rhetor-
ical flourish, what could be a higher intelligibly than that? However,
after a semester of being badgered by my current teaching assistants

(Forrest Hartman, Darien Shanske, and Dan Heider) I have come to see that Heidegger believes there is, indeed, a better form of intelligibility than everyday intelligibility and that this better intelligibility is constantly being undermined by the way language necessarily works. Of course, I still hold, as does Carman, that there is no other intelligibility than everyday intelligibility, so a better intelligibility cannot be some radically different way of making sense of things of the sort proposed by rationalist metaphysicians. The better form of intelligibility Heidegger has in mind is, rather, a richer and more appropriate way of coping with things and people than is available to the average person.

We can get a sense of what Heidegger thinks this richer form of intelligibility is if we turn to the truth chapter and remember Heidegger's example of an everyday true assertion, viz. someone saying, with his back turned to a crookedly hung picture, that the picture is askew. This assertion is true since it points out the picture as it, in fact, is.[1] But such an assertion glosses over, or, as Heidegger would say, levels, a richer truth that might well be revealed to an interior decorator, say, who sees how this particular way of hanging the picture in this particular room fits with the rest of the postmodern decor or to an admirer of Stella's works who sees that the work is hung exactly as it should be. What they understand by virtue of their special skills and current involvement cannot, according to Heidegger, be exhaustively captured in everyday language which is necessarily public and general, that is, meant to be used by anyone, skilled or not, as a tool for communication, that is, for passing the word along outside the current concrete situation. Not that an expert's practical wisdom can be captured in some private language either. It is just too fine grained and contextual to be grasped in average everyday discourse.

What Carman calls finite particularity is, I think, a misleading term for what shows up for an expert and only for an expert—misleading because it itself is too general. Again it helps to have in mind an example. An expert surgeon does not have names for the thousands of different way she knows how to cut, and even if she did, she could not pass on in the public language a description of each specific situation in which each way is appropriate. This implies that the

response to the concrete situation characteristic of an authentic individual, which I take to be based on having been intensely involved
in many similar situations in the past, is undermined by any attempt
to put that response into the generalities of public language.[2] There
is surely a way that two expert surgeons can use language to point
out important aspects of the situation to each other during a deli-
cate operation. Such an authentic language would presuppose a
shared background understanding and only make sense to experts
currently involved in a shared situation. It would, nonetheless, be
public in that anyone with enough talent, commitment, and training
could come to share it, but Heidegger only seems to consider a pejorative Kierkegaardian sense of public in which public means banal.
Because he lacks an account of authentic language in *Being and Time*,
Heidegger seems to hold that authentic Dasein must be reticent. But,
since acting in the world requires using our everyday public language, authentic Dasein is always in danger of losing touch with its
involved situational know-how and falling back into the indifference
and banalities of the average intelligibility of the one. This is my
version of Carman's suggestion.

But the phenomenon is more complicated. It may well be that one
needs to use the public leveled language in domains where he or she
is *not* an expert. So the interior decorator and the surgeon may well
have to say to their auto mechanic that they think their carburetor
is dirty because that is what the mechanic said the last time the car
acted the way it is acting now, without having any real understanding of what they were saying. But couldn't one at least remain reticent in the domain in which one was intensely involved and which
gave one one's identity so that, in areas that really mattered, one
would never need to fall out of reticence into banalities? If so, this
would call into question Carman's suggestion that one is always
forced, or at least pulled, into the average intelligibility of public
discourse.

But even supposing Carman has managed to give a satisfactory
answer to my question of why Dasein is pulled toward inauthenticity,
I cannot go along with his claim that authentic particularity has no
content of its own but is just a constant struggle against banality. I
agree that there is no separate other content—no independent

source of intelligibility than everyday intelligibility—just a richer content that grows out of the everyday intelligibility, but this richer content is surely more than just nonbanality. So I cannot agree with Carman that, for Heidegger, "authenticity consists in nothing over and beyond our ongoing resistance to the banalizing, leveling pressures that pull us away from any explicit recognition" of our finite particularity (25). Thus, I agree with Carman that, in its day-to-day affairs, Dasein "has no choice but to accommodate and exploit the prevailing criteria of intelligibility, which means at least to some extent trading the irreducible particularity of one's own factical situation for generally adequate, but always more or less loosely fitting means of expressing and communicating it" (21). But I do not agree with him that "resoluteness is not a stable, self-sufficient mode of existence, but a perpetual struggle against the reifying and banalizing forces inherent in discursive practice." I grant that expertise grows out of everyday intelligibility and so is not self-sufficient but I do not see why it cannot be stable. It seems to me that the surgeon has a stable grip on a positive, specific content, that is unavailable to the average person. Once one sees that what Heidegger calls a response to the Situation (*Situation* as opposed to *Lage*, which Heidegger defines as the general situation) requires the expertise (and historical awareness) that goes with having a specific identity, one can also see that Dasein is defined by this positive content, not just its struggle against banality. Of course, then one cannot explain why there has to be a constant struggle against banality in the domain important to any given Dasein, and I am still stuck with my nagging question.

Reply to Randall Havas

I find it hard to recognize my view in Randy's elegant chapter, but his critique does, nonetheless, provide me an opportunity to think through and correct some of the claims about Division II in the current version of my *Commentary*, so I would like to go over them in some detail.

I admit holding that in *Being and Time* the one (*das Man*) "explains" how meaning is possible, indeed, that the one is "the ontological source of intelligibility," or, as Heidegger puts it, that "the one itself articulates the referential context of significance."[3] I see no difference between these claims and Havas's assertion that "what something counts as depends in part on there already being a pattern of regular usage in place" (32) and I think Heidegger and I could both agree with Havas that, as long as we stick to describing the phenomenon and do not have recourse to traditional philosophical concepts such as constitution, there is nothing "philosophically problematic about the character of such 'dependence' " (347 n.7).

In *History of the Concept of Time* Heidegger, however, says that "The one . . . constitutes (sic) what we call the public,"[4] and I, to Havas's dismay, repeat this term in my claim that the one is "constitutive of worldhood and intelligibility."[5] Havas is right that if "constituting" intelligibility means more than articulating the shared practices—if, for example, it means, as it does in Husserl, that meaning is given to brute stuff by a self-sufficient subject to whom these meanings can be made completely clear—then Heidegger, as both Havas and I read him, should avoid the term and I should too. But one thing is clear, since Heidegger himself speaks of constitution, my using the term does not show that I have misunderstood Heidegger as Havas claims.

Havas's accusation that I have read Heidegger as making the one the philosophical ground of shared intelligibility in some traditional sense only sticks if I use "constitutes," "explains," and "ontological source" to mean more than "depends in part on," as if public practices were the self-grounding transparent ground of intelligibility. But I go to great pains to point out that Heidegger, like Wittgenstein, holds that public norms are not a philosophical ground but a "nonground [Un-ground]." I completely agree with Havas, Wittgenstein, and Heidegger on this important point and stress it in my *Commentary*.

Havas has a distressing way of arguing that consists in uncharitably interpreting other Heidegger interpreters as endorsing strong philosophical positions even when they use Heidegger's own words, so that he can then claim that, of course, Heidegger would never say such a thing. As far as I can understand it, the question of Dasein's self-determination is similarly a straw man. Havas accuses Bill Blattner of holding that, since Dasein must think and act in terms of the shared public meanings, Dasein must "renounce all attempts at self-determination." Since my view could be caricatured in the same way as Blattner's, I think it is important to point out that Heidegger does, indeed, reject Kant's demand for autonomy understood as pure self-determination. As Heidegger puts it, "Being-a-basis means *never* to have power over one's ownmost being from the ground up."[6] Havas himself recognizes that "A radically self-determining human being is not a human being at all" (311). But I would argue (and I think Blattner would agree) that Heidegger's denial of radical autonomy in no way means that Dasein cannot give itself a determinate content and take responsibility for what it does. As Heidegger makes abundantly clear in Division II, Dasein can take such responsibility by resolutely taking over its thrownness.

Havas and I do, however, genuinely disagree about what this taking of responsibility comes to. Although I am not clear just what Havas thinks Dasein is anxious about nor what he thinks resolute action is, I think his criticism of my account is justified. In my *Commentary* I thought of Dasein's resolute taking over of responsibility as anxiously accepting its ungroundedness and so changing the *form* or style, but not the *content*, of its life. But, as Havas points out, this supposes Dasein needs to be grounded and he rightly asks: why should we believe there is any such need? I would now try to stick more closely to what Heidegger says, which is that Dasein flees its nullity. This I take to mean that, for some reason that is not clear to me, Dasein finds it hard to live with the fact that it is essentially a discloser with no human nature and no essential content. In any case, Heidegger is clear that the radical change to authenticity (the *Augenblick*) is not merely a change in style but a new way of relating to the situation in its concreteness instead of its banal generality. Moreover, I now see I was wrong in saying authentic Dasein can achieve and needs to achieve only *formal constancy* in its life. Rather, resolute Dasein takes over a *determinate identity* that it is ready steadfastly to maintain even in adversity but also ready to give up when the identity becomes irrelevant to the current historical situation. Thus Dasein's current for the-sake-of-which or public role always gives it content, and the way it holds on to that identity can make it an authentic individual.

This being said, I do not think (pace Havas) that community and authentic individuality are, for Heidegger, "two sides of the same coin." As I read Heidegger, they could not be since there may never have been an authentic individual. There might well have been, and might someday be, only inauthentic Daseins or what Heidegger calls oneselves, whereas there have been some sort of communal practices and average intelligibility around as long as Dasein, and there would continue to be, whether or not there were any authentic individuals, that is, even if all Daseins manifested their mineness by "making the one their hero."

If Havas means that authentic individuals and the sort of *authentic* community Heidegger speaks of in Division II are correlative, then I completely agree, but he seems to think that even everyday community somehow depends on authentic individuals. His argument seems to be that otherwise Division II would not add something more primordial to the analysis of everydayness developed in Division I. The point of Division II, as I see it, is to spell out a higher form of intelligibility than the average intelligibility of Division I and to argue that an experience of this higher intelligibility reveals that Dasein is essentially a discloser. Heidegger can then draw on his own experience of authenticity to lay out the existential structure of being a discloser (whether individual or conformist does not matter) as the structure of the primordial temporality that ultimately grounds (or better un-grounds) all intelligibility. I look forward to hearing more from Randy on these issues.

Reply to John Haugeland

Every since I came to Berkeley in 1968, I have been discussing *Being and Time* with John, and our readings of *Being and Time*, though they may seem to have drifted apart as each of us tried to make Heidegger relevant to our central concerns, remained remarkably congruent. Thus, I focused my attention on Heidegger's implicit response to Cognitivism and to representationalism in general, whereas John focused on Heidegger's new understanding of the conditions of the possibility of knowledge, but we both wanted to explain what

Heidegger meant by the understanding of being and how this understanding made possible our encountering of entities as entities.

Now, both of us, after more or less ignoring Division II as something of an existentialist embarrassment, have tried to bring it into our account, and our paths seem to have finally diverged. I find that to make sense of Division II, I have to take seriously what I have hitherto ignored about Division I, viz. Heidegger's emphasis on Dasein's essence as the being whose being is an issue for it and on the inferiority of the average intelligibility constituted by the general standards of the one,[7] while John, in contrast, wants to fit even the seemingly existentialist elements in Division II, especially the discussion of death, guilt, and anxiety, into his reading of Division I as basically concerned with the possibility of getting it right about the entities we encounter.

The result of Haugeland's latest work is an amazingly coherent account of what Heidegger understood as resolute Dasein, and what he meant, or at least should have meant, by an "existential conception of science,"[8] all of which leads to the only convincing reading I have ever seen of the meaning and role of death in Heidegger's account of authenticity. My only reservation is that, by focusing on the relation between our knowledge and the objects known, Haugeland seems to accept a version of the very subject/object distinction Heidegger was trying so hard to overcome. Heidegger is not denying that getting our descriptions of entities right is something we sometimes need to do but, on my reading in my *Commentary*, Heidegger wants to shift the tradition's emphasis on getting our descriptions of objects right to Dasein's absorption in unimpeded coping with equipment. Heidegger focuses on activities like hammering, I hold, because this everyday form of encountering does not involve the correctness of assertions but, rather, shows that correctness is a derivative form of successful coping. From that pragmatist perspective getting things right, including getting hammers and nails to function properly, is in the service of more ongoing coping, whereas, for Haugeland, Dasein's goal is not just more coping, which is what animals do, but the understanding of entities as entities, and it is *for the sake of such understanding* that one checks up on one's equipment to make sure it functions properly and one checks to make sure one's assertions are correct.

I now think Haugeland is absolutely right in implicitly rejecting my pragmatist reading. But I think he rejects it for the wrong reasons. Heidegger is really quite clear that Dasein does not cope merely for the sake of more coping. Blattner is right; Heidegger is certainly no pragmatist. So I am wrong, but Haugeland seems to be wrong too. Dasein copes with equipment and pursues truth not merely for the sake of understanding entities in *their* being but ultimately for the sake of taking a stand on *its own* being. So I would now say that, although Haugeland's well worked out and convincing account of how Dasein is at once self-disclosing and disclosing of the being of entities makes clear that Heidegger is no pragmatist, it also reveals that Haugeland is no Heideggerian. He has gotten Heidegger's priorities reversed. *Dasein does not disclose itself in order to disclose the being of entities; Dasein discloses the being of entities in order to disclose itself.* This disagreement determines our divergent take on everything else.

Haugeland's focus on our relation to entities for the sake of making them intelligible to us rather than for the sake of manifesting our being through them is most apparent in his discussion of *disposedness*.[9] "Ontological sofindingness is *responsiveness* to ostensible possibilities in the current situation as something that *matters*," he tells us (56). Granted that it matters to us that our assertions point out objects as they are, I see no reason to think that, for Heidegger, mattering is paradigmatically concerned with double-checking possibilities and so confirming our truth claims, as Haugeland suggests. Such epistemological concerns matter to us only at the level of the unavailable or at the detached level of scientific theorizing. But, even if Haugeland has in mind the possibilities in the current situation for the successful use of equipment, something crucial seems to me to be left out of the account. Surely ontological moods, which Haugeland acknowledges are Heidegger's paradigm cases of disposedness, do not reveal what is and is not possible for *entities*; ontological moods like joy, boredom, despair, or anxiety reveal the global attunement or coloring of our whole world and so reveal "how things are going with us." By making us sensitive to what matters; they make us sensitive to our way of being.

What I find most challenging is the way Haugeland's powerful Kuhnian interpretation of what Heidegger means by death, guilt, and resoluteness parallels and yet opposes the account I would like to give of these same existential structures. First, the parallels. I find Haugeland's account of resolute being-towards-death as "living in a way that explicitly has everything at stake," very illuminating (73). It follows, as Haugeland once said to me, that resolute Dasein sticks with its identity without getting stuck with it, a slogan I use whenever I teach Division II. I have even recently argued that resolute Dasein has to be sensitive to anomalies in its life and, moreover, be ready for a possible crisis in which these anomalies reveal that its identity (its ultimate for-the-sake-of) is no longer relevant. I agree with Haugeland that in the face of such a crisis resolute Dasein must lucidly accept the collapse of its world,[10] its "way of life," so as to be open to disclosing a new world in which these anomalies are central and make sense. But, I would add, all for the sake of understanding its own being as a discloser.

Haugeland stunningly points out the striking parallel between the sense of scientific responsibility that can lead to a Kuhnian crisis and the way a resolute Dasein must be both steadfast in its commitments to its truth-claims and to the standards that are the basis of intelligibility, and yet be ready to take specific truth claims and even the whole projection of intelligibility back. Seeing this parallel allows Haugeland to give the most persuasive and illuminating account of what Heidegger must have meant by "an existential conception of science" that has yet been proposed. I will teach Heidegger's conception of science this way from now on, although I think Heidegger is more of a realist about the entities revealed by science than Haugeland takes him to be.[11]

But there is also a sharp opposition between our views as to what the parallel between scientific responsibility and resoluteness entails. This opposition comes out in Haugeland's attempt to model the responsibility of everyday Dasein on the Kuhnian model of normal science. I agree with Haugeland that both inauthentic Dasein in its everydayness and the responsible normal scientist accept the public standards of correct behavior, and feel obliged to live up to them. One type of fallenness surely consists in the failure to accept this responsibility. But Heidegger is clear that another way of falling is to embrace this responsibility and urgently obey the public rules. He glosses "Dasein's lostness in the one" as following "the tasks, rules, and standards, the urgency and extent, of concernful and solicitous being-in-the-world."[12] To defend his parallel with Kuhnian normal science, Haugeland consistently holds that what is inauthentic in this conformist way of life is not the following of the accepted general standards of rightness, but, rather, holding onto them even when they no longer work. So for Haugeland, resoluteness would consist in being sensitive to the anomalies that can develop in a life which obeys the public standards, and being ready to give up everything if the anomalies become too troubling. That is an important half of the story with which I fully agree, and the parallel with Kuhn brings it out beautifully. But clearly, for Heidegger, Dasein is lost in the one whenever it follows the public standards, whether or not it is resolutely ready to give them up. For Heidegger, when one is resolute one does not respond in the standard way at all. In Heidegger's terms, inauthentic Dasein responds to the general situation (*Lage*) whereas authentic Dasein responds to the concrete Situation (*Situation*).[13] As Heidegger puts it: "For the one . . . the Situation is essentially something that has been closed off,"[14] while resolute Dasein is in touch with the concrete Situation and so does not respond in the standard way the one does.

Since Haugeland and I both follow Heidegger in wanting to stick to the phenomenon, let's take Haugeland's firsthand description of being a teacher. According to Haugeland, a teacher can "*undertake . . . to do* what [he is] supposed to, that is, never to *act* in a way that is ruled out" (60). Haugeland seems unequivocally to approve of such law-abiding behavior as showing responsibility and, of course, Haugeland is right—a responsible teacher has to meet his classes on time, hand in his grades and so forth. But I think Heidegger would consider anyone for whom adherence to the rules was definitive of what it was to be a teacher, not a paradigm of professional responsibility but a victim of conformism. This may be why Heidegger says that resolute Dasein must be ready to fall back into irresoluteness.

To return to the phenomenon, in teaching I find that I often break the taken-for-granted rules, for example by teaching 200 students as if they were a discussion section, or by taping all my lectures and putting them on my course's web site so that students do not have to come to my lectures unless they really want to participate, or by trying to begin each lecture with a few minutes of repenting my mistakes in the previous one, if possible, naming the students who have convinced me that my previous claims were mistakes. Or, to take a more flagrant flouting of the rules, I once had a teaching assistant who scheduled his discussion sections late in the day and went on, usually for two or three hours, until each student felt that his or her questions had been fully answered. I would like to think that such nonconformity is a higher kind of responsibility than slavishly following the rules. It seems to me that in what is most important in life, for example in teaching or in love, the authentic person, rather than doing his or her "ordinary duties," uses the general rules as a background against which to innovate.

I agree with Haugeland that in science the standards and rules are much more precise and binding than those in everyday life and any deviation is, as Haugeland says, "irresponsible." Precisely because, as Haugeland, following Kuhn, emphasizes, "the tendency toward normality is *essential to science*," the *normal scientist* must scrupulously obey the rules of evidence and persistently try to normalize anomalies. What is important for my disagreement is that the *resolute scientist* too, precisely because he is ready to risk everything if he is wrong, is committed to "assiduous," "careful and persistent," "double checking" to make sure that he has followed all the rules and that his claims are therefore justified according to the accepted standards of evidence. Thus it is precisely the scientist's job always to respond to what Heidegger calls the general situation. Such scrupulous obedience to the accepted standards in a scientist or engineer would not be conformism but professionalism.

For Kuhn and Haugeland, then, science as a way of life allows no middle ground; the resolute scientist must either follow the normal standards as scrupulously as possible or face a crisis in which he has to "take everything back" and start again from scratch. There is no place in the special practices that define science for a resolute response to the concrete Situation. Theory, as Heidegger says, deals with the deworlded world, that is, with the universe, and in the universe there are no concrete Situations. Of course, we need to distinguish the laws and standards articulated within a scientific theory and its methodology from the techniques and rules of thumb informing the practices of the scientists themselves. But I do not think that distinction saves Haugeland's view since he holds that the scientist's practical skills are always exercised in the service of the science's rules and standards which themselves exist for the sake of articulating the laws internal to the theories. For Heidegger, on the contrary, responding to the concrete Situation is precisely what distinguishes authentic action. It is not just that I can make exceptions and flout custom in my teaching practices; a scientist can be unconventional and innovative in her problem-solving activity, too. It is rather that what I am trying to do when I teach is not teach *correctly* but rather teach *well* by responding to whatever the specific Situation demands.

There is, of course, even in resolute action something like getting it right. Heidegger's resolute individual, like Aristotle's *phronimos*, deviates from public standards to do the appropriate thing at the appropriate time in the appropriate way and, in the world of everyday involvement, such a resolute response is recognized, at least by other *phronimoi*, as the right thing to do in that concrete Situation, even though there are no rules that dictate that it was the *correct* thing to do in that *type* of situation. But the important point is that the resolute individual is not trying to get it right about a domain of rule-governed entities that exist independently of his activity or even to somehow express the inner truth of his own nature. When I am resolute I am called to disclose, through what I am doing, what it is to be me, and ultimately that I have no essential content because I am essentially a discloser. That is why responding to the concrete Situation manifests Dasein's being while a cautious and routine adherence to the general standards and rules of one's society or of normal science, no matter how ontologically risky, covers it up. Where my own being is concerned, there is literally nothing specific to get it right about.

Haugeland's Kuhnian reconstruction of *Being and Time* thus ends up illuminating Heidegger's book in a powerful and persuasive way by focusing on the understanding of being as that in terms of which we encounter entities as entities, and on authenticity as readiness for new understandings of being, but, in so doing, Haugeland's account leaves in the dark the dangers of conformism and Dasein's essence as the being whose way of being is to take a stand on its own being. As I see it, our two readings are complementary. I have learned a lot in writing this response, and it makes me happy to think that John and I still have a lot to learn from each other.

Reply to Charles Guignon

Charles Guignon, writing on the relation between authenticity and philosophizing and how in doing philosophy one is always on the way and never arrives at an answer, defends what he calls early Dreyfus against the later Dreyfus of my *Commentary*. He will be happy to learn that I have taken his objections and methodological suggestions to heart and in the second edition of my *Commentary* will leave behind much of what we could now call middle Dreyfus. The disagreement that Charlie's defense of early Dreyfus brings out is thus between early Dreyfus and the reading of Division II that I am presently working on.

I agree with Charlie that my Wittgensteinian reading of Division I of *Being and Time* neglected something important—viz. that in Division II, Heidegger wants to get beneath not only the traditional priority of theory that begins with Plato but also the acceptance of the routine or vulgar common sense championed by his favorite philosopher, Aristotle. As I said in my response to Taylor Carman, I now see that Heidegger makes a convincing case in Division II that average everyday intelligibility levels the particularity and richness revealed by what Guignon aptly calls "intense committed involvement" in the concrete Situation. I now think that, according to Division II, public understanding is always banalized, and that, when I become resolutely involved in a situation so as to give new meaning to my own existence, I thereby reveal an unrealized richness in the situation itself. I either renew the cultural meanings already latent in the situation or transform it so as to disclose a new local world.[15] Incidentally, it's important to note that, although Heidegger may have begun by thinking of such moments of commitment in terms of the *Augenblick* of total transformation in Christian scripture, by the time he has existentialized this phenomenon in *Being and Time*, Heidegger holds that any case of involvement in a situation so intense as to bring out its concrete richness is an *Augenblick*.

Guignon fills out Heidegger's account of the relation of theory and intense involvement by drawing on and elaborating the down-to-earth descriptions from Heidegger's 1919 lectures recounting the way theory "explodes" the unity of meaning that makes up a situation. Guignon's way of stating Heidegger's general critique of theory gives me an opportunity to take back an oversight, already in early Dreyfus, that Guignon no longer seems to fully accept but which he does not correct. According to Guignon, Heidegger learns from Kierkegaard (and no doubt Nietzsche) that, from a detached theoretical point of view, "If there were no care about things" — "that lets things show up as *significant* in determinate ways" — "experience . . . would become impossible" (83).

But we diverge after that. Guignon still seems to follow my early mapping of Heidegger's account of care onto what my favorite teacher, C. I. Lewis, called "concern." But I have since come to see that such a pragmatist approach levels the difference between the practical concerns that give us a differentiated world and the care that is definitive of a being that has to take a stand on its own being. Only Dasein's ultimate for-the-sake-of-itself gives it a world in which what shows up, not only matters for everyday coping, but can be worthy or unworthy, to use Charles Taylor's terms. Animals can presumably distinguish "the central from the peripheral" experiences because they have Lewis's kind of concern but they do not have Heideggerian care. This important difference not only distinguishes Heidegger from the pragmatists; it also distinguishes him from Merleau-Ponty who is interested in the sort of *être au monde* that we share with all organisms that move, perceive, and cope with things. I now want to stress, and hope Guignon would agree given what he says about "intense commitments," that only such commitments can give a life "content and meaning," that is, in Heidegger's terms, only such commitments in which the meaning of one's being is at stake, can open a world in which things are not only salient but, more importantly, have significance.

Responses to Part II

Reply to Alastair Hannay

I appreciate Alastair's focusing his knowledgeable attention on my interpretation of Kierkegaard's account of what was wrong with the Danish society of his time, especially since Alastair's discussion of what Kierkegaard means by levelling forces me to take back some of what I have said about authenticity and to get clear about an ambiguity in my understanding of nihilism.

To begin with, Hannay, like Haugeland and Havas, objects to my attempt, in the Appendix to *Being-in-the-World*, to make authenticity just a changed relation to the levelled world of *das Man*. Hannay helpfully points out that, for Kierkegaard, levelling is a condition that must be *overcome*, not just accepted in the right way, before one can go on to live a meaningful life. I now think that Heidegger has a similar view.

Hannay also objects to my claim that nihilism, understood as the levelling of qualitative distinctions, was the concern of Kierkegaard and his age. Hannay claims instead "that levelling in Kierkegaard's account is first and foremost a process at which people more or less consciously connive in order to avoid exactly any sense of there being a difficulty of the kind Dreyfus describes" (106). Hannay's objection helps me see that, according to Kierkegaard, both processes were going on. As Heidegger, drawing on Kierkegaard, would later put it, the public undermines meaningful distinctions and then helps people forget that they have forgotten them.

But, in spite of my agreement with many of his suggestions, I do have a different sense of the relevance of Kierkegaard than Hannay has. I would want to say that, for Kierkegaard, the most serious enemy was not the levelling of values and social roles, nor the covering up of this levelling, but rather the lack of enthusiasm or commitment brought about by what Kierkegaard calls reflection.[16] At one point Hannay seems to agree with my understanding of Kierkegaard's assessment of the danger in his age as lack of commitment but he then suggests that, at Kierkegaard's time, the danger was people's complacency—that the danger of indifference was still on the horizon and so was "not one that Kierkegaard saw as characteristic of his age" (107).

Much as I respect Hannay's knowledge of what was going on in Kierkegaard's time, it seems to me Kierkegaard was most concerned not with the complacency but with the detached attitude of his contemporaries. They acted as if they were spectators of life rather than throwing themselves into existence. Kierkegaard held that the reflection going on in the West since the Enlightenment was consummating the levelling of all worldly qualitative distinctions, and that Christianity's message to the modern world was that, if understood in the right way, this loss of worldly distinctions was really an advantage since it made clear that the essential way to have qualitative distinctions in one's life was by making an unconditional commitment to some specific cause or person. He called such a commitment an infinite passion for something finite.

The press, which we would now call the public sphere with its anonymity, critical detachment, and abstraction from local concerns, Kierkegaard held, was eliminating passionate involvement by substituting a safe commentator's perspective and so making concrete commitment more and more difficult. Thus Kierkegaard wrote in his *Journals* that "Actually it is the Press, more specifically the daily newspaper . . . which make[s] Christianity impossible."[17] Whether one emphasizes the complacency or the flight from involvement and risk, one thing is sure: Kierkegaard claimed that, especially in his day, there was a need for, and a resistance to, passionate commitments. To counter the lack of enthusiasm of the present age he attempts to attune his contemporaries to a call in existence—a call to make a risky leap—that has been covered up but must be heeded:

There is no more action or decision in our day than there is perilous delight in swimming in shallow waters. But just as a grown-up, struggling delightedly in the waves, calls to those younger than himself: 'Come on, jump in quickly'—the decision in existence . . . calls out. . . . Come on, leap cheerfully, even if it means a lighthearted leap, so long as it is decisive.[18]

Finally, Hannay and I differ, as we have for years, over what Kierkegaard thinks would be the outcome of such a leap. We agree that one would first land in what Kierkegaard calls the aesthetic sphere where pleasure and flexibility are the only qualitative distinctions and we also agree that the aesthetic way of life would not give the self any meaning. Hannay then claims that, in the end, one arrives at an ethical view of life which sustains "the belief that the world does indeed have a meaning" (122). Jane Rubin and I read Kierkegaard as holding that the qualitative distinctions once provided by an ethical life are no longer possible because the shared social distinctions that once gave public life meaning and orientation are being irrevocably eroded by reflection. So only religion is left as a way out. We agree with Hannay that *Sickness unto Death* is the place to look for Kierkegaard's account of the appropriate religious response. Hannay thinks that Jane and I misread Kierkegaard as proposing that one should define one's own world all by oneself. But we agree with Hannay that Kierkegaard would reject such an idea. He had already invented and written off Sartrean existentialism as an extreme form of despair. But the alternatives are not, either accepting the distinctions available in the public world, or inventing a private one. We take seriously Kierkegaard's claim that "in relating to itself," the self must "relate itself to something else."[19] We take this to mean that each person must make an unconditional commitment which, like love or devotion to a personal cause, will give that individual a world with its own meaningful distinctions. I realize that our ongoing disagreement with Alastair on this point underlies all the above issues, but it is too central a question for us to hope to settle here.

Reply to Michael Zimmerman

Michael Zimmerman offers a detailed analysis of Charles Spinosa's and my paper in which we attempt to show how Heidegger successfully answers the crucial question of our time: how can one have a positive relation to technology and still live a life that manifests what is essential to human being?[20] I'm grateful to Michael for having read the paper so carefully and for asking the question that really matters: does late Heidegger's response to nihilism in the name of world and thing save enough of early Heidegger's resolutely authentic strong identities to save us from becoming postmodern technological resources?

The technological understanding of ourselves as flexible resources, as manifest, for example, in the growing amount of time we spend on the World Wide Web, has already begun to undermine all our identities.[21] We suggest in our paper that one can only resist this postmodern way of life in the name of what Heidegger calls the saving power of the humble things. More specifically, we propose that we can cultivate those skills and sensitivities that enable us to be attuned to this technological world when that is appropriate, without losing our capacity to disclose other worlds too. Being able to open and dwell in a number of worlds, we argue, is as much integrity as a human being needs in order to resist becoming a flexible resource.

Zimmerman criticizes our proposal in the name of a modified Hegelian view he finds in Ken Wilber. Wilber claims that we must give up the modern strong identity as an end but we must still pass through it as a stage on the way to a higher Buddhist-like egolessness with compassion for all creatures. Zimmerman therefore rejects our Heideggerian proposal on the grounds that, if we gave up the stage of self-consistency, constancy, and sincerity, we would have nothing left to protect us from becoming postmodern morphers who take on and drop identities at will.

Zimmerman contends that going through a stage where one has a strong identity is essential to the development of authenticity, and so such a stage is to be found in any sufficiently developed culture. In some sense, then, each human being senses that he or she is called to become an "ego-subject, an individual, a rational agent, a competent adult" (140). Therefore, one must agree with Kierkegaard that human beings must learn to will one thing.[22]

But ego-subjects, individuals, rational agents, and competent adults are all modern notions. It amounts to a return to metaphysics to universalize and read back into our own cultural history our current need for sincerity, continuity, consistency, and integrity as a necessary requirement for a full human life. According to later Heidegger, integrity, constancy, and so forth, show up for us moderns as the best way to be on the basis of the Enlightenment understanding of subjectivity introduced by Descartes. Indeed, if Heidegger is right, it was precisely the Enlightenment virtues of integrity and autonomy that have led to the voluntaristic and totalizing will to power that in turn serves as the basis for the goalless technological "will to will" we are now moving into. Moreover, later Heidegger does not believe we can simply adopt a foreign way of life such as a variant of Buddhism to save our culture from the specifically Western problem of nihilism.[23] Given our culture's need for specific concerns that have authority for us, equal compassion for all beings can only be experienced as a levelling of all meaningful differences and so precisely as nihilism. Likewise, a self that is pure openness and nothing more is no longer a self that discloses and preserves worlds. Indeed, it is no self at all as Buddhists are happy to acknowledge.

Because a return to metaphysics ultimately returns us to our present predicament, Charles and I follow later Heidegger in rejecting both all total understandings of being (or nonbeing) and all universal developmental accounts of the necessary stages human beings must pass through to arrive at a fully human life. We defend instead a genuinely pluralistic view that there are many ways to manifest our human essence as world disclosers. For example, as later Heidegger points out, the Homeric Greeks encountered a plurality of gods who drew people into various worlds in each of which a particular god shone as a paradigm.[24] This was not willful morphing but receptivity to a plurality of authorities. Thus the Homeric Greeks were sensitive to and able to get in tune with various worlds such as Aphrodite's erotic world, Hera's domestic world, or Ares's world of warlike ferociousness, each with its own style.

Each person did not have one constant identity nor even a constant style but rather a family resemblance in the ways he or she acted when under the influence of each of the various gods. There is no reason to think, and every reason to doubt, that the Homeric Greeks (or people in Bali, Japan, or any other polytheistic culture) must pass though a stage of ego-centered integrity in order to deal with plurality and difference. Indeed, Heidegger held in "The Age of the World Picture" that the pre-Socratic Greeks were able to understand themselves as finite mortal opennesses without first being ego-subjects with private experiences.[25] Perhaps one of the mistakes later

Heidegger saw in *Being and Time* is that it describes as universal a kind of authenticity that depends on the anxious breakdown of bourgeois subjectivity.

In the world of the Homeric Greeks, pluralism was the highest good. Odysseus was admired as a cross-world voyager, and Zeus, his protector, was known primarily as the god of strangers and guests. A life like that of Odysseus would not resemble a novel but a series of interrelated short stories. (The attempt to read Odysseus as motivated constantly by a desire to get back to Penelope is a later imposition that does not fit the text.) Likewise, Helen understood herself both as the loving wife of Menelaus and as the paramour of Paris. And despite Zimmerman's modern doubts, she "function[ed] very well socially" (143) in each world—with Menelaus, as a gracious and resourceful hostess, who knew on every occasion just which drugs to drop into people's drinks, and with Paris, as a seductive and resourceful mistress who lured her lover to bed to help him forget he had just fled from the battlefield. She threw herself fully into each world without denigrating one or the other or ranking them and yet without "regressing to a pre-egoic state."[26] It is not that she was what Zimmerman calls "aperspectival" where this is said to mean "knowingly adopt[ing] several different perspectives" but "no longer strongly identify[ing] with [any] perspective" (358 n.27). That transpersonal way of life sounds exactly like the nihilism of postmodern Rortian ironic pragmatism. Helen, on the contrary, was fully identified with each world while she was in it.[27] Thus the Greek world and self were never coherent, as Zimmerman claims they must have been. In fact, Greece was at first polytheistic and then later became tragic when the various worlds collided as the culture tried in vain to make them coherent. In the pretragic world there was genuine pluralism—not nihilistic levelling but an acceptance of difference and of a nonmetaphysical form of authority.

In response to the return to polytheism envisioned in the salvation given us by things, Zimmerman might argue that having been through monotheism and the Enlightenment, we cannot return to polytheism. In making this argument he would even be following Heidegger's sense that any solution to our cultural problems must be drawn from our cultural history. It might seem that, if we cannot be saved by Buddhism (or any foreign understanding of being), then, for the same reason, we cannot be saved by polytheism either. But there is an important difference between Zimmerman's and our proposals. Zimmerman proposes adopting the ontology of another culture, as a stage beyond our own that also preserves the truth of our self-understanding.[28] Heidegger's proposes that we take up and strengthen both the ways of relating to things that exist in every culture and the unique form of pluralism still left in our language and marginal practices.[29] In particular, Heidegger explores the cross-cultural response to things thinging, which Borgmann spells out in his persuasive account of the focal power of celebratory events such as the family meal. And Heidegger also explores the remaining language and practices left over from the polytheistic Homeric Greeks. These practices enable us to understand why, for example, Marilyn Monroe could become an irresistible example of the feminine erotic and have the power to draw men and women into her world, and why, when she did, we called her a goddess. She was a shinning star who enabled us to see things in her light.

Since pluralistic, nonfoundational practices and language are still around in our culture, it makes sense to Heidegger and to us to try, in our response to postmodernity, to make a historical appropriation of these practices. By living in multiple worlds we can come to realize that no world is universal, and this draws us out of dispersion in technology. It is, therefore, as very late Heidegger says, in the name of thing and world—rather than in Hegel or Buddhism or even some new totalizing understanding of being—that we in the West can resist the nihilism of our totalizing technological practices. Moreover, we can resist while appreciating technological devices as offering one of several historical ways things can draw us to exercise our skills as disclosers and preservers of worlds.

Reply to Michel Haar

Michel continues a discussion of Heidegger that we started as students at the École Normale Supèrieure in 1959. Already then, and even more today, I'm awed by Michel's command of Heidegger's writings. No matter how fast the Hediegger corpus continues to grow—and now that he is dead Heidegger publishes more big books each year than he published in his entire lifetime—Michel reads them all and extracts important citations that no one else seems to have noticed.

My only reservation concerning Haar's illuminating chapter is that he does not distinguish clearly between Heidegger's rather banal critique of objectifying technology from the thirties and forties and his more prescient critique in the 1950s of a coming "postmodern" form of technology. Haar first lays out Heidegger's early critique from "Overcoming Metaphysics" written between 1936 and 1946 where Heidegger sees "nature objectified . . . politics directed" and describes the "systematic organization of all the domains of being" as "planned" and "controlled." But it seems to me that reading Nietzsche and understanding the will to power as having as its unthought the circularity of the will-to-will, frees Heidegger from this goal-directed view of technology and paves the way for "The Question Concerning Technology." There, as Haar notes, Heidegger speaks of "energy [as] unflaggingly produced, accumulated, distributed, transformed and consumed." But Haar's emphasis on consumption still flattens out the circle Heidegger had discovered. The important thing for Heidegger about energy—electricity in the technology essay—is that it is "switched about ever anew."[30] Goal-directed planning and consumption has been replaced by regulated flexibility. Of course, electricity is not an ideal example, since the electricity ends up turning a motor or lighting a room or heating a house. Heidegger already had a hunch, however, in his critique of what was then called cybernetics, that the perfect way beings were revealed by technology was as information—if talk of beings even makes sense here. Information is, indeed, "switched about ever anew" and its "consummation" produces more information, about the consumers, for example. Heidegger would have been delighted, I'm sure, to replace his account of the power station on the Rhine with an account of the self-regulating expansion of the Internet. The Internet has no goal, no one regulates it, and it does not satisfy pre-existing desires but rather creates ever new ones. Human beings truly become resources (*Bestand*) when they are caught up in this flexible, ever expanding net.

In his discussion of Heidegger's difficult idea of a new beginning of the history of the West, Haar raises another important question that, again, can only be clarified and responded to by looking at the phenomenon—something Heidegger often does, while Haar, like most French Heideggerians, seems content to contemplate the texts. If one actually describes what happens when a thing things and how the ahistorical worlding of a thing can take place even in the "unworld" of contemporary technology, one sees how the metaphysical history of being that culminates in our technological understanding of being can exist side by side with a new beginning in the name, as Heidegger later says, of "world and thing." Albert Borgmann has done a pioneering job of laying out the phenomenon of what he calls "focal practices" in his *Technology and the Character of Contemporary Life* [31] and Charles Spinosa and I have tried to work out the relation of focal practices to technology in our paper "Highway Bridges and Feasts: Heidegger and Borgmann on How to Affirm Technology."[32]

Reply to Béatrice Han

Béatrice Han's chapter has opened up for me a whole new way of thinking about Nietzsche and truth. The idea that for Nietzsche a master of truth speaks the truth by virtue of incarnating it in his life also seems to be applicable, with some modification, to Foucault's concern with self-stylization and his way of living his own philosophy. Not that Foucault wanted to attract disciples, but the master of truth need not want followers. His way of life simply attracts them. I hope to explore these ideas next fall when Béatrice and I will teach a Foucault seminar along with Paul Rabinow and Judith Butler.

Reply to Julian Young

Julian Young's beautiful meditation on Heidegger's understanding of dwelling and the poetic made me appreciate how far middle and later Heidegger are from the world of rootless Dasein standing out into the nothing described in *Being and Time*. It also reminded me of our conversations in Auckland which consisted in Julian's drawing my attention to phenomena important to Heidegger that I had over-looked, and I insisting that, once we had these phenomena in view, we needed to make further distinctions. Here, it is Julian's elucidat-ing of the gods that has been most challenging to me.

I think we need to distinguish more clearly the god of "The Origin of the Work of Art" and, in general, of the middle Heidegger, from the gods (plural) of the Heidegger of things thinging. We know that for Heidegger the work of art is a cultural paradigm and that the Greek temple is a paradigm paradigm. (Jesus, whom Kierkegaard calls "the paradigm," would have be an even better exemplar.) It is the temple-god that shines so that everything shows up in its light, and that has what Young aptly calls "charismatic ethical authority." It is this god that articulates or rearticulates the culture's understand-ing of being by embodying the cultural heritage. This god is pre-sumably now the unknown God of which the divinities bring traces and messages, and which Heidegger, when he is in his more theistic frame of mind, thinks must return if we are to be saved.

All this, it seems to me, is a long way from the gods of Homer's polytheism and the gods of the thing thinging. When things shine, a god (one of many) attunes mortals to the current situation by means of his or her local authority, whether it be Aphrodite attun-ing everyone at a party to the erotic, or the god of a place attuning passersby to the peculiar feel of that locale. Such gods have little to do with an understanding of being, so it is not surprising that being is hardly ever mentioned in "The Thing" and in "Building, Dwelling, Thinking." The job of these gods is getting mortals in tune with their current world. It is this function that the very late Heidegger has in mind when, in his seminar on the lecture "Time and Being," he remarks that "from the perspective of appropriation [the ten-dency in the practices to bring things out in their ownmost] it becomes necessary to free thinking from the ontological differ-ence."[33] And continues, "From the perspective of appropriation, [letting-presence] shows itself as the relation of world and thing, a relation which could in a way be understood as the relation of being and beings. But then its peculiar quality would be lost."[34] Poetry and dwelling, so helpfully evoked by Julian, belong to this very late stage of Heidegger's thinking.

Reply to Jeff Malpas

I am deeply indebted to Jeff not only for his chapter but also for this whole Festschrift. The fact that Jeff was never a student or a colleague of mine, but is nonetheless intellectually near, even while he is geographically far away, makes his dedication to producing this book all the more moving. The very existence of this collection, conceived in Berkeley and nurtured in Germany, and this paper, begun in France and completed in Tasmania, shows that technology has overcome space and time in a way that no one could regret, and yet Heidegger claims that some important kind of nearness and dwelling is being threatened by technology. It is important to figure out just what is being lost and Malpas rises to the occasion.

I think Heidegger would like Malpas's chapter because it leaves the reader not with answers but some very hard questions. If place and dwelling are necessary for disclosing, as Malpas claims, then they must be preserved even in technology since technology is a mode of disclosing. In that case, as Jeff suggests, what concerns Heidegger is not that place and dwelling are disappearing but that we no longer experience them and so we no longer understand ourselves as disclosers. But why should that matter? What difference does it make in the quality of our lives? Or does the loss of a sense of dwelling and place mean that disclosing itself changes so that, instead of continuing to be the sort of disclosers we became in pre-Socratic Greece, we are in danger of actually becoming resources, and instead of disclosing a world we are in danger of disclosing what Heidegger sometimes calls an unworld? If so, it looks like an account of place and dwelling must not only give us an account of what we no longer *experience* but of something that is ceasing to *be*. But what, then, is the phenomenon being lost, and why should it matter to us that technology as mode of disclosing is disclosing an unworld in which dwelling has no place? We need an account not merely of what we postmoderns overlook, but what we have lost and why we should care.

Standing on Malpas's shoulders, I will try to suggest some phenomena that might help answer these questions. One line to take would be that technology, while surely a mode of disclosing, is not a mode of *gathering* but of *dispersion*. This is Albert Borgmann's important contribution to understanding Heidegger. Technology is wiping out what Borgmann calls focal practices so that we lack any center to our lives. Given Borgmann's approach, nearness and place can be redefined, and technology resisted, by bringing together in a focal activity, skills, mattering, a sense of mortality, and a sense of gratitude—Heidegger's fourfold—which does not require geographical proximity nor any "bounded place." Borgmann's version of what was once "oriented, located, embodied engagement" is thus very abstract. As I understand Borgmann's account of how a thing gives nearness, while Jeff and I have been working on this volume, nearness has not been obliterated. Rather, our collaboration involves mattering, skills, mortality, and gratitude, and gives our lives focus for a while, even though we are at opposite ends of the earth. If dwelling means this kind of gathering, it seems clear that technology's distance-diminishing gadgets do not make dwelling impossible but can even augment it.[35]

Malpas's approach is quite different from Borgmann's. He sees the loss of gathering or focal practices as a special case of a more general loss, the loss of being open to several different modes of revealing. Technology reveals things as resources and thus blocks access to them as creatures, objects, as things thinging and so forth. We cope, but we don't dwell; things function but they are not revealed *as* things. This raises the important question: why does technology block other modes of revealing in a way that seeing things as creatures, or objects does not block other ways or encountering them? Jeff offers the plausible answer that this special kind of loss has to do with the way technology eliminates embodiment and thus the complex interrelatedness of ourselves, things, and their location.[36] We thus lose a sense of the concreteness of things and of ourselves as capable of disclosing new aspects of things and new worlds. Heidegger would add that when we thus cease to be innovators, our world becomes an unworld in which freedom is lost and we are caught up in the eternal return of the same.

I thank Jeff doubly, both for this collection and for his chapter, which has given me a lot to think about. What better gifts could there be?

Responses to Part III

Reply to William Blattner

I've learned a lot from everything Bill has written, even his under-graduate papers. The same is true of this thorough chapter arguing that Heidegger cannot be considered a pragmatist. I do not always agree with Blattner (we differ on our understanding of anxiety, death, and whether Heidegger is a metaphysical realist or a tempo-ral idealist) but, this chapter has convinced me that, although Hei-degger is similar to Dewey in important respects, he is certainly not a pragmatist. I have not always been clear on this point but, thanks to Bill, I will be from now on.

Reply to Dagfinn Føllesdal

In the late 1950s I wrote my dissertation under Dagfinn Føllesdal, working out his interpretation of Husserl's *noema* and transcenden-tal reduction and using these ideas to support Merleau-Ponty's claim that Husserl's transcendental phenomenology led Husserl directly to the existential phenomenology later worked out by Heidegger and himself.[37] As I studied and taught *Being and Time*, however, I began to think that my thesis was all wrong (which is why I have resisted all attempts to publish it). I began to see Heidegger's and Merleau-Ponty's existential phenomenology as radically opposed to Husserl's transcendental phenomenology, and I have been having a friendly and productive disagreement with Dagfinn on the subject ever since.

In the latest round of this debate, Føllesdal's chapter challenges my reading of Heidegger's relation to Husserl on three points. He claims: (1) that Heidegger respected Husserl as philosopher; (2) that Heidegger gets many of his views from Husserl (especially from *Ideas II*), although he fails to acknowledge the extent of his debt; and (3) that *Being and Time* is not a subversive attack on Husserl's account of intentionality as I contend, and that it is I, not Heidegger, who mis-understands Husserl as the last Cartesian. These are big issues, and I can only touch on them briefly here.

1. There is one thing I am sure of: Heidegger did not respect Husserl as a philosopher. In spite of his dedication of *Being and Time* to Husserl, whose chair he hoped to inherit, Heidegger wrote in a letter to Karl Löwith in 1923.

In the last seminar class I publicly burned and destroyed the *Ideas* to such an extent that I dare say that the essential foundations for the whole [of my work] are now clearly worked out. . . . Husserl was never a philosopher, not even for a second in his life. He becomes ever more ridiculous.[38]

This devastating assessment exculpates Heidegger from the sin of "not giving enough credit to Husserl" only to show him "with the even greater moral flaw" of being a disgusting hypocrite, but no one ever said Heidegger was an admirable human being.

2. Føllesdal in an earlier exchange showed convincingly that Husserl was interested in the constitutive role of practical activity. I responded by showing that this did not change his commitment to the transcendental reduction since one could, like John Searle, separate mental intention from bodily movement and thereby preserve a subject/object split.[39] I then claimed that Heidegger's contribution was to show that in transparent coping there was no ego or subject coping with an object, but that the agent was absorbed into the situation, or, in more fancy Heideggerian terminology, "Dasein *is* its world existingly."[40]

Now, Føllesdal wants to argue that Husserl was onto absorbed coping long before Heidegger was. But without more context and interpretation it is hard to tell what Føllesdal's quotations from *Ideas II* are supposed to show. Husserl often comes up with phenomenological observations that might well have inspired Heidegger or Merleau-Ponty, only to distort them to fit into his account of the constitutive role of transcendental subjectivity. For example, motivation might mean, as it does in Merleau-Ponty, a gestalt tension that elicits a bodily response to bring the body/situation into equilibrium, but if, for Husserl, motivation has to do with willing, as Føllesdal claims, then motivation might be like Searle's intention in action, and, whether one is thematically aware of such an intention in action or not, it is, as Searle is happy to affirm, compatible with the transcendental reduction.[41]

I have discussed elsewhere the claim that, long before *Being and Time*, Husserl had already described the background that lies before and is presupposed by all comportment.[42] I pointed out that if Husserl had this important insight, he lost it when he tried to fit it into his transcendental phenomenology. Thus, in *Crisis*, he describes the background as a kind of atmosphere that cannot be objectified but is presupposed by all objectification (Føllesdal now suggests that Husserl had such a phenomenon in mind already in *Ideas II*. If so, Husserl did indeed beat Heidegger to this very important notion). But in *Crisis*, after describing the background in Heideggerian terms (by 1938 Husserl had read *Being and Time* twice), Husserl immediately treats the background as a belief system—what he sometimes calls a network of beliefs—so that the intentional content of the whole background can be pulled into transcendental subjectivity and brought under the reduction.

[W]e move in a current of ever new experiences, judgments, valuations, decisions . . . none of these acts, and none of the validities involved in them is isolated: in their intentions they necessarily imply an infinite horizon of inactive validities which function with them in flowing mobility. The manifold acquisitions of earlier active life are not dead sediments; even the background . . . of which we are always concurrently conscious but which is momentarily irrelevant and remains completely unnoticed, still functions according to its implicit validities.[43]

I do not have the space to take up the rest of Føllesdal's examples of where Husserl has anticipated Heidegger's insights into the practical and into the development of skills, and it would not be profitable to do so anyway until Føllesdal spells out his views more completely. Then, I am sure, we will have yet another round of fruitful discussion.

3. As to my inventing the dramatic confrontation between Husserl. and Heidegger, I simply follow Heidegger in understanding Husserl as a benighted Cartesian. As Heidegger understands the transcendental reduction, it introduces a Cartesian gulf between the inner world of senses, noemata, or intentional content—transcendental

subjectivity—and the world of referents to which these meanings are directed. The job of transcendental phenomenology is to study the meanings while bracketing the referents. (This is what Dagfinn taught me back in the 1950s). Heidegger has many texts to back him up in this way of reading Husserl. I'll quote Heidegger from *Basic Problems*:

[The] distinction between subject and object pervades all the problems of modern philosophy and even extends into the development of contemporary phenomenology. In his *Ideas*, Husserl says: "The theory of categories must begin absolutely from this most radical of all distinctions of being—being *as consciousness* [*res cogitans*] and being as being that 'manifests' itself in consciousness, 'transcendent' being [*res extensa*]." "Between consciousness [*res cogitans*] and reality [*res extensa*] there yawns a veritable abyss of meaning." Husserl continually refers to this distinction and precisely in the form in which Descartes expressed it: res cogitans—res extensa.[44]

Heidegger clearly did not want to disagree with Husserl in *Being and Time*, the book on the basis of which he hoped to get a Chair at Freiburg, so he never mentions Husserl and intentionality directly, but in his lectures in Marburg he explains clearly that he is looking for the conditions of possibility of intentionality and that that concern is not dealt with in Husserl's work.

The task of bringing to light Dasein's existential constitution leads first of all to the twofold task, intrinsically one, of *interpreting more radically the phenomena of intentionality and transcendence*. With this task . . . we run up against a central problem that has remained unknown to all previous philosophy and has involved it in remarkable, insoluble aporia.[45]

He then announces the anti-Husserlian thesis of *Being and Time*:

It will turn out that intentionality is founded in the Dasein's transcendence and is possible solely for this reason—that transcendence cannot conversely be explained in terms of [intentionality].[46]

To conclude, I am simply trying to remain true to the Husserl Dagfinn taught me. Where my interpretation differs from Dagfinn's, I am always ready to defer to his expertise. Sometimes, however, I cannot reconcile what he says with the texts. For example, Dagfinn says that, according to Husserl, "we do not perceive physical objects and synthesize them into tools," yet Husserl says:

Anything built by activity necessarily presupposes, as the lowest level, a passivity that gives something beforehand . . . an existent mere physical thing (when we disregard all the . . . "cultural" characteristics that make it knowable as, for example, a hammer . . .) is given . . . in the synthesis of passive experience . . . beforehand to "spiritual" activities, which begin with active grasping.[47]

Otherwise, I am grateful to Dagfinn for the rest of his corrections, although most of the "mistakes" he cites (numbers 4–7) are Heidegger's, not mine. I will, nonetheless, correct them all in the second edition of my *Commentary* and continue to be indebted to Dagfinn both for his frank criticism and his friendship.

Reply to David Cerbone

David has taken up an issue where Searle and Heidegger disagree— the role of arguments for the existence of the external world—and given a convincing and subtle defense of Heidegger's view. I so much agree with his chapter that I wish I had written it, and will draw from it in rewriting my *Commentary* on Division I of *Being and Time.*

There is room for further discussion, however, in that Cerbone seems to me unclear on a issue about which Heidegger too seems to waver. Is being-in-the-world a form of intentionality or isn't it? Or, to put it another way, does the fact that transcendence toward the world is an ontological notion, as Cerbone says, imply that it cannot be a form of intentionality? Sometimes, as Cerbone points out, Heidegger sounds like Searle in claiming that being-in-the-world makes intentionality possible, and therefore couldn't, on pain of regress, itself be a kind of intentionality. At least it couldn't be a kind of ontic intentionality like particular coping activities. This side of Heidegger's view is reflected in Cerbone's remark that "what Heidegger calls 'primal transcendence', is the understanding of being, which is not a matter of the fulfillment of any particular intentional states." But then Cerbone also notes that "being-in-the-world is a kind of intentionality that Heidegger sometimes calls 'primordial intentionality'"

(275). He adds, "Were it not, the connection between it and intentional states like beliefs and desires would be hard to make out" (275). That is, it would be hard to see how, if being-in-the-world was some non-intentional behavior, it could make intentionality possible. So Heidegger seems to have good reasons pushing him in two opposed directions and, there are, indeed, quotes that suggest he cannot make up his mind whether the understanding of being, which he equates with being-in-the-world, is or is not a kind of intentionality. I worried about this question in my *Commentary* and tried to figure out what phenomenon Heidegger could have in mind that was a kind of intentionality without content. I came to the puzzling conclusion that the global familiarity that makes up our understanding of being does not have conditions of satisfaction and yet this global familiarity seems to be nothing more than a lot of interconnected coping capacities which do have content. I wish that David would help me out by filling out his elegant and subtle analyses with some account of the phenomenon in question.

Reply to Mark Okrent

I always learn a lot from reading Mark because I always disagree with him. In the past he has succeeded in showing similarities between Heidegger and Davidson and I have argued that he neglected important differences, but I have not been clear what these differences were, or if I have, I have only focused on methodological differences. Now in this lucid and carefully worked out chapter, Okrent himself points out an important difference, viz. that for Heidegger, but not for Davidson, "every intentional state in *some* way involves a self reference" (289). That helps me see that, by leaving aside the fact that Heidegger's argument for his claims is not based on rational reconstruction but on phenomenology, Okrent necessarily misses the biggest difference of all. If I'm right, Okrent's chapter is instructive because it shows how, if one does not explicitly pay attention to the phenomenon Heidegger is laying out and interpreting, one leaves out what is most essential in Heidegger's thought.

I call what Okrent and Davidson are doing rational reconstruction because they are interested in actions insofar as they are rationally explainable. Heidegger would say, I'm fairly sure, that philosophers have long been at work on the project of working out how we make our activity intelligible to ourselves and others, but that working out this network of reasons does not get at what is actually going on in our everyday activity. That, therefore, he is interested in *describing* action not in *explaining* it. In one's everyday action one is constantly orienting oneself in a familiar world (circumspection) and dealing with equipment by doing whatever one is solicited to do by the current situation. This activity gets passed over in our explanations because it is normally invisible to us. We only give reasons when something goes wrong. Then we understand ourselves and others as trying to achieve goals based on beliefs and desires. Heidegger uses the example of opening the door and coming into the classroom as a case of transparent circumspective dealing, and he would, I'm sure, contrast it with *trying* to open the door because one *desires* to get into the room and *believes* that turning the knob is how to do it. The second sort of activity only takes place if the door is stuck. Heidegger is explicit that our everyday pressing into possibilities is not like trying to achieve a goal. Nonetheless, we do have to understand ourselves and others in terms of their goals, desires, and beliefs when we reflect on our or their activity. Then we find the network of reasons rational reconstruction describes. There is nothing wrong with this rationalized description as long as one realizes it is what Heidegger calls "a construction" and so does not read it back into the phenomena of everyday action. But it is the phenomenon of everyday coping with the available, not struggling with the unavailable, that Heidegger thinks is the basis of all intelligibility and which he claims he is the first to describe.

Dasein cannot be understood as a self-sufficient subject, but not because its mental states have to be related in the right way to beings other than itself, but because mental states and other beings only make sense on the background of Dasein's circumspective coping. As Heidegger says, being-in-the-world[48] as ecstatic temporality is the condition of the possibility of all intentionality. Thus there are different ways of being anti-Cartesian and just being anti-Cartesian is not enough to make Heidegger and Davidson similar. It is not just a question of whether one prefers rational reconstruction or phenomenological description as ways to reach the same conclusion. Rather, one could say in simple terms that Davidsonian rational reconstruction with its talk of things, other people, and mental states, misses Dasein's world disclosing because its account of Dasein's activity comes in one stage too late. Or one could say, in a more fancy Heideggerian way, that Davidson, like Aristotle and all traditional philosophers, passes over being-in-the-world and so knows nothing of the ontological difference. No matter what the similarities between Heidegger and Davidson may be, this is a big difference to miss.

The same issue comes up in Okrent's ingenious account of self-reference. Okrent concludes from Heidegger's claim that "Each one of us is what he pursues and cares for" that for Heidegger "every intentional state involves . . . a self-referential intention directed toward the person with that state"(290). Okrent thinks that Heidegger must be holding that if one is a shoemaker working on a pair of shoes one also intends oneself as a shoemaker. And he asks the right question: "what is it to intend oneself in that way?" (291) He sees that the crucial point is that, "for Heidegger every act involves . . . an interpretation and constitution of oneself as an agent of some definite type" (294–295). But, because he has no sense of being-in-the-world, he sees this self-interpretation as an intention somehow directed toward Dasein itself. This leads him to a complicated and ingenious explanation of the norms involving using tools and the necessity of acknowledging those norms in order to be, for example, a shoemaker. But this is not convincing. John Haugeland introduced the idea that for Heidegger, tools have to be used the right way, but neither John nor Okrent has ever cited a passage where Heidegger says as much. As far as I can see, this claim, while true, plays no role in any of Heidegger's arguments. Moreover, I would have thought one could be a shoemaker as long as one made shoes even if one misused all of one's tools.[49]

For Heidegger the self-referentiality is much less direct. It takes place not on the level of individual acts but on the level of worldhood. The clue to what Heidegger has in mind is in the phrase which Okrent quotes, "The Dasein as existing is there for itself," if one remembers that for Heidegger "existing" is a technical term referring to the way a Dasein has to take a stand on its own being by way of its activity in the world. Okrent quotes the relevant passage where Heidegger says that, in understanding, Dasein "has assigned itself to an 'in-order-to', and it has done so in terms of a potentiality-for-Being for the sake of which it itself is" (299). But, because he is always thinking in terms of making particular actions intelligible, Okrent does not see what Heidegger is getting at. According to Heidegger, to assign oneself to a for-the-sake-of-which does not mean that one "choose, intend, and constitute oneself as one of those who accept that style of norm" (300). It means that a role or identity organizes all of one's activity. One does not have an identity because one acknowledges tool using norms as Okrent claims, but one uses tools and people, normally or idiosyncratically, in order to manifest one's identity. I can only be a professor by giving lectures, keeping office hours, grading papers, and so forth and so a self-reference is *indirectly* involved in each such action. Self-reference is not a feature of each act; it is the way many of one's actions are organized or coordinated. Thus, self-referentiality, as Heidegger understands it, is not a directedness toward at all. This is what Heidegger means when he says that the for-the-sake-of-which is an essential structure of worldhood and that worldhood is not itself a kind of intentionality but the condition of the possibility of all intentional acts.

Notes

Foreword

1. Edmund Husserl, *Cartesian Meditations: An Introduction to Phenomenology*, trans. Dorion Cairns (Dordrecht: Kluwer, 1995).

2. Martin Heidegger, *Sein und Zeit, Gesamtausgabe*, vol. 2, ed. Friedrich-Wilhelm von Hermann (Frankfurt am Main: Vittorio Klostermann, 1977). Henceforth cited as *SZ* (citations in general are to page numbers of the eighth edition [Tübingen: Max Niemeyer, 1957]). Volumes in the *Gesamtausgabe* henceforth cited as *GA*.

3. Jacques Derrida, *La Voix et la Phénomène* (Paris: Presses Universitaires de France, 1967).

4. Hubert L. Dreyfus, *What Computers Can't Do: A Critique of Artificial Reason* (New York: Harper & Row, 1972).

5. *What Computers Still Can't Do: A Critique of Artificial Reason* (Cambridge: MIT Press, 1992).

6. Gilbert Ryle, *The Concept of Mind* (New York: Barnes & Noble, 1949).

7. Martin Heidegger, *Being and Time*, trans. John Macquarrie and Edward Robinson (New York: Harper & Row, 1962), henceforth cited as *BT*.

Introduction

1. The way Dreyfus describes the relationship (though certainly not Searle's preferred description) is that he (Dreyfus) plays Heidegger to Searle's Husserl.

2. Hubert. L. Dreyfus, *What Computers Still Can't Do: A Critique of Artificial Reason* (Cambridge: MIT Press, 1992), xi.

3. See John R. Searle, "The Limits of Phenomenology," in *Heidegger, Coping, and Cognitive Science*, eds. Mark A. Wrathall and Jeff Malpas (Cambridge: MIT Press, 2000), 71–92.

4. Richard Rorty, *Philosophy and the Mirror of Nature* (Princeton, N.J.: Princeton University Press, 1980). Stanley Cavell's *The Claim of Reason: Wittgenstein, Skepticism, Morality, and Tragedy* (New York: Oxford University Press, 1979), also appeared in the same year, but while Cavell's work was undoubtedly significant, and, like Rorty's, also promoted an engagement with the "continental" tradition, it has not had quite the same philosophical impact.

5. In 1974 all three appeared on the program of a symposium called "Perspectives on Heidegger" at the University of San Diego along with J. Glenn Gray, Marjorie Grene, Jürgen Habermas, Erich Heller, Bernd Magnus, Herbert Marcuse, and Frederick Olafson. In 1979 Dreyfus, Rorty, and Taylor were the three participants in a well-known exchange on the question "What is Hermeneutics?" at the 18th annual meeting of the Society for Phenomenology and Existential Philosophy held at Purdue University, which was later published in the *Review of Metaphysics* 34 (September 1980): 3–55.

6. In 1966 Dreyfus received the Baker Award for Outstanding Teaching and in 1968 the Harbison Prize for Outstanding Teaching.

7. Randall Havas, Taylor Carmen, William Blattner, David Cerbone, Theodore Schatzki, Sean Kelly, Charles Spinosa, Patricia Benner, Fernando Flores, and also Mark Wrathall all studied with Dreyfus at Berkeley or had Dreyfus on their Ph.D. committees.

8. The list of Institutes is as follows: 1980, "Perspectives on Intentionality"; 1988, "Interpretation"; 1990, "Heidegger and Davidson: Critics of Cartesianism"; 1992 "Principles and Practices"; 1994, "The Body"; 1997, "The Background of Intelligibility".

9. Martin Heidegger, *Kant and the Problem of Metaphysics*, 5th ed., trans. Richard Taft (Bloomington: Indiana University Press, 1997), xx.

10. "Teaching between Skill and Philosophy by a Philosopher of Skills," an interview with Hubert Dreyfus by Tone Saugstad Gabrielsen. Berkeley, April 7, 1998.

11. Hubert L. Dreyfus, *Being-in-the-World: A Commentary on Heidegger's Being and Time, Division I* (Cambridge: MIT Press, 1991).

12. Ibid., vii.

13. John Haugland, "Truth and Finitude," this Volume, 43–77.

14. *Being-in-the-World*.

15. Hubert L. Dreyfus and Charles Spinosa, "Highway Bridges and Feasts: Heidegger and Borgmann on How to Affirm Technology," *Man and World* 30 (1997):159–177.

16. "Teaching between Skill and Philosophy by a Philosopher of Skills."

Notes

Chapter 1: Must We Be Inauthentic?

1. Hubert L. Dreyfus and Jane Rubin, "Appendix: Kierkegaard, Division II, and Later Heidegger," in Dreyfus, *Being-in-the-World*, 333.

2. Søren Kierkegaard, "To Need God Is a Human Being's Highest Perfection," in *Eighteen Upbuilding Discourses*, ed. and trans. Howard V. Hong and Edna H. Hong (Princeton: Princeton University Press, 1990), 309, 311. Similarly, in "He Must Increase; I Must Decrease," Kierkegaard refers to "the fullness of the joy that is the incorruptible apparel of self-denial." Ibid., 288. Religiousness A is thus not unlike Hegel's notions of stoicism and unhappy consciousness in *Phenomenology of Spirit.*

3. Søren Kierkegaard, *Concluding Unscientific Postscript to Philosophical Fragments*, ed. and trans. Howard V. Hong and Edna H. Hong, vol. 1 (Princeton, N.J.: Princeton University Press, 1992), 574. Thus Kierkegaard's pseudonym, Johannes Climacus, insists, "I have never called Religiousness A Christian or Christianity." Ibid., 561n.

4. Unclosedness and determination are, respectively, the literal and the ordinary senses of the word *Entschlossenheit.* "Owning up" is an English idiom, but it compensates for the fact that the translation of *Eigentlichkeit* as "authenticity" masks its connection with the root *eigen* (own). Heidegger says, for example, that being "authentic" (*eigentlich*), for Dasein, "means being its own" (*sich zueigen*). *Sein und Zeit*, 15th ed. (Tübingen: Max Niemeyer, 1979), 42, henceforth cited as *SZ.* All translations of Heidegger are mine.

5. *Being-in-the-World*, 333.

6. Ibid., 334.

7. Ibid. Earlier, at 229, Dreyfus writes: "If Heidegger derives falling as absorption from falling as fleeing, he makes authenticity impossible."

8. Ibid., 334.

9. My aim in this paper is to urge *that* falling and fleeing can be, not to describe exactly *how* they are, internally related yet logically distinct. A fuller treatment of the problem would have to explain in greater detail precisely how falling in its "intensified" or "aggravated" form often degenerates into full-fledged motivated irrationality.

10. "Falling is an existential determination of Dasein itself . . . The ontological-existential structure of falling would also be misunderstood, if one wanted to attribute to it the sense of a bad and deplorable ontical property, which could possibly be eliminated in more advanced stages of human culture. . . . An *existential mode* of being-in-the-world is documented in the phenomenon of falling" (*SZ*, 176). "Falling reveals an *essential* ontological structure of Dasein itself, which, far from characterizing its dark side (*Nachtseite*), constitutes all its days in their everydayness" (*SZ*, 179). "The term 'falling' . . . once again must not be taken as a value judgment, as if the term marked something like an occasionally occurring defect of Dasein's that is to be deplored and perhaps rectified in advanced stages of human culture. Falling, like uncoveredness, being-with, and being-in, indicates a constitutive structure of the being of Dasein." *Prolegomena zur Geschichte des Zeitbegriffs*, GA 20 (Frankfurt am Main: Vittorio Klostermann, 1979), 378.

11. Dreyfus distinguishes between falling as a "tendency" and fleeing as a "temptation" (*Versuchung*), ascribing the fomer to the structural and the latter to the motivational account. See *Being-in-the-World*, 228, 233. But I think the tendency and the temptation to flee pose essentially the same problems of interpretation and that the structural story can accommodate both.

12. Ibid., 228.

13. Ibid., 355 n2.

14. Ibid., 235.

15. Ibid., 233–234. In his 1925 lectures Heidegger says, "Dasein, essentially given over to the world, gets *entangled* in its own concern. It can yield to this tendency of falling to such an extent that, in doing so, it loses sight of the possibility of returning to itself, i.e. no longer even understands such a thing." *Prolegomena zur Geschichte des Zeitbegriffs*, GA 20, 389.

16. In referring to this last element, Heidegger may have in mind Husserl's distinction between the communication of objective content and the "intimation" of subjective mental acts. To say "the sky is blue" is at once to communicate a proposition and to intimate or convey a belief. In purely expressive speech acts, for example apologizing, the two moments coincide, and indeed elsewhere Heidegger himself collapses the distinction.

17. The original discussions occur in Kierkegaard's essay, "The Present Age." Heidegger takes over the notion of "leveling." See Søren Kierkegaard, *Two Ages: The Age of Revolution and the Present Age*, ed. and trans. Howard V. Hong and Edna H. Hong (Princeton, N.J.: Princeton University Press, 1978), 84 *et passim*. Heidegger uses the term "ambiguity" to refer to what Kierkegaard calls "superficiality," namely the deterioration of the distinction between revealing and concealing. Ibid., 102. Heidegger's own treatment of the phenomena is analogous with but not identical to Kierkegaard's, for whereas the latter regards them as historical contingencies peculiar to modernity, Heidegger attributes them to the basic ontological constitution of being-in-the-world.

18. Dreyfus anticipates my argument when he himself describes Heidegger's structural account on analogy with gravity: "*Falling-for* the non-primordiality of the one" (*das Man*), he writes, "is not a positive act; it just happens to one like falling in a gravitational field. Thus undifferentiated Dasein literally has no choice . . . Resisting falling requires constant effort." *Being-in-the-World*, 236. But Dreyfus dismisses this interpretation of falling as incomplete and problematic for a full account of inauthenticity. Incomplete it may be, but I think it promises to meet the charge of incoherence Dreyfus and Rubin subsequently pose.

19. Jean-Paul Sartre, *L'être et le néant: Essai d'ontologie phénoménologique* (Paris: Gallimard, 1943), 97. Translated as *Being and Nothingness: An Essay on Phenomenological Ontology*, trans. Hazel E. Barnes (New York: Philosophical Library, 1956), 61.

20. It is no accident, then, that Heidegger mentions the "rebound" effect in the opening sentences of §32 of *SZ*, which spells out his conception of interpretation. It is worth asking what kind of "explicitness" is at stake in interpretation. I argue elsewhere that it should be understood as expressive and communicative explicitness, that is, as rooted in discourse.

21. Jean-Paul Sartre, "Cartesian Freedom," in *Literary and Philosophical Essays*, trans. Annette Michelson (New York: Collier Books, 1962).

Chapter 2: The Significance of Authenticity

1. Notwithstanding the "terrible" means by which such calculability is brought about, this first dimension of human intelligibility is trivial from a philosophical point of view. In insisting on the necessity of what he calls "calculability" Nietzsche means neither to be providing a philosophical explanation of how communication is possible, nor to be pointing to something that itself demands a philosophical account.

2. I am indebted to Edward Minar for this way of putting the point.

3. This usage of the term "constitutive" can be found in Dreyfus, *Being-in-the-World*. See, for example, page 154 where he speaks of "constitutive *conformity*" to norms as the condition of the possibility of understanding.

4. William Blattner explores such a reading in his "Existential Temporality in *Being and Time*," in *Heidegger: A Critical Reader*, ed. Hubert L. Dreyfus and Harrison Hall (Cambridge: Blackwell, 1992), 99–129.

5. Although in his view Division I revealed the essentially self-interpretative character of human life, Heidegger nevertheless felt compelled to acknowledge that our self-interpretations tend by and large to cover up the fact that they *are* interpretations. As he sees it, it must therefore be possible for the existential phenomenologist to circumvent our tendency to misinterpret the interpretative character of our lives if he is to claim with any confidence to have done a better job than has the philosophical tradition of understanding human being. The investigation into authenticity is therefore meant to validate the results of Divison I by showing us that it is indeed possible to see human being for what it is. My claim here is simply that an apparently powerful interpretation of Division I threatens our ability to understand what Heidegger's conception of human being actually involves.

6. "[Z]u einem gewissen Grade nothwendig, einförmig, gleich unter Gleichen, regelmässig und folglich berechenbar." Friedrich Nietzsche, *On the Genealogy of Morals*, trans. Walter Kaufmann and R. J. Hollingdale (New York: Vintage, 1967), 58–59. Henceforth cited as *GM*.

7. What Nietzsche and Heidegger both deny is that there is anything philosophically problematic about the character of such "dependence". Nietzsche's remark functions simply as a reminder of what the philosopher has to forget in order to get philosophy off the ground.

8. "The tremendous labor of that which I have called "morality of mores"—the labor performed by man upon himself during the greater part of the existence of the human race, his entire *prehistoric* labor, finds in this its meaning, its great justification, notwithstanding the severity, tyranny, stupidity, and idiocy involved in it: with the aid of the morality of mores and the social straitjacket, man was actually *made* calculable." *GM*, 59.

9. Of course, we can say that, in another sense, the pot boils "in response" to heating it. In this context, however, we are no longer talking about intelligibility. Boiling is

not a way of making sense of having been put on a flame. Nietzsche's "argument" against someone who wanted to insist that the notion of intelligibility needs to be reduced to responsiveness of the former sort can be found in §110 of Friedrich Nietzsche, *The Gay Science*, trans. Walter Kaufmann (New York: Vintage, 1974); henceforth cited as *GS*. The main thing to avoid here is the philosophical inflation of the fact that what distinguishes us from the boiling pot is the presence of "normativity" in the former case, and its absence in the latter. There is nothing *mysterious* about the kind of calculability to which Nietzsche is drawing our attention in the passage we are considering.

10. In other words, that calculability requires what he calls—somewhat indifferently—"training" and "breeding".

11. More is at stake in *Being and Time* than just the accuracy of the epistemologist's description of human being, but *at least* this much is (and is so explicitly). The broader target is the idea that there is a meaningful philosophical question to be asked about the source of the sense the world makes to us. But it is easiest to set the problem up in terms of Heidegger's rejection of epistemology.

12. And this in a particular way: "fallenly." Thus, neither I myself nor the world in which I live are, in the first instance, objects of knowledge. But this is so for a slightly different reason in each case. Things are what they are primarily as they are encountered in the course of one's practical dealings with them. On the other hand, I am who I am primarily as someone concerned to conform to the expectations of others. I am ignoring this asymmetry difference here. However, I think Heidegger's insistence on the "common" world is primarily to be understood in terms of the fact of our conformism.

13. See *Being-in-the-World*.

14. Frederick A. Olafson, *Heidegger and the Philosophy of Mind* (New Haven: Yale University Press, 1987).

15. Ibid., 146.

16. Ibid., 147.

17. See *Being-in-the-World*, 144. Dreyfus addresses this issue most recently in "Interpreting Heidegger on *Das Man*," *Inquiry* 38 (1995): 423–430.

18. *Being-in-the-World*, 145.

19. I am omitting a large part of Dreyfus's story here—in particular, Dreyfus's account of the public character of equipment. This part of his story seems to me seriously to stretch interpretative credibility. He understands "distantiality" to be a concern with conforming one's activity to the norms that govern the sense of that activity, while Heidegger seems pretty clearly to be thinking of distantiality to be a concern with conformity in the sense of conform*ism*. I am not entirely confident about this last point, but nothing hangs on it for our purposes here.

20. See *Being-in-the-World*, 151, 154.

21. Ibid., 155 (emphasis supplied).

22. Olafson himself speaks of a "theory" in this connection. See *Heidegger and the Philosophy of Mind*, 147.

23. As Edward Minar makes abundantly clear in his "Feeling at Home in Language," *Synthese* 102 (1995): 413–452.

24. This line of argument is helpfully pursued in Edward Minar, "The Heideggerian Response to the 'Scandal of Philosophy'," unpublished manuscript.

25. See subtitle to chapter 8, section C, *Being-in-the-World*, 161.

26. "There is certainly something unsettling about Heidegger's discovery. Traditionally all meanings have been traced back to some final self-intelligible, most real, occurrent source, e.g., the Good, God, or the transcendental ego. The one [i.e., the community] as ultimate reality . . . cannot supply this sort of intelligibility." Ibid.

27. According to the Platonist, for example, unless our speaking is "grounded" in knowledge of the Forms, it's not really speaking at all, only mooing of some sort.

28. *Being-in-the-World*, 162 (emphasis in original).

29. See, for example, the appendix to Dreyfus's commentary on *Being and Time*, on which I will concentrate here. Harrison Hall and Charles Guignon also recommend such a reading. See Harrison Hall, "Intentionality and World: Division I of *Being and Time*," in *The Cambridge Companion to Heidegger*, ed. Charles Guignon (Cambridge: Cambridge University Press, 1993), 122–140; Charles Guignon, "Heidegger's 'Authenticity' Revisited," *Review of Metaphysics* 38 (December 1984): 321–339.

30. Hubert L. Dreyfus and Jane Rubin, "Appendix: Kierkegaard, Division II, and Later Heidegger," in *Being-in-the-World*, 337.

31. *BT*, 331.

32. *Being-in-the-World*, 332.

33. *Being-in-the-World*, 329.

34. Dreyfus suggests that Heidegger's account in *Being and Time* confronts a dilemma: "If . . . Dasein is dependent upon the one in the same way as the social person is derived from transcendental intersubjectivity, then Heidegger is faced with a dilemma: either the activity of the public is taken as fundamental, in which case . . . Heidegger must be doing sociology or anthropology instead of philosophy, or else Heidegger is doing philosophy, in which case the one itself must have some kind of self-intelligible transcendental source. In *Being and Time* Heidegger's response to the dilemma is unclear. On the one hand, he feels he must find some sort of transcendental source to answer Husserl, and in Division II he seems to suggest that a source for the everyday world and the self in originary temporality. Yet on the other hand, his description of the phenomenon of everydayness in Division I affirms the one as *ens realissimum*—as the end of the line of explanations of intelligibility." *Being-in-the-World*, 353. Rather than attributing a dilemma to Heidegger here, we should try to see how he might respond to the dichotomy between anthropology and philosophy with which Dreyfus presents him. As I read him, Heidegger is saying that it is precisely that distinction that has not been sufficiently motivated by the tradition.

If we take it for granted, then his appeals to community can have no philosophical significance. From that point of view, they *are* merely anthropological. But Heidegger means to ask us what licenses our assurance that there *is* a specifically philosophical point of view in the first place. Nothing I have said in this paper shows that there is no such standpoint. But it should be clear that *Being and Time* aims to replace a *philosophical* problem about individual and community/universal with an *existential* one. Dreyfus recognizes this fact, but does not appear adequately to appreciate its radicality.

35. *GM*, 59.

36. *Ibid.*

37. *GM*, 60.

38. According to *GM*, it is primarily this sense of indebtedness that we tend to conceive in terms of a moralized notion of guilt.

Chapter 3: Truth and Finitude: Heidegger's Transcendental Existentialism

1. Martin Heidegger, *Hegels Phänomenologie des Geistes* (Frankfurt: Vittorio Klostermann, 1980), an edited transcript of lectures delivered in 1930–31, 13. Translated as *Hegel's Phenomenology of Spirit* by Parvis Emad and Kenneth Maly (Bloomington: Indiana University Press, 1980). This translation, as well as all translation of *Sein und Zeit*, henceforth cited as *SZ*, is my own.

2. This implies, of course, that animals do not have genuine intentionality—a thesis that I, like Heidegger, endorse (but will not argue here).

3. Since these relationships concern what is possible and impossible, the actuality of an entity of one determinate kind can be seen as enabling, requiring, or precluding the actuality of another, in accord with their respective physical determinations; hence, physical actuality can also be explicated in terms of (a physical species of) causal efficacy and affectability.

4. It is illuminating to consider how so-called "functional explanations"—say, of how mechanisms or organisms work—are another special case, partaking of elements from each of the foregoing examples; but that cannot be pursued here.

5. In his summer 1927 lectures, Heidegger identifies and examines a deeper form of ontological articulation: the distinction, in the being of any entity (of whatever sort), between its that-it-is (existence or actuality, for instance) and its what-it-is (essence or reality, for instance). *Die Grundprobleme der Phänomenologie* (Frankfurt: Vittorio Klostermann, 1975), an edited transcript of lectures delivered in 1927, 10–12. Translated as *The Basic Problems of Phenomenology*, trans. Albert Hofstadter (Bloomington: Indiana University Press, 1982). Elsewhere he occasionally also includes a third member in this articulated set, corresponding to what the medievals called accidental-being. See, for instance, *Die Grundbegriffe der Metaphysik: Welt-Endlichkeit-Einsamkeit* (Frankfurt: Vittorio Klostermann, 1983), an edited transcript of lectures delivered in 1929–30, 476–481. Translated as *The Fundamental Concepts of*

Metaphysics: World, Finitude, Solitude, trans. William McNiell and Nicholas Walker (Bloomington: Indiana University Press, 1995). He calls these distinctions the articulation of *being*. And the question he always asks is: *why* is being articulated in just this way? But, so far as I know, he never succeeds in answering that question.

6. With this survey of the three moments of disclosedness we are in a better position to see some of the ways in which it differs from Kant's transcendental apperception. Most conspicuously, the architectonic is different. For Kant, there are two distinct faculties that *jointly* make knowledge possible: sensibility and understanding. The first is the capacity to be affected by objects, and the second is the capacity to make judgments that are about them and bound by them. But apperception is associated exclusively with the latter. For Heidegger, by contrast, there is only disclosedness. The closest thing to a "partner" for disclosedness, in the way that sensibility is the partner of understanding, would be the world itself. But even that isn't quite right, because disclosedness is the same as being-in as such, the "middle" element in the triune structure of being-in-the-world. Disclosedness is "between" the self and the world.

But that implies a more particular—and particularly striking—difference. If disclosedness is "between" the self and the world in the structure of being-in-the-world, then it is no more to be identified with the self than with the world. Yet Kant explicitly identifies transcendental apperception with the "I that thinks" and the "transcendental self."

Closely related to this difference is a third. If understanding is basically skillful know-how, then, like comportment toward entities in general, it is not exclusively, or even primarily, *mental* (let alone, intellectual). Rather, it is primarily a moment of skillful worldly activities—and the same goes for telling and sofindingness. (One might suppose that moods, at least, are somehow "mental," were it not for the fact that Heidegger explicitly disavows that as an implication of what he means: "Being-attuned [in a mood] is not related in the first place to the psychical, and is not itself an inner state." *SZ* 137). Clearly, disclosedness cannot be equated with consciousness (or the mind) in any familiar sense.

Finally, on my (controversial) reading, disclosedness is not even primarily private or individual. Rather, in the first place and usually, it is cultural and historical, hence *public*. Indeed, Heidegger's specific term for *unowned* disclosedness is *publicness* (*Öffentlichkeit*) (*SZ*, 167). To be sure, particular instances of know-how, articulation, and responsiveness are found in individual people. But that's like pointing out that particular scientific experiments and speech acts are performed by individuals. Nevertheless, science and language themselves are clearly cultural/historical *public* phenomena; and that's the way I believe we should understand disclosedness. Needless to say, Kantian apperception is not public in this way.

7. Without putting it in the same way, what this paragraph describes (and so promises to explicate) is what Heidegger calls the three "priorities" of Dasein. *SZ*, 12f.

8. The basic point is that, if scientists were not *tenacious* in their efforts to solve even highly recalcitrant puzzles (that is, in preference to giving up on their paradigm), then hard but solvable puzzles would seldom get solved. Yet it is precisely these solutions that are often the most valuable achievements of science. Moreover, if and when a paradigm shift does become inevitable, it will be largely driven and guided by those very intransigent puzzles which could only have been identified as such through persistent efforts to solve them, and which, once so identified, can prove particularly revealing. See Thomas S. Kuhn, *The Structure of Scientific Revolutions* (Chicago: University of Chicago Press, 1962; second enlarged edition, 1970), 64f., 151f.

9. In other words, owned Dasein faces up to and takes over the ultimate *riskiness* of its life as a whole—it lives resolutely as and only as ultimately *vulnerable*. According to this interpretation, then, it is ironic (to say the least) that the character of Religiousness B that Dreyfus and Rubin specifically identify as *omitted* from ownedness is risk and vulnerability. *Being-in-the-World*, 298, 335f. Their concluding critical observation that the position they attribute to Heidegger "makes no sense" strikes me as telling.

Chapter 4: Philosophy and Authenticity: Heidegger's Search for a Ground for Philosophizing

1. Martin Heidegger, *Sein und Zeit*, henceforth cited as *SZ*, 437.

2. Heidegger's marginalia are included in the *Gesamtausgabe* edition of *Sein und Zeit*, and are included in Joan Stambaugh's translation of *Being and Time* (Albany: SUNY, 1996).

3. Karl Löwith, for example, describes Heidegger as a magician "who knew how to cast a spell insofar as he could make disappear what he had a moment before presented." His lecture technique, according to Löwith, "consisted in building up an edifice of ideas which he then proceeded to tear down, presenting the spellbound listeners with a riddle and then leaving them empty-handed." Cited from Karl Löwith, *Mein Leben in Deutschland vor und nach 1933* (Stuttgart: J. B. Metzler, 1986), 43, by Richard Wolin, "Hannah and the Magician," *New Republic* 213 (October 9, 1995): 30. For the English version, see Löwith, *My Life in Germany Before and After 1933* (Urbana: University of Illinois Press, 1994), 45.

4. Martin Heidegger, *On the Way to Language*, trans. Peter D. Hertz (New York: Harper & Row, 1971), 92.

5. Martin Heidegger, "What is Metaphysics?" in *Basic Writings*, ed. David F. Krell (New York: Harper & Row, 1977), 93.

6. Martin Heidegger, *Beiträge zur Philosophie (Vom Ereignis)*, GA 65 (Frankfurt: Klostermann, 1989), 13–14. I am indebted to Richard Polt for calling my attention to this and the previous passage.

7. Dreyfus and Rubin, "Appendix: Kierkegaard, Division II, and Later Heidegger," in *Being-in-the-World*, 283–340.

8. Martin Heidegger, *Zur Bestimmung der Philosophie*, GA: 56/57 (Frankfurt: Klostermann, 1987), Freiburg lectures of 1919. Henceforth cited as *ZBP*.

9. Martin Heidegger, *Phänomenologische Interpretationen zu Aristoteles: Einführung in die Phänomenologische Forschung*, GA 61 (Frankfurt: Klostermann, 1985), 60 (Freiburg lectures of 1921/22). Henceforth cited as *PIA*. Quoted in John van Buren, *The Young Heidegger: Rumor of the Hidden King* (Bloomington: Indiana University Press, 1994), 245.

10. Søren Kierkegaard, *Concluding Unscientific Postscript*, trans. David F. Swenson and Walter Lowrie (Princeton: Princeton University Press, 1941), 173.

Notes

11. Ibid., 176.

12. Paul Ricoeur, *Time and Narrative*, 3 vols., trans. Kathleen McLaughlin and David Pellauer (Chicago: University of Chicago Press, 1984–88), especially vol. 1, 60–64, and vol. 3, 60–96.

13. In choosing "the artist" as a paradigm of the "genuine" life, Heidegger probably had in mind Vincent van Gogh. Having read van Gogh's letter's during the war (they appeared in German in 1914), Heidegger praised them as a more authentic manifestation of the artist's existence than anything provided by academic art history. See Otto Pöggeler, "Heidegger on Art," in *Martin Heidegger: Politics, Art, and Technology*, ed. Karsten Harries and Christoph Jamme (New York: Holmes & Meier, 1994), 113. Just as van Gogh struggled against the influence of urban living and tried to stay close to nature, so "Heidegger's thinking was also intended to face the problems of life without the academic safeguards." Ibid. Heidegger strove to approach life in a way that was unmediated by the schematizations and styles of interpretation sedimented into university life.

14. *SZ* 145. Cf. Martin Heidegger, *Introduction to Metaphysics*, trans. Ralph Manheim (New Haven: Yale University Press, 1959), 101.

15. Quoted from unpublished parts of the transcript from Heidegger's 1919 lectures by Theodore Kisiel in *The Genesis of Heidegger's Being and Time* (Berkeley: University of California Press, 1993), 17.

16. Ibid., 189.

17. Ibid. On the kairotic "moment of illumination" by virtue of which all of factic life experience is actualized in every moment, see ibid., 186.

18. Nearly all the main characteristics of being-toward-death are developed in Martin Heidegger, *The Concept of Time*, trans. William McNeill (Oxford: Blackwell, 1992).

19. *SZ*, 307.

20. I have discussed the account of authentic historicity and its relation to world-history in *Heidegger and the Problem of Knowledge* (Indianapolis: Hackett, 1983) sections 6 and 16, and more recently in "History and Commitment in the Early Heidegger," in *Heidegger: A Critical Reader*, ed. Hubert L. Dreyfus and Harrison Hall (Oxford: Blackwell, 1992), 130–142.

21. The claim that *Being and Time* leads to decisionism has been argued forcefully by Jürgen Habermas in *The Philosophical Discourse of Modernity: Twelve Lectures*, trans. Frederick G. Lawrence (Cambridge: MIT Press, 1987), and Richard Wolin in *The Politics of Being: The Political Thought of Martin Heidegger* (New York: Columbia University Press, 1990).

22. This is, of course, Gabriel Marcel's well-known criticism of Sartre. See his *The Philosophy of Existentialism*, trans. Manya Harari (New York: Citadel Press, 1956), 86–88.

23. "The Origin of the Work of Art," trans. Albert Hofstadter in *Poetry, Language, Thought* (New York: Harper & Row, 1971), 15–87, henceforth cited as OWA.

24. Here I am building on ideas developed by Dreyfus in "Heidegger on the Connection Between Nihilism, Art, Technology, and Politics," in *The Cambridge Companion to Heidegger*, ed. Charles Guignon (Cambridge: Cambridge University Press, 1993).

25. Martin Heidegger, "Phenomenological Interpretations with Respect to Aristotle: Indication of the Hermeneutical Situation," trans. Michael Baur, *Man and World* 25 (1992): 355–393. Henceforth cited as PIRA.

26. Jean Grondin points out that the word "finitude," in *Being and Time* reserved for references to Dasein's mortality, begins to be used in its wider sense in the works that appear immediately after *Being and Time*. See "Prolegomena to an Understanding of Heidegger's Turn," in Jean Grondin, *Sources of Hermeneutics* (Albany: State University of New York Press, 1995), and his *Le Tournant dans la Pensèe de Martin Heidegger* (Paris: Presses Universitaires de France, 1987).

27. Martin Heidegger, *The Metaphysical Foundations of Logic*, trans. Michael Heim (Bloomington: Indiana University Press, 1984), 156. Henceforth cited as *MFL*.

28. For example, Heidegger says that "Dasein is thrown, factical, thoroughly amidst nature through its bodiliness," and that "as factical, it remains environed by nature" (*MFL* 166).

29. *The Concept of Time*, 20.

30. Ibid.

31. My thanks to Steven Crowell, Richard Polt, Robert Scharff, and Dieter Thomä for helpful suggestions and criticisms. An earlier version of this paper was read at the Piaget Institute in Portugal in November, 1997; my thanks to the participants at that conference, and especially to Dorothea Frede for her comments.

Chapter 5: Kierkegaard's Present Age and Ours

1. Søren Kierkegaard, *En literair Anmeldelse* (1846), in *Samlede Værker*, vol. 14, ed. A. B. Drachmann, J. L. Heiberg and H. O. Lange (1991), 92; *Samlede Værker* henceforth cited as *SV*.

2. Hubert L. Dreyfus, *Being-in-the-World*, 283–341. This is an extended and slightly revised version of Hubert L. Dreyfus and Jane Rubin, "You Can't Get Something for Nothing: Kierkegaard and Heidegger on How Not to Overcome Nihilism," *Inquiry* 30, no. 1–2 (1987): 33–75.

3. Hubert L. Dreyfus and Jane Rubin, "Kierkegaard on the Nihilism of the Present Age: The Case of Commitment as Addiction," *Synthese* 98, no. 1 (1994): 3–19.

4. Ibid., 6–7.

5. "Appendix," 283.

6. Ibid., 284.

7. Martin Heidegger, *History of the Concept of Time: Prolegomena*, trans. Theodore Kisiel (Bloomington: Indiana University Press, 1985), 246 (emphasis in original).

8. Ibid.

9. *SV*, vol. 1, 130. See also *The Concept of Irony*, in *Kierkegaard's Writings*, vol. 2, trans. Howard V. Hong and Edna H. Hong (Princeton: Princeton University Press, 1989), 79.

10. *SV*, vol. 10 (cited in n. 1, above), 181. See Søren Kierkegaard, *Concluding Unscientific Postscript*, 450, where the rather vague translation is: "Irony is a specific culture of the spirit."

11. *SV*, vol. 10 (cited in n. 1, above); *Concluding Unscientific Postscript*, 449.

12. See *SV*, vol. 14 (cited in n. 1, above), 73, quoted by Dreyfus and Rubin in "Kierkegaard on the Nihilism of the Present Age," 5.

13. See *History of the Concept of Time*, 283.

14. Ibid.

15. "You Can't Get Something for Nothing," 34.

16. *En literair Anmeldelse*, 73. Quoted in "Kierkegaard on the Nihilism of the Present Age," 6.

17. *History of the Concept of Time*, 246.

18. *SV*, vol. 14, 78–79.

19. Ibid., 79.

20. Ibid., 80.

21. Ibid. The press, aided by the "apathy and reflective nature of the age," begets that "phantom of abstraction: the public."

22. See Søren Kierkegaard, *Søren Kierkegaards Papirer*, vol. 1 B 2, ed. P. A. Heiberg and V. Kuhr, enlarged ed. N. Thulstrup (Copenhagen: Gyldendal, 1968).

23. *SV*, vol. 14, 86.

24. See ibid., 88.

25. Cf. Heidegger: "The public is involved in everything but in such a way that it has already always absolved itself of it all." *History of the Concept of Time*, 246–247.

26. *SV*, vol. 14, 88.

27. *Søren Kierkegaards Papirer*, vol. VII 1 B 43.

28. Ibid., vol. X 1 A 107; Søren Kierkegaard, *Kierkegaard's Papers and Journals: A Selection* (Harmondsworth: Penguin, 1996), 365, translation amended, original emphasis.

29. *History of the Concept of Time*, 248; *SV*, vol. 9, 164. There is a parallel (though how close remains unclear) with Climacus's assertion that, however much the existing subject is made "infinite in imagination's eternity," it "remains at the same time most definitely itself"; *Concluding Unscientific Postscript*, 176. The translation is amended.

30. *SV*, vol. 14, 78.

31. Martin Heidegger, *Basic Writings*, ed. David Farrell Krell, 221. There may even be a parallel here with Kierkegaard's actual claim, namely that the age is a reflective one. That might be so if we can read him as saying that the reflectiveness of the age is manifested, not in a disposition on the part of individuals to think before they act, but in the nature of the background against which they act unthinkingly.

32. *SV*, vol. 14, 80.

33. Ibid., 98.

34. "Kierkegaard on the Nihilism of the Present Age," 5.

35. Søren Kierkegaard, *The Concept of Dread*, trans. Walter Lowrie (Princeton: Princeton University Press, 1957), 55; *SV*, vol. 6, 55, "*griber Endeligheden at holde sig ved.*"

36. "Kierkegaard on the Nihilism of the Present Age," 8–9.

37. Ibid., 14–16.

38. *History of the Concept of Time*, 245. Translated as "apartness," sometimes as "distantiality."

39. These and other points are also discussed in my "Kierkegaard's Levellings and the *Review*," in *Kierkegaard Studies: Kierkegaard Yearbook*, 1999, ed. J. N. Cappelørn and Hermann Deuser (Berlin: Walter de Gruyter, 1999).

40. I am very grateful to Camilla Serck-Hanssen for comments on the penultimate draft of this essay which helped a great deal to clarify the presentation.

Chapter 6: The End of Authentic Selfhood in the Postmodern Age?

1. Kenneth J. Gergen, *The Saturated Self: Dilemmas of Identity in Contemporary Life* (New York: Basic Books, 1992). An earlier version of this essay included a more detailed discussion of this important book.

2. "Flexible raw material" is a free rendering of Heidegger's word, *Bestand*, often translated as "standing reserve." Heidegger views the noun *Bestand* as being related to the verb *stellen*, to place or posit. In his account of modern technology he frequently uses verbs with the *stellen* stem to describe the tendency of modern technology to shift things about, to order and reorganize them, to make them available, and so on. For Heidegger, modern technology discloses things as virtually interchangeable (thus flexible) phenomena whose sole value lies in their use (raw material) for

human projects. Here, one may think of the contemporary push for total digitiliza-
tion of all phenomena as a continuing instance of this process.

3. Hubert L. Dreyfus and Charles Spinosa, "Highway Bridges and Feasts: Heidegger
and Borgmann on How to Affirm Technology"; citation is from 163. Henceforth cited
as "Highway Bridges."

4. Sherry Turkle, *Life on the Screen: Identity in the Age of the Internet* (New York: Simon
and Schuster, 1995), as cited by Hubert Dreyfus and Charles Spinosa in "Highway
Bridges," 165.

5. Ibid.

6. Ibid., 171 (emphasis supplied).

7. Ibid., 171–172.

8. Ibid., 172.

9. This passage is found in the *electronic* version of "Highway Bridges," which includes
at least one paragraph omitted in the version published in *Man and World*. The electronic version (found at http://www.focusing.org/dreyfus.html) was published in
connection with the "After Postmodernism" conference held at the University of
Chicago, November 14–16, 1997.

10. This passage is also found in the electronic version.

11. "Highway Bridges," 173.

12. Ibid.

13. Ibid.

14. Ibid., 175.

15. Albert Borgmann, *Crossing the Postmodern Divide* (Chicago: University of Chicago
Press, 1992), 144, as cited by Dreyfus and Spinosa, "Highway Bridges," 174.

16. In my view, Dreyfus sometimes reads Heidegger so much in line with Wittgens-
tinian and pragmatist views of practices, that he overlooks the transcendental neo-
Kantian and Aristotelian dimensions of Heidegger's thought, dimensions that cannot
readily be understood in terms of practices. Discussion of this is an issue that must
be postponed for another essay, however.

17. Spinosa, personal communication, February 16, 1998.

18. For Dreyfus's own analysis of the *Angst* phenomenon's relation to authenticity,
see his essay (co-authored with Jane Rubin), "You Can't Get Something for Nothing:
Kierkegaard and Heidegger on How Not To Overcome Nihilism."

19. Martin Heidegger, "What Are Poets For?" trans. Albert Hofstadter in *Poetry,
Language, Thought* (New York: Harper & Row, 1971), 96.

20. Heidegger, "The Thing," in *Poetry, Language, Thought,* 178–179.

21. On this issue, see Dreyfus, *Being-in-the-World,* and Michael E. Zimmerman, *Eclipse of the Self: The Development of Heidegger's Concept of Authenticity* (Athens: Ohio University Press, 1986).

22. Heidegger writes: "In his story 'The Death of Ivan Ilyitch,' Leo [L.N.] Tolstoi has presented the phenomenon of the disruption and breakdown of having 'someone die'." *BT,* 495; *SZ,* 254.

23. Calvin O. Shrag, *The Self After Postmodernity* (New Haven: Yale University Press, 1997), 33.

24. See Ken Wilber, "The Pre/Trans Fallacy," in *Eye to Eye: The Quest for the New Paradigm* (Boston: Shambhala, 1996), 198–243.

25. Among a number of other books by Ken Wilber, see *Up From Eden: A Transpersonal View of Human Evolution* (Garden City, N.Y.: Anchor Press/Doubleday, 1981); Wilber, *Eye to Eye: The Quest for the New Paradigm;* Wilber, *Sex, Ecology, Spirituality: The Spirit of Evolution* (Boston: Shambhala, 1995).

26. Scott Bukatman, *Terminal Identity: The Virtual Subject in Postmodern Science Fiction* (Durham: Duke University Press, 1993), and Claudia Springer, *Electronic Eros: Bodies and Desire in the Postindustrial Age* (Austin: University of Texas Press, 1996).

27. The term "aperspectival" refers to people who no longer strongly identify with the perspective that they formerly took to be the Truth about self and world, and who knowingly adopt several different perspectives.

28. See his latest book, Ken Wilber, *The Marriage of the Senses and the Soul: Integrating Science and Religion* (New York: Random House, 1998).

29. "Highway Bridges" 168.

30. See for example, Brian Swimme and Thomas Berry, *The Universe Story: From the Primordial Flaring Forth to the Ecozoic Era—A Celebration of the Unfolding of the Cosmos* (San Francisco: HarperSanFrancisco, 1992).

31. My thanks to Charles Spinosa for his very helpful criticism that allowed me to improve this essay. Any shortcomings remain exclusively my responsibility, however.

Chapter 7: "The End of Metaphysics" and "A New Beginning"

1. Hubert L. Dreyfus, "Heidegger on the Connection Between Nihilism, Art, Technology, and Politics."

2. Martin Heidegger, "Überwindung der Metaphysik," in *Vorträge und Aufsätze* (Stuttgart: Günther Neske, 1954), 86. Subsequent citations are to the English translation, "Overcoming Metaphysics," in *The End of Philosophy,* trans. Joan Stambaugh (New York: Harper & Row, 1973).

Notes

3. "Overcoming Metaphysics," 93.

4. Martin Heidegger, *Nietzsche* vol. 3, trans. David Farrell Krell (San Francisco: HarperSanFrancisco, 1987), 137.

5. Friedrich Nietzsche, *Kritische Gesamtausgabe: Werke*, ed. Giorgio Colli and Mazzino Montinari, 30 vols. in 8 parts. (Berlin: Walter de Gruyter, 1967–78), III:3, 207. Henceforth cited as *KGW*.

6. *KGW*, VII:3, 386.

7. Ibid.

8. *Nietzsche* vol. 3, 176.

9. Ibid.

10. Ibid., 172.

11. Ibid., 170.

12. In *Nietzsche* vol. 3, 178–80.

13. Friedrich Nietzche, *The Will to Power*, trans. Walter Kaufman and R. J. Hollingdale (New York: Vintage Books, 1967), §491; henceforth cited as *WP*.

14. *Ibid.*, §489.

15. Friedrich Nietzsche, *On the Genealogy of Morals*, III, §12. Henceforth cited as *GM*. See also [translator's note: the author doesn't refer to a specific passage in which Heidegger discusses these passages. But see *Nietzsche* vol. 4, 137].

16. *GM*, III, §12.

17. *KGW*, VIII:3, 353, quoted at *Nietzsche* vol. 4, 129.

18. *WP*, §493.

19. *Nietzsche* vol. 4, 134.

20. *GS*, §179.

21. *Nietzsche*, vol. 3, 218.

22. *Neitzsche*, vol. 4, 148.

23. *Nietzsche*, vol. 3, 229.

24. Ibid., 205.

25. Ibid., 230.

26. Ibid., 233.

27. Ibid., 233.

28. "Overcoming Metaphysics," 101.

29. *Nietzsche*, vol. 3, 200. Between pages 197 and 200, the terms "quantum," "measure," "number," and "reckoning" are repeated a dozen times in reference to the will to power.

30. "Overcoming Metaphysics," 93.

31. Ibid., 105.

32. Ibid., 106.

33. Ibid., 107.

34. Ibid., 104.

35. Ibid., 106.

36. Ibid., 108.

37. Ibid., 108.

38. Heidegger, *Beiträge zur Philosophie (vom Ereignis)*, 183. Henceforth cited as *Beiträge*.

39. "Overcoming Metaphysics," 86.

40. Martin Heidegger, *Basic Questions of Philosophy: Selected "Problems" of "Logic"*, trans. Richard Rojcewicz and André Schuwer (Bloomington: Indiana University Press, 1994), 108. The texts of 1936–38 include the *Beiträge* (1936–38), and the *Basic Questions of Philosophy*, a course taught the winter semester of 1937/38.

41. For example, *Beiträge*, 229.

42. Ibid.

43. Martin Heidegger, "Question Concerning Technology," in *Basic Writings*, 330–331.

44. Martin Heidegger, "The Turning," in *The Question Concerning Technology* and *Other Essays*, trans. William Lovitt (New York: Harper & Row, 1977), 44.

45. *Beiträge*, 185.

46. Ibid., 187.

47. "The Eternal Recurrence of the Same and the Will to Power," in *Nietzsche* vol. 3, 182–183; "Nietzsche's Metaphysics," in *Nietzsche* vol. 3, 191. They are also found at the conclusion of "The Will to Power as Knowledge," *Nietzsche* vol. 3, 157.

48. Martin Heidegger, *Nietzsche: Der Wille zur Macht als Kunst*, GA 43 (Frankfurt: Klosterman, 1985), 277.

49. *WP*, "Preface," §2, 3.

50. *KGW*, V:2, 514 (emphasis in original).

Chapter 8: Nietzsche and the "Masters of Truth": The Pre-Socratics and Christ

1. Many commentators have studied this point: see Maudemarie Clark on the "problem of self-reference," *Nietzsche on Truth and Philosophy* (Cambridge: Cambridge University Press, 1990), 3, or Alexander Nehamas on the "paradox of interpretation," *Nietzsche: Life as Literature* (Cambridge: Harvard University Press, 1985), 66.

2. Cf. Heidegger, *Nietzsche*, vol. 3, chapters 19–21.

3. To mention a few: Walter Kaufmann, *Nietzsche: Philosopher, Psychologist, Antichrist*, 4th ed. (Princeton: Princeton University Press, 1974); Jean Granier, *Le problème de la vérité dans la philosophie de Nietzsche* (Paris: Editions du Seuil, 1966); or Arthur C. Danto, *Nietzsche As Philosopher* (New York: MacMillan, 1965).

4. One should note, however, that the question is more complex than it seems. Admittedly, the first text that Nietzsche explicitly devoted to truth is already strongly critical in that it stipulates that our truths are "illusions we have forgotten are illusions"—they are linguistic transpositions of reality born from the needs intrinsic to communication itself, and whose metaphoric character has been covered up by their repeated use. Friedrich Nietzsche, "On Truth and Lie in a Nonmoral Sense," in *Philosophy and Truth: Selections from Nietzsche's Notebooks of the Early 1870's*, trans. Daniel Breazeale (Atlantic Highlands, N.J.: Humanities Press, 1979), 84. Yet as shown by Maudemarie Clark, the early Nietzsche's attacks against language-borne truth remain metaphysical: the metaphorical character that condemns our truths to falsity stems from the impossibility for language to be a faithful reflection of the In-itself. Thus, "we believe we know something about the things themselves when we speak of trees, colors, snow, and flowers; and yet we possess nothing but metaphors for things— *metaphors which correspond in no way to the original entities*," ibid. 82–83 (emphasis supplied). Therefore, Nietzsche's early claims about truth implicitly rest upon the (Kantian) infra-structure of Schopenhauer's *World as Will and Representation*, which presupposes both a noumenal essence for phenomena (the "things themselves," their "original essence") and an adequationist conception of truth (the reason why linguistic metaphors are false is that they do not "correspond" to the things in themselves). Although he recognizes the impossibility of any correspondence with the noumenal, the young Nietzsche remains enough of a metaphysician to deplore its lack.

5. Friedrich Nietzche, *Gay Science*, §54, 116; henceforth cited as *GS*.

6. The relationship between truth, schematization and falsification of reality is one of the major contributions of Heidegger's analysis of Nietzsche. See *Nietzsche* vol. 3, chapter 11. About the Nietzschean critique of categories, see Michel Haar, Nietsche and metaphysics, trans. Michael Gendre (Albany: SUNY Press, 1996), especially chap. 1.

7. Friedrich Nietzche, §487, 269; henceforth cited as *WP*.

8. Thus, truth is defined as "the kind of *error* without which a certain species of life could not live," ibid., §493, 272 (emphasis supplied). This statement in itself presupposes that efficiency cannot be the determining criterion for thinking truth. About the criticism of the so-called Nietzschean pragmatism, see Alexander Nehamas, *Nietzsche: Life as Literature* (Cambridge: Harvard University Press, 1985), 52–55; Maudemarie Clark, *Nietzsche on Truth and Philosophy*, 12–13, 31; John T. Wilcox, *Truth and Value in Nietzsche: A Study of his Metaphysics and Epistemology* (Ann Arbor: University of Michigan Press, 1974); and especially Wilcox, "Nietzsche Scholarship and 'The Correspondence Theory of Truth': The Danto Case," *Nietzsche-Studien* 15 (1986): 337–357.

9. Richard Rorty, *Consequences of Pragmatism: Essays, 1972–1980* (Minneapolis: University of Minnesota, 1982).

10. See Michel Haar, chapter 3, in *Nietzsche and Metaphysics*.

11. *Human, All Too Human: A Book for Free Spirits*, trans. R. J. Hollingdale (Cambridge: Cambridge University Press, 1986), §261, 123. Henceforth cited as *HH*.

12. Marcel Détienne, *Les Maîtres de vérité dans la Grèce archaïque* (Paris: Pocket, 1994). All subsequent translations are mine.

13. *Early Greek Philosophy*, quoted in Leslie P. Thiele, *Nietzsche and the Politics of the Soul: A Study of Heroic Individualism* (Princeton: Princeton University Press, 1990), 25.

14. *Gesammelte Werke* vol. 16, 245 (emphasis supplied).

15. *Early Greek Philosophy*, no. 8, 66; *KGW*, III:2.

16. *Early Greek Philosophy*, later preface (1879), 79 (emphasis supplied); *KGW* III:2, 298.

17. Ibid.

18. On this question, see Tracy B. Strong's excellent analyses *Friedrich Nietzsche and the Politics of Transfiguration* (Berkeley: University of California, 1975), particularly chapter 6.

19. Friedrich Nietzche, *Beyond Good and Evil*, trans. Walter Kaufmann (New York: Vintage Books, 1989) section 6, §202. Henceforth cited as *BGE*.

20. Arthur Rimbaud, "Lettre du Voyant," in *Complete Works*, 304, ed. Wallace Fowlie (Chicago: University of Chicago Press, 1966).

21. Ibid. (emphasis supplied).

22. Cf. Sarah Kofman, *Nietzsche and Metaphor* (Stanford: Stanford University Press, 1993).

23. Friedrich Schlegel, *Philosophical Fragments*, trans. Peter Firchow (Minneapolis: University of Minnesota Press, 1991) §242, 51.

24. *KGW*, VIII:3, 370 (emphasis supplied).

25. *HH*, §262, 125. The theme of "severity" is recurrent in *BGE*, in which Nietzsche, closes the circle of Western history by describing the "philosophers of the future" as "severe spirits." See §210.

26. *HH*, §261, 123.

27. Ibid.

28. *Les Maîtres de vérité dans la Grèce archaïque*, 7.

29. Ibid., 41.

30. Ibid., nouvelle préface, 6 (emphasis supplied).

31. Ibid., 66 (emphasis supplied).

32. Such as an alibi, for example.

33. *Les Maîtres de vérité dans la Grèce archaïque*, 6. According to the same logic, the Seer's truth cannot be tested against reality because it *shapes* it. By predicting the future, the seer transforms it (cf. Sophocles, *Oedipus at Colonnus*).

34. Ibid., 132 (emphasis supplied).

35. Jacques Derrida, *Spurs: Nietzsche's Styles* (Chicago: University of Chicago Press, 1979). See Friedrich Nietzsche, *Twilight of the Idols: Or, How to Philosophize with the Hammer*, trans. Richard Polt (Indianapolis: Hackett, 1997), "History of an Error," §2, 23 (hereafter: *TI*).

36. See for example *BGE*, §239.

37. *Les Maîtres de vérité dans la Grèce archaïque*, 194.

38. Friedrich Nietzsche, *The Birth of Tragedy* (with *The Case of Wagner*), trans. Walter Kaufmann (New York: Vintage, 1966), chapter 15.

39. Gilles Deleuze, *Nietzsche et la philosophie* (Paris: Presses Universitaires de France, 1962), 183–189.

40. *Les Maîtres de vérité dans la Grèce archaïque*, 69.

41. Cf. *HH*, §261, 123: "With the Greeks everything goes quickly forwards, but it likewise goes quickly downwards; the movement of the whole machine is so accelerated that a single stone thrown into its wheels makes it fly to pieces. Socrates, for example, was such a stone."

42. In fact, this is a reversed form of Hegelianism: in the *Aesthetics*, the beauty of the Greek God's statue was construed by Hegel as the plastic expression of the harmony between spirit and matter (itself symbolized by the uninterrupted line of the God's nose, that link (ed.) his brow [spirit] to his lower face [matter]. According to a similar reasoning, Socrates' ugliness appears as a testimony to the fundamental disharmony that governs him.

43. *WP*, §433, 237: "to make a tyrant of shrewdness:—but for that the drives must be tyrants."

44. It is worth mentioning that Détienne too sees in the birth of Greek democracy the major cause of the decline of the magisterial understanding of truth. Thus, "The hoplitic reform signifies the end of the warrior as a particular individual, and the extension of his privileges to the citizen" (*Les Maîtres de vérité dans la Grèce archaïque*, 132): the disappearance of the Homeric hero's aura is accompanied by the apparition of a "common space" (*meson*) in which the right to speak and the goods are shared. The "*es meson*" speech is related to the interest of the group, and must be addressed to all the members of the assembly (ibid., 143). It is mostly a "dialogue-speech, mostly egalitarian" (ibid., 145), which "is mostly grounded in the social group's agreement, itself manifested by approbation or disapprobation" (ibid., 146).

45. *WP*, §166, 100.

46. Friedrich Nietzsche, *The Antichrist*, in *The Portable Nietzsche*, trans. Walter Kaufmann (New York: Penguin Books, 1968), §33, 607. Henceforth cited as *AC*.

47. Christ is said to be a "naïve" and a "great symbolist." See *AC*, §34. On this point, see Michel Haar, *Par-dela le nihilisme: Nouveaux essais sur Nietzsche* (Paris: Presses Universitares de France, 1998), chapter 1: "Decadence et nihilisme."

48. Friedrich Nietzsche, *Daybreak: Thoughts on the Prejudices of Morality*, trans. R. J. Hollingdale (Cambridge: Cambridge University Press, 1982) §68, 40. Henceforth cited as *DB*.

49. *WP*, §150, 95.

50. See *WP*, §167, 101: "He understood what the pagan world *had the greatest need of*" (emphasis supplied). See also *GS*, §139, 189: "People like St. Paul have an evil eye for the passions . . . hence their idealistic tendency aims at the annihilation of the passions, and they find perfect purity in the divine. Very differently from St. Paul and the Jews, the Greeks directed their idealistic tendency precisely toward the passions and loved, elevated, gilded, and deified them."

51. Cf. *AC*, §40. The "History of an Error," in *TI*, indicates clearly the link between Plato's invention of the intelligible world and the way it was taken up (under a moralizing form) by Christianity.

52. *WP*, §169, 101. Nietzsche gives the following examples: "a god who died for our sins: redemption through faith; resurrection after death."

53. Cf. the invention by Roman Law of the notion of the juridical person as opposed to that of the individual.

54. *BGE*, 6, §207, 122–123. One will recognize in this vocabulary Paul's "counterfeits."

55. Friedrich Nietzsche, *Ecce Homo*, trans. Walter Kaufmann (New York: Vintage Books, 1967) preface, §3, 218. Henceforth cited as *EH*.

56. Quoted in Thiele, *Nietzsche and the Politics of the Soul: A Study of Heroic Individualism*, 131.

57. *HH*, §221, 155. The rest of the passage, however, shows the same optimism as in the last chapters of the *Birth of Tragedy* in that it concludes on the possibility of a renewal of the Golden Age: "The sorrow he feels was widely compensated by the joy from knowing that they had been realized in the past and that we can still partake of this achievement." Yet Nietzsche will give up this hope later on, along with the faith in a renewal of Dionysus through Wagner's opera.

58. Which is also the meaning given by Foucault to the expression in Michel Foucault, *The Use of Pleasure: The History of Sexuality, Volume 2*, trans. Robert Hurley (New York: Vintage, 1985).

59. Nehamas, *Nietzsche: Life as Literature*, chapter 1.

60. Thiele, *Nietzsche and the Politics of the Soul.*

61. Which is also a point in common with Ted Sadler's interpretation, for whom Nietzsche has a "heroic" conception of writing. Cf. *Nietzsche: Truth and Redemption Critique of the Postmodern Nietzsche* (London: Athlone Press, 1995).

Chapter 9: What Is Dwelling? The Homelessness of Modernity and the Worlding of the World

1. Martin Heidegger, "Building Dwelling Thinking," *Poetry, Language, Thought*, 143–162. *Poetry, Language, Thought* henceforth cited as *PLT*. This translation is at times seriously unreliable and I have made frequent emendations.

2. Heidegger identifies 1930 as the year of the "the turn." "Letter on Humanism," in *Basic Writings*, 231; *Basic Writings* henceforth cited as *BW*. But in the La Thor seminar of 1969, he identifies a further turn as having occurred during the period of the *Beiträge zur Philosophie*, 1936–38, the transition from pre-"*Ereignis*" thinking to "*Ereignis*" thinking. Hence, in his final taxonomy, his "path of thinking" has three stages to it. Martin Heidegger, *Seminare*, GA 15, ed. F. W. von Herrmann (Frankfurt am Main: Klostermann, 1986), 344, 366. By "early Heidegger" I thus refer to Heidegger before 1930 and by "late Heidegger" Heidegger after 1936. The Heidegger from 1930 to 1936 I shall variously call "earlier" "later" or "middle" Heidegger, as the occasion warrants.

3. Martin Heidegger, ". . . Poetically Man Dwells . . ." in *PLT*, 211–229.

4. The translation of the untranslatable "*heimisch*" as "homely" I take over from William McNeill and Julia Davis's translation of Martin Heidegger, *Hölderlin's Hymn "The Ister"* (Bloomington: Indiana University Press, 1996). Though initially unpromising-looking it is necessitated by the need to distinguish between being "*heimisch*" and being "*zuhause*" (at-home) and has the advantage of reflecting the structure of the German word.

5. Martin Heidegger, *Denkerfahrungen 1910–1976* (Frankfurt am Main: Klostermann, 1983), 187; henceforth cited as *Denkerfahrungen.*

6. *Being and Time.* References are to the pagination of the 7th German edition of *Sein und Zeit* given by Macquarrie and Robinson in the margins.

7. At a column-and-a-half in Macquarrie and Robinson's splendid index it receives more space than any other entry—more than "being," "time," "Dasein," and (just) more than "authentic."

8. Notice how this list, just by itself, constitutes a kind of (very) short story, a story with an unmistakable plot and tone.

9. Though the term "clearing" appears in *Being and Time*, late Heidegger emphasizes that its character was not properly thought out until the late period. *Holzwege, GA* 5, ed. F. W. von Herrmann (Frankfurt am Main: Klostermann, 1977), 1 fn. a.

10. *Hölderlin's Hymn "The Ister,"* 20.

11. In the omitted part of this passage Heidegger indicates that *Schonen*, care and protection, is reciprocal. The homeland is experienced as caring for and protecting the dweller who, in return, cares for and protects, conserves, it. For further expositions of this theme, see *PLT*, 140; Martin Heidegger, *Die Grundbegriffe der Metaphysick: Welt-Endlichkeit-Einsamkeit, GA* 29/30, ed. F. W. von Herrmann (Frankfurt am Main: Klostermann, 1983), 86–88; Martin Heidegger, *Erläuterungen zu Hölderlins Dichtung, GA* 4, ed. F. W. von Herrmann (Frankfurt am Main: Klostermann, 1981), 120, 124.

12. Martin Heidegger, *Identität und Differenz* (Pfullingen am Main: Neske, 1957), 28; henceforth cited as *ID*. See also *PLT*, 151.

13. *GA* 15, 363.

14. Ibid.

15. *PLT*, 124. Two points. (1) Late Heidegger's understanding of being and nothingness—being *as* nothingness—is, I believe, no more than a proper thinking out of the account of truth as "disclosure" first presented in section 44 of *Being and Time*. So in a sense late Heidegger is present in early Heidegger. In my view, however, much of *Being and Time* is inconsistent with section 44. Late Heidegger makes this point by saying, as already observed, that though the concept of truth as "the clearing" is present in his early works, its nature is "still withheld" until his late period. *GA* 5, 1 fn. a. (2) In my view the nothing is still understood as an absolute nothing in the 1929 "What is Metaphysics?" in *BW*, 89–110. One way of thinking of "the turn" which Heidegger identifies as beginning with the 1930 "On the Essence of Truth," in *BW*, 111–138, is to think of it as the beginning of his reassessment of the character of the nothing.

16. Martin Heidegger, *Hölderlins Hymnen "Germanien" und "Der Rhein", Gesamtausgabe* vol. 39, ed. F. W. von Herrmann (Frankfurt am Main: Klostermann, 1980), 86–88; *GA* 4, 102, 174.

17. One might be tempted, here, by the thought that late Heidegger's own account of truth as disclosure which is simultaneously concealment is itself, in this sense, "metaphysics." But this would be a mistake. Though Heidegger affirms something to be—absolutely—true, it seeks to absolutize no horizon *of beings*, in fact denies the possibility of such absolutizing.

18. The quotation is from a poem which begins "In lovely blueness." That the poem is authentic Hölderlin has been challenged by some scholars, a challenge Heidegger rejects in "Das Wohnen des Menschen," in *Denkerfahrungen*, 153–160.

19. Surely late Heidegger's "earth" which "rise[s] up into plant and animal" (*PLT*, 149).

20. Martin Heidegger, *Hölderlins Hymne "Andendken"*, *Gesamtausgabe* vol. 52, ed. F. W. von Herrmann (Frankfurt am Main: Klostermann, 1982), 15.

21. *GA* 4, 60; *GA* 52, 193; *Hölderlin's Hymn "The Ister,"* 138.

22. Martin Heidegger, *The Question Concerning Technology and Other Essays*, 49; henceforth cited as *QCT*. See also *PLT*, 150.

23. Much of the time Heidegger prefers to talk of "the divinities (*die Göttlichen*)" rather than "the gods (*die Götter*)." The distinction should not, however, be overstressed, since the preference is by no means universal or systematic. Insofar as there is a point to the preference—apparent, for example, in the well-known statements of the fourfold—the point, I think, is to move us away from thinking of Heidegger's gods as needing to be identified with the gods of some familiar religion or theology. It is a serious mistake to suppose that Heidegger's talk of the "return of the gods" has anything to do with the return of organized religion.

24. *GA* 4, 20. Notice that angels (Rilke's (*PLT*, 134–135) or Wim Wender's) are almost always bearers of tidings rather than possessors of power. Angels do not, cannot, perform miracles. We should thus expect the same to be true of Heidegger's gods—compare the previous footnote.

25. Martin Heidegger, "Hölderlin and the Essence of Poetry," in *Existence and Being*, ed. Werner Brock (London: Vision Press, 1968), 288; henceforth cited as HE.

26. *Hölderlin's Hymn "The Ister,"* 116.

27. Ibid.

28. The nonexistent cannot be "absent."

29. This post-enlightenment understanding of the character of ethical authority is, of course, *dangerous*. It is what led Heidegger, for a time, to think of Hitler as a new god and is why, having recovered himself, he warns against the worship of "idols" and manufactured gods (*PLT*, 150)—the power of Hitler's charisma being the product of his, and Goebbel's, pioneering understanding of the manipulative use of the mass media. The ethical task is, then, to distinguish between the "holy sway" and false glamour. It would be nice, perhaps, if there were, as Kant dreamt, rules, algorithms, for doing this. But, such is life, there are not. As the Greeks understood and Heidegger emphasizes in the *Ister* lectures, life is essentially a *Wagnis*, a risk, in which illusion—"dissembling" (*PLT*, 54)—constantly threatens to conceal truth.

30. Jeff Malpas, *Place and Experience: Philosophical Topography* (Cambridge: Cambridge University Press, 1999).

Chapter 10: Uncovering the Space of Disclosedness: Heidegger, Technology, and the Problem of Spatiality in *Being and Time*

1. Heidegger, "The Thing," in *Poetry, Language, Thought*, 165.

2. See Ken Goldberg, ed., *The Robot in the Garden: Telerobotics and Telepistemology on the Internet* (Cambridge: MIT Press, 2000).

3. See "The Thing"; see also Martin Heidegger, "The Question Concerning Technology," in *The Question Concerning Technology and Other Essays*, 3–35.

4. On the concept of *Bestand* (and also the concept implied by talk of "en-framing"— namely *Gestell*) see especially "The Question Concerning Technology."

5. "The Question Concerning Technology," 27.

6. See Martin Heidegger, *Being and Time*, H54.

7. "The Thing," 182.

8. See Martin Heidegger, "Building Dwelling Thinking," in *Poetry, Language, Thought*, 151ff. Only in the nearness of things—in their being disclosed in this way—do things appear as either close or far away (see "The Thing," 177–178).

9. Although the argument in these pages is developed with particular reference to Heidegger, the ideas at issue are also presented, in much more detail and in a way that is more directly tied up with the understanding of place, in my *Place and Experience*.

10. Heidegger himself notes the spatial connotations associated with terms such as "Situation" (see *Being and Time*, H299) and "environment" (*"Umwelt"*—see *Being and Time*, H66).

11. Hubert L. Dreyfus, *Being-in-the-World*, 129.

12. *Being and Time*, H54.

13. Ibid.

14. *Being-in-the-World*, 43.

15. See for instance, Descartes's discussion in the *Principles of Philosophy*, in *The Philosophical Writings of Descartes*, vol. I, trans. John Cottingham, Robert Stoothoff, and Dugald Murdoch (Cambridge: Cambridge University Press, 1985), 227. For an introduction to some of the history of space and place that is at issue here see Edward S. Casey, "Smooth Spaces and Rough-Edged Places: The Hidden History of Place," *Review of Metaphysics* 51 (1997), 267–296.

16. See Albert Einstein, Foreword to Max Jammer, *Concepts of Space*, 2nd ed., (Cambridge: Harvard University Press, 1970), xiii.

17. *Being and Time*, H54.

18. On this point, see also the discussion in Martin Heidegger, *What is a Thing?* trans. W. B. Barton Jr. and Vera Deutsch (Chicago: Henry Regnery, 1968), 98–106.

19. *Being and Time*, H55. See below, 216–217, for more on this issue in relation to the idea of containment.

20. *Being and Time*, H54. Notice the way in which corporeality is, in this passage, deemphasized.

21. Ibid., H66.

22. *Being and Time*, H367–369.

23. In "Spatiality, Temporality, and the Problem of Foundation in *Being and Time*" (*Philosophy Today* 40 [1996], 36–46), Yoko Arisaka claims that the discussion in §70 does not in fact address the question of derivation, but of "foundation." I must admit to finding this distinction obscure.

24. Indeed, Heidegger never completely abandons the idea that a certain sort of priority is to be accorded to temporality—see especially "Time and Being," in *On Time and Being*, trans. Joan Stambaugh (New York: HarperTorch book, 1972), 1–24.

25. See *What is a Thing?* 16 and "On Time and Being," 23.

26. The argument for this claim is set out in detail in my *Place and Experience* .

27. As Edward Casey notes in *The Fate of Place* (Berkeley: University of California Press, 1997), 245.

28. *Physics* IV, 212a36 in *Aristotle's Physics Books III and IV*, trans. Edward Hussey (Oxford: Clarendon Press, 1983); see also 212a20.

29. See "The Thing," 166ff.

30. See Einstein's comments in Jammer, *Concepts of Space*, xv, and also in "The Problem of Space, Ether and the Field in Physics," in Albert Einstein, *Ideas and Opinions*, trans. Sonja Bargmann (New York: Crown, 1954), 276–285.

31. See, once again, the discussion in *Place and Experience* 26–31.

32. *Being-in-the-World*, 129.

33. Ibid. 132. Yoko Arisaka takes issue with Dreyfus's reading of Heidegger's account of spatiality in "Heidegger's Theory of Space: A Critique of Dreyfus" (*Inquiry* 38 [1995], 455–467). One of Arisaka's main criticisms is that Dreyfus's emphasis on the necessarily public character of existential spatiality turns existential spatiality into something indistinguishable from the levelled-out spatiality associated with merely occurrent entities ("world-space"). That spatiality does indeed have to be understood as a public structure derives from the nature of the spatial and the public as such; and while there is an important sense in which the "objective space" of occurrent entities can be derived from equipmental space by means of the public

character of that space (see my "Space and Sociality," *International Journal of Philosophical Studies* 5 [1997], 53–79, for a discussion of some of the issues that arise here in a more general context), this does not mean that the two are thereby simply collapsed. The public space of equipmentality remains a space ordered by places and regions in a way that the space of the merely occurrent is not. Unfortunately Arisaka's account offers little in the way of an illumination of the issues at stake here. She emphasizes that "the key to understanding Heidegger's theory of space is his attempt to redescribe spatial experience without presupposing objective space" ("Heidegger's Theory of Space," 464), but this provides only a preliminary description of what is really at issue here. Unfortunately Arisaka does not offer much more than this, essentially using the discussion of spatiality as a means to advance Frederick Olafson's existential reading of *Being and Time* against that of Dreyfus.

34. See *Being-in-the-World*, 131–136.

35. The connection between the spatial and the public is one that I explore further in my "Space and Sociality"—there I argue for the necessarily spatial character of our being-with-others.

36. See Dreyfus's discussion in *Being-in-the-World*, 137 and also my *Place and Experience*, 109ff.

37. See *Being and Time*, §70, H368; the discussion of *res cogitans* versus *res corporea* at §19, H89–92; and the passage from §12, H54 quoted above.

38. In this respect, I take disclosedness to be less a matter of what Albert Borgmann calls "focal practices" (see his *Crossing the Postmodern Divide*) as of a focus brought about through relatedness to *things* and locatedness in *place*—although this should not obscure important points of continuity between my account and Borgmann's.

39. "Seminar in Le Thor 1969," in *Seminare*, *Gesamtausgabe* 15 (Frankfurt: Klostermann, 1986), 344.

40. In this respect *Being and Time* remains a thoroughly "metaphysical" project. Such metaphysicality is, however, notably absent from Heidegger's later thinking.

41. For more on the methodological issues at stake here, and also the focus on place, see *Place and Experience*, especially 31–43.

42. On the concept of "topology" in Heidegger see Otto Poeggeller, "Heidegger's Topology of Being," in Joseph J. Kockelmans, ed., *On Heidegger and Language* (Evanston: Northwestern University Press, 1972), 107–146 and also *Martin Heidegger's Path of Thinking*, trans. Daniel Magurshak and Sigmund Barber (Atlantic Highlands, N.J.: Humanities Press, 1987), 232–238.

43. See "Building Dwelling Thinking" and "The Thing."

44. The connection, via "*stellen*," between "*Vorstellen*" and "*Gestell*" should not be overlooked here. See also "The Age of the World Picture," in *The Question Concerning Technology*, 115–154, for more on the idea of "representation."

45. On the nature of mortality as tied to "locatedness" and to place see my "Death and the Unity of a Life," in Jeff Malpas and Robert C. Solomon, eds., *Death and Philosophy,* (London: Routledge, 1998), 120–134; and also *Place and Experience,* 190–193.

46. See my discussion in "Acting at a Distance and Knowing from Afar: Agency and Knowledge in the World of Telerobotics," in Goldberg, ed., *The Robot in the Garden: Telerobotics and Telepistemology on the Internet* (Cambridge, Mass.: MIT Press, 2000).

47. "The Turning," in *The Question Concerning Technology,* 39.

Chapter 11: The Primacy of Practice and Assertoric Truth: Dewey and Heidegger

1. All references to *Being and Time* are to *SZ,* 15th ed. (Tübingen: Max Niemayer Verlag, 1979).

2. Richard Rorty, "Heidegger, Contingency, and Pragmatism," in *Essays on Heidegger and Others.* Philosophical Papers, vol. 2 (Cambridge: Cambridge University Press, 1991), 33.

3. Ibid., 32.

4. Rorty officially identifies "de-intellectualizing" understanding with the claim that "beliefs and desires must be ascribed together," which he quotes from Okrent, who is interpreting Heidegger's notion of understanding. *Essays on Heidegger and Others,* 32. See Mark Okrent, *Heidegger's Pragmatism* (Ithaca: Cornell University Press, 1988), 64. But this is puzzling, for there is hardly a philosopher today who does not agree with that much!

5. My use of Rorty is more as a prop than as an interlocutor, for he rejects the pragmatist theory of truth, or at least, the version of it that I shall attribute to Dewey. See Richard Rorty, "Pragmatism, Davidson and Truth," in *Objectivity, Relativism, and Truth.* Philosophical Papers, vol. 1 (Cambridge: Cambridge University Press, 1991), 126–150. For this reason, my arguments to follow are not a commentary on Rorty's own philosophical position.

6. John Dewey, "Does Reality Possess Practical Character?" in *The Middle Works, 1899–1924,* vol. 4, ed. Jo Ann Boydston (Carbondale: Southern Illinois University Press, 1977), 125–142, henceforth cited as *RPPC.*

7. John Dewey, "The Reflex Arc Concept in Psychology," in *The Early Works, 1882–1898,* vol. 5, ed. Jo Ann Boydston (Carbondale: Southern Illinois University Press, 1972), 96–109, henceforth cited as *RA.*

8. In the antiquated sense of the term, "common sense," rather than in its contemporary sense, "courage" or even "chutzpah."

9. Hubert L. Dreyfus is the foremost exponent of this way of reading Heidegger. Among others who approach Heidegger by way of the primacy of practice, one should mention Carl Friedrich Gethmann, *Dasein: Erkennen und Handeln. Heidegger im phänomenologischen Kontext* (Berlin: Walter de Gruyter, 1993), 137–168; Charles B.

Guignon, *Heidegger and the Problem of Knowledge* (Indianapolis: Hackett Publishing Co., 1983); John Haugeland, "Heidegger on Being a Person," *Noûs* 16 (1982): 15–26, and "Dasein's Disclosedness," in *Heidegger: A Critical Reader*, ed. Hubert L. Dreyfus and Harrison Hall (Oxford: B. Blackwell, 1992), 27–44; Mark Okrent, *Heidegger's Pragmatism*; Rorty *Essays on Heidegger and Others*; Richard Schmitt, *Martin Heidegger on Being Human* (New York: Random House, 1969); and Charles Taylor, "Engaged Agency and Background in Heidegger," *The Cambridge Companion to Heidegger*, ed. Charles B. Guignon (Cambridge: Cambridge University Press, 1993), 317–336, many of whom, like me, have been directly influenced by Dreyfus. Recently Dreyfus's practice-oriented approach to Heidegger has come under critical scrutiny from Carleton B. Christensen, "Heidegger's Representationalism," *Review of Metaphysics*, 51 (1997): 77–103; and "Getting Heidegger Off the West Coast," *Inquiry* 41 (1998): 65–87. Christensen's criticisms deserve a detailed response, which I hope to be able to offer on another occasion.

10. All translations of *Being and Time* are my own, although of course I have relied heavily on Macquarrie and Robinson's English translation: *Being and Time*.

11. An existentiale is an essential feature of human being.

12. Heidegger's term for human beings, "the entity each of us in each case is" (*SZ*, 41).

13. Or a "break [*Bruch*] in the referential connections that are uncovered in circumspection" (*SZ*, 75). By "reference" (*Verweisung*) Heidegger means the way in which our environment hangs together for precognitive practice (circumspection, *Umsicht*). Reference is a practical, means-ends relation, in which one thing or status is appropriately used in some activity.

14. Here I borrow a common term from contemporary literature. The term has, of course, many uses; I restrict my use to that stated in the text.

15. This is also the most plausible near relative to the performative theory of the truth predicate propounded by P. F. Strawson, "Truth," *Analysis* 9 (1949): 83–97.

16. In a more comprehensive context, in which one sets out comparatively to evaluate the early Heidegger and pragmatism in all its forms, one would want to look into the deflationary theme and how it relates to the primacy of practice. I hope to do this in future work.

17. Robert B. Brandom, "Pragmatism, Phenomenalism, and Truth Talk," in *Midwest Studies in Philosophy* 12 (Minneapolis: University of Minnesota, 1987), 75–93.

18. Robert B. Brandom, *Making It Explicit: Reasoning, Representing, and Discursive Commitment* (Cambridge: Harvard University Press, 1994).

19. John Dewey, "What Pragmatism Means by Practical," in *The Middle Works, 1899–1924*, vol. 4, ed. Jo Ann Boydston (Carbondale: Southern Illinois University Press, 1977), 98–115, henceforth cited as WPMP.

20. This idea is attributed originally to Alexander Bain. See Fisch's "Introduction," in *Writings of Charles S. Peirce: A Chronological Edition*, Vol. 1, ed. Max H. Fisch (Bloom-

ington: Indiana University Press, 1982–1993), xxxi; as well as Karl-Otto Apel, *Der Denkweg von Charles S. Peirce* (Frankfurt am Main: Suhrkamp, 1975). James takes this over from Peirce and endorses it in *Pragmatism: A New Name for Some Old Ways of Thinking*, ed. Fredson Bowers, reprinted in *The Works of William James* (Cambridge: Harvard University Press, 1975), 28–29; see Charles S. Pierce, "How to Make our Ideas Clear," in *Writings of Charles S. Peirce: A Chronological Edition*, vol. 3, ed. Christian J. W. Kloesel (Bloomington: Indiana University Press, 1986), 263. Ideas are plans of action, and one's belief in the idea is "measured" by one's willingness to act on that plan. William James, *The Principles of Psychology*, authorized ed., vol. 2 (1890; reprint, New York: Dover, 1950), 283; Charles S. Peirce, "The Fixation of Belief," in *Writings of Charles S. Peirce: A Chronological Edition*, vol. 3, 242–257. Although Dewey's understanding of ideas and their meaning derives historically from these sources, he provides an explicit foundation for it in his biologism.

21. John R. Searle, *Intentionality: An Essay in the Philosophy of Mind* (Cambridge: Cambridge University Press, 1983), 7f.

22. Michael Clark has argued that the truth-predicate has no direction of fit. "Truth and Success: Searle's Attack on Minimalism," *Analysis* 57 (1997): 205–209. Direction of fit is a concept that applies to illocutionary forces, such as asserting and ordering (as well as to their mental counterparts, such as believing and intending), whereas truth applies to propositional content. If I assert (or believe) that Jones is opening the door, the propositional content of my assertion is true if and only if Jones is in fact opening the door. The assertion *qua* assertion has word-to-world direction of fit. But if I order Jones to open the door, then the order *qua* order has world-to-word direction of fit. The propositional content of the order, however, is identical with that of the assertion, and it has the same truth-conditions. So, Clark argues that although illocutionary force determines direction of fit, whether there is fit at all is determined by a correspondence between propositional content and the facts. This objection to the manner in which I motivate Dewey's position can be overcome by the discussion below of Gethmann's interpretation of Heidegger. For there we see that the relation between a problem and a solution, which is the relation that explains truth for Dewey and the operationalists, is not a form of identity or matching. And even on Clark's pared down approach to the truth predicate, the core of the relation between content and fact is one of correspondence, matching, or identity.

23. John Dewey, "Propositions, Warranted Assertibility, and Truth," in *Later Works, 1925–1953*, vol. 14, ed. Jo Ann Boydston (Carbondale: Southern Illinois University Press, 1981), 168–188, henceforth cited as *PWAT*.

24. Dewey is no doubt motivated here by residual elements of the analytic enterprise of defining the meaning of the ordinary predicate "is true." His cooptation of "correspondence" arises in the context of the defense of his methodology against the criticisms leveled by Russell to the effect that Dewey had not properly *defined* or *analyzed* truth as warranted assertibility, but rather, *substituted* warranted assertibility for truth. Dewey had left himself open to such a criticism in his earlier work, where he confusingly mixed analytic and ontological arguments for his pragmatic theory of truth, for instance in his 1906 "Experimental Theory of Knowledge" in *The Middle Works, 1899–1924*, vol. 3, ed. Jo Ann Boydston (Carbondale: Southern Illinois University Press, 1977), 107–127, henceforth cited as *ETK*. By his *Logic* however, he has become clear that he is offering a revisionary (because clarificatory) definition of "truth." *Logic: The Theory of Inquiry*, in *The Later Works, 1924–1953*, vol. 12, ed. Jo Ann Boydston (Carbondale: Southern Illinois University Press, 1986), henceforth cited as *Logic*.

It is uncharitable at best, a distortion at worst, to characterize this as "substitution," as if Dewey were guilty of a bait-and-switch.

25. Tom Burke, *Dewey's New Logic* (Chicago: University of Chicago Press, 1994).

26. *Logic.* See note 24.

27. Okrent, *Heidegger's Pragmatism*, chatper 4; Carl Friedrich Gethmann, *Dasein: Erkennen und Handeln.*

28. Because the distinction between meaning in the cognitive-representational sense and intention in the action-theoretic sense is so important to this discussion, I shall translate the Husserlian and Heideggerian term "*meinen*" and its derivatives by the English cognate "to mean" and its derivatives. The standard translation as "to intend" can cause confusion, when the distinction is as important as it is here.

29. With this expression "the entity shows itself in itself" Heidegger does not intend to refer to any Kantian realm of noumena. Rather, throughout *Being and Time* "in itself" contrasts with "in disguise." Here he means only to exclude the case in which something shows itself "in disguise" or "in semblance," that is, as it is not.

30. Assertions do not just point entities out, they also "determine" them as thus and so. Note, however, that Heidegger's conception here appears to be guided by the traditional, but misleading, fixation on predication as the only or paradigmatic form of assertion, a fixation that makes it hard, indeed sometimes impossible, to do justice to other forms of assertion, such as conditionals and disjunctions. To develop and defend Heidegger's account here, we would need to introduce serious reforms into his official presentation.

31. Our grip on the hammer referred to by "The hammer is too heavy," is plausibly initially provided for us by our practical engagement with the everyday world. But what are we to say about mathematical assertions and the assertions of highly theoretical physics? To answer this question, we would have to turn to Heidegger's "existential conception of science" (§ 69b). There he argues that all sciences are grounded in an existential, practical grasp on a domain of scientific activity and objects. See Joseph Rouse, *Knowledge and Power: Toward a Political Philosophy of Life* (Ithaca: Cornell University Press, 1987); Dreyfus, *Being-in-the-World*; Carl Friedrich Gethmann, "Der existenziale Begriff der Wissenschaft," *Lebenswelt und Wissenschaft: Studien zum Verhaltnis von Phanomenologie und Wissenschaftstheorie*, ed. Carl Friedrich Gethmann (Bonn: Bouvier Verlag, 1991), 181–208; William D. Blattner, "Decontextualization, Standardization, and Deweyan Science," *Man and World* 28 (1995): 321–339.

32. It is important to insist that an assertion can point an object out without revealing it to us either cognitively *or practically*, for a central element of Okrent's account is that the revelation in question may be a practical, precognitive one. He views Heidegger as having extended traditional verificationism (of the sort found in Husserl, for example) to include precognitive, practical evidence. My point is that even *given* this extension, Heidegger is still not properly viewed as a verificationist.

33. Heidegger here formulates his theory of assertoric truth in a manner directly modeled on Husserl's, as Heidegger indicates in a note to *SZ* page 218.

34. Martin Heidegger, "Vom Wesen der Wahrheit," in *Wegmarken, Gesamtansgabe* 9 (Frankfurt: Klostermann, 1976), especially §1.

35. Of course, the fore-having and fore-sight are two of the technical elements of the "fore-structure" of interpretation presented in *SZ*, 32. The third element is the fore-grasp (*Vorgriff*), which is also mentioned in this paragraph from pages 156–157.

36. Mark Okrent, *Heidegger's Pragmatism*, 98–99. Of course, one might wonder what sort of ontological status ought to be ascribed to the entity *as meant*, in contrast with the entity as it is. Heidegger does not directly confront this worry. And if he cannot answer it, then we have found a fatal objection to his account of assertion. The closest we get to an answer is this: "We do not in advance restrict the concept of sense to the signification of 'content of judgment' ['*Urteilsgehalt*'], but rather, we understand it as the existential phenomenon, which we have already characterized, in which the formal framework [*Gerüst*] of what is disclosable in understanding and Articulable [*Artikulierbaren*] in interpretation becomes visible for the first time" (*SZ*, 156). This could suggest that the entity as meant is to be construed as a *sense*, in Heidegger's use of the word. A sense is a position in the articulated framework of everyday activity, a location sketched out in advance by our basic disclosure of the practical world.

37. I will translate Husserl's term "*Intention*" with "meaning" in order, once again, to underscore the distinction between the cognitive sense "intention" and the action-theoretic. "Intention" is the standard translation of the term in Husserl's works, however.

38. Charles S. Pierce, "How to Make Our Ideas Clear," in *Writings of Charles S. Peirce: A Chronological Edition*, vol. 3, 257–276.

39. Dewey incorporates this aspect of the relation between a problem and a solution into his official definition of "inquiry" in *Logic*: "*Inquiry is the controlled or directed transformation of an indeterminate situation into one that is so determinate in its constituent distinctions and relations as to convert the elements of the original situation into a unified whole*" (108).

40. Heidegger regards this more basic phenomenon as a more originary form of truth. Indeed, the practical disclosure of the contours of our worldly environment in the end rests, for Heidegger, on the most basic form of truth discussed in *Being and Time*, what he calls "the truth of existence," namely, the disclosure of the being of Dasein, and ultimately, being in general, through Dasein's self-understanding. "*With* and *through* [the disclosedness of Dasein] is uncoveredness; thus, with the *disclosedness* of Dasein we reach for the first time the *most originary* phenomenon of truth" (*SZ*, 220–221). In this paper I have been concerned only with assertoric truth. How Heidegger's views on disclosedness and the truth of existence relate to Dewey and the other American pragmatists is a question I hope to answer elsewhere.

41. If Heidegger did operationalize his conception of truth, then he could not regard theoretical, natural science as seeing past the context of use to a domain of objects (the occurrent or present-at-hand, *die Vorhandenen*) that are independent of any involvement in human practices. In my "Decontextualization, Standardization, and Deweyan Science," I argue (in agreement with Joseph Rouse) that he should have abandoned this view of science in favor of the Deweyan. See Rouse, "Science and the Theoretical 'Discovery' of the Present-at-Hand," in *Descriptions*, ed. Don Ihde and Hugh J. Silverman (Albany: SUNY Press, 1985), 200–210; and *Knowledge and Power*. For a defense of Heidegger's philosophy of natural science, see Dreyfus, *Being-in-the-World*, and Gethmann, "Der existenzial Begriff der Wissenschaftstheorie."

42. I would like to thank the departments of philosophy at the University of Virginia, the University of Kentucky, and the Universität Tübingen, where I read earlier versions of this chapter, and who are responsible for significant changes to it. Also, I thank Taylor Carman, Bert Dreyfus, Toni Koch, and Terry Pinkard for comments on earlier drafts of this paper or on some of the ideas contained in it. Finally, I thank the Graduate School of Georgetown University for a summer research grant to work on this paper and the Alexander von Humboldt-Stiftung, who provided me with a fellowship year during which I worked on the general project of which this chapter is a part.

Chapter 12: Absorbed Coping, Husserl, and Heidegger

1. Dagfinn Føllesdal, "Husserl and Heidegger on the role of actions in the constitution of the world," in *Essays in Honour of Jaakko Hintikka*, ed. E. Saarinen, R. Hilpinen, I. Niiniluoto, and M. Provence Hintikka (Dordrecht: Reidel, 1979), 365–378.

2. Edmund Husserl, *Gesammelte Werke, Husserliana* V. 124, 41–43; henceforth cited as *Husserliana*. Translations of *Husserliana* IV are from Edmund Husserl, *Ideas Pertaining to a Pure Phenomenology and to a Phenomenological Philosophy*, Second Book, trans. Richard Rojcewicz and André Schuwer (Norwell, Mass.: Kluwer Academic Publishers, 1989).

3. Dagfinn Føllesdal, "Husserl on evidence and justification," in *Edmund Husserl and the Phenomenological Tradition: Essays in Phenomenology*, ed. Robert Sokolowski, Vol. 18, Studies in Philosophy and the History of Philosophy; proceedings of a lecture series in the fall of 1985 (Washington: The Catholic University of America Press, 1988), 107–129.

4. Edmund Husserl, *Erfahrung und Urteil*, § 4, p. 12; trans. Churchill and Ameriks, p. 20. See also pp. 21, 23, and 68 of *Erfahrung und Urteil*, corresponding to pp. 27, 29, and 65 of the English translation.

5. *Erfahrung und Urteil*, §14, pp. 68–69; Churchill and Amiks, pp. 65–66.

6. Kristiana Arp, "Husserlian Intentionality and Everyday Coping," in *Issues in Husserl's Ideas II*, eds. Thomas Nenon and Lester Embree, Contributions to Phenomenology (Dordrecht: Kluwer, 1996), 162–171.

Chapter 13: Proofs and Presuppositions: Heidegger, Searle, and the "Reality" of the "External" World

1. The influence of Searle may be attributed to more than institutional proximity: Dreyfus has detected in Searle's views deep and striking parallels with the philosophy of Edmund Husserl, the founder of the phenomenological movement and Heidegger's teacher. See, for example, Dreyfus's introductory remarks on Searle in *Husserl, Intentionality, and Cognitive Science*, eds. Hubert Dreyfus and Harrison Hall (Cambridge: MIT Press, 1982), see especially 4–9.

2. Immanuel Kant, *Critique of Pure Reason*, trans. Norman Kemp Smith (New York: St. Martin's Press, 1965), Bxxxix.

Notes

3. Martin Heidegger, *Being and Time* (*BT*), 249.

4. G. E. Moore, "Proof of an External World," in his *Philosophical Papers* (London: George Allen and Unwin, 1959), 146.

5. Here we might recall Wittgenstein's remark at the opening of *On Certainty*, ed. G. E. M. Anscombe and G. H. von Wright, trans. Denis Paul and G. E. M. Anscombe (New York: Harper & Row, 1972): "If you do know that *here is one hand*, we'll grant you all the rest" (2e). It's precisely one's entitlement to that first step that is in question when a proof for the external world is demanded, and so one cannot simply use that step as a way to meet the demand. See also Michael Williams, *Unnatural Doubts: Epistemological Realism and the Basis of Scepticism* (Princeton: Princeton University Press, 1996) for similar criticisms of Moore; see especially chapters 1 and 2.

6. *BT*, 102. Compare what Heidegger says here about world with his remarks about *being* in the First Introduction to *Being and Time*: "*what is asked about* is being—that which determines entities as entities, that on the basis of which entities are already understood." (*BT*, 25–26) If, as Heidegger maintains, being cannot be explained in terms of beings, the same is true in the case of world; hence, his dissatisfaction with Moore's proof.

7. John R. Searle, *Intentionality: An Essay in the Philosophy of Mind*, henceforth cited as *Intentionality*, 141.

8. See, for example, Barry Stroud's discussion of Searle on the Background, which begins with a version of such a regress argument. Stroud attributes the argument to Wittgenstein, though he sees it at work in Searle as well. See "The Background of Thought," in *John Searle and His Critics*, eds. Ernest LePore and Robert van Gulick (Cambridge: Blackwell, 1991).

9. It would seem that there is as much reason to place scare-quotes around "commitment" as around "realism": the Background consists of strictly non- or pre-intentional phenomena, while talk of commitment suggests a "vocabulary of first-order Intentional states." As we will see below, part of Heidegger's dissatisfaction with a response like Searle's to the demand for proof is with this talk of commitment, as something that has been incurred by one's speaking meaningfully or by one's having contentful intentional states.

10. John R. Searle, *The Construction of Social Reality* (New York: The Free Press, 1995), 181, henceforth cited as *CSR*.

11. See *Intentionality*, 154.

12. Martin Heidegger, *History of the Concept of Time*, 215–216.

13. *CSR*, 195 (my emphasis). Note especially Searle's talk of one's being "committed to the truth of a proposition." One problem with understanding this commitment lies in reconciling it with Searle's claim that the Background is non-intentional: how can this commitment at one and the same time have propositional content, as a commitment to the truth of a particular proposition, while at the same time function as part of the non- or pre-intentional Background? Furthermore, Searle's talk of *commitment*, despite his attempt to understand it in non-intentional terms, continues to invite the question of justification: if I'm committed to something, what entitles me to that commitment? If, given the fundamental nature of the commitment, no

entitlement can be furnished, we are still left with the feeling that something is lacking. One way of understanding why Heidegger would be dissatisfied with Searle's talk of presupposition and commitment is by means of his rejection of Husserl's characterization of our everyday predicament as: "the natural attitude." In *History of the Concept of Time*, Heidegger maintains, contra Husserl, that "Man's natural manner of experience ... cannot be called an attitude" (113), by which he means that it does not consist of a set of either explicit or implicit commitments.

14. We get a glimpse of Searle's continued allegiance to a traditional, and from Heidegger's point of view problematic, conception of the world in the dichotomy he draws in his articulation of External Realism, between the world understood as involving human beings and activity and the world understood in "objective" or "independent" terms. One of Heidegger's principal claims in *Being and Time* is that considerable care is required in disentangling these two conceptions of world, and that in doing so, one must not read the latter as having priority over the former.

15. More specifically, §10 Martin Heidegger, *The Metaphysical Foundations of Logic*, henceforth cited as *MFL*.

16. See *BT*, 79–81 for Heidegger's discussion of the sense of "in" in the locution "being-in-the-world."

17. There is, in other words, no getting behind or outside of intelligibility, which is what a proof for the existence of the world would require. At the same time, part of Heidegger's efforts here are to question whether we can make sense of this talk of "getting behind or outside." That is, he can be seen as asking just what it is that, when faced with the demand for proof, we *cannot* do.

18. The invocation of Plato in this context should come as no surprise, given the epigraph to *Being and Time* from Plato's *Sophist*: "For manifestly you have long been aware of what you mean when you use the expression 'being'. We, however, who used to think we understood it, have become perplexed." Heidegger's phenomenology is thus permeated more generally with the contrast between forgetfulness and recollection: his engagement with skepticism is but one example or application.

19. A version of this chapter was presented to the Continental Philosophy Workshop at the University of Chicago. I would like to thank the members of the workshop for their comments and criticisms, especially Rachel Zuckert, who discussed a draft with me at length. Thanks also to Mark Wrathall for many helpful comments, both editorial and philosophical. My greatest debt is obviously to Hubert Dreyfus, with whom I first studied *Being and Time* and from whom I continue to learn.

Chapter 14: Intending the Intender (Or, Why Heidegger Isn't Davidson)

1. Martin Heidegger, *The Basic Problems of Phenomenology*, 171; henceforth cited as *BPP*.

2. Rene Descartes, *Descartes: Selected Philosophical Writings*, trans. John Cottingham, Robert Stoothoff, and Dugald Murdoch (Cambridge: Cambridge University Press, 1988), 152.

3. Ibid., 130.

4. Ibid., 152.

5. Rene Descartes, "Principles of Philosophy," in *Descartes: Selected Philosophical Writings*, 177.

6. Donald Davidson, "Mental Events," in *Essays on Actions and Events* (Oxford: Clarendon Press, 1980), 211.

7. Ibid.

8. Donald Davidson, "Thought and Talk," in *Inquiries into Truth and Interpretation* (Oxford: Clarendon Press, 1984), 159.

9. Immanuel Kant, *The Critique of Pure Reason*, 331–332.

10. Donald Davidson, "What is Present to the Mind," in *The Mind of Donald Davidson*, ed. Johannes Brandl and Wolfgang L. Gombocz (Amsterdam: Rodopi, 1989), 4, 6.

11. Donald Davidson, "The Myth of the Subjective," in *Relativism: Interpretation and Confrontation*, ed. Michael Krausz (Notre Dame: University of Notre Dame Press, 1989), 159–72.

12. Martin Heidegger, *History of the Concept of Time*, 35.

13. *BPP*, 63.

14. *History of the Concept of Time*, 159.

15. *BPP*, 159.

16. Ibid., 158–159.

17. "Thought and Talk," 159.

18. *BPP*, 159.

19. Heidegger, *Being and Time*, 98.

20. *BPP*, 292.

21. Ibid., 164.

22. *Being and Time*, 119.

23. *BPP*, 171.

Chapter 15: Responses

1. See William Blattner's clear explication of this claim and its implications. (242–244)

2. See my objections to John Haugeland's emphasis on the necessity of obeying public standards of correctness (315–318).

3. Martin Heidegger, *Being and Time*, 167.

4. Martin Heidegger, *History of the Concept of Time*, 246.

5. Hubert L. Dreyfus, *Being-in-the-World*, 151.

6. *Being and Time*, 330.

7. I explain in my *Commentary* why I think the least misleading way to translate *das Man* is simply as the one, as in "One drives on the right in the U.S."

8. *Being and Time*, 408.

9. I prefer disposedness as a translation of *Befindlichkeit*, because it sounds a little more like English, but I have to admit that John's translation is more accurate.

10. See Charles Spinosa, Fernando Flores, Hubert L. Dreyfus, *Disclosing New Worlds* (Cambridge: MIT Press, 1997). Especially footnote 25 on p. 193. Of course, one never risks one's eternal salvation as in Kierkegaard. Another way to see the same point is to see that in Heidegger, but not in Kierkegaard, one can change one's identity without going through grief.

11. See Hubert L. Dreyfus and Charles Spinosa, "Coping with Things-in-Themselves: A Practice-Based Phenomenological Argument for Realism," *Inquiry* 42(1999):25–78.

12. *Being and Time*, 312.

13. *Being and Time*, 346.

14. Ibid.

15. See the discussion of articulation and reconfiguration in *Disclosing New Worlds*.

16. See my "Kierkegaard on the Internet: Anonymity vrs. Commitment in the Present Age," http://socrates.berkely.edu/~hdveyfus/htnie/papers.html.

17. Pap. X, 2A 17: J & P no. 2163, cited in Hakon Strangerup, "His Polemic with the Press," in *Kierkegaard as a Person*, ed. Niels and Marie Thulstrup (Copenhagen: C.A. Reitzels Forlag), 1983.

18. Søren Kierkegaard, *The Present Age*, trans. Alexander Dru (New York: Harper & Row, 1962), 36, 37. As is often the case, we here find Heidegger borrowing without acknowledgment from Kierkegaard. As Haugeland stresses, Heidegger claims that conscience is always calling Dasein to risk its concrete identity.

19. Søren Kierkegaard, *The Sickness unto Death*, trans. Alastair Hannay, (Harmandsworth: Penguin Books, 1989), 43.

20. Hubert L. Dreyfus and Charles Spinosa, "Highway Bridges and Feasts: Heidegger and Borgmann on how to Affirm Technology."

21. We are not "enthusiastic" about morphing on the Internet. In the quotation from our paper Zimmerman cites (126), we are simply describing phenomena that support Heidegger's contention that a new flexible technological understanding of being is beginning to replace the modern attempt to cultivate one unified and continuous identity. Far from endorsing this change, we favor trying to recover the practices of cultivating local worlds as a way of resisting this development. Zimmerman acknowledges this on the very next page where he gives a lucid sketch of the postmodern way of being and our proposal for avoiding this dehumanized form of life.

22. Since Zimmerman brings up Kierkegaard's defense of a single unconditional commitment as a necessary stage on the way to pure egolessness, it is worth noting that, according to Kierkegaard, the life of commitment which Kierkegaard calls Religiousness B *supersedes* a life in which the self accepts its "self annihilation," which Kierkegaard calls religiousness A. Kierkegaard thereby reverses the Hegelian order Zimmerman, following Wilber, defends. To reverse Zimmerman's slogan, for Kierkegaard, to be someone (an individual) you first have to be no one. Later Heidegger would reject any such claims of necessary priority as metaphysical.

23. For the sake of the record, I should note that I have not changed my mind that a life of Zen, yoga, Hindu meditation and so forth is inauthentic. I still hold that such a life takes up practices that are not in our culture's tradition and so amounts to playing at getting into tune with the various worlds these practices make possible. Only if a person is willing to spend years in each world acquiring the different embodied practices that make each one of these worlds possible, can he or she live in one or more of them.

24. See Charles Spinosa's paper in vol. II.

25. There are moments when Zimmerman seems to think that by finitude and mortality we mean that there are a limited number of possibilities open to man. At other times he sees that, by finitude and mortality, we mean that human beings, as world disclosers, can have no single content that defines them. Zimmerman aptly calls this lack of a single defining content our "finite/mortal openness for being" and "the nothingness that makes world-disclosure possible." No doubt we should have been clearer that, on our view, we are never wholly defined by one world. Thus, familiarity with multiple worlds reveals that man is never at home but always a stranger, the way anxiety revealed the uncanniness of existence in *Being and Time.*

26. When Helen saw that her life with Paris was going to bring about the destruction of Troy, she regretted she had ever run off with him. But that regret is different from regretting her passion. Presumably, if things had gone well, she could have lived happily with Paris or gone back to Menelaus, depending on which mood or goddess had authority over her at the time.

27. When back with Menelaus after the war, Helen describes her former self as "the wanton that I was" but she does not blame herself, and, strikingly, Menelaus does not blame her either. Apparently she does not feel strongly committed to the feeling and actions of her former self so she can recognize them as hers and take responsibility for them without feeling guilt. A monotheistic Christian self would feel obliged to continue to feel guilt until she had expiated her sin.

28. Hegelian development is not supposed to be just a narrative but a narrative in which the truth of the earlier stages is preserved and better and better articulated.

As Zimmerman says, "Transpersonal existence . . . involves *incorporating* the constructive elements of personal subjectivity, including integrity and sincerity." But it is hard to see what is preserved of authentic content, consistency, and personal integrity, and so forth when one passes to what Zimmerman, following Wilber, calls the post-egoic stage. Perhaps this is why Zimmerman refers to the Wilber story as a "developmental narrative." A developmental account does not have to preserve the stages one develops through, it just "presupposes . . . the prior stages."

29. Zimmerman seems to think that Heidegger either has to believe that the West has been dominated by a series of monolithic understandings of being or, if there are still marginal practices around, that there have never been any such total understandings. Heidegger, however, has a subtler view. There are both dominant and marginal practices. Thus there have been such total understandings of what counts as real as the Medieval view that everything was a creature. But that dominant Christian understanding marginalized, without eliminating, such incompatible Pagan practices as carnival and witchcraft.

30. Martin Heidegger, "The Question Concerning Technology," 16.

31. Albert Borgmann, *Technology and the Character of Contemporary Life* (Chicago: University of Chicago Press, 1984).

32. "Highway Bridges," see note 20.

33. Martin Heidegger, "Summary of a Seminar on the Lecture 'Time and Being,'" in *On Time and Being*, 37.

34. Ibid.

35. This is not to deny that our sort of collaboration would have been impossible if we had not for several months been bodily present to each other in two bounded places, first in Berkeley and then in Perth, so as to establish the sort of trust and understanding which I think would be difficult if not impossible to establish by e-mail alone. But, as Jeff says, the necessity of this embodied nearness tends to be covered up and forgotten.

36. I don't think that this sort of loss can be caused by *representing* things, as Jeff suggests. Although Heidegger himself is not always clear on the point, being an *object* of *representation* belongs to the modern, Cartesian understanding of being not to the postmodern, technological understanding of things as resources. So the interesting question returns: what is there about treating things as *resources* that is more "one-dimensional" than treating them as *representations*? If, as Jeff plausibly claims, representations are already disembodied, how can treating things as resources be any more dangerous?

37. Hubert Dreyfus, "Husserl's Phenomenology of Perception: From Transcendental to Existential Phenomenology," (Ph.D. diss., Harvard University 1964).

38. Letter to Karl Löwith, February 2, 1923. Cited in Martin Kusch, *Language as Calculus vs. Language as Universal Medium: A Study in Husserl, Heidegger, and Gadamer* (Dordrecht: Kluwer, 1989), 151.

39. Hubert Dreyfus, "Heidegger's Critique of the Husserl/Searle Account of Intentionality," *Social Research* 60, No. 1 (Spring 1993).

40. *Being and Time,* 416.

41. See my response to Searle in volume II. Motivated action certainly need not be rule following, and Husserl is certainly not a computationalist. Insofar as I interpreted Husserl's claim that the noema was a "strict rule" to show Husserl was a cognitivist, I was clearly mistaken. Ronald McIntyre pointed this out in his article, "Husserl and the Representational Theory of Mind," *Topoi* 5 (1986). I still think, however, that Husserl was the grandfather of AI. See my response to McIntyre in the second edition of my anthology, *Husserl, Intentionality and Cognitive Science* (Cambridge: MIT Press, forthcoming).

42. See my introduction to *Husserl, Intentionality and Cognitive Science.*

43. Edmund Husserl, *The Crisis of European Sciences and Transcendental Phenomenology,* trans. D. Carr (Evanston, Ill.: Northwestern University Press, 1970), 149.

44. Martin Heidegger, *The Basic Problems of Phenomenology* (Bloomington: Indiana University Press, 1982), 124–125. (Heidegger's brackets).

45. Ibid., 162.

46. Ibid.

47. Edmund Husserl, *Cartesian Meditations,* 78.

48. Mark does not talk much about being-in-the-world, and when he does he mistakenly equates it with being-in. He says for example, "producing a widget . . . is a paradigmatic case of being-in-the-world" (292) and "to produce a widget is a paradigm of being in" (293), but for Heidegger an activity like production is still a kind of intentionality *within* the world, for example, working on something with something, and so presupposes being-in-the-world. (Incidentally, working on something, unlike production, which involves a relation with a possible future object, necessarily involves a relation between the agent and the object that the agent is working on right now.)

49. One way to see that something has gone wrong here, is to note that the explanation of self reference has to work even for those who don't have a profession and are not using tools that have to be used in the right way. One's for-the-sake-of-which might be delivering the morning paper by throwing it on people's doorstep. For Heidegger, being a newsboy is just as self referential as being a shoemaker or a professor even if one needs no tools to be one.

References

Apel, Karl-Otto. *Der Denkweg von Charles S. Peirce.* Frankfurt: Suhrkamp, 1975.

Arisaka, Yoko. "Heidegger's Theory of Space: A Critique of Dreyfus." *Inquiry* 38 (1995): 455–467.

Arisaka, Yoko. "Spatiality, Temporality, and the Problem of Foundation in *Being and Time.*" *Philosophy Today* 40 (1996): 36–46.

Aristotle, "Physics IV." In *Aristotle's Physics Books III and IV.* Translated by Edward Hussey. Oxford: Clarendon Press, 1983.

Arp, Kristiana. "Husserlian Intentionality and Everyday Coping." In *Issues in Husserl's Ideas II,* edited by Thomas Nenon and Loster Embree. Contributions to Phenomenology, 162–171. Dordrecht: Kluwer, 1996.

Blattner, William D. "Decontextualization, Standardization, and Deweyan Science." *Man and World* 28 (1995): 321–339.

Blattner, William D. "Existential Temporality in *Being and Time.*" In *Heidegger: A Critical Reader,* edited by Hubert L. Dreyfus and Harrison Hall, 99–129. Oxford: Blackwell, 1992.

Borgmann, Albert. *Crossing the Postmodern Divide.* Chicago: University of Chicago Press, 1992.

Borgmann, Albert. *Technology and the Character of Contemporary Life.* Chicago: University of Chicago Press, 1984.

Brandom, Robert. *Making It Explicit: Reasoning, Representing, and Discursive Commitment.* Cambridge: Harvard University Press, 1994.

Brandom, Robert. "Pragmatism, Phenomenalism, and Truth Talk." In *Midwest Studies in Philosophy* 12, 75–93. Minneapolis: University of Minnesota, 1987.

References

Bukatman, Scott. *Terminal Identity: The Virtual Subject in Postmodern Science Fiction.* Durham, N.C.: Duke University Press, 1993.

Burke, Tom. *Dewey's New Logic.* Chicago: University of Chicago Press, 1994.

Casey, Edward S. *The Fate of Place.* Berkeley: University of California Press, 1997.

Casey, Edward S. "Smooth Spaces and Rough-Edged Places: The Hidden History of Place." *Review of Metaphysics* 51 (1997): 267–296.

Cavell, Stanley. *The Claim of Reason: Wittgenstein, Skepticism, Morality, and Tragedy.* New York: Oxford University Press, 1979.

Christensen, Carleton B. "Getting Heidegger off the West Coast." *Inquiry* 41 (1998): 65–87.

Christensen, Carleton B. "Heidegger's Representationalism." *Review of Metaphysics* 51 (1997): 77–103.

Clark, Maudemarie. *Nietzsche on Truth and Philosophy.* Cambridge: Cambridge University Press, 1990.

Clark, Michael. "Truth and Success: Searle's Attack on Minimalism." *Analysis* 57 (1997): 205–209.

Danto, Arthur C. *Nietzsche as Philosopher.* New York: Macmillan, 1965.

Davidson, Donald. "Mental Events." In *Essays on Actions and Events,* 207–224. Oxford: Clarendon Press, 1980.

Davidson, Donald. "The Myth of the Subjective." In *Relativism: Interpretation and Confrontation,* edited by Michael Krausz, 159–172. Notre Dame: University of Notre Dame Press, 1989.

Davidson, Donald. "Thought and Talk." In *Inquiries into Truth and Interpretation,* 155–170. Oxford: Clarendon Press, 1984.

Davidson, Donald. "What Is Present to the Mind." In *The Mind of Donald Davidson,* edited by Johannes Brandl and Wolfgang L. Gombocz, 3–18. Amsterdam: Rodopi, 1989.

Deleuze, Gilles. *Nietzsche et la philosophie.* Paris: Presses Universitaires de France, 1962.

Derrida, Jacques. *Spurs: Nietzsche's Styles.* Chicago: University of Chicago Press, 1979.

Derrida, Jacques. *La Voix et la Phènomène.* Paris: Presses Universitaires de France, 1967.

Descartes, René. *Descartes: Selected Philosophical Writings.* Translated by John Cottingham, Robert Stoothoff, and Dugald Murdoch. Cambridge: Cambridge University Press, 1988.

Descartes, René. *The Philosophical Writings of Descartes,* vol. 1. Translated by John Cottingham, Robert Stoothoff, and Dugald Murdoch. Cambridge: Cambridge University Press, 1985.

References

Détienne, Marcel. *Les Maîtres de vérité dans la Grèce archaïque*. Paris: Pocket, 1994; *The Masters of Truth in Archaic Greece*. Translated by Janet Lloyd. New York: Zone Books, 1996.

Dewey, John. *Logic: The Theory of Inquiry*. In *The Later Works, 1925–1953*, vol. 12, edited by Jo Ann Boydston, 3–5. Carbondale: Southern Illinois University Press, 1986.

Dewey, John. "Does Reality Possess Practical Character?" In *The Middle Works, 1899–1924*, vol. 4, edited by Jo Ann Boydston, 125–142. Carbondale: Southern Illinois University Press, 1977.

Dewey, John. "Experimental Theory of Knowledge." In *The Middle Works, 1899–1924*, vol. 3, edited by Jo Ann Boydston, 107–127. Carbondale: Southern Illinois University Press, 1977.

Dewey, John. "Propositions, Warranted Assertibility, and Truth." In *Later Works, 1925–1953*, vol. 14, edited by Jo Ann Boydston, 168–188. Carbondale: Southern Illinois University Press, 1981.

Dewey, John. "The Reflex Arc Concept in Psychology." In *The Early Works, 1882–1898*, vol. 5, edited by Jo Ann Boydston, 96–109. Carbondale: Southern Illinois University Press, 1972.

Dewey, John. "What Pragmatism Means by Practical." In *The Middle Works, 1899–1924*, vol. 4, edited by Jo Ann Boydston, 98–115. Carbondale: Southern Illinois University Press, 1977.

Dreyfus, Hubert L. *Being-in-the-World: A Commentary on Heidegger's* Being and Time, *Division I*. Cambridge: MIT Press, 1991.

Dreyfus, Hubert L. *What Computers Can't Do: A Critique of Artificial Reason*. Cambridge: MIT Press, 1972.

Dreyfus, Hubert L. *What Computers Still Can't Do: A Critique of Artificial Reason*. New York: Harper & Row, 1992.

Dreyfus, Hubert L. "Heidegger on the Connection Between Nihilism, Art, Technology, and Politics." In *The Cambridge Companion to Heidegger*, edited by Charles Guignon. Cambridge: Cambridge University Press, 1993.

Dreyfus, Hubert L. "Heidegger's Critique of the Husserl/Searle Account of Intentionality." *Social Research* 60, no.1 (spring 1993).

Dreyfus, Hubert L. "Husserl's Phenomenology of Perception: From Transcendental to Existential Phenomenology." Ph.D. diss., Harvard University, 1964.

Dreyfus, Hubert L. "Interpreting Heidegger on *Das Man*." *Inquiry* 38 (1995): 423–430.

Dreyfus, Hubert L., and Harrison Hall, eds. *Husserl, Intentionality, and Cognitive Science*. Cambridge: MIT Press, 1982.

Dreyfus, Hubert L., and Jane Rubin. "Kierekegaard on the Nihilism of the Present Age: The Case of Commitment as Addiction." *Synthese* 98 (1994): 3–19.

References

Dreyfus, Hubert L., and Jane Rubin. "You Can't Get Something for Nothing: Kierkegaard and Heidegger on How Not To Overcome Nihilism." *Inquiry* 30 (1987): 33–75.

Dreyfus, Hubert L., and Charles Spinosa. "Coping with Things-in-Themselves: A Practice-Based Phenomenological Argument for Realism." *Inquiry* 42, no.1 (1999): 25–78.

Dreyfus, Hubert L., and Charles Spinosa. "Highway Bridges and Feasts: Heidegger and Borgmann on How to Affirm Technology." *Man and World* 30 (1997): 159–177.

Einstein, Albert. *Ideas and Opinions.* Translated by Sonja Bargmann. New York: Crown, 1954.

Einstein, Albert. *Concepts of Space,* 2d ed. Cambridge: Harvard University Press, 1970.

Føllesdal, Dagfinn. "Husserl and Heidegger on the Role of Actions in the Constitution of the World." In *Essays in Honour of Jaakko Hintikka,* edited by E. Saarinen, R. Hilpinen, I. Niiniluoto, and M. Provence Hintikka, 365–378. Dordrecht: Reidel, 1979.

Føllesdal, Dagfinn. "Husserl on Evidence and Justification." In *Edmund Husserl and the Phenomenological Tradition: Essays in Phenomenology,* edited by Robert Sokolowski, 107–129. Washington, D.C.: The Catholic University of America Press, 1988.

Foucault, Michel. *The Use of Pleasure: The History of Sexuality,* vol. 2. Translated by Robert Hurley. New York: Vintage, 1985.

Gergen, Kenneth J. *The Saturated Self: Dilemmas of Identity in Contemporary Life.* New York: Basic Books, 1992.

Gethmann, Carl Friedrich. *Dasein: Erkennen und Handeln. Heidegger im phänomenologischen Kontext.* Berlin: Walter de Gruyter, 1993.

Gethmann, Carl Friedrich. "Der existenziale Begriff der Wissenschaft." In *Lebenswelt und Wissenschaft: Studien zum Verhaltnis von Phanomenologie und Wissenschaftstheorie,* edited by Carl Friedrich Gethmann, 181–208. Bonn: Bouvier Verlag, 1991.

Granier, Jean. *Le problème de la vérité dans la philosophie de Nietzsche.* Paris: Editions du Seuil, 1966.

Goldberg, Ken, ed. *The Robot in the Garden: Telerobotics and Telepistemology on the Internet.* Cambridge: MIT Press, 2000.

Grondin, Jean. *Sources of Hermeneutics.* Albany: SUNY Press, 1995.

Grondin, Jean. *Le Tournant dans la Pensée de Martin Heidegger.* Paris: Presses Universitaires de France, 1987.

Guignon, Charles. *Heidegger and the Problem of Knowledge.* Indianapolis: Hackett, 1983.

Guignon, Charles. "Heidegger's 'Authenticity' Revisited." *Review of Metaphysics* 38 (December 1984): 321–339.

References

Guignon, Charles. "History and Commitment in the Early Heidegger." In *Heidegger: A Critical Reader,* edited by Hubert L. Dreyfus and Harrison Hall, 130–142. Oxford: Blackwell, 1992.

Haar, Michel. *Nietzsche and Metaphysics.* Translated by Michael Gendre. Albany: SUNY Press, 1996.

Haar, Michel. *Par-dela le nihilisme: Nouveaux essais sur Nietzsche.* Paris: Presses Universitaires de France, 1998.

Habermas, Jürgen. *The Philosophical Discourse of Modernity: Twelve Lectures.* Translated by Frederick G. Lawrence. Cambridge: MIT Press, 1987.

Hall, Harrison. "Intentionality and World: Division I of *Being and Time.*" In *The Cambridge Companion to Heidegger,* edited by Charles Guignon, 122–140. Cambridge: Cambridge University Press, 1993.

Hannay, Alastair. "Kierkegaard's Levellings and the *Review.*" In *Kierkegaard Studies: Kierkegaard Yearbook,* 1999, edited by J. N. Cappelörn and Hermann Deuser. Berlin: Walter de Gruyter, 1999.

Haugeland, John. "Dasein's Disclosedness." In *Heidegger: A Critical Reader,* edited by Hubert L. Dreyfus and Harrison Hall, 27–44. Oxford: Blackwell, 1992.

Haugeland, John. "Heidegger on Being a Person." *Noûs* 16 (1982): 15–26.

Heidegger, Martin. *Basic Questions of Philosophy: Selected "Problems" of "Logic."* Translated by Richard Rojcewicz and André Schuwer. Bloomington: Indiana University Press, 1994.

Heidegger, Martin. *Basic Writings.* Edited by David Farrell Krell. New York: Harper & Row, 1993.

Heidegger, Martin. *Beiträge zur Philosophie (Vom Ereignis),* Gesamtausgabe 65. Frankfurt: Klostermann, 1989.

Heidegger, Martin. *The Concept of Time.* Translated by William McNeill. Oxford: Blackwell, 1992.

Heidegger, Martin. *Denkerfahrungen 1910–1976.* Frankfurt: Klostermann, 1983.

Heidegger, Martin. *Die Grundbegriffe der Metaphysik: Welt-Endlichkeit-Einsamkeit,* Gesamtausgabe 29/30. Frankfurt: Klostermann, 1983; *The Fundamental Concepts of Metaphysics: World, Finitude, Solitude.* Translated by William McNeill and Nicholas Walker. Bloomington: Indiana University Press, 1995.

Heidegger, Martin. *Die Grundprobleme der Phänomenologie,* Gesamtausgabe 24. Frankfurt: Klostermann, 1975; *The Basic Problems of Phenomenology.* Translated by Albert Hofstadter. Bloomington: Indiana University Press, 1982.

Heidegger, Martin. *The End of Philosophy.* Translated by Joan Stambaugh. New York: Harper & Row, 1973.

References

Heidegger, Martin. *Erläuterungen zu Hölderlins Dichtung,* Gesamtausgabe 4. Frankfurt: Klostermann, 1981.

Heidegger, Martin. *Hegels Phänomenologie des Geistes,* Gesamtausgabe 22. Frankfurt: Klostermann, 1980; *Hegel's Phenomenology of Spirit.* Translated by Parvis Emad and Kenneth Maly. Bloomington: Indiana University Press, 1982.

Heidegger, Martin. *History of the Concept of Time: Prolegomena.* Translated by Theodore Kisiel. Bloomington: Indiana University Press, 1985.

Heidegger, Martin. *Hölderlin's Hymn "The Ister."* Translated by William McNeill and Julia Davis. Bloomington: Indiana University Press, 1996.

Heidegger, Martin. *Hölderlins Hymne "Andendken,"* Gesamtausgabe 52. Frankfurt: Klostermann, 1982.

Heidegger, Martin. *Hölderlins Hymnen "Germanien" und "Der Rhein,"* Gesamtausgabe 39. Frankfurt: Klostermann, 1980.

Heidegger, Martin. *Holzwege,* Gesamtausgabe 5. Frankfurt: Klostermann, 1977.

Heidegger, Martin. *Identität und Differenz.* Pfullingen: Neske, 1957.

Heidegger, Martin. *Introduction to Metaphysics.* Translated by Ralph Manheim. New Haven: Yale University Press, 1959.

Heidegger, Martin. *Kant and the Problem of Metaphysics,* 5th ed. Translated by Richard Taft. Bloomington: Indiana University Press, 1997.

Heidegger, Martin. *The Metaphysical Foundations of Logic.* Translated by Michael Heim. Bloomington: Indiana University Press, 1984.

Heidegger, Martin. *Nietzsche.* 4 vols. Translated by David Farrell Krell. San Francisco: HarperSanFrancisco, 1979–1987.

Heidegger, Martin. *Nietzsche: Der Wille zur Macht als Kunst,* Gesamtausgabe 43. Frankfurt: Klostermann, 1985.

Heidegger, Martin. *On Time and Being.* Translated by Joan Stambaugh. New York: HarperTorch Book, 1972.

Heidegger, Martin. *On the Way to Language.* Translated by Peter D. Hertz. New York: Harper & Row, 1971.

Heidegger, Martin. *Phänomenologische Interpretationen zu Aristoteles: Einführung in die Phänomenologische Forschung,* Gesamtausgabe 61. Frankfurt: Klostermann, 1985.

Heidegger, Martin. *Poetry, Language, Thought.* Translated by Albert Hofstadter. New York: Harper & Row, 1971.

Heidegger, Martin. *Prolegomena zur Geschichte des Zeitbegriffs,* Gesamtausgabe 20. Frankfurt: Klostermann, 1979.

References

Heidegger, Martin. *The Question Concerning Technology and Other Essays.* Translated by William Lovitt. New York: Harper & Row, 1977.

Heidegger, Martin. *Sein und Zeit,* Gesamtausgabe 2. Frankfurt: Klostermann, 1977; *Being and Time.* Translated by John Macquarrie and Edward Robinson. New York: Harper & Row, 1962; also translated by Joan Stambaugh. Albany: SUNY Press, 1996.

Heidegger, Martin. *Seminare,* Gesamtausgabe 15. Frankfurt: Klostermann, 1986.

Heidegger, Martin. *Vorträge und Aufsätze.* Stuttgart: Günther Neske, 1954.

Heidegger, Martin. *Wegmarken,* Gesamtausgabe 9. Frankfurt: Klostermann, 1976.

Heidegger, Martin. *What Is a Thing?* Translated by W. B. Barton Jr. and Vera Deutsch. Chicago: Henry Regnery, 1968.

Heidegger, Martin. *Zur Bestimmung der Philosophie,* Gesamtausgabe 56/57. Frankfurt: Klostermann, 1987.

Heidegger, Martin. "Hölderlin and the Essence of Poetry." In *Existence and Being,* edited by Werner Brock, 270–291. London: Vision Press, 1968.

Heidegger, Martin. "Phenomenological Interpretations with Respect to Aristotle: Indication of the Hermeneutical Situation." Translated by Michael Baur. *Man and World* 25 (1992): 355–393.

Husserl, Edmund. *Cartesian Meditations: An Introduction to Phenomenology.* Translated by Dorion Cairns. Dordrecht: Kluwer, 1995.

Husserl, Edmund. *The Crisis of European Sciences and Transcendental Phenomenology.* Translated by D. Carr. Evanston, Ill.: Northwestern University Press, 1970.

Husserl, Edmund. *Erfahrung und Urteil. Untersuchungenzur Genealogie der Logik.* Edited by L. Landgrebe. Prague: Akademie Verlagsbuchhandlung, 1939; *Experience and Judgment: Investigations in a Genealogy of Logic.* Translated by James S. Churchill and Karl Ameriks. Evanston: Northwestern University Press, 1973.

Husserl, Edmund. *Husserliana: Gesammelte Werke.* The Hague: Nijhoff, 1950–1988.

Husserl, Edmund. *Ideas Pertaining to a Pure Phenomenology and to a Phenomological Philosophy.* Second Book. Translated by Richard Rojcewicz and André Schuwer. Norwell, Mass.: Kluwer Academic Publishers, 1989.

James, William. *Pragmatism: A New Name for Some Old Ways of Thinking.* Edited by Fredson Bowers. Reprinted in *The Works of William James.* Cambridge: Harvard University Press, 1975.

James, William. *The Principles of Psychology,* vol. 2. New York: Holt, 1890; New York: Dover, 1950.

Jammer, Max. *Concepts of Space: The History of Concepts of Space in Physics,* 2d ed. Cambridge: Harvard University Press, 1969.

References

Kant, Immanuel. *Critique of Pure Reason*. Translated by Norman Kemp Smith. New York: St. Martin's, 1965.

Kaufmann, Walter. *Nietzsche: Philosopher, Psychologist, Antichrist*, 4th ed. Princeton: Princeton University Press, 1974.

Kierkegaard, Søren. *The Concept of Dread*. Translated by Walter Lowrie. Princeton: Princeton University Press, 1957.

Kierkegaard, Søren. *The Concept of Irony*. In *Kierkegaard's Writings*, vol. 2. Translated by Howard V. Hong and Edna H. Hong. Princeton: Princeton University Press, 1989.

Kierkegaard, Søren. *Concluding Unscientific Postscript*. Translated by David F. Swenson and Walter Lowrie. Princeton: Princeton University Press, 1941.

Kierkegaard, Søren. *Concluding Unscientific Postscript to Philosophical Fragments*, vol. 1. Edited and translated by Howard V. Hong and Edna H. Hong. Princeton: Princeton University Press, 1990.

Kierkegaard, Søren. *Eighteen Upbuilding Discourses*. Edited and translated by Howard V. Hong and Edna H. Hong. Princeton: Princeton University Press, 1990.

Kierkegaard, Søren. *Kierkegaard's Papers and Journals: A Selection*. Harmondsworth: Penguin, 1996.

Kierkegaard, Søren. *The Sickness unto Death*. Translated by Alastair Hannay. Harmondsworth: Penguin Books, 1989.

Kierkegaard, Søren. *Søren Kierkegaards Papirer*, vol. 1. Edited by P. A. Heiberg and V. Kuhr, enlarged ed. N. Thulstrup. Copenhagen: Gyldendal, 1968.

Kierkegaard, Søren. *The Present Age*. Translated by Alexander Dru. New York: Harper & Row, 1962.

Kierkegaard, Søren. *Two Ages: The Age of Revolution and the Present Age*. Edited and translated by Howard V. Hong and Edna H. Hong. Princeton: Princeton University Press, 1978.

Kisiel, Theodore. *The Genesis of Heidegger's Being and Time*. Berkeley: University of California Press, 1993.

Kofman, Sarah. *Nietzsche and Metaphor*. Stanford: Stanford University Press, 1993.

Kuhn, Thomas S. *The Structure of Scientific Revolutions*. Chicago: University of Chicago Press, 1962; second enlarged edition, 1970.

Kusch, Martin. *Language as Calculus vs. Language as Universal Medium: A Study in Husserl, Heidegger, and Gadamer*. Dordrecht: Kluwer, 1989.

Löwith, Karl. *Mein Leben in Deutschland vor und nach 1933*. Stuttgart: J. B. Metzler, 1986; *My Life in Germany Before and After 1933*. Translated by Elizabeth King. Urbana: University of Illinois Press, 1994.

References

Malpas, Jeff. *Place and Experience: Philosophical Topography.* Cambridge: Cambridge University Press, 1999.

Malpas, Jeff. "Acting at a Distance and Knowing from Afar: Agency and Knowledge in the World of Telerobotics." In *The Robot in the Garden: Telerobotics and Telepistemology on the Internet,* edited by Ken Goldberg. Cambridge: MIT Press, 2000.

Malpas, Jeff. "Death and the Unity of a Life." In *Death and Philosophy,* edited by Jeff Malpas and Robert C. Solomon, 120–134. London: Routledge, 1998.

Malpas, Jeff. "Space and Sociality." *International Journal of Philosophical Studies* 5 (1997): 53–79.

Marcel, Gabriel. *The Philosophy of Existentialism.* Translated by Manya Harari. New York: Citadel Press, 1956.

McIntyre, Ronald. "Husserl and the Representational Theory of Mind." *Topoi* 5 (1986).

Minar, Edward. "Feeling at Home in Language (*What Makes Reading* Philosophical Investigations *Possible?*)." *Synthese* 102 (1995): 413–452.

Moore, G. E. "Proof of an External World." In *Philosophical Papers,* 127–150. London: George Allen and Unwin, 1959.

Nehamas, Alexander. *Nietzsche: Life as Literature.* Cambridge: Harvard University Press, 1985.

Nietzsche, Friedrich. *Beyond Good and Evil.* Translated by Walter Kaufmann. New York: Vintage Books, 1989.

Nietzsche, Friedrich. *The Birth of Tragedy* (with *The Case of Wagner*). Translated by Walter Kaufmann. New York: Vintage, 1966.

Nietzsche, Friedrich. *Daybreak: Thoughts on the Prejudices of Morality.* Translated by R. J. Hollingdale. Cambridge: Cambridge University Press, 1982.

Nietzsche, Friedrich. *Early Greek Philosophy and Other Essays.* Translated by Maximilian A. Mügge. London: Foulis, 1911.

Nietzsche, Friedrich. *Ecce Homo.* Translated by Walter Kaufmann. New York: Vintage Books, 1967.

Nietzsche, Friedrich. *The Gay Science.* Translated by Walter Kaufmann. New York: Vintage, 1974.

Nietzsche, Friedrich. *Human, All Too Human: A Book for Free Spirits.* Translated by R. J. Hollingdale. Cambridge: Cambridge University Press, 1986.

Nietzsche, Friedrich. *Kritische Gesamtausgabe: Werke.* 30 vols. Edited by Giorgio Colli and Mazzino Montinari. Berlin: Walter de Gruyter, 1967–1978.

References

Nietzsche, Friedrich. *On the Genealogy of Morals.* Translated by Walter Kaufmann and R. J. Hollingdale. New York: Vintage Books, 1967.

Nietzsche, Friedrich. *Philosophy and Truth: Selections from Nietzsche's Notebooks of the Early 1870's.* Translated by Daniel Breazeale. Atlantic Highlands, N.J.: Humanities Press, 1979.

Nietzsche, Friedrich. *The Portable Nietzsche.* Edited and translated by Walter Kaufmann. New York: Penguin Books, 1968.

Nietzsche, Friedrich. *Twilight of the Idols: Or, How to Philosophize with a Hammer.* Translated by Richard Polt. Indianapolis: Hackett, 1997.

Nietzsche, Friedrich. *The Will to Power.* Translated by Walter Kaufmann and R. J. Hollingdale. New York: Vintage Books, 1967.

Okrent, Mark. *Heidegger's Pragmatism.* Ithaca: Cornell University Press, 1988.

Olafson, Frederick A. *Heidegger and the Philosophy of Mind.* New Haven: Yale University Press, 1987.

Peirce, Charles S. *Writings of Charles S. Peirce: A Chronological Edition.* 5 vols. Bloomington: Indiana University Press, 1982–1993.

Pöggeller, Otto. *Martin Heidegger's Path of Thinking.* Translated by Daniel Magurshak and Sigmund Barber. Atlantic Highlands, N.J.: Humanities Press, 1987.

Pöggeller, Otto. "Heidegger on Art." In *Martin Heidegger: Politics, Art, and Technology,* edited by Karsten Harries and Christoph Jamme, 106–124. New York: Holmes & Meier, 1994.

Pöggeller, Otto. "Heidegger's Topology of Being." In *On Heidegger and Language,* edited by Joseph J. Kockelmans, 107–146. Evanston, Ill.: Northwestern University Press, 1972.

Ricoeur, Paul. *Time and Narrative.* 3 vols. Translated by Kathleen McLaughlin and David Pellauer. Chicago: University of Chicago Press, 1984–1988.

Rimbaud, Arthur. "Lettre du Voyant." In *Complete Works, Selected Letters,* edited by Wallace Fowlie, 304–311. Chicago: University of Chicago Press, 1966.

Rorty, Richard. *Consequences of Pragmatism: Essays 1972–1980.* Minneapolis: University of Minnesota Press, 1982.

Rorty, Richard. *Essays on Heidegger and Others.* Philosophical Papers, vol. 2. Cambridge: Cambridge University Press, 1991.

Rorty, Richard. *Philosophy and the Mirror of Nature.* Princeton: Princeton University Press, 1980.

Rorty, Richard. "Pragmatism, Davidson and Truth." In *Objectivity, Relativism, and Truth.* Philosophical Papers, vol. 1, 126–150. Cambridge: Cambridge University Press, 1991.

References

Rouse, Joseph. *Knowledge and Power: Toward a Political Philosophy of Life*. Ithaca: Cornell University Press, 1987.

Rouse, Joseph. "Science and the Theoretical 'Discovery' of the Present-at-Hand." In *Descriptions*, edited by Don Ihde and Hugh J. Silverman, 200–210. Albany: SUNY Press, 1985.

Ryle, Gilbert. *The Concept of Mind*. New York: Barnes & Noble, 1949.

Sadler, Ted. *Nietzsche: Truth and Redemption Critique of the Postmodern Nietzsche*. London: Athlone Press, 1995.

Sartre, Jean-Paul. *L'être et le néant: Essai d'ontologie phénoménologique*. Paris: Gallimard, 1943; *Being and Nothingness: An Essay on Phenomenological Ontology*. Translated by Hazel E. Barnes. New York: Philosophical Library, 1956.

Sartre, Jean-Paul. "Cartesian Freedom." In *Literary and Philosophical Essays*. Translated by Annette Michelson. New York: Collier Books, 1962.

Schlegel, Friedrich. *Philosophical Fragments*. Translated by Peter Firchow. Minneapolis: University of Minnesota Press, 1991.

Schmitt, Richard. *Martin Heidegger on Being Human*. New York: Random House, 1969.

Searle, John R. *The Construction of Social Reality*. New York: The Free Press, 1995.

Searle, John R. *Intentionality: An Essay in the Philosophy of Mind*. Cambridge: Cambridge University Press, 1983.

Searle, John R. "The Limits of Phenomenology." In *Heidegger, Coping, and Cognitive Science*, edited by Mark A. Wrathall and Jeff Malpas, 71–92. Cambridge: MIT Press, 2000.

Shrag, Calvin O. *The Self after Postmodernity*. New Haven: Yale University Press, 1997.

Spinosa, Charles, Fernando Flores, and Hubert L. Dreyfus. *Disclosing New Worlds*. Cambridge: MIT Press, 1997.

Springer, Claudia. *Electronic Eros: Bodies and Desire in the Postindustrial Age*. Austin: University of Texas Press, 1996.

Strangerup, Hakon. "His Polemic with the Press." In *Kierkegaard as a Person*, ed. Niels and Marie Thulstrup. Copenhagen: C. A. Reitzels Forlag, 1983.

Strawson, P. F. "Truth." *Analysis* 9 (1949): 83–97.

Strong, Tracy B. *Friedrich Nietzsche and the Politics of Transfiguration*. Berkeley: University of California Press, 1975.

Stroud, Barry. "The Background of Thought." In *John Searle and His Critics*, edited by Ernest LePore and Robert van Gulick, 245–258. Cambridge: Blackwell, 1991.

References

Swimme, Brian, and Thomas Berry. *The Universe Story: From the Primordial Flaring Forth to the Ecozoic Era—A Celebration of the Unfolding of the Cosmos.* San Francisco: HarperSanFrancisco, 1992.

Taylor, Charles. "Engaged Agency and Background in Heidegger." In *The Cambridge Companion to Heidegger,* edited by Charles B. Guignon, 317–336. Cambridge: Cambridge University Press, 1993.

Thiele, Leslie P. *Friedrich Nietzsche and the Politics of the Soul: A Study of Heroic Individualism.* Princeton: Princeton University Press, 1990.

Turkle, Sherry. *Life on the Screen: Identity in the Age of the Internet.* New York: Simon and Schuster, 1995.

van Buren, John. *The Young Heidegger: Rumor of the Hidden King.* Bloomington: Indiana University Press, 1994.

Wilber, Ken. *Eye to Eye: The Quest for the New Paradigm.* Boston: Shambhala, 1996.

Wilber, Ken. *The Marriage of the Senses and the Soul: Integrating Science and Religion.* New York: Random House, 1998.

Wilber, Ken. *Sex, Ecology, Spirituality: The Spirit of Evolution.* Boston: Shambhala, 1995.

Wilber, Ken. *Up From Eden: A Transpersonal View of Human Evolution.* Garden City, N.Y.: Anchor Press/Doubleday, 1981.

Wilcox, John T. *Truth and Value in Nietzsche: A Study of his Metaphysics and Epistemology.* Ann Arbor: University of Michigan Press, 1974.

Wilcox, John T. "Nietzsche Scholarship and 'The Correspondence Theory of Truth': The Danto Case." *Nietzsche-Studien* 15 (1986): 337–357.

Williams, Michael. *Unnatural Doubts: Epistemological Realism and the Basis of Scepticism.* Princeton: Princeton University Press, 1996.

Wittgenstein, Ludwig. *On Certainty.* Translated by Denis Paul and G. E. M. Anscombe. New York: Harper & Row, 1972.

Wolin, Richard. *The Politics of Being: The Political Thought of Martin Heidegger.* New York: Columbia University Press, 1990.

Wolin, Richard. "Hannah and the Magician." *New Republic* 213 (October 9, 1995): 27–37. Review of Elizbieta Ettinger, *Hannah Arendt/Martin Heidegger.* New Haven: Yale University Press, 1995.

Zimmerman, Michael E. *Eclipse of the Self: The Development of Heidegger's Concept of Authenticity.* Athens: Ohio University Press, 1986.

Contributors

William D. Blattner is Assistant Professor in Philosophy at Georgetown University.

Taylor Carman is Assistant Professor in Philosophy at Barnard College, Columbia University.

David R. Cerbone is Assistant Professor of Philosophy at West Virginia University.

Dagfinn Føllesdal is Professor of Philosophy at the University of Oslo.

Charles Guignon is Professor of Philosophy at the University of Vermont.

Michel Haar is Professor of Philosophy at the University of Paris XII.

Béatrice Han is Lecturer in Philosophy at Essex University.

Alastair Hannay is Professor of Philosophy at the University of Oslo.

John Haugeland is Professor of Philosophy at the University of Pittsburgh.

Randall Havas is Assistant Professor in Philosophy at Willamette College.

Jeff Malpas is Professor of Philosophy at the University of Tasmania.

Mark Okrent is Associate Professor in Philosophy at Bates College.

Richard Rorty is Professor of Comparative Literature at Stanford University.

Julian Young is Associate Professor in Philosophy at the University of Auckland.

Michael E. Zimmerman is Professor of Philosophy at Tulane University.

Index

Index

Index